THE DORR WAR

THOMAS WILSON DORR.

The Dorr War

or

The Constitutional Struggle in Rhode Island

by

ARTHUR MAY MOWRY, Ph. D.
(HARVARD)

WITH AN INTRODUCTION BY

ALBERT BUSHNELL HART
PROFESSOR OF AMERICAN HISTORY, HARVARD UNIVERSITY

PROVIDENCE, R. I.
PRESTON & ROUNDS CO.
1901

PRESS OF
E. L. FREEMAN AND SONS
PROVIDENCE, RHODE ISLAND

CONTENTS.

ILLUSTRATIONS.

PREFACE.

THIS book is designed to set forth with fullness and accuracy the long protracted struggle for an extended suffrage in Rhode Island. The author has examined with care all available material, in order to frame from original sources a consistent account of this peculiar controversy from the early days of the charter to the present time. Valuable aid has been received from old documents and records in the Rhode Island State Library, in the archives of the City Hall, Providence, and in the collections of the Rhode Island Historical Society; also from the reports of the Supreme Court of the State of Rhode Island and of the United States; and from the journals of Congress and various State legislatures. The newspapers have proved to be a fruitful source for information, and scores of files of papers published not only in Rhode Island but also in other portions of New England, in New York, and in more distant States, have been turned over in an exhaustive search for the truth.

Thanks are due to the late Amos Perry, Secretary of the Rhode Island Historical Society, and to the librarians and attendants of the public libraries of Providence and Boston; the Harvard Library, at Cambridge; the Library of the American Antiquarian Society, Worcester; the Astor and Lenox libraries, of New York City; and many other public and private libraries, for their interest and courteous attention. Particular acknowledgments are credited to Professor Albert Bushnell Hart, Ph.D., who has kindly written the Introduction; to Professor Edward Channing, Ph.D., and to Professor James B. Thayer, LL.D., of Harvard University, for valuable assistance rendered; to Professor James B. Scott, D. C. L., Dean of the Law School of Illinois State University, and Professor James A. Hoose, Ph.D., of the University of Southern California, for reading the manuscript and for important suggestions; and to Clarence S. Brigham, Librarian of the Rhode Island Historical Society, and the many friends who have assisted in the search for illustrations.

The work is submitted to the people of Rhode Island and to the students of history throughout the country in the hope that it will bring to them much information, in readable form, upon this very important and hitherto neglected history.

INTRODUCTION.

BY PROFESSOR ALBERT BUSHNELL HART.

"*Certainly, the great multiplication of Vertues upon Humane Nature, resteth upon Societies well Ordained, and Disciplined. For Commonwealths, and Good Governments, doe nourish Vertue Growne, but doe not much mend the Seeds.*"

So wrote great Bacon three centuries ago. The observation applies to no Commonwealth and to no Good Government more than to the colony and State of Rhode Island, where for nearly two centuries one instrument of government sufficed for the interests of a thriving and advancing community; yet where from the beginning there were seeds of dissension, from which sprang eventually a dangerous civil war.

Rhode Island has had the fortune to illustrate several different phases of that abounding American life which found expression in a dozen other colonial governments: Rhode Island was one of the earliest American homes of religious toleration; Rhode Island was an example of a loose kind of federation; Rhode Island was one of the few American commonwealths which had a thoroughly democratic government, choosing its own governor as well as its own assembly. In the federal history of America, also, Rhode Island has gone through several interesting crises: Rhode Island was one of the earliest commonwealths to purge itself of the crime of human slavery; Rhode Island was one of the most vigorous defenders of State rights, against what it thought the aggressions of the national government in 1814; Rhode Island was the only State in the Union to pass through a revolution of its own after the great uprising of the Revolution and before the overthrowings of the Civil War period.

Rhode Island has also been, if not singular, at least fortunate, in the loyalty of its own sons. When some years ago Mr. Arthur May Mowry, at much personal sacrifice, sought the opportunity of enlarging his training in historical work, it was my fortune to be acquainted with his purpose and frequently to discuss with him the subject which he had chosen for investigation. It seemed to him that in the history of his State the Dorr Rebellion was the most important episode, and that at the same time it was the least studied and perhaps the most misconstrued. He therefore set himself steadily and pertinaciously to become acquainted with the prime materials on that subject; and he soon learned where to find the pamphlet, periodical, and fugitive material upon which a skillful writer might draw. He left no stone unturned: he searched libraries far and near: he unearthed forgotten newspapers and rare broadsides: he went through the neglected records of courts and legislatures: no collection of sources which was open to the investigator was neglected in his search.

After many months of labor, extending through several years' time, he began to arrange his materials, to come to conclusions, and carefully to prepare this history. His method was always inductive: he came to estimate men and measures because those judgments seemed to him inevitable, borne in upon him by wide evidence: he was a careful, painstaking, and reflective writer. About the time that his manuscript was completed, disease came upon him. When he began to see that his days were numbered, he took the pains to revise his manuscript again and yet again, pruning and completing and coming to a final judgment. The results of what amounts in the aggregate to several years of well-directed labor, appear in this volume, which is at the same time the author's monument and a tribute to his beloved State.

The first significance of the work is its study of the development of an unwritten constitutional law, side by side with the written charter of Rhode Island. In his early chapters, therefore, Mr. Mowry presents a view of the political and constitutional history of one of the States in the Union, interesting not only to Rhode Island, but to the increasing number of persons who are seeking to understand the development of popular government in America.

In chapters iv to vii Mr. Mowry begins a careful study of the great constitutional struggle in Rhode Island which led up to the rival conventions of 1841, a struggle important in the as yet unwritten history of American constitutions; and he brings out clearly how far the whole question was affected by the rise of manufacturing communities and the inflow of foreigners. In one sense, therefore, the issue in the Dorr Rebellion was commercial—the recognition of the industrial class; but, on the other hand, the broad belief in a widely-distributed suffrage as a right principle of human government comes out as the ruling motive of those who were to direct the new movement.

Rhode Island is not the only State in the Union in which there have been rival constitutions and rival governments. In New Orleans, after the Civil War, two legislatures sat for a time simultaneously; in Ohio, in 1849, a House of Representatives organized in one corner of the official hall, and another House in another corner, and they remained for some weeks in hostility to each other; in Kentucky there have been two governors at the same moment, each threatening the other. Nevertheless the danger of duality, the impossibility of two trains passing on a single track, has never been so clearly brought out as in the rivalries of Rhode Island from 1841 to 1842; and it is to the credit of the good order and peaceful instincts of the Rhode Island people that the collision was so long postponed.

The preliminaries of the Dorr Rebellion are really an account of the power of public sentiment working upon an unwilling legislature and constitutional convention. The most significant and the fundamental difference between the Freeman's and People's constitutions was simply that the official Freeman's convention did not yield the vexed question of a property requirement for the suffrage, while the People's Constitution, which was shortly to become revolutionary, followed the system of neighboring States in a gradually enlarging suffrage. In chapters ix, x, and xi the story grows more interesting as we come to the parallel votes upon the two constitutions, and the important statute declaring the proceedings under the People's Constitution to be criminal.

The second half of Mr. Mowry's book, from chapter xii, is the history—hitherto never adequately written—of the actual revolution, or attempt at revolution, in Rhode Island. Everybody knows that appeal was made by both sides to President Tyler before hostilities began; not everybody knows the details of the two rival governments in May, 1842; and still fewer people are acquainted with the singular history of Mr. Dorr's visit to New York and appeal to Tammany Hall for sympathy and assistance.

The drama now grows more intense as military preparations are made on both sides. Mr. Mowry gives us a clear and faithful picture of the conditions and failure of the People's government, and the final military collision, ending with the fiasco at Acote's Hill, in June, 1842. The remaining chapters of the book deal with the punitive action of Rhode Island against Dorr, and his trial and conviction for treason. We have here a valuable study of the great constitutional question of the relation of the United States to the government of Rhode Island, involving important issues of State rights.

From this brief summary it will be seen that the book is not only well prepared, but that it includes a careful discussion of the disputed questions which arose throughout the whole controversy. Mr. Mowry's judgment is that the People's party were ill advised in attempting to fight the regular State government; and that their ends might have been substantially reached without violence; but he does not lack sympathy with the patriotic and in some ways heroic elements in the whole controversy. Mr. Mowry is convinced that in this, as in most similar difficulties, violence defeats its own ends, and leads to counter violence. Perhaps the main lesson of the whole controversy, and the lesson to which Mr. Mowry especially addresses himself, is the power of strong, moderately phrased, and continuous public protest, and its superiority to forcible revolution.

One part of the book remains to be noticed: the illustrations are what pictures ought to be in such a work; not a modern artist's conception of what an artist on the spot might have sketched, but reproductions of the rough wood cuts and maps of the time, and excellent portraits of the principal characters.

The merits of Mr. Mowry's book I have had many opportunities to judge: he has chosen a very dramatic and a very suggestive episode: he has treated it with thoroughness, with candor, and with good judgment: he has well told the story of a movement which had roots deeper than Narragansett bay and broader than the territory of Rhode Island; for the Dorr Rebellion is one of the most distinct and striking incidents of the long American struggle for manhood suffrage. To the Rhode Islander, to the student of constitutional development, to the believer in the righteousness and the success of popular government, Mr. Mowry has rendered a great service.

CHAPTER I.

INTRODUCTORY.

A LITTLE more than fifty years ago the State of Rhode Island passed through a struggle which not only led to civil war within the State itself but also aroused great interest in other parts of the country. The contest was unique: in its causes it finds no parallel in the annals of any State of the Union; history records few civil wars in which the antagonism of parties was so intense, few which collapsed so completely and so suddenly, and yet few which accomplished a more definite result. It would be worthy of study, even were the causes less significant; but the causes illustrate, as almost no other episode of this century, the development of democratic government. The Dorr War, as the struggle has commonly been designated, has not been "famed in song and story;" and yet the dual government in Rhode Island in May, 1842, and the short military contest which followed, were among the most noticeable features of the quiet administration of President Tyler, and attracted the attention of the members of both political parties and of all classes of people throughout the country.

The popular interest in the "Rhode Island Question" was primarily due to the sympathy which the people of the other States felt for the "non-freemen" of that little State. Though this sympathy was doubtless to a considerable extent spontaneous, it was carefully fostered by the politicians of the day. The opinion was current that these "oppressed" persons, though greatly preponderating in numbers, had been unjustly deprived of certain "rights;" that these non-freemen had long struggled for these rights, and that no course was now left open to them but an appeal to arms. This widespread interest did not diminish even when the struggle was over; for the victorious government, though secure in its strength, showed little clemency to the vanquished, and singled out the leader for condign punishment. The story was spread broadcast, and everywhere sympathy was publicly expressed for the "fallen hero," the "martyr to popular liberty." Thus the war became widely known, and deserves permanent place in the annals of the country.

The current notions of the Rhode Island struggle are almost entirely derived from the general histories of the United States, in which the story is necessarily briefly told, and in no case appears to have been based on a first-hand study of the subject. Very few investigations have been made into the constitutional troubles in Rhode Island since the time when the bitterness of the struggle passed away; hence the conventional view really represents only the loose ideas that prevailed in the Union at large during the struggle among those not personally acquainted with the facts of the case. Careful investigation makes it certain that in 1842 and the subsequent years public opinion greatly erred in its estimate of the real questions at issue in Rhode Island. The political animosities in the contest were exceedingly strong, and neither side sent out impartial accounts to the general public. The domestic character of the war was marked; families were divided, sons were ranged against fathers, and brothers were found on opposing sides. The seat of the war was limited in extent, and even in the most densely settled portions of the State the population was comparatively small. It was impossible, under such circumstances, for even disinterested persons to obtain fair statements and unprejudiced reports.

The troublesome Rhode Island question was discussed in Congress and in the newspapers of the day, and popular enthusiasm was marked in the leading cities of the country. The universal assumption was that two questions were involved in the contest, and but two: a struggle for freer suffrage, and the purpose of might to be the oppressor of right. No other possible causes for the war were seen, and an almost universal popular sympathy was shown by the suffrage advocates in the various States for the "rightful demands" of the non-freemen of Rhode Island who were seeking the suffrage. The era was one of advancing democracy, and in all directions restrictions on the suffrage were being removed, or at least lessened. The cry arose that Rhode Island must be brought into line. As attentive observers watched the struggle for the franchise, it was only natural that the position of the legal voters should be generally condemned. They appeared to be relying upon their inherited power and once again to be refusing to grant equal political rights to the less favored. That the general public should see only these two issues was natural, especially as their knowledge of the conflict was limited to the crisis itself. The early movements in the State, especially during the eighteen months preceding the outbreak, the steps taken by each party, and the legal and constitutional issues involved were almost entirely unknown. The newspapers, outside of the State, did not begin to give prominence to the news from Rhode Island until well into the month of April, 1842; the two months of armed controversy which followed were extremely dramatic, and the transactions during this period alone made much impression upon the public mind.

The true struggle was, in fact, something more than a mere quarrel over the extent of the suffrage restrictions, and the length of the controversy may be measured by years rather than by weeks. The main issue was constitutional, and therefore the contest deserves the attention of publicists as well as of historians. That it was a constitutional issue does not imply merely that questions arose as to the validity of certain laws or actions during the three years in which the contest was raging; the main point at issue was the making of a constitution for the State. Inasmuch as no method of procedure had been provided by the existing "fundamental law," the Charter of 1663, there was great diversity of opinion. The demand for a constitution primarily came from the non-voters, and they, with some show of reason, claimed a share in the process. The questions soon came up: "Who are the people?" "Have not the people a right to make constitutions for their government?" Thus, though the contest was local and confined within a limited area, the questions presented were national in importance. If the inhabitants of Rhode Island had the legal right to rise in their might, to throw off all existing control, and to make a new fundamental law at pleasure, no State in the Union could consider itself safe from a similar proceeding. If, in Rhode Island, such a movement should be prevented, and thereby proclaimed revolutionary, a valuable precedent would be furnished for the protection of other State governments.

When the peaceful legal contest was beginning to develop into an armed controversy, new political and constitutional issues were brought to the front. As each party realized its own weakness, it appealed to the national government for aid. Here was presented the then novel issue of rival State governments calling upon the President of the United States to decide which of them had legal authority. What were his powers in such a case? Did the Constitution of the United States, notwithstanding the doctrine of State sovereignty, make him an arbiter in such crises in the commonwealths?

Another method of settlement suggested during the struggle was to refer the matter at issue to one of the Houses of Congress. Although the House of Representatives found no opportunity to act directly as arbitrator, it nevertheless forced itself into the controversy by an attempt to investigate the action of the President toward the establishment—or, perhaps, rather the overthrow—of a government in Rhode Island.

Failing to obtain assistance from either the executive or the legislative departments of the national government, as a last resort one of the rival parties appealed to the Supreme Court. Here an insurmountable obstacle was found in the time-honored conservatism of the highest tribunal in the land. A decision was rendered in the case of Luther *vs.* Borden, which determined the exact status of the Supreme Court on constitutional questions, but did not settle the Rhode Island controversy.

Besides raising serious questions as to its internal relations with the three departments of the national government, the struggle in Rhode Island is interesting because of its connection with other States. Public mass meetings were held in many of the large cities of the country, which inflamed the passions of the hostile parties in Rhode Island. However unfortunate such action may have been, it was not illegal, perhaps not improper. But all upholders of the internal autonomy of the State must be strongly opposed to the official position taken by some of the State legislatures in making appeals to Congress. The refusal of certain governors to honor the requisition of the governor of Rhode Island to hold in arrest the fugitive leader of the defeated party adds another complication to the situation.

Three other issues, judicial as well as constitutional, grew out of the Dorr Rebellion, and present matters of interest to all students of criminal as well as constitutional law. The first arose when the governor, under a vote of the General Assembly, declared martial law throughout the State—taking a step far beyond any which the people of any State had ever witnessed. No study of martial law is complete without a careful review of the decision of the Supreme Court of the State of Rhode Island and the individual opinion of Justice Woodbury of the Federal Supreme Court. The second legal issue came after the war was ended, the new constitution adopted, and matters in the State had quieted down. The State government arrested the leader of the insurrection and brought him to trial for treason. Prosecution and defense were in practical accord as to questions of fact; the question at issue was the legality of a revolution. The defence also took the unusual position that there could be no such thing as treason against a State, but only against the United States. The third political issue arose several years after the conviction of the so-called "traitor," and well illustrates the Anglo-Saxon rivalry between legislature and judiciary. The General Assembly, in 1854, passed a statute declaring the decision of the Supreme Court null and void, and ordering that the account of the conviction and sentence be expunged from the records of the State.

There are, then, at least ten distinct issues bound up in the Rhode Island constitutional contest, which may be briefly summed up as follows:

(1) The general right of the people to adopt constitutions;

(2) The character of the amendatory method adopted in Rhode Island, whether revolutionary or legal;

(3) The powers of the national executive in cases of State controversies;

(4) The powers of the national legislature in such cases;

(5) The powers of the national judiciary in such cases;

(6) The interference of States in the affairs of other States;

(7) The right of governors to decline requisitions for persons charged with crime;

(8) The declaration of martial law;

(9) The possibility of treason against a State;

(10) The power of a legislature to annul the acts of the judiciary.

In this monograph it is intended to present a complete narrative of the short civil war of May and June, 1842, with its causes and results; and further to state and comment upon the important issues which were brought into prominence during the movements for a constitution and for universal suffrage which have been more or less before the people of Rhode Island since 1776, and some of which have continued to agitate the State even to the present decade.

CHAPTER II.

THE RHODE ISLAND CHARTER.

THE written instrument which the Rhode Island suffragists were anxious to replace by a new constitution was the charter granted by Charles II in 1663, under which the people of Rhode Island had lived and prospered for more than a century and three-quarters. Undemocratic as the government of the State under the charter may seem in the light of the nineteenth century, yet its practice was unusually liberal for the seventeenth century; it simply remained stationary while popular ideas steadily progressed. For nearly two hundred years the charter was considered the fundamental law by all the inhabitants, and under it the General Assembly met, executive and judicial officers were chosen, and statutes were enacted and enforced. No one questioned its authority or constitutional supremacy until, in 1841, some of the suffrage agitators declared that the State had no constitution, much less a written constitution, and that the government was in the hands of an usurping "landocracy." An analysis of this charter and a study of the constitutional development of the colony and State under it form the most appropriate starting point in the discussion of the Rhode Island controversy.

If the Charter of 1663 can properly be called the Constitution of the State, it must be shown to conform to the requisites of a modern constitution of a republic. First, the document must be the fundamental law; all other laws, statutes, ordinances or acts must be subordinate to it, and legislative enactments must be treated as null and void if inconsistent with any of its provisions. Secondly, this fundamental law should contain provisions for the machinery of the government and also for the performance of legislative, executive, and judicial functions. Third, such a document, in order to be valid, must have been at some time adopted by the people of the State or by their properly-chosen representatives. Fourth, the authority of the document must, formally or informally, be continuously acknowledged by immigrants and later generations; for, though once adopted by the State, a constitution which has lost its authority, and is no longer accepted as binding by the citizens, may be considered to have lapsed, even if it has not been formally superseded by another. Were these conditions fulfilled by the Rhode Island charter as it was operated in 1841?

The first settlement within the colony was made at Providence, in 1636, by a wanderer fleeing from the jurisdiction of Massachusetts Bay. Two years later a home was provided at Portsmouth, on the Island of Rhode Island, for another fugitive from Massachusetts. The next year a third settlement was made, at Newport, by seceders from Portsmouth. In each of these towns the democratic spirit was marked, and in each local pride engendered a strong feeling of jealousy towards the other towns. In 1640 the two towns on the Island entered into a federation—each, however, retaining nearly all of its former independence.(1) Three years later the three towns obtained from a committee of Parliament a patent, entitled an "Incorporation of Providence Plantations in the Narragansett Bay in New England."[2] The rivalry was strong enough to delay the acceptance of this patent and the formation of a government under it, so that not till 1647 was sufficient harmony obtained to enable the first general assembly of the colony to be held at Portsmouth. A fourth town, Warwick, was then admitted to the group, and a legally constituted government was inaugurated. Jealousy, however, soon broke out again, and in 1651 a separation took place between the northern or mainland colonies on the one hand and the southern or island colonies on the other.[3] Providence and Warwick continued the government under the patent of 1643, while Portsmouth and Newport formed a confederation under a new patent obtained by Coddington. Three years later this latter patent was waived, and a reunion took place.[4] This movement was entirely voluntary, and the people of each of the four towns deliberately chose to be governed under the patent of 1643. This federal government was, however, almost a nullity in practice, as the towns continued to exercise nearly all the powers which they possessed previous to the formation of the confederacy.

Thus matters stood when the Restoration of 1660 took place. Though Rhode Island had, in some respects, less to fear from the accession of King Charles than the adjoining colonies, still prudence suggested to the little colony to win the friendship of the new king if possible. Much of the king's hostility to the northern colonies would doubtless be directed against the New England Confederacy, from which Rhode Island had been ungratefully excluded. Yet the patent of 1643 had been obtained from the parliamentary government which had made war upon the king's father, and therefore would hardly be considered legal by him or his ministers. Again, the hostile attention of the churchmen around King Charles would be quickly attracted to the religious liberty prevailing in the colony. For these reasons, the necessity was very evident to the Rhode Island leaders of obtaining the goodwill of the king at the outset, and seeking from him a new charter as liberal as could be obtained.

Accordingly, John Clarke, the agent of the colony, was commissioned to present their allegiance to the crown and to take all possible steps to secure a ratification of their territorial limits in the form of a charter. Mr. Clarke met with almost wonderful success in his undertaking—a success less easy to explain than that of Governor Winthrop of Connecticut a year earlier. The charter, evidently patterned after that of Connecticut so recently issued, was dated July 8, 1663, and was immediately sent to the colony. The first portion, or preamble (not in the Connecticut charter), referred to the religious position of the settlements, and, both in thought and wording, was noticeably like a letter sent by the agent to the king. This resemblance, and the fact that the Rhode Island Court of Commissioners planned to send definite instructions to the agent,[a] have led some writers to state that a draft, which formed the basis of the charter, was drawn up in Rhode Island and sent over to Clarke.[5] This statement seems very doubtful, especially as the charter proper differs so slightly from that of Connecticut, granted fifteen months earlier.

The anxiously awaited charter reached the colony in November, 1663, and caused great rejoicing in each of the four settlements.

---

[a] The General Assembly, May 21, 1661, appointed a committee of four "for the drawinge up of somethinge to consider with respecte of sending a man for England." (*Rhode Island Colonial Records*, I, 441.) In accordance with the resolutions prepared by this committee, the Assembly resolved that selectmen from each town should "draw up our addresses unto his majestie, in all humble manner, by way of petition, in terms intreating of our dutifull prostration at his royall feett of ourselves and services, as it becometh the humble subjecks of so gracious a prince; as also procure the Generall Recorder's hand unto the sayd addresses in the name and behalfe of the colony." (*Idem*, I, 445.)

The colony commissioners were summoned to meet at Newport and the colonists also were requested to be present in large numbers. A record of the proceedings of this assembly reads as follows:

" At a very great meeting and Assembly of the Freemen of the Colony of Providence Plantations, at Newport, on Rhode Island, in New England, November, 24, 1663,—

" The above said Assembly being legally called, and orderly met for the solemn reception of his Majestyes Gracious Letters patent unto them sent, and having in order thereto chosen the President Benedict Arnold, Moderator of the Assembly,—

" It was ordered and voted *nemine contradicente*,

" Voted 1. That Mr. John Clarke, the colony Agent's letter to the President, Assistants and Freemen of the colony be opened and read, which accordingly was done with good delivery and attention.

" Voted 2. That the box in which the King's gracious Letters were enclosed be opened, and the Letters, with the Broad Seale thereto affixed, be taken forth and Read by Captayne George Baxter, in the Audience and view of all the people; which was accordingly done and the said Letters, with his Majestyes Royal Stampe and the Broad Seale with much beseeming gravity held up on high and presented to the perfect view of the people, and so returned into the Box and locked up by the Governor in order to the safe keeping it.

" Voted 3. That the most humble Thanks of this colony, unto our gracious Sovereign Lord, King Charles the Second of England, etc. for the high and Inestimable, yea incomparable grace and favor unto the colony in giving these his gracious Letters patents unto us; thankes may be presented and returned by the Governor and Deputy-Governor in the behalf of the whole colony.

" Voted 4. That for present and until the colony can otherwise declare, than by words their obligations unto the most honorable Earl of Clarendon, Lord High Chancellor of England, for his Exceeding great care and love unto this Colony, as by our Agent above mentioned hath always been acknowledged in his letters. The Governor and Deputy-Governor are desired to return unto his Lordship the humble thanks of the whole colony."[(b)]

After the establishment of the government under this charter, which had thus been formally accepted—or, one might almost say, adopted—by the colonists, no constitutional or revolutionary change took place for twenty-five years. Then, for a short time, during the Andros regime in New England, Rhode Island was deprived of the charter; but, after its restoration, affairs in the colony went on exactly as before, and political conditions remained unchanged until the breaking out of the Revolution of 1775. The charters of Connecticut and Rhode Island were already so liberal and democratic that little political change was necessary. The only step taken to change His Majesty's colony of Rhode Island and Providence Plantations into a free and independent State was that of formally renouncing allegiance to Great Britain.[(6)] By the same act direction was given to erase the name and titles of the king from all commissions, writs, processes, or other instruments, from all oaths, and from the names of all courts, etc. This act, declaring independence, was passed by the General Assembly, May 4, 1776, two months before the Declaration by the United Colonies at Philadelphia. It made no change in the government of the State and did not violate the wording of the charter, however much

---

(b) This account is printed in the Minority Report of the Select Committee of the United States House of Representatives, to which the "Memorial of the Democratic Members of the Rhode Island General Assembly" was referred. This report is commonly called "*Causin's Report.*" *House Reports*, 28 Cong., I Sess., III, No. 581, pp. 50–52. The Majority Report, or "*Burke's Report*," *House Reports*, 28 Cong., I Sess., III, No. 546, has been separately published, and copies of it, though rare, are still obtainable. These two reports will be referred to as *Burke's Report* and *Causin's Report*, respectively. See, also, Arnold, *Rhode Island*, I, 284; *Rhode Island Colonial Records*, I, 509.

it may have been in opposition to its spirit. The charter was not modified in any way by the ratification of the Declaration of Independence by the State of Rhode Island, July 19, 1776, when the General Assembly solemnly promised to support the General Congress with their lives and fortunes.[7] Here, as well as in the act of the preceding May, the action was taken by the legislature and not submitted to the people for adoption; nor was any other constitution adopted by popular vote before 1842.

In February, 1778, the General Assembly sent instructions to the three "Delegates from Rhode Island in Congress" recommending "amendments and alterations" in the proposed Articles of Confederation, which they deemed of very great importance; and yet they instructed the delegates, even in case of the rejection of the amendments, "not to decline acceding, on behalf of this State, to the Articles."[8] The people of the State had, directly, no part in this ratification of the final national Constitution; and the Assembly which preferred the act owed its existence to the King Charles charter. The adoption of the Articles of Confederation by the thirteen States had no permanent effect upon the charter of Rhode Island, for they were soon superseded by the Constitution of 1787. As is well known, Rhode Island ratified this Constitution in due form, May 29, 1790, after a protracted struggle of more than two years.

From this brief narrative of the external constitutional changes in the colony and the State, it is readily seen that the old charter had never been abolished or abandoned. Government continued under it, officers took oath to support it, and nowhere did the people show any signs of questioning its authority or legality. Neither the act renouncing allegiance, nor the approval of the Declaration of Independence, nor the acceptance of the Articles of Confederation, nor the ratification of the Constitution of the United States, can be said to have repealed or seriously altered the charter as a fundamental law. The practical effects of the ratification of the Constitution of the United States upon the Rhode Island Charter of 1663 must have been exactly identical with its effects upon the Massachusetts Constitution of 1780—namely, to modify but not to abolish. The proposition is clear, then, that up to June, 1790, the old charter remained in force; and it is also true that no further constitutional change took place previous to the year 1842. Unless the colony had changed the charter—directly or indirectly—by some ordinary statute, which would not attract public attention, and which might perhaps be styled an amendment to the charter, then the King Charles charter must be regarded as a written constitution in 1841.

The Charter of 1663 (*Appendix A*) was granted to the existing "Colony of Providence Plantations, in the Narraganset Bay, in New England," and re-established it as a "body corporate and politic" under the title of "The Governor and Company of the English Colony of Rhode Island and Providence Plantations, in New England, in America." It provided that the government of the colony should be in the hands of a governor, a deputy-governor, ten assistants, and a General Assembly consisting of freemen chosen from the different towns, together with the above officers. To this Assembly was given authority to establish such other offices and choose thereto such officers as might seem necessary, together with entire legislative power and the constitution of courts of jurisdiction. The "sovereign power" of the General Assembly—its practical control over all the branches of the government—was not merely a possibility, but was to a marked degree a reality. There was under the charter no such separation of the three departments of government as is common in our State constitutions; and the General Assembly exercised, throughout its entire existence under the charter, an almost omnipotent sway. The governor had absolutely no official authority except as a member of the Assembly, and acted as its executive agent, merely carrying out its orders. The judiciary was practically under the control of the legislature by virtue of its annual appointment by the Assembly.

The two most noticeable features of the charter related to the suffrage qualifications and to the apportionment of the representation from the different towns in the Assembly. These are important enough to warrant exact quotations of the words of the charter. "They [the General Assembly] shall have, and have hereby given and granted unto them, full power and authority, from time to time, and at all times hereafter, . . . to choose, nominate and appoint, such and so many other persons as they shall think fit, and shall be willing to accept the same, to be free of the said Company and body politic, and them into the same to admit." "Forever, hereafter, twice in every year, that is to say, on every first Wednesday in the month of May, and on every last Wednesday in October, or oftener, in case it shall be requisite, the Assistants and such of the freemen of the said Company, not exceeding six persons for Newport, four persons for each of the respective towns of Providence, Portsmouth, and Warwick, and two persons for each other place, town or city, who shall be, from time to time, thereunto elected or deputed by the major part of the freemen of the respective towns or places for which they shall be so elected or deputed, shall have a general meeting or assembly, then and there to consult, advise and determine, in and about the affairs of the said Company and Plantations." These two sections furnished the basis for nearly all the attacks upon the charter during the half-century ending in 1843. Much more attention was paid, on the whole, to the suffrage clause than to the other, though the demand for a reapportionment of the representation held a prominent position in all the discussions and, indeed, antedated the demand for the suffrage by many years. These provisions need a careful exposition, as they are the key-notes to the whole controversy.

The apportionment article is simple, and its practical working is easy to understand. By it the members of the General Assembly consisted, in 1663, of the Governor, the Deputy-Governor, the ten Assistants, and eighteen Deputies. The latter represented the towns, four each being sent from Portsmouth, Warwick, and Providence, and six from Newport, while the other officers were elected at large, thereby representing the whole colony. It may be said with perfect truth that this apportionment was just and fair to each town in 1663. Newport was larger than the others, which were of nearly equal population and importance. The charter, it will be noticed, very properly assigns two Deputies each to any new towns that might be formed, anticipating that these would be weaker and smaller than the older settlements. This assignment of Deputies was a permanent apportionment, however, as no arrangement was made for a later equalization of the representation. It did not occur to Englishmen of the seventeenth century that their own borough representation was defective, and that membership in Parliament should be allotted to the boroughs more in accordance with their importance; much less would it be expected that they would make any provision for such a possible future need in the colony of Rhode Island. The number of Deputies was increased to twenty in 1669 by the formation of the town of Westerly, and before 1700 to twenty-eight by the addition of four other towns. The nine towns at the beginning of the eighteenth century had become thirty at its close — furnishing seventy Deputies to the General Assembly. The formation of the town of Burrillville, in 1806, increased the numbers to thirty-one and seventy-two, respectively, at which point they remained for thirty-seven years. Thus, at the beginning of the agitation for a constitution, in 1840, the General Assembly consisted of the Governor, the Deputy-Governor, and the ten Assistants, or Senators, chosen by the freemen at large; and the seventy-two Deputies, or Representatives, chosen, two each from twenty-seven towns, four each from Providence, Portsmouth, and Warwick, and six from Newport. Had Newport remained the largest town in the State, had the other three original towns retained comparatively equal populations, and had none of the new towns become more important, the justice of the representation might never have been questioned.

Turning to the other important provision of the charter, we find that, contrary to the belief which prevailed throughout the country in 1842, and is generally believed to-day, the Charter of 1663, granted by King Charles the Second, did not specify the suffrage qualifications in Rhode Island. Just as the Constitution of the United States does not name the successor to the presidency, in case of the inability of both President and Vice-President to act, but leaves it to Congress to make rules with regard to the succession, so the Rhode Island charter placed it in the hands of the General Assembly of the colony to admit as freemen whomsoever it pleased. There was nothing in this word "freemen" that could even indirectly cast a slur upon the non-freemen. By freemen was meant simply the members of the Company, sharing its rights and privileges as well as its duties and obligations. The non-freemen were merely non-members, and held a position in the colony on the whole similar to that of unnaturalized foreigners in the United States to-day. In time, as the Company developed into a political community, the freemen came to be considered merely as voters, and the expression non-freemen became identical with non-voters.

Among the first acts passed by the General Assembly, as early as May, 1664, was one limiting the right to vote on all affairs of the Company and Plantations to the freemen.[(9)] This was purely formal, merely putting into the form of a law the unexpressed but evident intention of the charter. The next May, the General Assembly — in response to a request of the King's Commissioners — voted that "so many of them that take the aforesaid Engagement, and are of Competent Estates, Civil Conversation, and Obedient to the Civil Magistrate, shall be admitted freemen of this colony, upon their express desire therein declared to the General Assembly, either by themselves, with sufficient testimony of their fitness and Qualifications as shall by the Assembly be deemed satisfactory, or . . . by the Chief Officer of the Towne . . . where they live."[(10)] The next year the Assembly deputed the business of admitting freemen to the several towns, merely reserving the right of supervision, which was seldom, if ever, exercised.[(11)] It seems probable that the requirements of the law as to "Civil Conversation" and to be "Obedient to the Civil Magistrate" did not prevent many applicants from being admitted as freemen. As to the words "Competent Estates," no action was taken for sixty years looking to any official decision as to the requisite size of a competent estate.

In 1723–4, the General Assembly passed an act granting admission as freeman to a "freeholder of lands, tenements, or hereditaments in such town where he shall be admitted free, of the value of one hundred pounds, or to the value of forty shillings per annum, or the eldest son of such freeholder; any act, custom, or usage to the contrary hereof, notwithstanding."[12] While the wording of this act would allow any town to refuse the rights of freemanship. even to those possessing real estate of the requisite value, in actual practice this property requisite became the sole qualification for admission to the privilege of the suffrage. The relic of primogeniture which is found in this act—namely, that the eldest son of a freeman is exempted from the property qualification—continued to be a law in Rhode Island until 1843, and furnished an additional opportunity for criticism of the "landed aristocracy." An act of 1742 is of great significance in the change of the meaning of the word freeman from that of a membership in a corporation to that of a person possessing the right to vote.[13] In substance, it took away the right of suffrage from those freemen who, admitted at some former time, did not, at any election, possess the requisite real estate. In other words, to be once admitted as a freeman did not convey a life right of suffrage, as the privilege of voting at any election depended upon the possession of the necessary amount of real estate at that particular time.

In 1729 the one hundred pounds test was increased to two hundred, and in 1746 to four hundred pounds.[14] The qualification continued at this value until 1760, when it was placed at forty pounds.[15] When the General Assembly revised the laws in 1798—the English money system having gone out of official use—the value of the requisite real estate was declared to be one hundred and thirty-four dollars, or a rental of seven dollars per annum.[16] It was permitted, at this time, that the property should lie within the State; not, as before, necessarily within the town in which the candidate for admission as a freeman presented his request. In brief, then, the qualification was at first one hundred pounds, then two hundred pounds, later four hundred pounds, then forty pounds, and finally one hundred and thirty-four dollars. This fluctuation is at first sight an indication of fickleness in the character of the Assembly, but an explanation has been given which appears reasonable. It is claimed that real estate worth, in the money of the day, one hundred pounds in 1723 would cost not far from four times as much in 1746, and still be of about forty pounds value in 1760. At any rate, it is certain that the value of the currency changed between 1720 and 1760 in much greater degree than is suggested by these values of land.

Such are the most important features of the Charter of 1663 as interpreted by the later history of the colony. It remains to examine some of the acts of the Assembly which have sometimes been described as contrary to the charter and as proofs that the charter was never considered binding as a fundamental law. The first is the statute, already described, by which the Assembly in 1666 delegated to the separate towns the right to admit freemen, though the charter placed the "power and authority" to admit persons into the Company in the General Assembly: the question is merely a constitutional doubt as to the right or power of a legislative body to delegate an executive act to another subordinate body. The second is an act of 1669 granting the freemen the choice either to come in person to Newport, on the first Wednesday in May, to vote for the general officers of the colony, or to send a proxy vote to be cast in their stead,[17] apparently in violation of the words of the charter directing that these officers shall be chosen "by such greater part of the Company . . . as shall be then and there present." Whatever the usurpation, it was increased by a statute of 1760, taking away altogether the privilege of attending the general election at Newport and voting there; all freemen were henceforth required to vote in their respective towns.[18] These two acts may be considered merely as based on the legal fiction that the freemen were still present at Newport in their proxies, which were always carried there to be counted; or they may be considered amendments to the charter, adopted by the legislature and tacitly accepted by the freemen. The third change was brought about by a vote of the General Assembly, in 1796, to sit in two bodies:[19] the later claim that it thereby ceased to be a "general assembly" in the sense of the charter is hypercriticism, as is also the complaint because in 1798 the Assistants were renamed Senators.[20] Such minor details are almost unworthy of notice and hardly deserve the name of amendments, though technically they are changes of the fundamental law. The fourth allegation of unconstitutional action is the statute passed by the Assembly providing who should act as Governor in case of the Governor's absence: though the charter said nothing on this point, the statute is surely not hostile to the charter.[21] Fifth, the resolution of 1771, refusing the right of appeal to the king in council, unless the matter in controversy were worth three hundred pounds, does not seem to have been usurpatory, in view of the very comprehensive legislative powers which the Assembly had received from the charter: "Power to make, ordain, constitute or repeal such laws, statutes, orders and ordinances, forms and ceremonies of government and magistracy, as to them shall seem meet."[22]

Having thus eliminated minor questions of changes in procedure and organization, we are ready to consider whether the Rhode Island charter was lawfully the Constitution of the State in 1840. Applying the criteria mentioned above, we must accept the constitutional working of the charter. First, it was the fundamental law: except for a few amendments of slight importance, made by legislative acts and confirmed by the tacit consent of the people, all the laws, statutes, ordinances, and acts had been subordinate to the charter. Second, the charter contained the requisite provisions for the formation of the government and for the performance of legislative, executive, and judicial functions. Third, the charter was accepted by the "great concourse" of freemen when, in 1663, they received the document with "great joy." Fourth, the charter had been continuously acknowledged by the later inhabitants of the State, and it, therefore, had never lost its authority. Though, at infrequent intervals, complaints had been made against the charter, these never went farther than words, and no open rebellion or secret opposition had ever weakened its force.

The conclusion is inevitable that the charter granted by King Charles, accepted by the people, creating a new government of the colony, remaining unimpaired, unimpeached, supreme, and scarcely amended for nearly two centuries, was the Constitution of the State in 1840, as it had been in 1663, in 1776, and in 1790. This conclusion — reached from internal facts — is corroborated by external conditions. Members of the Continental Congress, Senators and Representatives in the United States Congress, had been accepted without question, although the provisions for their elections were made by the General Assembly sitting in accordance with the regulations of the charter. The President of the United States, and the National Supreme Court as well, had practically acknowledged the charter Constitution by dealing with the charter government. Though this fundamental question of the constitutional character of the charter scarcely needed discussion here, it has given an opportunity to place the document in its proper light, to explain and illustrate its characteristics and workings, and to bring before us the original causes of the demand for a constitution, which, after many years of ebb and flow, culminated in the Dorr Rebellion and, a little later, in the adoption of the present Constitution of the State.

AUTHORITIES.—**1** Arnold, *History of Rhode Island*, I. 143. **2** Arnold, I, 114–115. **3** Arnold, I, 238. **4** Arnold, I, 251. **5** Arnold, I, 279–280. **5** Potter, *Considerations on the Rhode Island Question*, 5. **6** *R. I. Col. Records*, VII, 522–526. **7** *R. I. Col. Records*, VII, 581–582. **8** *R. I. Col. Records*, VIII, 364–365. **9** *R. I. Col. Records*, II, 58. **10** *R. I. Col. Records*, II, 113; *Causin's Report*, 53. **11** *Digest of 1730*, 16; Arnold, I, 237. **12** *Digest of 1730*, 131; Arnold, II, 77–79. **13** *R. I. Col. Records*, V, 57. **14** *Digest of 1730*, 209; *Digest of 1752*, 12. **15** *R. I. Col. Records*, VI, 257. **16** *Digest of 1798*, 114–126. **17** *R. I. Col. Records*, II, 62. **18** *R. I. Col. Records*, VI, 256. **19** *R. I. Col. Records*, III, 313. Compare *Idem*, II, 63, 144, 151, 181. **20** *Digest of 1798*, 127. **21** *R. I. Col. Records*, II, 71. **22** *R. I. Col. Records*, IV, 250.

CHAPTER III.

EARLY MOVEMENTS FOR A CONSTITUTION.

1775–1838.

IN the war of words which broke out in Rhode Island during the summer of 1842, one of the most important causes of dispute was connected with some previous movements for a constitution and for an enlarged suffrage. The most extreme view of the Suffragists of 1842 was well presented by a "Member of the Boston Bar," who claimed that the people of Rhode Island had, "for more than forty years, been quietly endeavoring, by petition and appeal to the legislature of the State, to procure for themselves what every other member of our federal republic had long possessed—a constitution; and whose prayers [had], for nearly a century, been alternately refused and insulted."[a] Radically opposed was the view held by many of the leading citizens of the State, whose ideas were thus expressed by Francis Wayland, President of Brown University: "It is proper to add that, until very lately, it has been really doubtful whether a change was actually

---

[a] *Review of President Wayland's Discourse*, 3. This brochure, written by a "Member of the Boston Bar," has been commonly attributed to John A. Bolles.

4

desired by any large number of our citizens. Petitions on this subject were, it is true, several times presented, but they never seemed to arise from any strong feeling, nor to assume a form that called for immediate action. It has really been a matter of surprise to me that the question awakened so little attention."(1) It is important to ascertain which of these positions more nearly accords with the facts of history. To understand the position of the non-freemen of Rhode Island in 1842, it is necessary to trace the history of the various steps which had been previously made in behalf of, and in opposition to, a more liberal constitution and a freer suffrage, and to ascertain the strength of the previous demand. Could the non-freemen claim the same right to inaugurate a revolution as their forefathers undeniably had in 1776? Could they as truthfully say: "In every stage of these oppressions We have Petitioned for Redress in the most humble terms; Our repeated Petitions have been answered only by repeated injury?"

FRANCIS WAYLAND,
PRESIDENT OF BROWN UNIVERSITY, 1827-1855.

The years of the American Revolution were a period of constitution-making throughout the Union. Eleven States had drawn up and adopted written "forms of government" before the Federal Convention promulgated the Constitution of the United States. Even Connecticut, while satisfied with her existing charter government, deemed it best to take the formal action of adopting her charter as the Constitution of the State. In Rhode Island the matter was brought up in the legislature in September, 1777; and an able committee of five, headed by the Deputy-Governor, was appointed "to form a Plan of Government for this State." The unsettled condition of the State, due mainly to the presence of the British forces on the island of Rhode Island and to the inevitable dread and uncertainty, was not favorable to the preparation of a new constitution; and, since the State did not need any different government from that of her colonial days, no further record has been found of a "Plan of Government."

Twenty years later, in 1797, the idea of a new constitution was again presented, but met with the adverse action of the General Assembly in a form and for reasons of which no record has been discovered.[(b)] The chief interest of this period lies in the Fourth of July oration delivered by Colonel George R. Burrill, a leading lawyer and a brother of United States Senator James Burrill—an argument in favor of the rights of the majority and criticising the charter apportionment.[(2)] "Representation always supposes proportion," says the orator. "Equal representation is involved in the very idea of a free government." Burrill had, however, come to realize that any change in the government would be difficult to obtain. "To petition this legislature for equal representation is to require the majority to surrender their power—a requisition which

---

(b) The records of the General Assembly of a hundred years ago contained no allusion to bills that failed of passage, and no account of this movement has been found in the newspapers of the day.

it is not in human nature to grant." Hence he saw no method left but to ignore the General Assembly and proceed to form a constitution without its aid. This movement of 1797 failed for lack of support, and nothing further is heard of any demand for constitutional tinkering for fourteen years.

An enlargement of the suffrage was proposed in 1811 which may only indirectly be called a demand for a constitution, inasmuch as it seems to have been the general opinion that the General Assembly had entire power to change the suffrage qualifications by virtue of the provisions of the charter. An act was proposed to extend the suffrage to all male citizens, twenty-one years of age or over, who paid a poll or property tax or were enrolled in the militia, and who had resided in the town for a year. This bill passed the Senate, but was laid upon the table by the House.[3] The final action was preceded by a long debate, in the course of which a remarkable petition in favor of the bill was presented by several freemen.[c] Instead of the usual arguments in favor of an extension of the suffrage, the petitioners declared themselves opposed to the existing qualifications on the ground that they presented an opportunity for fraud. In order to manufacture the one hundred and thirty-four dollar real-estate qualification a large landowner would give a *quasi* life-lease of land on the condition that the lease should be forfeited at the end of the year if the rent were unpaid. The lessee thus, says the petition, becomes a freeholder of landed property which he does not use, has not purchased, and for which he does not intend to pay any rent. The petitioners preferred an almost universal suffrage to a suf-

[c] Both bill and petition are said to have been prepared by John Pitman, later United States Judge of the District Court of Rhode Island, and a prominent opponent of the suffrage movement of 1842. *Burke's Report*, 206–209.

frage thus fraudulently enlarged, and which admitted only bribable votes.[d]

In 1818, after a long and thorough discussion, Connecticut laid aside her charter and adopted a new constitution. The influence of this agitation was evidently felt in Rhode Island, since as early as October, 1817, a tentative resolution looking toward a constitution passed the House of Representatives.[4] By this bill, a committee was appointed to draft a call for a "Convention of the people to consider the expediency of forming a Constitution for this State." The committee, within a few days, reported a call for a convention, and the House, after a full debate, postponed consideration until the February session, though it ordered that the call be printed. The postponement was considered at the time "tantamount to a rejection," a prophecy which was fulfilled, inasmuch as the matter was not brought up again in the legislature for more than three years.

Scarcely a word of complaint is to be found during this interval, and it required the meeting of the Massachusetts Constitutional Convention of 1820 once more to interest the Rhode Islanders in the matter. This time the movement began with the newspapers of Providence, in editorials and communications, all of which criticised the omnipotence of the General Assembly or the subordinate position of the State judiciary. No mention is made of the representative apportionment nor of the suffrage qualifications. As a result of this agitation an act passed both houses, without opposition, at the February session, 1821, requesting the freemen, at the

---

(d) No record has been preserved of the debate in the House, but the feeling of conservative Rhode Islanders may be seen in the brief comments of the newspapers of the day. "After a long debate, in which the evil and wickedness of the bill were fully discussed, it was postponed until next session." *Rhode Island American*, March 5, 1811; *Newport Mercury*, March 9, 1811.

regular April election, to cast their ballots for or against the holding of a Constitutional Convention.(6) Unfortunately, the question of the convention became involved in a bitter sectional contest over the governorship. For more than thirty years the governor had been a Providence man; but, in 1821, William C. Gibbs, of Newport, was elected Governor by a plurality of a thousand in a total vote of sixty-six hundred.(7) The advocates of a new constitution belonged mainly to the Providence party, and the natural result was the defeat of the convention: out of 3,500 votes cast on the question, 1,600 were in favor and 1,900 against the proposition.(8) The votes in favor of the convention came almost entirely from the northern part of the State.(e)

Except for a brief discussion in the newspapers,(9) in September, 1821, which ceased, however, almost as soon as it began, the next appearance of the matter was in January, 1822, when the General Assembly again asked the people their wish in the matter.(10) No special interest seems to have been taken in the question, nor in fact in any political matter. The convention was defeated by a majority of about a thousand at the April election, when the total vote for governor was scarcely over two thousand.(11) The *Rhode Island American* declared that "in the present state of political affairs" the defeat was "a source of congratulation rather than regret to many of the warmest friends of a well-balanced constitution."(12)

In spite of these two defeats of 1821 and 1822, the demand for a constitution was renewed in the autumn of 1823. The agitation led to the appointment, at the October session of the legislature, of

(e) The Providence county vote stood 1,100 to 200; Bristol county, 177 to 8. On the other hand, in Newport county, the no majority was about 8 to 1; in Washington county, 7 to 1; and in Kent county, 3 to 1. *Providence Gazette*, May 9, 1821.

a committee of ten to report to the next session "on the subject of a written Constitution for the State."[13] In January, 1824, a bill was reported calling a "Convention for the purpose of forming a written Constitution of government for this State."[14] A long discussion followed a motion of Asher Robbins, later United States Senator, to strike out the main section of the bill; the principal arguments against the convention lay in the fact that the people had not asked for it and the presumption that they did not want it.[f] The amendment failed by a vote of 11 to 54, and the bill calling the convention was passed. During all the discussion, the only suggestion as to the possible content of a new constitution was the remark of Mr. Hazard, of Newport, that he would be willing to vote for a constitution which should provide a fair and equal representation.[15]

The call for the convention limited to the freemen the right to choose delegates, and apportioned these to the towns in equal number with their representatives.[16] These two features of the call were only natural, especially as there does not seem to have been any demand for any other arrangement. The election of delegates was set for the April town meetings; the convention was directed to meet at Newport in June; and the constitution formed was to be ratified by a three-fifths vote of all the freemen at a special election. The proposed convention aroused little interest among the people, and the vote for delegates was light.[17] There is no way of ascertaining the exact vote, but the election for governor indirectly shows the absence of enthusiasm.[g]

---

[f] The Speaker of the House, Albert C. Greene, later Attorney-General of the State for eighteen years, suggested that if the people did not want the convention they might refuse to elect delegates. *Rhode Island American*, January 20, 1824.

[g] James Fenner, who had been Governor from 1807 to 1810, was elected Governor again in 1824, and annually re-elected until 1831; he was again entrusted with the chair in 1843 and 1844.

The convention met as directed, June 21st, 1824, and on July 3d issued a plan for a constitution of the usual form:[18] it distributed the powers of government, arranged for the legislative, the executive, and the judiciary departments, contained a Bill of Rights, and provided for elections, suffrage, amendments, etc. No change of importance was made in the suffrage qualifications, except that the eldest son of a freeholder was no longer exempted from the real estate requirement. A proposition had been made in the convention, by Dutee J. Pearce, to extend the suffrage, but it was voted down, three votes only being cast in its favor.[19] As to the representation, the convention tried to arrange an apportionment which should satisfy large and small towns alike. Leaving the election of the ten Senators as it had been—that is, at large—it provided for the House of Representatives a scheme of proportionate representation.[h] This apportionment would have furnished, according to the census of 1820, a House of Representatives of seventy-three members—six towns choosing three members each, Newport four, Providence five, while two each would come from the twenty-three other towns. It would be a matter of surprise if this apportionment had not aroused great opposition in several towns and if it had awakened much enthusiasm in any.

The State remained very quiet during the summer and early autumn of 1824, before the special election of October. The Providence newspapers, after favorable editorials in the early part of July, when the constitution was published, were willing to let matters take their own course. The question before the people

---

In 1824, however, he received but 2,100 votes to 600 for his opponent, a total little more than one-third that of the election of 1821. *Rhode Island Manual, 1896–7*, 97, 99, 102.

[h] No town was granted more than seven Representatives, nor less than two; towns having over 3,000 inhabitants were assigned three Representatives; over 5,000, four; over 8,000, five; over 12,000, six; and over 17,000, seven.

was quite different from that three years before: in 1821 it was the desirability of holding a constitutional convention; in 1824 it was the adoption or rejection of a proposed constitution. In 1821 the referendum was taken at the end of a hotly-contested gubernatorial campaign; in 1824 no extraneous questions were before the people which might confuse their vote on the constitution. The number of votes at a special election would be less; but this would be offset by the interest which might be expected in an actually submitted constitution.

The usual vote for governor from 1819 to 1829 was under 3,000; in 1821 the total vote for governor was 6,602, and the sum of the "yes" and "no" votes on the convention reached 3,543; in April, 1824, 2,751 votes only were cast for governor,[20] and in October 4,792 ballots expressed the opinions as to the constitution. These figures conclusively show that the interest of the freemen in the constitutional question was marked, and make the comparison between the "yes" and "no" votes of much importance. The constitution received 1,668 votes in its favor and 3,206 against it—being lost by a vote of nearly two to one.[21] The sectional issue is again prominent—the two northern counties being nearly a unit for the constitution, while the three southern counties were strongly ranged on the other side.[i] Inasmuch as there has come down to us no record of the reasons for the rejection, we can only surmise what they were:[j] first, natural conservatism; the feeling that the

(i) Newport county gave 33 "yes" out of 1,095 votes; Washington county recorded 70 "yes" out of 793; and Kent county 169 out of 777. Providence county gave 677 votes, out of 1,885, against the constitution; the comparatively large negative vote being mainly due to two towns, Scituate and Foster, that adjoined Kent county. Adding the vote of the other eight towns in this county to that of Bristol county, we find 265 "no" votes out of a total of 1,634.

(j) The apportionment clause in the proposed constitution does not seem to have noticeably affected the vote. Providence, Smithfield, and Bristol, which would have gained in representation, did not give a proportionally greater "yes" vote than the neighboring towns; and the towns in charter was working satisfactorily and that no change was needed: second, the pronounced rivalry between the northern and the southern counties; the demand for a constitution coming mainly from the city of Providence.

The movements in favor of a new constitution have been now traced through the last quarter of the eighteenth and the first quarter of the nineteenth centuries. In summing them up, we must conclude that little consistency was shown by the leaders who demanded a change. They do not seem to know what they wanted; and we are almost tempted to declare that the agitation was, for the most part, the result of a mere desire for change. The people of the State seemed to have but little real interest in the movement; and it is evident that the majority of the voters were opposed to any innovation, while the non-freemen were seldom, if ever, heard from. Not until some definite plan was presented, not until the agitators were certain of their desires, not until they persistently and consistently urged their demands, could it be expected that the Rhode Island freemen would annul, or even amend, their time-worn charter.

The whole movement for a constitution now underwent an entire change: suffrage became the central question when the agitation was resumed. It will be remembered that not one of the preceding attempts to obtain a constitution had been made by those desirous of enlarging the franchise: the bill and petition of 1811 were for a change in the suffrage qualifications to be made by the General Assembly, and not for a constitution; and the movement, at that time, was led by those who claimed that universal suffrage might offset the prevalent fraudulent voting. As these men subsequently

---

the southern part of the State, which were accorded an extra Representative, gave almost a unanimous negative vote.

showed no desire for an increased suffrage, the isolated movement of 1811 may well be ignored. After 1825 the agitation was wholly in the hands of the suffragists. At first their cause seemed a desperate one and their various attacks invariably failed, the leaders deserting the cause and new leaders coming to the front. The struggle was, thereafter, never abandoned—although there were several resting spells—until the cause finally triumphed in 1842–3. A demand that the freemen, who possessed the right to vote, should give this privilege to a large class of non-voters would not at first, to say the least, be likely to obtain a hearing. Before a privileged class can be prevailed upon, of their own free will, to admit another large group to a share in their advantages, a "campaign of education" is always necessary. Years of agitation and the clearly expressed desire of the non-freemen would, inevitably, be necessary to bring about so radical a change.

In 1829, public agitation began again in the form of petitions to the legislature. At the May session of that year, Mr. Arnold presented to the General Assembly a memorial from 998 citizens of Providence, of whom 369 were said to be freeholders,[(22)] asking for an extension of suffrage. Similar memorials were presented from about 300 people of Bristol, Warren, and North Providence, nearly half of whom were claimed to be freeholders. These were local petitions, it is true, but they deserved recognition by the legislature; for it is evident that a large minority, at least, of the citizens of Providence would favor the movement, even making allowance for the carelessly signed names which are found on almost any petition. The 629 non-freemen of Providence also deserved to be listened to respectfully, even though they had no legal footing and were supported by no special backing. The House referred the memorials to a committee, of whom Benjamin Hazard, of New port, was chairman, and upon which was but one member who had presented memorials. At the next (June) session they reported adversely, and the petitioners were "allowed to withdraw."

The report of this committee—containing about 15,000 words—was evidently drawn by the chairman, and has always been called "Hazard's Report."[23] Its animus toward the petition may be seen from the opening words: "The committee . . ask leave to report: That they find nothing in these memorials, either of facts or of reasoning, which requires the attention of the House. If there is anything noticeable in them it is the little sense of propriety manifested in the style in which they are drawn up." The committee continued that they were confident that the people of the State did not desire to introduce the "new and untried system" of universal suffrage, but for the sake of the citizens who have not this confidence they will explain the subject of the franchise. The most remarkable feature of the report is its constitutional doctrine. It declared that the legislature had no power in the matter whatever: "The right of suffrage, as it is the origin and basis of every free elective government, so it is the peculiar and exclusive prerogative of the people, and cannot, without infringing that prerogative, be subjected to any other control than that of the people themselves. If representatives of the people, chosen for the ordinary purpose of legislation, could assume a control over this right, to limit, curtail, or extend it at will, they might, on the one hand, disfranchise any portion of their own electors; might deprive them of the power ever to remove them; and thus reduce the government to a permanent aristocracy. . . Such are the ordinances which our ancestors thought necessary to preserve the rights and liberties of themselves and their posterity; by preserving the elective franchise in the hands of the sound part of the community—the substantial freehold inhabitants of the State. Had they not a right to adopt these provisions? And have not their descendants, and those whom they have associated with them in conformity to those provisions, equally a right to preserve and adhere to them? . . Complainers mistake their right; which is, a right to qualify themselves as the laws require—not a right to be voters without such qualifications." The rest of this document consists of arguments upholding the freehold qualifications, and denouncing democracy as the curse of every nation which has ever yielded to its charms. In spite of its inconsistencies, in spite of the failure to treat the petitioners respectfully, the report accomplished its purpose, and the memorialists were unable to do anything further. The suffrage agitation was quiescent for a few years after this blow, and all movements for a constitution seemed at rest. How far party rivalries affected this result will be discussed in the next chapter.

In 1834, for the first time, we find an attempt at systematic action in place of the individual movements which have been noted in previous years. Before attempting to make any effort with the legislature, the leaders sought to mould public sentiment. This was done in various ways, but special trust was put in educating the people up to a realization of the need of a new constitution. Early in the year two northern towns of Providence county, Cumberland and Smithfield, invited the towns of the State to send delegates to a convention to be held at Providence, "to promote the establishment of a State Constitution."(24) Providence, North Providence, Cranston, Johnston, and Burrillville, as well as Smithfield and Cumberland, responded to this invitation by sending delegates. Bristol and Warren, of Bristol county, were represented, and also the town of Newport. These delegates from ten towns met February 23d, 1834, and organized by electing Nathan A. Brown president. The principal business done was the appointment of a committee of five to prepare an "Address to the People of Rhode Island," and to report at an adjourned session, which was held March 12th, at which time Scituate, in Providence county, and North Kingstown, in Washington county, were also represented.[k]

The masterly report of this committee is the first clear statement of the position of those who desired a new constitution; boldly attacking the charter and the legislature, it is throughout clear and unusually logical, and seizes upon the critical points with rare judgment.[25] It was a document of more value for its purpose than any of the many publications which the greater agitation of eight years later produced. Even those who most bitterly oppose its theories and conclusions must acknowledge its merit and give due credit to its author, Thomas W. Dorr, who thus first appears in the controversy.

The report opens with a declaration of loyalty to the "ancient sturdy spirit of Rhode Island patriotism;" with a request to lay aside all party predilections, to avoid the "too much man-worship" of the past and to form a constitutional party, "in the spirit of concession and compromise upon matters of local politics." The claim is made that political reforms are necessary in the State and can only be obtained by a written constitution, especially as the "discretionary regulation of the elective right, and of the judicial system, can never be properly and safely vested in the legislature." Frequency of election is not a sufficient safeguard: the constitution should be the fundamental law of the State, coming directly from the *free* and *sovereign* people. "When the American States severed the political tie which formerly bound them to Great Britain,

---

[k] This committee consisted of Thomas W. Dorr, Joseph K. Angell, David Daniells, William H. Smith, and Christopher Robinson.

all obligation to acknowledge obedience to a British charter as a constitution of government was, of course, dissolved; and the people of each State were left free and sovereign." "The sovereignty of the King of England passed, not to the Governor and Company of Rhode Island, but to the people at large, who fought the battles of the Revolution, and to their descendants." "That the people of Rhode Island retain their inherent right to establish (in their original, sovereign capacity) a constitution, cannot for a moment be doubted."

THOMAS W. DORR.
Aged about 35 Years

The next eight pages are devoted to a brief resumé of the character of the charter as an instrument of government, and to a more complete statement of the minor defects of the charter and of the provisions which the legislature had changed. Six pages are given to a treatment of the inequality of the representation, in which the claim is put forward that Rhode Island has not a republican government—"a government resulting from the will of the majority, ascertained by a just and equal representation." Rather the government is that of "an oligarchy, or the rule of a few." The demand is made that population, considered nearly proportional with wealth, be made the basis of apportionment.

One-half of the document is devoted to the subject of the extension of the suffrage. "We contend *that a participation in the choice of those who make and administer laws, is a natural right, which cannot be abridged, nor suspended any farther than the greatest good of the greatest number imperatively requires.*" The exclusion of women from the franchise is declared to be right because based "upon a just consideration of the best good of society including that of the sex itself." The justice of the exclusion of minors is discussed, and the rule that twenty-one is a suitable age for acquiring the right of the suffrage is accepted. "No man should be excluded from the exercise of [the suffrage], except from circumstances of unavoidable necessity." Arguments follow that the landed qualification acts unjustly and operates "differently from what it did in early times," and is also opposed to the spirit of the Constitution of the United States and to the theory and practice of most of the States. Every voter ought to show some sign of sufficient honesty and intelligence to exercise the privilege consistently with the best good of the whole people: therefore a small tax as a requisite for voting, and a distinction between native and naturalized voters, and a strict registration of voters are suggested. Then comes a brief discussion concerning improvements in the judiciary, especially urging life tenure and competent salaries for the judges. In closing, the people are urged to call, through their representatives, a convention to frame a "liberal and permanent constitution," and the report requests the legislature, "which has imposed a landed qualification not spoken of in the charter, . . . to suspend it, for the single purpose of facilitating the exercise by the people of the great, original right of sovereignty in the formation of a constitution."

The convention and its report met with a response from the legislature, at its June session, 1834,[26] and it issued a call for a convention, worded very much like that of 1824. As many delegates were to be chosen by the towns as they had representatives, and in the usual manner. The hint that a broader suffrage be granted for the occasion was ignored in arranging both for the election of delegates and for the voting on the constitution, if formed. The convention met as called, September 1st, and started upon its work; but the sessions were noted for the absence of interest, and frequent lack of a quorum. After a few days it adjourned until November, then again until February, 1835, and finally to June, when its members simply did not come together, and it thus expired.

From the very beginning this convention was doomed to failure. There was not even the interest shown that had been manifested ten years before. Many of the delegates thought that the labor of framing a constitution would be uselessly expended. They remembered that the same demand had, in 1821, 1822, and 1824, been distinctly and completely rejected by the freemen. Apparently the leaders in the movement thought that they had chosen a very opportune time to bring up their proposition: when neither party had a safe hold on the State, it might be expected that at least

6

one, if not both, of them would make a bid for the new voters. The inability to elect a governor the year before, and the unusual number of seven candidates for Representative to Congress, indicates a period of political dissatisfaction. But the hopes of the suffragists were in vain; neither party gave them any assistance, and their attempt to form a new party, definitely pledged to a constitution, was a failure from the beginning.

Two definite movements toward universal suffrage, in connection with a new constitution, had now been made: the first by petitions from four towns, including freemen and non-freemen; the second from a convention of delegates from about a third of the towns, nearly all in the northern part of the State. For the dismal failures of both attempts two reasons may be given: the freemen, as a rule, had no desire to extend the suffrage, and it was not to be expected that they should have; the sectional character of the demand also tended to create a prejudice in the other sections from the start. The attempt of 1834 was, hence, premature: the "campaign of education" had not been complete enough to overcome the traditions of generations.

Undoubtedly the non-freemen desired the franchise, and realized the fact that men like themselves had the ballot in almost every other State. But they were powerless: they could not vote suffrage to themselves; they had petitioned, but they had been laughed to scorn: they had obtained a convention, but it simply fell to pieces; they had no newspapers to speak for them: they were debarred from urging their point at town meetings; they had not succeeded in forming any kind of organization. Therefore they were practically unable to make their desires known. The freemen had not, as yet, really been impressed with any clear notion of their legitimate demands. The failure in 1834 was evidently decisive against the constitutional party, even though it struggled along for a few years and went so far as to nominate two candidates for Representatives to Congress in 1837.[(1)] The party and the movement were dead; and when a new attempt was begun, the leaders of 1834 declined, for a long time, to have anything to do with it.

We are now prepared to come to some conclusion as to the dispute between President Wayland and the "Boston Lawyer." It seems very evident that the latter was entirely wrong in speaking of any strong demand for a voice in the government as coming from the non-freemen previous to 1829. Beginning with that date we find a change. The landless residents began to awaken to a desire for what are called their political rights. But there had not been sufficient time to reach anything like the desired result: the first lessons had been learned, and the movement was destined to advance more rapidly when next taken up. The conclusion is inevitable that President Wayland was very nearly right. It might have been "a matter of surprise that the question had awakened so little attention," but before 1840 there was no definite general demand for a change. The movements had all been irresponsible and had not shown a strong feeling of injustice.

[(1)] At this election, Thomas W. Dorr received 72 votes, and Dan King 25, out of a total of 7,615. *Rhode Island Manual, 1896–7*, 160.

AUTHORITIES.—**1** Wayland, *The Affairs of Rhode Island*, 14. **2** *Burke's Report*, 271–274. **3** *Rhode Island American*, Mar. 5, 1811. *Newport Mercury*, Mar. 9, 1811. **4** *Newport Mercury*, Nov. 1, 1817. **5** *Manufacturers and Farmers Journal*, Nov. 27, Dec. 11, Dec. 25, 1820; Jan. 11, Jan. 14, Feb. 19, 1821. *Rhode Island American*, Feb. 13, 1821. *Providence Gazette*, Jan. 24, 27, 31; Feb. 10, 17, 24; March 3, 1821. See, also, Turner, *Report of The Trial of Thomas W. Dorr*, 77. **6** *Manufacturers and Farmers Journal*, March 1, 1821. *Rhode Island American*, Feb. 27, Mar. 2, 1821. *Providence Gazette*, Feb. 28, 1821. **7** *Rhode Island Manual, 1896–7*, 99. **8** *Idem*, 126. **9** *Rhode Island American*, Sept. 14, 28, 1821. *Manufacturers and Farmers Journal*, Sept. 17, 1821. *Providence Gazette*, Sept. 22, 1821. **10** *Manufacturers and Farmers Journal*, Jan. 28, Feb. 4, 1822. **11** *Rhode Island Manual, 1896–7*, 126. See, also, *Manufacturers and Farmers Journal*, Apr. 22, 1822. **12** *Rhode Island American*, Apr. 23, 1822. **13** *Manufacturers and Farmers Journal*, Nov. 11, 1823. **14** *Providence Gazette*, Jan. 17, 1824. *Rhode Island*

American, Jan. 20, 1824. **15** *Providence Gazette*, Jan. 17, 1824. **16** *Burke's Report*, 642–643. **17** *Rhode Island American*, Apr. 16, 1824. **18** *Burke's Report*, 209–219. *Providence Gazette*, July 10, 1824. *Manufacturers and Farmers Journal*, July 12, 1824. *Rhode Island American*, July 9, 1824. **19** *Burke's Report*, 722. **20** *Rhode Island Manual, 1896–7*, 99. **21** *Manufacturers and Farmers Journal*, Nov. 4, 1824. *Rhode Island Manual, 1896–7*, 127. **22** *Rhode Island American*, May 12, 1829. **23** *Burke's Report*, 377–401. See, also, *Providence Journal*, May 21, 22, 1841. **24** *Burke's Report*, 151. **25** *Address to the People of Rhode Island from the Convention assembled at Providence, Feb. 23 and March 12, 1834: To Promote the Establishment of a State Constitution. Burke's Report*, 151–185. **26** *Burke's Rebort*, 643–644.

CHAPTER IV.

THE RHODE ISLAND SUFFRAGE ASSOCIATION.

WHEN the question of an enlargement of the suffrage first came into prominence in 1829, the politicians had no wish to increase the number of their constituents; for they knew what to count upon and could not calculate the effect of a large additional voting list. The personal popularity of James Fenner kept him in office until 1829, but the next year his election was hotly contested, and in 1831 he was defeated by Lemuel H. Arnold, the Whig candidate. In 1832 the ascendency of the Whigs was threatened; the two parties were evenly matched, while a thousand independents prevented an election of governor, although five attempts were made. Though the State gave its electoral vote to Clay, the Whigs lost the governorship and did not regain it until 1838. The early defeats of the suffrage clause, therefore, seem not due to either party, but rather to the marked indifference or conservatism of the average voter.[a]

---

[a] In January, 1833, the legislature chose Asher Robbins, a Whig, to be United States Senator, giving him 41 out of the 78 votes cast. In November of the same year the newly-elected Assembly showed the change of sentiment politically by declaring the previous election void and choosing Elisha R. Potter, a Democrat, Senator. (*Rhode Island Manual, 1846-7*, 39) The United States Senate refused to give the seat to Potter and declared Robbins legally elected. (Senate Journal, 1 Sess. 23 Cong. 1833-34, page 285)

In 1839 neither party was able to elect its candidate for governor, and the Whig representatives received but a slight plurality over the opposing candidates. It would not be accurate to place Rhode Island in either political camp during this decade, but Whig principles were proving more attractive throughout the country, and Rhode Island felt the tidal wave.

LEMUEL H. ARNOLD.

In election of April, 1840, the Whigs elected Samuel Ward King their governor by a plurality of nearly fourteen hundred votes over Thomas F. Carpenter and carried nineteen of the thirty-one towns.[1] The House had a Whig majority of two to one[b] and the General Assembly chose a Whig senator, James F. Simmons. In the national election in November, General Harrison received about 5,000 votes in a total vote of 8,000.[c]

[b] The twelve towns that had Democratic majorities chose each two representatives, making twenty-four in all, or one-third of the entire membership. The strong Democratic towns, at this time, were Burrillville, Glocester, Foster, Scituate, Charlestown, Exeter, and North Kingstown. The close towns were Tiverton, West Greenwich, Richmond, Hopkinton, Jamestown, New Shoreham, and Coventry. These towns, for the most part, were entirely agricultural, and remote from the centres, such as Providence, Newport, Bristol, and Warwick.

[c] *Newport Mercury*, Nov. 7, 1840. Eight towns only gave a majority for President Van Buren: Burrillville, Glocester, Scituate, Foster, Exeter, Richmond, North Kingstown, and Tiverton.

Such were the political conditions in the winter of 1840–1. Not only was the Whig party victorious in the nation, with a majority in both branches of Congress; in the State of Rhode Island national political interests predominated over State interests in a way unusual in that community: the senators and representatives had been chosen with reference merely to their national political preferences, and there was every reason to believe that the Whigs would vote almost as a unit on most of the matters that would come before the State government.

On the other hand, the Democratic party was, apparently, in a forlorn condition, about to lose all control of the national government, and already driven out of power in State affairs. In the campaigns of 1840 the Democratic rank and file had shown very little enthusiasm; they had never before known what an overwhelming defeat was; it seemed to them that their party was doomed, and they knew not in what direction to turn. In the spring of 1841 the Democrats failed to nominate candidates either for governor or for Representatives to Congress, and the Whig candidates were elected by default.[2]

JAMES F. SIMMONS.

The first appearance of the question of suffrage and constitutions, after the final collapse of the previous agitation in 1838, was in an "Address to the citizens of Rhode Island, who are denied the right of suffrage," which appeared in January, 1840, in a brochure of eight pages, purporting to come from the "First Social Reform Society of New York." In this address we find a development of the propositions that had been made forty years earlier by Colonel Burrill; a definite scheme is set before the readers by which, in spite of the opposition of the government, a liberal constitution might be obtained.

An important part of the address was the "preliminary suggestions as to holding a *State Convention.*" It advised the holding of primary meetings to call a convention, to name the time and place, and to apportion the number of delegates from each county and town. It advised that all male citizens over twenty-one years of age should be allowed to vote for delegates, and that lists of such voters should be kept, "duly certified by those appointed to receive the votes, and appended to the credentials of the delegates." The next step suggested was that the assembled delegates should count the votes cast, and if "the whole number of votes cast exceeds the whole vote of the previous general election for Representatives to Congress, then the convention will unquestionably represent the majority of the people, and will, therefore, as unquestionably have the sovereign right to frame a constitution for the State." Having framed a constitution, they should appoint time and manner of electing State and congressional officers. Then the members of Congress, thus elected, might claim their seats at Washington, "and the responsibility would then devolve upon Congress of deciding whether members from a majority of the people, elected under a Republican Constitution, framed by the people themselves, shall have seats in the councils of the nation, or members from an incorporated body of land *Lords*, and their eldest sons, who, by virtue of a royal charter, are stockholders of the elective franchise, and of the government."

It will be interesting to see how far this novel proposition was followed. At first there seemed to be an inherent promise of success: if the non-freemen were numerous enough, or if they could find sufficient freemen who sympathized with their movement, there seemed no reason why they could not induce Congress to acknowledge the legality of a new constitution. So far as the preliminary course of action went, the advice was gladly received; but when the time came, the proposed appeal to Congress was not made.

This address was distributed broadcast throughout Rhode Island, and soon came to the notice of the newspapers. The Whigs identified it with the Van Buren New York Democracy, and claimed that it indicated the desires of the Democrats of Rhode Island, even if, perhaps, it were not prepared by them.[(3)] This charge the *Republican Herald* — the Democratic organ — denied "in the most solemn and unequivocal terms."[(4)] Instead, it claimed that the Democracy of Rhode Island was "firmly attached to the present laws regulating the elective franchise. . . . For our own part we view the proffered advice and interference of any body of men in New York with the political affairs of our State as an indecent and unwarrantable assumption; and as the *New York Evening Post* has had the kindness to volunteer to republish the above-named pamphlet in its columns, we should esteem it quite as much an act of kindness should the *Post* give us light on the origin of it." However, the belief was very strong that the "Address" was prepared in Rhode Island, and that the so-called Social Reform

Society was either a myth, or was used in the interest of Rhode Islanders who were about to inaugurate a suffrage movement. How much influence the address had in shaping the movement in the State cannot be determined; but the close connection between the proposition and the movement itself is quite remarkable. Acting in accordance with this advice, the Rhode Island Suffrage Association was organized in the autumn of 1840 by certain inhabitants of Providence, for the purpose of inaugurating a new agitation for a constitution with freer suffrage. Many, if not most, of

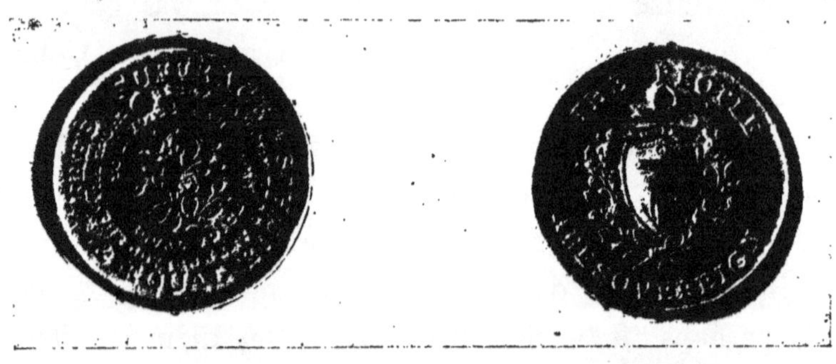

SUFFRAGE MEDAL.

(COLLECTION OF CHARLES GORTON.)

the members were non-freemen.[5] This was soon followed by the establishment of the Woonsocket Suffrage Association, and by other similar suffrage societies throughout the State.[6] Before the spring of 1841 nearly every town in the State had an organization of this kind.

The plan of these societies was from the beginning in accord with the propositions of the address before described. The Rhode Island Suffrage Association issued a Declaration of Principles, which was generally adopted by the societies.[7] In this declaration, the propositions were laid down that:

(1) All men are created free and equal;

(2) Possession of property should not create political advantages for its holder;

(3) That every body politic should have for its foundation a bill of rights and a written constitution;

(4) That Rhode Island had neither;

(5) That the charter lost its authority when the United States became independent;

(6) That every State is entitled to a republican form of government;

(7) That any State is anti-republican which keeps a majority of of the people from participating in its affairs;

(8) That by every right, human and divine, the majority should govern; and

(9) That the time had gone by for submission to most unjust outrages upon social and political rights.

These propositions led to the resolutions:

(1) "That the power of the State should be vested in the hands of the people, and that the people have a right, from time to time, to assemble together, either by themselves or their representatives, for the establishment of a republican form of government;

(2) "That whenever a majority of the citizens of this State, who are recognized as citizens of the United States, shall, by their delegates in convention assembled, draught a Constitution, and the same shall be accepted by their constituents, it will be, to all intents and purposes, the law of the State."

It will be seen that, from the outset, the leaders of the suffrage movement proposed to ignore the legally constituted government of the State. They did not intend merely to agitate the question, to "educate" the people, to furnish means by which an expression of the desires of the people could be obtained. Rather, it was their plan to prepare the people for a peaceful revolution. They would make use of what they called the "original sovereign right of the people" to ignore all previous forms of government, to lay aside all allegiance to the existing order, and to evolve, at their own pleasure and in their own method, a new government which should suit their convenience. The germ of this doctrine was destined to grow until it led to the complications of the next year.

It cannot be too strongly urged that the suffrage agitation in Rhode Island in the early forties was not begun by either party.[d] The Whig newspapers kept entirely aloof from the movement; they were absorbed in the presidential campaign and had no thoughts for any such outside matters. The Democratic papers also ignored the matter until the November election was over. The leaders, both Democratic and Whig, as a rule, refused to have anything to do with the agitation, even during the year 1841. Nevertheless, the organizers of this new movement would seem to have wisely chosen the time for their agitation: the Democratic party throughout the country had been the "party of reform," so far as the franchise was concerned: as soon as the Rhode Island Democrats should have recovered from the stunning blow which they had received in the elections, the suffrage leaders hoped that they would grasp the opportunity to make a strong bid for support, however

---

[d] As an illustration of the non-partisan character of the movement, it may be noted that the president of the Woonsocket Suffrage Association was an ardent Democrat, while the secretary was a thorough Whig. *Burke's Report*, 247. (Testimony of Welcome B. Sayles.)

indifferent they had been, when in power, to the wrongs of the non-freemen. These hopes were doomed to disappointment, for the Democratic party did not officially ally itself with the movement.

The effect of the election of 1840 was, nevertheless, soon apparent. The *Republican Herald*, in spite of its strong statement in the previous winter against any change, began gradually to feel its way toward an expression of sympathy with the suffragists, and, two days after the election, editorially remarked: (8) "There are at least 14,000 men in Rhode Island who had not the privilege of voting for President of the United States, on Monday last—men who in all respects are equal to those who enjoyed that privilege—and who, had they lived in any other State of the Union, could have exercised the inestimable right of freemen. They are deprived of the right, because they are not land-owners." The angry feeling of the defeated party was still further shown ten days later, in another editorial, in which the thought was brought forward that the election might have been different if the 14,000 had voted; and that even if defeat had still been encountered, it would have been much pleasanter to realize that it had come in a vote of "the whole people and not a select few merely." (9) The editor then offered to throw open his columns to a discussion upon the subject of a freer suffrage.

The suffrage associations wisely determined to keep free from entangling alliances with either of the great parties, and decided to establish an official organ for themselves. November 20, 1840, the first number of the *New Age* appeared in Providence, and devoted its leading editorial to a word of advice "to the Non-Freeholders of Rhode Island." It considered that the time—immediately after the great political excitement of the national election—was particularly appropriate for a consideration of the unrepresented thousands who were deprived of the privilege of voting, by the discrimination of the charter and subsequent legislation. In brief, it claimed that "the present system of franchise in Rhode Island is unjust, inasmuch as it concedes privileges to a certain wealthy class, thereby tending to build up among us an aristocratic class, with special privileges and immunities."

About the first of December the association held a meeting, which voted that the association would "support the paper entitled the *New Age* for the term of three months." A committee of two from each ward in the city of Providence was appointed to "collect subscriptions and act as agents for the paper." The *New Age* appeared weekly, and each number was carefully prepared for the purpose of leading its readers on step by step. The issue of December 4, 1840, contained an editorial entitled "What We Want," which was a disquisition on the use made by the paper of the term "universal suffrage." While claiming that the personal opinion of the editor was that *no one* should be excluded from the right to vote, it suggested that the qualifications then existing in Massachusetts — payment of a poll tax and residence within the town — made a close approach to universal suffrage. It concluded the editorial with the advice that a convention of the *whole people* be called "to put, in a clear and decisive form, an exposition of the wants of the non-freeholders." The next issue of the paper restates the belief of the editor in the right of universal suffrage, but acknowledged that this opinion had received a severe condemnation from the suffrage associations, and that the explanation of the willingness of the editor to abide by the decision of the convention had not proved satisfactory to his "keepers." This was a sufficient hint that the committee on printing of the Rhode Island Suffrage

Association claimed the right of control over the principles which the paper should set forth.[e]

The agitation was now fairly under way, and preparations were made for a vigorous "campaign of education," to be carried on early in the year 1841. Communications now began to appear in the other newspapers of the State, most of them anonymous, and few presenting any new or important material. One writer did suggest a feasible plan of operations, and showed the position which the leaders were ready to assume when the right moment arrived:[10] "I would first propose to call a general convention of all the 'freeholders and non-freeholders' in favor of adopting a constitution for this State, and then appoint a committee in every town to call on every freeman, and take the names of all those who will pledge themselves to support such a measure; and if there is a minority of them (which no doubt there will be), then to make up the deficiency from among the non-freeholders, who will qualify themselves expressly for this purpose by a purchase of $134 of real estate. Could this be done everything would go smoothly without a civil revolution between our present Lordly Freemen and their vassals, and save a deal of time and political acrimony. I am for trying all peaceable means first, by the ballot box, to effect this object; and should that fail, I would then say, 'We the people' *will* have a constitution for this State, and rise in the majesty of our strength, form a constitution and establish a government."

---

[e] This committee consisted of Asa W. Davis, James Stone, Jesse Calder, Augustus Arnold, W. C. Thayer, W. C. Spencer, James Manchester, J. M. Wheeler, Benjamin Arnold, James A. Smith, Edwin Field, and Colonial Hopkins.

AUTHORITIES.—1 *Newport Mercury*, Apr. 18, 1840; *Rhode Island Manual, 1896-7*, 102. 2 *Rhode Island Manual, 1896-7*, 102. 3 *Providence Journal*, Jan. 29, Feb. 5, 1840. 4 *Republican Herald*, Feb. 1, 1840. 5 *Burke's Report*, 16, 108, 247, 724. 6 *Burke's Report*, 247. 7 *Burke's Report*, 108-109, 403-404; *New Age*, Feb. 19, 1841. 8 *Republican Herald*, Nov. 4. 1840. 9 *Idem*, Nov. 14, 1840. 10 *New Age*, Dec. 25, 1840

CHAPTER V.

TWO CONVENTIONS CALLED.

IT is evident that the suffrage associations had no confidence that any help would come from the legislature; when the right time came it was their intention to ignore the government and act independently of it. Nevertheless, there were some ardent agitators who deemed it best to make one more trial, and the following petition was prepared and published in the official organ: (1)

"To the Honorable the General Assembly of the State of Rhode Island: The undersigned, inhabitants and citizens of the State of Rhode Island, would respectfully represent to your honorable body, that they conceive, that the dignity of the State would be advanced, and that the liberties of the citizens better secured, by the abrogation of the Charter granted unto this State by King Charles the Second of England, and by the establishment of a constitution which should more efficiently define the authority of the Executive and Legislative branches, and more strongly recognize the rights of the citizens.

"Your petitioners would not take the liberty of suggesting to your honorable body, any course which should be pursued, but would leave the whole affair in your hands, trusting to the good sense and discretion of the General Assembly.

"Your petitioners would further represent to the General Assembly, that they conceive that an extension of the suffrage to a greater portion of the white male residents of the State, would be more in accordance with the spirit of our institutions, than the present system of the State and for such an extension they ask. Your petitioners would not suggest any system of suffrage, but would leave the matter to the wisdom of the General Assembly.

"Upon both the prayers of your petitioners, they would ask the immediate and efficient action of the General Assembly, and as in duty bound will ever pray."

The *New Age*, in commenting editorially upon this petition, made the important concession that there could be no doubt of the right of the legislature to amend the laws of the State, among them that establishing the suffrage qualifications, which had already been "from time to time altered and amended at pleasure."[2] At the same time the editorial took occasion to reaffirm a belief in the "right of the people to assemble in convention, and raise their voice in the work of reform." "We wish to regain our rights and, as the easiest way of so doing, we, in respectful terms, ask of the freeholders, through their representatives, that they be restored. If our request is refused, there is no reason why other steps should not be taken to regain that which has been taken from us. If a thief steals my property, there is no impropriety in my first asking him to return it, and if he refuses, I shall have to take other measures to obtain my own." The petition was respectfully worded, but this explanatory editorial was not calculated to win votes in favor of acceding to the request of the petitioners.

The petition was received by the General Assembly and at once laid on the table, from which it was never taken.[3] This action has been condemned by many writers: for instance, the "Boston Lawyer" stated that "the petitions were insultingly passed by without any notice, or action, on the part of the Assembly."[4] The temper of the legislature cannot be fully understood[a] without some discussion of the reception of a memorial from the town of Smithfield, at the same January session, which was presented and referred to a select committee, of which Asher Robbins was chairman.[5] The memorial prayed the General Assembly to "take the subject of the extreme inequality of the present representation from the several towns under consideration, and, in such manner as seems most practicable and just, to correct the evil complained of."[6]

The committee reported that the regular and rightful way of obtaining the object prayed for was by a convention of the freemen, and presented the resolution "that it be recommended to the freemen of the State, at the several town meetings in April, to instruct their representatives as to their wishes for a State Convention to frame a new Constitution for this State, in whole or in part, with full power for that purpose."[7] After much discussion and a recommittal of the resolution, it was voted to call a convention without the preliminary process of asking the freemen to make known their desires in the matter. On February 6, 1841, the General Assembly passed the act calling a convention to frame a new constitution, in whole or in part; "and, if only for a Constitution in part, that said Convention have under their special consideration the expediency of equalizing the representation of the towns in the House of Representatives."[8] The freemen were requested to choose delegates at the August election, and the convention was appointed for November, at Providence. The call directed that the result of the work

[a] Elisha R. Potter, Representative in Congress from Rhode Island, declared, in a speech in the House, that the name which headed this list of 581 petitioners, Elisha Dillingham, was that of a man who had been in the Massachusetts state prison for eighteen years. Potter, *Considerations*, 7

of the convention should be submitted to the freemen at whatever time it should deem best. It was also provided that the votes of the people should be counted by the General Assembly, and that the constitution, or amendments, should go into effect if approved by a majority of the freemen voting.

The vote of the representatives calling this convention is significant: 37 in favor, 16 against; and 18 absent or not voting,[9] of whom 12 were probably in favor of the measure; while 3, at least, of the negative votes were due to objection to particular features of the bill.[10] The actual majority in favor of granting the request and calling a convention was, therefore, something like three to one; and among the members of each party a majority was in favor of the bill.[b]

It will be seen that the legislature, in giving this direct reply to the Smithfield memorial, indirectly answered the Dillingham petition. The memorial asked for a reapportionment: a convention was summoned, and it was especially directed, whatever it chose to do or refrain from doing, to rectify the apportionment. The petition asked for a new constitution: the call for a convention was a step in the direction of obtaining such a result. The petitioners also desired an extension of the franchise: a new constitution would be likely to define the suffrage qualifications, and the General Assembly tacitly left the question of the franchise to the convention. Apparently the General Assembly had fully answered both memorial and petition.

The position taken by the suffragists, immediately after the passage of this call, is shown by an editorial as follows:[11] "Though we have but little confidence in the results of the deliberations of

---

[b] Of the 49 Whig members in the House, 28 voted "yes," 9 "no," and 12 were absent; of the Democrats, 9 voted "yes," 7 "no," and 6 were absent—22 in all.

the Convention ordered by the General Assembly, yet the very fact that such a Convention has been ordered proves conclusively that there is a growing disposition on the part of the freeholders of the State to consider and remedy the abuses of its government. There has been a time when a petition like the one of Smithfield would have been quietly laid upon the table. But the General Assembly know that it would not do at this late day to pass over in contempt a document of such character. As for this *Convention for the framing of a Constitution*, which they have called, we do not suppose it will do anything for the advancement of freedom in our State. It will be seen that the representation in the Convention will be nothing more than a representation of freemen, and taking this into view, it will be only the General Assembly elected over again, and therefore we have no more to hope from such a body than we have from the General Assembly. Of course the over-represented towns will send their quota of representatives, and the under-represented towns will be voted down in precisely the same manner as if the General Assembly had themselves taken up the question of a Constitution. We are of the opinion that the whole affair will result precisely as did the last attempt of the kind. These contradictions only show the necessity of the people's taking the matter into their own hands. They are the persons most interested in the result; it is no partial body of freemen who take an interest in the result. If then the General Assembly will not meet the wants of the people, nor in all probability will a Convention acting under them, it is high time *they* took the matter into their own hands, resolved if they cannot obtain redress of their grievances in the ordinary way, they will take extraordinary measures to obtain it."

The suffragists had not forgotten the defeats of 1824 and 1834, and conceived that the coming convention offered no prospect of a better result. Hence they continued the agitation, as though the legislature had not voted, except that the convention seems to have stimulated them to greater energy, and the movement developed with great rapidity.

The Whig campaign of 1840 was still fresh in the minds of all. What better means for agitating the cause of "constitution and suffrage" than to adopt the essential features of that campaign Processions and mass conventions were in some respect new features in political affairs, and they were destined to be used with good effect by the leaders of the new movement in Rhode Island. The organ of the "Suffrage party," as the suffragists now began to be called, as early as the last week in February, strongly urged the holding of a mass convention of the non-freeholders of the State.(12) Such a convention, though never yet attempted, would, doubtless, "eventuate as successfully as any one can desire." A few days later a letter appeared in the same paper, purporting to come from a fifty-dollar tax-payer, enlarging upon the advisability of such a convention. The writer thought that it might easily be arranged and that it would be the largest assembly that Rhode Island had ever witnessed.

Meanwhile, public meetings were being constantly held, especially in the city of Providence, many of which were given up to debate. One of the most remarkable of these discussions, extending over three evenings, was on the question, "Is it expedient for the non-freeholders to refuse to do military and fire duty?"(13) Another debate was held on the subject, "Is it expedient for the non-freeholders to form associations for the purpose of military discipline?"[14] This, the first hint that has been found of the possible need of arms in the controversy, evidently caused some hesitation. The fifty-dollar tax-payer, above alluded to, acknowledged that the organization of military companies would "strike a terror to some who have but small organs of combativeness, and a great fear of anything that has the appearance, or can in any way be construed into a semblance, of revolution or nullification."[15] The writer, however, went on to explain that the power of a government consisted in the arms of the government, and that there was no power in the State "to ensure the citizen's safety from foreign invasion or extensive internal commotion." He then claimed the right to keep and use firearms, and also the right of the people to assemble together in a peaceable manner to perfect their knowledge of the art of using firearms. This letter, of March, 1841, is interesting in the light of the later events of May and June, 1842.

At a meeting of the "friends of suffrage," Saturday, March 20, 1841, a committee was appointed to report on the subject of a parade. They reported the next Wednesday, recommending that the non-freemen and other persons interested in an extension of the suffrage should "parade the streets of Providence, with appropriate banners, and partake of a collation on Jefferson Plains," in the afternoon. They also requested that citizen's dress should be worn, and that efforts be made to preserve order and decorum throughout the day. This was to be the first demonstration of a series, and the leaders expected great results from such a united demand for what they considered their rights. Their organ, of course, was boiling over with enthusiasm;[16] and the *Republican Herald* swung around into line, expressing the belief that the right of the elective franchise belonged to everyone, and hoping that the parade might be the "precursor of a signal success, equal to the importance and justice of the object."[17]

The parade and feast, on April 17, must have fully come up to the hopes of the leaders of the movement. Although a great part of the day was unpleasant, there was an immense concourse of people, and many thousands turned out to see the parade, which consisted of from 2,500 to 3,500 men, about 200 mounted, and a very few in carriages.[18] All of these wore the suffrage badge, with the words, "I am an American citizen." Many banners were carried, bearing such legends as, "I die for liberty;" "Worth makes the man, but sand and gravel make the voter;" "Virtue, Patriotism, and Intelligence versus $134 worth of dirt;" "Peaceably if we can, forcibly if we must." The collation fed the multitude and provided an opportunity for orations by Dutee J. Pearce, Samuel Y. Atwell, and others.[19] The suffrage organ was naturally very much elated, and predicted that "People's Day" would be honored in Rhode Island side by side with Independence Day.[20]

It must not be forgotten that curiosity played a great part in enlarging the numbers of the spectators in Providence on April 17; nor should it be supposed that all the persons taking part in the parade were "white male citizens over twenty-one years of age." Nevertheless, an unusual opportunity was afforded of sowing suffrage seeds; many came to look on, and went away to think. The non-freeholders were awakened; those who had previously had no desire for the privilege of voting now began to look upon it as a boon not to be despised; those who had abandoned hope were now encouraged by organized effort. Many freemen, who had never before thought much about the matter, were awakened to the feeling that others besides the freemen had equally as good a right to the suffrage.

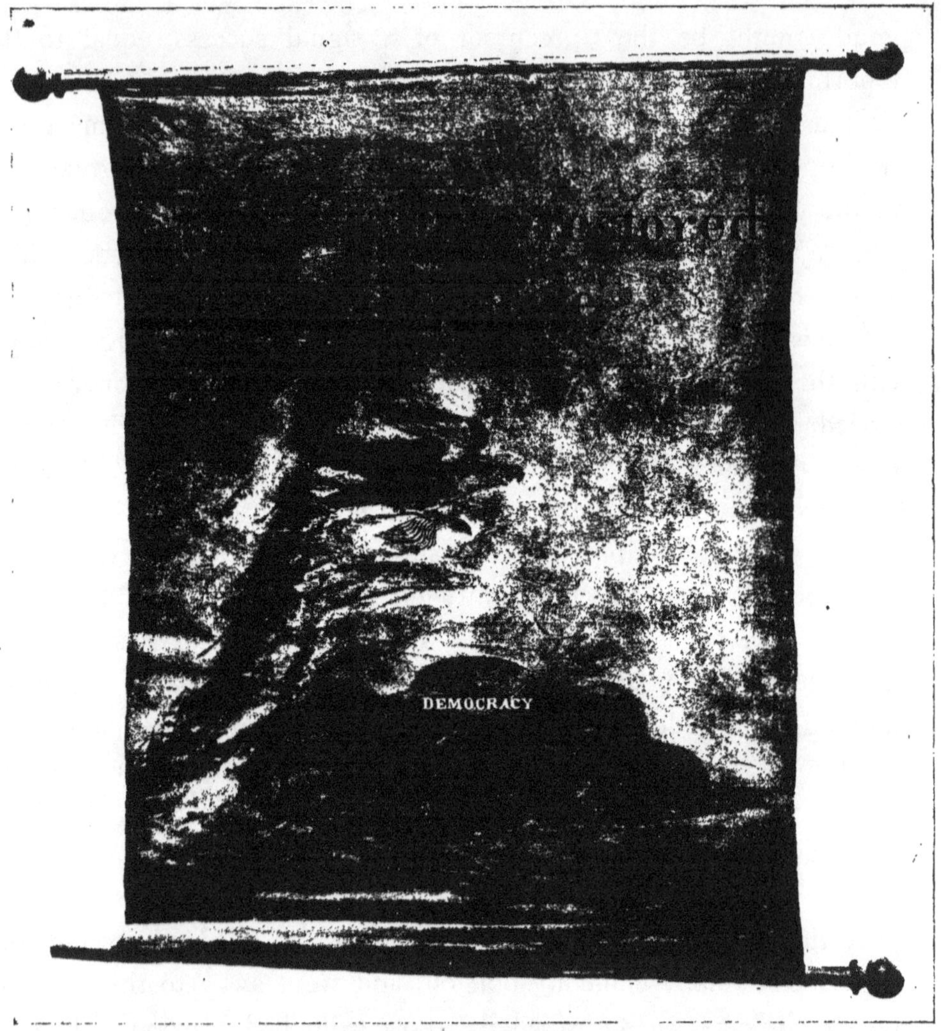

BANNER USED IN SUFFRAGE PARADE.
(ORIGINAL IN COLLECTION OF RHODE ISLAND HISTORICAL SOCIETY.)

The parade had accomplished so much that the agitators immediately began a movement for a mass convention in Newport on "Election Day," May 5.[(21)] This term has always been used to mean the day when the new government of the State entered upon its duties, and has always been a time of special interest, one of the holidays of the State. Time and place were well chosen for this convention, which it was hoped would bring together, as could not have been done in larger States, a vast assemblage of interested persons, and would be likely to produce an effect upon the incoming legislature. The number in the procession was, however, barely half that in the previous parade in Providence; about a third of those who took part were armed, either with guns or swords,[(22)] but certain companies of the State militia advertised to appear were not present.[(23)] The smaller number was disappointing, but not inexplicable, even from the standpoint of the suffragists: Newport and the neighboring towns were much smaller than Providence and its vicinity, and were geographically separated from most of the State. Moreover, the centre of the discontent with regard to the existing conditions was at Providence, while Newport headed the opposition to any change in the form of government. The number and enthusiasm shown in behalf of free suffrage at Newport on this occasion ought to have satisfied even the most earnest suffragist in the State.

The meeting on "Election Day" was not merely a procession, a mark of interest in the movement of the day. The convention, at which only badge-wearers were supposed to be present, listened to addresses by General Stoddard (the presiding officer), Dutee J. Pearce, James A. Greene, and William Ennis.[(c)] A series of resolutions was reported by the committee on resolutions,[(d)] which criticised the "Charter of a British King as a Constitution of political

(c) The convention was presided over by General Martin Stoddard; John Sterne, Franklin Cooley, Samuel H. Wales, James A. Greene, Silas Sisson, and James A. Brown were chosen vice-presidents; and Samuel Thomas and Francis B. Peckham, secretaries. *Republican Herald*, May 8, 1841.

(d) This committee consisted of William Ennis, Edward Field, David Parmenter, Jesse Calder, and Simeon Anthony.

government," deeming it "insufficient and obsolete;" declared that the "whole body of the people of this State" had the right, "in their original and sovereign capacity," to make their own constitution, and that this right was not barred by the lapse of time, and that the proper time had arrived; criticised the "undefined and uncontrolled" legislative power, the unequal representation in the General Assembly, and the restricted suffrage; declared that a government of property was inconsistent with the American idea; denied all connection with any political party; criticised the unequal and limited representation in the convention called by the General Assembly; advised the suffragists to perfect their organization in every town; appointed a State committee to carry forward the cause, and to "*call a convention of delegates to draught a constitution* at as early a day as possible;" requested the State committee to obtain "a list of all the citizens in the several towns who were ready to vote for and sustain a constitution based on the principles hereinbefore declared," and to prepare an address to the people; and directed that copies of the resolutions be sent to the various executive and legislative officers of the State.[24] The resolution establishing the State committee[e] and assigning its duties is the most significant portion of the action of the convention. The advice to call a convention, and to obtain a list of pledged supporters, indicated a determination to go forward with a constitution and to ignore the legislature and its legally-called convention. The convention adjourned to meet in Providence on Independence Day, Monday, July 5, 1841.

---

[e] This committee, as appointed May 4, consisted of Charles Collins and Dutee J. Pearce, of Newport county; Samuel H. Wales, Welcome B. Sayles, and Benjamin Arnold, Jr., of Providence county; William S. Peckham and Sylvester Himes, of Washington county; Silas Weaver and Emanuel Rice, of Kent county; and Samuel Allen and Benjamin M. Bosworth, of Bristol county.

The next movement in the drama consisted in the "Address of the State Suffrage Committee, setting forth the principles of the suffrage movement," sent out to the public June 11, 1841. This address presented the usual arguments for a constitution, criticised the omnipotent power of the Assembly, and claimed that there were but two methods by which an improvement could be obtained. The ballot box was open to them, or they might resume "their original and natural rights and powers;" but the "disfranchised majority" were excluded from the ballot box, and there was little hope from the freemen at the polls. An important concession was made: "The committee are happy to believe that a very considerable change has taken place in this respect, within a short period; and that a very respectable body of the landholders are now advocates for a written constitution, to be framed and adopted by the people, and a liberal and permanent system of suffrage placed beyond the reach of legislative control and interference. The committee congratulates the friends of the cause on this auspicious circumstance; still it must not be disguised that much remains to be done." The address urged the "people—'the numerical force'—to proclaim their will, resume their original powers, and assert their original rights." It closed with a promise that, in due time, a call would be issued for the holding of primaries prior to a State convention.[25]

Another effort was made, however, to obtain more liberal provisions from the General Assembly. On the second day of the May session, a resolution was introduced apportioning the delegates to the convention more in accordance with the population,[26] and was immediately passed by a vote of 48 to 20:[27] It allowed one delegate from towns under 850 inhabitants; two from towns with a population between 850 and 3,000; three from towns of 3,000 to 6,000; four, from 6,000 to 10,000; five, from 10,000 to

15,000; and six, if over 15,000 inhabitants.[28] That is, six delegates from Providence; four each from Newport, Warwick and Smithfield; three each from Tiverton, Bristol, Scituate, North Providence, Coventry, and South Kingstown; one each from Jamestown and Barrington; and two each from the other towns; making seventy-seven in all.[29] This concession to the suffrage party was received with scorn. At a meeting of the Rhode Island Suffrage Association, immediately following this action of the legislature, the following resolutions were adopted:[30] "Resolved that this Association believes that the action of the General Assembly, May 6th, to proportion the delegates to the whole People for the Convention in November, is but a feint to draw the attention of the friends of equal rights from the object they have in view. Resolved, that we will relax no exertion, but redouble our energies in the cause, and shrink not until our rights, and the rights of the People be acknowledged."

Early in the May session Samuel Y. Atwell introduced a bill, which was taken up at the June session, referred to the committee on the judiciary, and by them endorsed "not recommended."[31] The main features of the proposed act[32] related to the representation in the convention and to the qualifications of the electors of the delegates. The franchise, for election of delegates and upon the question of ratification, was granted to "every male inhabitant of the State, of the age of twenty-one years, who is a citizen of the United States, and who has resided in the State two years, and in the town or city where he offers to vote for three months next previous to the day of town or ward meetings, (persons insane, under guardianship, or convicts excepted)". The apportionment allowed eighteen delegates to Providence; nine to Smithfield; eight to Newport; seven to Warwick; five to Cumberland: four each to

Scituate, South Kingstown, and North Providence; three each to Tiverton, Cranston, North Kingstown, Coventry, and Bristol; one each to Middletown, Little Compton, New Shoreham, Jamestown, Charlestown, Richmond, West Greenwich, and Barrington; and two each to the other ten towns, making 102 in all. A long debate took place on this bill, occupying the whole day.[33] The arguments advanced pro and con are of little importance. The one notable incident of the debate was the moment when Mr. Atwell, in order to "prevent," as he said, "any more violent appeal, solemnly and earnestly appealed to the Assembly to be wise in their determination."[34] The vote was taken June 25, and the bill was defeated, ten to fifty-two, with ten absentees. Five of the seventeen Democrats were absent, and seven voted in favor of the bill; five of the fifty-five Whigs were also absent, three voted yes, and forty-three no.[35] The objection to the bill lay mainly to the suffrage clause, though the apportionment was unpopular with many representatives.[f]

The Election Day Convention met again at Providence July 5. The usual procession was held, banners and mottoes were carried, orations were delivered. It is difficult to ascertain the exact number of persons in the procession; while one account acknowledged that it consisted of some 1,600,[36] another declared that it was the largest concourse ever assembled in the State, though it granted that "owing to the heat and the length of the route, less persons marched over the route than on April 17."[37] It stated also that 1,200 persons came over the Stonington railroad.

The important feature of this meeting was the series of resolutions passed,[38] the most important of which was the following:

---

[f] The votes in favor of the bill came from Glocester, Burrillville, Charlestown, North Kingstown, North Providence, and Cumberland.

"Resolved, That we unanimously and cordially reaffirm the views, sentiments and plans set forth in their resolutions by the convention of the friends of equal rights, held at Newport on the 5th day of May last; and that, inasmuch as the General Assembly of this State, at their last session, in June, have finally decided that the freeholders are exclusively the people of Rhode Island, and have denied to the great majority of the people, so far as it is in their power thus to deny, any participation in the convention to be held in November next, the time has now fully arrived for the people, in their original and sovereign capacity, to exercise their reserved rights; and that we hereby approve the call by the State committee of the people's convention, on the basis of the resolutions aforesaid, at an early day, for the formation of a constitution. Resolved, That when the constitution, so framed, shall be adopted by a majority of the whole people of the State, by their signatures or otherwise, as the convention may provide, we will sustain and carry into effect said constitution, by all necessary means; and that, so far as in us lies, we will remove all obstacles to its successful establishment and operation; and we hereunto solemnly pledge ourselves to each other and the public."[g]

The State committee met in Providence, July 20, and acted in accordance with these instructions.[39] Samuel H. Wales, of Providence, was chairman, and Benjamin Arnold, of Providence, secretary. The committee issued a call[40] for the election of delegates

---

[g] The convention added to the State committee: Silas Sisson, of Newport county; Henry L. Webster, Philip B. Stiness, and Metcalf Marsh, of Providence county; John Brown and John B. Sheldon, of Kent county; Abijah Luce, of Bristol county; and Wager Weeden and Charles Allen, of Washington county; making eighteen in all. John Brown (who afterwards voted against the "People's Constitution") and William S. Peckham did not act with the committee. It is of interest to note that most of these eighteen, if not all, were freemen. *Burke's Report*, 474–622 · "List of Persons voting on the People's Constitution."

to take place August 28; these delegates to attend a convention to be held at the State House, in Providence, October 4, for framing a constitution to be laid before the people for their adoption. They directed that "every American male citizen, of twenty-one years of age and upwards, who has resided in this State one year preceding the election of delegates," should vote for delegates; that every meeting held for the election of delegates should organize by the election of a chairman and secretary, whose signatures would be needed by the delegates; that every town of 1,000 inhabitants or less should have one delegate; that for every additional thousand one delegate should be allowed; and that Providence should elect three delegates from each ward.

SAMUEL H. WALES.

We have thus brought the story to the point where two conventions have been called, each for the framing of a constitution for the State: one under an act of the legislature; the other by an extra-constitutional machine. This seems to be a fitting opportunity to pause in the narrative, and discuss the issue now fairly before the people.

AUTHORITIES.—1 *New Age*, Dec. 18, 1840; *Burke's Report*, 402-403. 2 *New Age*, Dec. 18, 1840. 3 *Rhode Island House Journals*, Jan. 21, 1841; *Providence Journal*, Jan. 22, 1841. 4 *Review of President Wayland's Discourse*, 20. 5 *Rhode Island House Journals*, Jan. 22 and

29. 1841. **6** *Providence Journal*, Jan. 23, 1841. **7** *Providence Journal*, Feb. 6 and 8, 1841; *Rhode Island House Journals*, Feb. 5, 1841. **8** *Rhode Island House Journals*, Feb. 6, 1841; *Rhode Island Acts and Resolves*, Jan., 1841, 85; *New Age*, Feb. 12, 1841; *Burke's Report*, 401–402, 644–645. **9** *Rhode Island House Journals*, Feb. 6, 1841; *Providence Journal*, Feb. 8, 1841. **10** *Republican Herald*, Feb. 10, 1841. **11** *New Age*, Feb. 12, 1841. **12** *New Age*, Feb. 26, 1841. **13** *New Age*, Feb. 26 and Mar. 5, 1841. **14** *New Age*, Mar. 12, 1841. **15** *New Age*, Mar. 19, 1841. **16** *New Age*, Apr 9, 1841. **17** *Republican Herald*, Apr. 17, 1841. **18** *Republican Herald*, Apr. 21, 1841; *Providence Journal*, Apr. 19, 1841; *New Age*, Apr. 23, 1841; See, also, the Testimony of Jacob Frieze, *Burke's Report*, 663–665. **19** *Providence Journal*, Apr. 19, 1841. **20** *New Age*, May 14, 1841. **21** *Republican Herald*, Apr. 24, 1841. **22** *Providence Journal*, May 4, 1841; *Newport Mercury*, May 8, 1841. See, also, Testimony of Martin Stoddard: *Burke's Report*, 660; of Jacob Frieze, *Burke's Report*, 663. **23** *Providence Journal*, May 4, 1841. **24** *Burke's Report*, 256–259, 405–407. **25** *Burke's Report*, 261–268. **26** *Rhode Island House Journals*, May 6, 1841; *Newport Mercury*, May 8, 1841. **27** *Rhode Island House Journals*, May 6, 1841. **28** *Burke's Report*. 409, 645–646. **29** *Newport Mercury*, May 15, 1841. **30** *New Age*, May 14, 1841. **31** *Newport Mercury*, June 26, 1841. **32** *Burke's Report*, 439–441. **33** *Rhode Island House Journals*, June 25, 1841; *Providence Journal*, June 26, 1841; *Republican Herald*, July 3, 1841. **34** *Providence Journal*, June 28, 1841. **35** *Providence Journal*, June 28, 1841; *Burke's Report*, 441. **36** *Providence Journal*, July 7, 1841. **37** *Republican Herald*, July 7, 1841. **38** *Burke's Report*, 259–261, 407–409. **39** *New Age*, July 23, 1841; *Newport Mercury*, July 24, 1841. **40** *Burke's Report*, 269–271, 410–412.

CHAPTER VI.

THE CHARTER CRITICISED.

IN the calls of these two conventions may be found the real controversy and the positions held by the two parties. The call issued first, for what later came to be called the Landholders' or Freemen's Convention, was directed to the freemen of the different towns, requesting them to choose, at the regular election, a certain number of delegates to a convention for framing a new constitution;[1] the second call was directed to male citizens of the United States, resident within the State of Rhode Island, requesting them to elect, on a specified day, a certain number of delegates to what has been commonly called the People's Convention.[2] The first call was issued by the General Assembly of the State, which claimed the right from a clause in the charter granting to the General Assembly power "from time to time, to make, ordain, constitute or repeal such laws, statutes, orders and ordinances, forms and ceremonies of government, and magistrates;" the second call was issued by a committee of eighteen, chosen by mass meetings—some at a convention at Newport, and the others at another convention at Providence, and acting under instructions from these irregular meetings of the "people." The first call took the form of a set of resolutions, witnessed and sent out to the public by the Secretary of State; the second, of a series of votes, passed by the committee of eighteen, one of which directed the chairman and secretary to sign the proceedings of the meeting, and to cause them to be printed and distributed throughout the State.

The Freemen's Convention was to be made up of delegates elected nominally "on the basis of population"—from one to six delegates from each of the towns; the People's Convention was to have a more proportionate representation—from one to eighteen delegates from each town. The electors to the Freemen's Convention were naturally the freemen of the State: that is, the male inhabitants who owned $134 worth of real estate and had qualified, together with their eldest sons; the People's Convention was made up of delegates chosen by "every American male citizen of twenty-one years of age and upwards, who has resided in the State one year preceding the election of delegates." The Freemen's Convention was directed by the call to submit the constitution formed to the freemen in open town meetings, whose vote was to ratify or fail to ratify; the People's Convention was restricted in no way by the call, though the resolutions of July 5th promised to uphold the constitution which should "be adopted by a majority of the whole people of the State, by their signatures or otherwise, as the convention may provide." Behind the Freemen's Convention and its work was the legal government of the State; authority for the People's Convention could be found only in the irresponsible committee of eighteen and the mass meetings. The Freemen's Constitution, if adopted, would have the approval of a majority of the legal voters of the State; behind the People's Constitution, if it became the law of the land, would be an unproved majority of the male inhabitants of the State, voting at extra-legal meetings held without legal restrictions.

Both movements showed that there was a genuine need of a more modern constitution. The inequalities and inconsistencies in the Charter Constitution became apparent with very little study, as may be seen by a brief resumé of the most important causes of the grievances which were set forth during the years of controversy.

First and foremost always were the suffrage qualifications, which, though established by the legislature, had become practically a part of the constitution. The relative proportion between the freemen and the non-freemen in 1841 is difficult to ascertain, since there were no enrollments of all the freemen: the largest number of votes cast in the State had been 8,402 in 1818, and 8,283 in 1840.[(3)] A conservative estimated that there were about 11,000 qualified voters,[(4)] but the secretary of the People's Convention asserted that there were not more than 9,600 freemen;[(5)] the true number in 1841 was probably about 10,000.

The number of possible voters, under an enlarged suffrage, is even more difficult to ascertain. The suffragists estimated 25,674 free white males over twenty-one, or nearly one-quarter of the entire number of inhabitants; subtracting 3,000, the number of "aliens, *non-compos*, insane, under guardianship, and criminals," they claimed 22,674 as the number of probable voters, under a system of universal suffrage. The conservatives, on the other hand, taking as their model "of a greatly extended franchise" the suffrage qualifications in Massachusetts, found that about one in six of the population voted in 1840, and counting the same rate in Rhode Island the population of 108,837 would give 18,139 voters in that State. These rival figures make it certain that the 10,000 or more actual freemen were scarcely one-half of the possible voters, and that the limitations on the suffrage in Rhode Island were greater than those of any other State.[a]

The advisability of rendering the suffrage less restricted was acknowledged by many of the opponents of the suffrage party. "We cannot blame those whom the existing laws exclude from the suffrage, for desiring to be included; . . . Let us, then, while we steadily adhere to the main principle of our compact, so modify our laws in extension of that principle, that every man among us, who has a real interest in our prosperity, may, if he desires it, find a ready, easy, peaceful, and lawful admission to our suffrage, with an equal right to be chosen to the offices which we dispense."[6] President Wayland, of Brown University, said: "I believe it to be at present universally conceded that it would have been better if a change in the elective franchise had been made many years since."[7]

It must not be overlooked that the proportionate number of persons excluded from the suffrage was continually on the increase. So long as Rhode Island remained an agricultural community, with

---

[a] In a few States the ownership of land was a restricting or an alternative qualification: in Connecticut, either a freehold of $7 00 yearly value, or a year's performance of military duty, or the payment of taxes, together with good moral character, were required; in Virginia, either a freehold of $25.00 value, or reversion in land worth $50.00, or occupancy of a leasehold estate at a rent of $20.00, or a housekeeper and head of a family who paid a State tax, were necessary; in South Carolina, a freehold of fifty acres or a town lot; in North Carolina, to vote for Senator, a freehold of fifty acres of land. The following States required, as a necessary—or at least as an alternative—qualification, the payment of taxes: Connecticut, Delaware, Georgia, Louisiana, North Carolina, Ohio, Pennsylvania, and Virginia. The States that had no requirements except those of residence, the franchise demanded by the suffrage party in Rhode Island, were: Alabama, Illinois, Indiana, Kentucky, Maine, Maryland, Michigan, Mississippi, Missouri, New Hampshire, New York, Tennessee, and Vermont. In addition, it may be noted that Georgia, Louisiana, Massachusetts, New Hampshire, New Jersey, New York, North Carolina, South Carolina, and Virginia required a landed qualification of the governor or the members of the State legislature, or both. The universal suffrage demanded by the leaders of the movement in Rhode Island was the rule in about half of the States, and it was, doubtless, somewhat unwise to attempt to replace the very limited suffrage by one so extremely broad, and one not granted by any of the neighboring States. Poore's *Charters and Constitutions*. See, also, *Address of the Convention of 1834*, *Burke's Report*, 176–178.

sparse population and cheap land, it had been easy to obtain the property required. But when the State became a manufacturing and commercial community, the "political power of the State had passed into the hands of a minority," or, to quote a somewhat extravagant address to the people: "A chartered minority, or less than one-third of the male adult population, governs the majority, comprising more than two-thirds of the citizens; imposes taxes on them at will; denies them all natural and social rights of equality; divests them of the best guarantee of freedom (the elective franchise), and excludes them from any representative voice in legislation or government."

The second criticism of the charter government lay in the disproportionate apportionment, to remedy which the Freemen's Convention was primarily called. A fixed apportionment is always subject to two difficulties: old communities may stand still or decay, and thus have undue representation; new communities may spring up, with inadequate representation; both causes worked unfavorably in Rhode Island. At the first census, in 1708, the nine towns had a total population of 7,181; Newport's six Deputies represented 2,203 persons, and the four from Providence represented 1,446, thus making an unusually equal apportionment; the other towns that had four Deputies, Warwick and Portsmouth, had, however, a population of but 480 and 628 respectively; and the five towns with but two Deputies each varied from 206 in Jamestown to 1,200 in Kingstown. In 1776 quite a different story may be read out of the statistics: 161 persons in Jamestown were represented by a Deputy in the Assembly, and 1,644 in Scituate had the same representation. These numbers illustrate the greatest divergence, but not the most undesirable features of the apportionment. Less complaint would have been made if all the towns had been equally represented, without regard to population; but the double and triple representation of the four original towns was the cause of the greater part of the difficulty. Warwick, with its 2,376 inhabitants, had twice as many Deputies as either Glocester, Scituate, Smithfield, North or South Kingstown, each of which boasted a larger population than Warwick. Sixteen towns registered a greater number of inhabitants than Portsmouth, though each of them had but half its representation.

By 1840 the unfairness of the fixed apportionment had become greatly intensified. The only apparent remedy was to divide the large towns and thus secure more members. This process had been frequently used, but there was a limit to it, as a glance at the map of the State in 1840 will show; and the unequal growth of the indivisible towns like Providence prevented any general correction of the abuse except by means of reapportionment. A few of the inconsistencies may be briefly noted. Sixteen of the thirty-one towns had a total population of 22,995, and sent to the Assembly thirty-four Representatives; but the 23,172 inhabitants of the town of Providence were represented by only four Representatives. Smithfield had a population which lacked but sixty-four of equaling that of nine other towns which together were allowed ten times its representation. A Representative from Jamestown represented 182 and one from Barrington 274 persons, while one from Smithfield had a constituency of 4,757, and from Providence, 5,793. The average population which each Representative from Newport county represented was 844; from Washington county, 1,024; from Bristol county, 1,080; from Kent county, 1,308; from the whole State 1,512. On the other side of the scale may be placed Providence county, which sent one Representative to the General Assembly for every 2,640. The comparison by counties shows that the contest must become sectional, for Providence county, occupying the entire northern portion of the State, had a population, in 1840, of 58,073, against 54,500 in all the rest of the State; but by the charter and the number of its towns the county was restricted to twenty-two out of the seventy-two Representatives.

The possibility of obtaining any change, or at least a change radical enough to satisfy the large towns, seemed very doubtful to the suffrage party—since the apportionment of delegates to the Freemen's Convention showed illiberal views as to what would be a fair proportionate representation: Providence, with its 23,172 inhabitants, had but six times as many delegates in the convention as had Jamestown, with its 365 inhabitants. The General Assembly was, in this respect, extremely conservative—making as little change from the charter apportionment as possible, and yet not daring to refuse to grant a partial relief. Very few reasons were stated in opposition to a fairer apportionment, except the claim that the existing system had worked well; that both branches of the legislature ought not to be based on population; that other States—as, for instance, Connecticut and Vermont—were no better off; and that, in any case, but slight changes were necessary, as all the towns, except Providence and Portsmouth, were within one of their proportionate number of representatives.[(8)] Nevertheless, the inequalities were glaring, and this second cause of grievance needed a remedy.[(9)]

The third trouble arose from the great power committed to the General Assembly. The restrictions placed upon it by the charter were inconsiderable; custom only restrained the legislature from being omnipotent. The criticism of Mr. Dorr, in his trial, upon the power of the legislature, is scarcely too strong:[(10)] "The General Assembly had so long acted according to their mere will and pleasure, that they deemed themselves and virtually became omnipotent within their sphere." An amusing instance of the general feeling is found in an alleged remark in the midst of a legislative debate:[(11)] "Mr. Speaker, the member from —— is very much mistaken when he supposes that this General Assembly can do anything that is unconstitutional. Sir, I conceive that this body has the same power over the non-freeholders of this State that the Almighty has over the Universe."

Some other criticisms of the charter as a constitution were occasionally brought forward, though they had little influence in the agitation. Thus, the charter contained no Bill of Rights—that "important bulwark of the liberties of the people."[(12)] The levying of taxes upon the non-freemen, and also the requirements of military and fire duty, seemed unjust, and led some to join the suffrage party.[(13)] Complaint was made that non-freemen had not complete protection of their property, since without the assistance of a freeman they could not appeal to the law for the collection of a debt.[(14)] The fact that only freemen could serve upon a jury was another cause of complaint, and the statement was common that trial by one's "peers" was not granted the non-freeholders.[(15)] Finally, the charter was set forth as the gift of an autocratic monarch of a country from which the State had successfully revolted, and a constitution should be the act of a free people providing for their own government.

Although the non-freeholders had many good and sufficient reasons for complaint,[(b)] their social and economic position was not

---

(b) "We happen to know that for about fifteen years the author of the 'Discourse' has resided in Rhode Island, paying taxes every year, yet never allowed to vote, nor to exert his influence, or lift up his voice, in the affairs of government, nor to sit upon a jury, nor to claim the protection of law by sueing out his writ. All this may, in *his* opinion be no injury, no infringement of liberty, no more than an inconsiderable loss. *Answer to Wayland*, 12."

so oppressive as might be judged from the list of grievances. Few felt maimed by the lack of the rights and privileges for which they clamored. Elisha R. Potter, a Representative in Congress from Rhode Island, was too strong an opponent of the suffrage party to be sensitive to the hardships of the non-freemen; nevertheless, there is much truth in his statement: "Under that old charter we have enjoyed more happiness and better government than any other State in this Union; we have had very little class legislation; we pay no high salaries; we have had no direct taxes for twenty years; the taxes paid by the banks support our government; we had good courts, and our laws were cheaply and economically administered, so that the poorest could obtain redress for injuries."(16) The *New York Courier and Enquirer* declared that the general content was shown by the "records of the Republic, the history of that State in particular, and the testimony of every man of intelligence in the country."(17) "This charter of government," says George Bancroft, the historian, "constituting, as it then seemed, a pure democracy, and establishing a political system which few besides the Rhode Islanders themselves believed to be practicable, remained in existence till it became the oldest constitutional charter in the world. The probable population of Rhode Island, at the time of its reception, may have been 2,500. In 170 years that number increased forty fold; and the government, which was hardly thought to contain checks enough on the power of the people to endure even among shepherds and farmers, protected a dense population, and the accumulations of a widely-extended commerce. No where in the world were life, liberty, and property safer than in Rhode Island."(18)

However, with a government based upon an antiquated fundamental law, with a limited suffrage, with unequal representation, with a legislature under no legal control but the semi-annual elections, and without a Bill of Rights, it was not strange that the non-freemen, paying taxes, serving as firemen and in the militia, and kept out of the jury box, should manifest a desire for a new constitution. The strange thing is that the desire had not been expressed earlier and more plainly. But how was this coveted result to be obtained? Was there a likelihood that a constitution could be drawn out of the "landholders?" Or, if they did provide a new frame of government, was it probable that it would be satisfactory? Had not the freemen refused to call a convention in 1821 and again in 1822? Had they not voted down a constitution in 1824 which contained but few of the changes now desired? Had they not failed to form a constitution in 1834, because the interest of the freemen in the matter was not sufficient to keep a quorum together?

Besides the failures in the past and the more recent legislative rebuffs, the suffrage party had good reason to feel that, *a priori*, the freemen would not grant their requests; that they had the same feeling in 1841 that Colonel Burrill expressed forty-four years earlier: the natural repugnance of the "ins." Under such circumstances how could the non-freemen obtain their desires? Early in the movement, before the April parade, came the answer of the suffrage party.(19) "There are two remedies for this—either the whole people may form a constitution, or in the Supreme Court of the United States, they may try the constitution of our present government. The former course the suffrage party have decided upon, although we think that the whole matter will eventually be settled in Congress or the Supreme Court."

The plan for "the whole people" to form a constitution is the key note to the whole controversy that raged in Rhode Island until finally the United States Supreme Court was reached. Before this question all controversies as to franchise or apportionment, all discussions as to universal suffrage or the rights of the majority to rule, are matters of little consequence. The claim was made that the call for this People's Convention was right; that the convention had a *prima facie* legality; that the constitution which it should form would be the fundamental law of the State, if ratified by a majority of "the people." The simplest statement of this claim, as made by the suffrage party, is found in the words of Benjamin F. Hallett, in his argument before the Supreme Court of the United States: "It is a right of the people to change, alter, or abolish their government, in such manner as they please; a right, not of force, but of sovereignty."

AUTHORITIES.—**1** *Burke's Report*, 644–645. **2** *Burke's Report*, 269–271, 410–412. **3** *Rhode Island Manual, 1896–7*, 98, 102. **4** *Providence Journal*, May 1, 1841. The method of estimating was as follows: In the city of Providence there were 1,721 names on the ward lists, of which 1,312 voted. At the same rate, the 8,283 votes cast in the State would indicate 11,000 voters. **5** *Burke's Report*, 120–121. **6** *Providence Journal*, Aug. 21, 1841. **7** Wayland, *Affairs of Rhode Island*, 13. **8** *Providence Journal*, May 25, 1841. **9** *Providence Journal*, Feb. 10, 1841. **10** Turner, *Trial of Thomas W. Dorr*, 53; see, also, *Burke's Report*, 270. **11** *New Age*, Jan. 8, 1841. **12** *Burke's Report*, 270. **13** *Reply to Wayland*, 12; *Burke's Report*, 12, 163, 249. **14** *Burke's Report*, 13, 249. **15** *Burke's Report*, 13. **16** *Congressional Globe*, I Sess., 28 Cong., 1843–44, App. XIII., 268. **17** *New York Courier and Enquirer*, as copied in the *National Intelligencer*, May 19, 1842. **18** Bancroft, *History of the United States*, 10th Ed., II, 64. **19** *New Age* Mar. 26, 1841

CHAPTER VII.

THE ISSUE.

THIS is not the place to enter into any thorough or exhaustive discussion of the questions of sovereignty and constitution-making. Instead, we will merely set forth a few of the arguments that were advanced by the advocates and opponents of the doctrine cited at the close of the preceding chapter, and thus determine the real status of the Rhode Island movement—whether it may be called legal or revolutionary.

The suffragists came out boldly with their doctrine. The Suffrage Association, in its Declaration of Principles,[(1)] "Resolved, That the *power* of the State should be vested in the hands of the *people*; and that the people have the right from time to time to assemble together, either by themselves or their representatives, for the establishment of a republican form of government. Resolved, That whenever a majority of the citizens of this State, who are recognized as citizens of the United States, shall, by their delegates in convention assembled, draught a constitution, and the same shall be accepted by their constituents, it will be, to all intents and purposes, the law of the State." The State Suffrage Committee declared that a "majority of the '*governed*' have, at any time, and on any occasion, a right to change their government—a right which, being inherent, unalienable, and indefeasible, not even they can part with by their free and voluntary act."[2] Thomas W. Dorr, in the People's Convention, said: "We ask for no authority from the legislature to empower the people to assemble in convention, or to vote for or against the doings of that convention. We need, and can have, no higher commission for our proceedings, than that is derived from the sovereign power of the State."[3] But the suffragists took a more pronounced position, and presented arguments to support a legal right of amending the constitution at will. They claimed that "what was a revolutionary right merely, a right of war, in countries where the sovereignty was not held to reside in the people, had here, by the act of the people, been transplanted into the pale of government itself, by our declarations and constitutions, which recognize the right of the people, on the outside of all organizations, to act for themselves. A right which is thus recognized, though in a general way, and, of course, without prescribed forms of proceedings, ceases to be revolutionary, and has become regular and definite."[4]

In reply to these opinions, the conservatives attempted to show to what results they would lead. In an article in the *New Englander*, an illustration of these principles was thus set forth:[5] "If it should happen in any State that an actual minority should elect a governor, the majority could immediately get rid of him in a legal way, by assembling on the authority of this right of revolution, either in mass or by delegates, and framing a new constitution, and under it electing a new governor, who would be the legal chief magistrate to whom civil obedience is due, while through the silent operation of law the former governor becomes at once guilty of treason, if he remains longer in office." President Wayland declared that "the principles which have been avowed, seem to me as utterly subversive of all other governments as they are of our own If an established government may be overturned on the principles which have been advocated, . . no constitution in the land is worth the parchment on which it is written. The only law that would be known would soon be the law of force. The only principle of action would come to be the love of plunder. All that would be necessary, in order to establish unlimited power over us, would be without form of law, to lay claim to a majority, and assemble a sufficient number of armed men to carry its decisions into effect."[6] Judge Pitman considered that "majorities, real or pretended, will find all things lawful and all things expedient, and should they be fettered by constitutions, or forms of government, they have only to resolve themselves into '*their original sovereign capacity*,' and they may act their pleasure, until another faction, stronger than they, shall arise to make them feel, in their turn, the miseries of such licentiousness and anarchy."[7]

After suggesting the possibilities underlying this doctrine of sovereignty, the opponents of these principles declared that such acts were without law and against the laws of the State. They declared that a constitution so obtained would be "voted for without the forms of law, and of course in such a manner that none could pretend to determine what expression of the wishes of the people it really sanctioned."[8] Dr. Channing was quoted as saying that a constitution was "the act of a people imposing limits on itself, setting guard on its own passions, and throwing obstructions in the way of legislation, so as to compel itself to pause, to deliberate, to hear all remonstrances, to weigh all rights and interests before it acts."[9] Another reply to the arguments in favor of the legality of this method of constitution-making is directed to Governor Morton of Massachusetts. "You have confounded in your own mind, or would confound in the minds of others, the great distinction between revolution and reform. Revolution is not to be regulated by law. This is an appeal to force against the law and the government. But the right of reform is to be exercised in conformity with the fundamental laws of the State and the rights of the government, and if a portion of the people, under the pretense of reform, violate their allegiance to the government, and set up a government upon their own authority, this is rebellion and treason, and it is the duty of the government to put it down."(10) One of the "Law and Order" Representatives to Congress declared in the House that "he did not deny the right of revolution to the people; he did not deny the right of the people to change the form of their government, when it was administered contrary to the principle on which it was established, or when it was oppressive and could not be endured; but he did not admit that they could change it as often as they pleased, without law, against law, and without any cause."(11)

Some of the lawyers of the suffrage party made a thorough search of the writings of the leading exponents of the Constitution of the United States, and brought together the paragraphs, sentences, and clauses which appeared to support their position that "the people of Rhode Island had the right, of their own sovereign will, and without the consent of, the existing authorities of the State, to change, alter, reform, or abolish the government."(a) They cited first the Declaration of Independence: "Governments are instituted among men, deriving their just powers from the consent of the governed; when any form of government becomes destructive of these ends [that is, the rights just enumerated] it is the right

---

(a) These are the words of the majority of the select committee. *Burke's Report*, 25.

of the people to alter or abolish it." They quoted from the farewell address of President Washington that: "The basis of our political systems is the right of the people to make and alter their constitution of government." They found Justice Wilson's statement that the people "always retain the right of abolishing, altering, or amending their constitution, in whatever manner they shall deem expedient,"(12) and that "the people may change their constitution whenever and however they please."(13) Mr. Justice Iredell is quoted as affirming that "those in power are servants and agents; the people, without their consent, may new-model the government whenever they think proper."(14) As a further list of authorities, the Bills of Rights of the various States were drawn upon. Twenty of the twenty-five State constitutions declared that sovereignty lay in the people, and that they had the right to change the government. Eight of these constitutions granted the people the right to alter the form of government "in such manner as they may think proper," or "as they may think expedient;" and Virginia specifically declared that "when any government shall be found inadequate or contrary to these purposes, a majority of the community hath an indubitable, unalienable, and indefeasible right to reform, alter, or abolish it, in such manner as shall be judged most conducive to the public weal."(15)

In commenting upon these authorities, it is hardly necessary to do more than call attention to the context to show that they had a different background and connection from that used in this controversy. The Declaration of Independence was an act of revolution, justified itself by grievances, and called for resistance to England as a deduction from the right of the people to alter their government: this is simply a statement of the right of revolution. In like manner, there is no authority, in the quotation from Washington, for the legal right of the people to alter their constitutions at will, without the consent of the existing government. Mr. Justice Wilson, in the passage from which the first quotation was taken, was criticising Blackstone because of his opinion that the discussion of the right of revolution did not come under the province of law. He considered that though "revolution principles" are not recognized by the English constitution, yet the English constitution cannot destroy those principles; and he described the principle that the people "may change their constitution and government whenever they please" as a "revolution principle."[16] The other sentence quoted from Mr. Justice Wilson was taken from a speech in the Pennsylvania convention which ratified the Constitution of the United States. The judge here desired to bring about this ratification, which could be the result of nothing but a revolution. There is nothing in the words of Mr. Justice Iredell to indicate that the right spoken of was not the right of revolution; the extract was taken from his speech in the North Carolina convention which ratified the Constitution of the United States. The Bills of Rights were, for the most part, patterned after the Declaration of Independence, and it was evidently the intention of their framers to leave to the people, besides the right to amend legally, the great moral right of revolution. An efficient answer to the assertion that this was considered to be a legal right in Virginia, at least, is shown by the fact that in that State, by her laws,[17] "those who may attempt to set up a constitution of government, without the permission of the Legislature, are guilty of treason, and are liable to be punished with death."[b]

[b] It is said that John Randolph, who opposed the insertion in the Virginia constitution of a clause regarding amendments, did so because he "desired to prevent any change for ages to come," declaring that "he would as soon interpolate the marriage ceremony with a clause providing for a divorce." Elmer, *Speech in the House of Representatives*, Feb. 28, 1845, p. 6.

Having examined the state of public opinion in Rhode Island at the time of the great constitutional controversy, we are prepared to examine the legitimacy of Mr. Hallett's argument that "the right of the people to change, alter or abolish their government, in such manner as they please, is a right, not of force, but of sovereignty." It is not necessary to discuss here, at great length, the meaning and scope of the words "sovereign" and "sovereignty." Sovereignty lies in the people, associated into a body politic, in their political capacity; or, in other words, in those persons who possess the elective franchise.[c] The use of the sovereign power must be either regular, in accordance with the established rule, or irregular, in opposition to the established rule, or the constitution and laws. An irregular exercise of sovereignty would be a possibility, but, not being regular, it cannot be called legal and must be revolutionary. Revolutions may be of three kinds:[18] those causing war, like the contest of 1861–65; those that do not result in bloodshed, but which almost lead up to military encounters, such as the "Dorr Rebellion" proved to be; and those which are brought about so peaceably that the revolutionary character is not realized, as in the case of the adoption of the Constitution of the United States, and as would have been the case in Rhode Island in 1842, had the People's government quietly taken possession in the month of May.

(c) "The theory of our political system is that the ultimate sovereignty is in the people, from whom springs all legislative authority." Cooley, *Constitutional Limitations*, 6 Ed 39. "The word *people* itself presupposes association—for if you suppose a million of inhabitants congregated on a spot of earth ten miles square, they would not constitute a people." J. Q. Adams, *The Social Compact*, 7. "Sovereignty resides in the *society* or *body politic;* in the corporate unit resulting from the organization of many into one, and not in the individuals constituting such unit, nor in any number of them as such, nor even in all of them, except as organized into a body politic and acting as such." Jameson, *Constitutional Convention*, § 21. "As a practical fact the sovereignty is vested in those persons who are permitted by the Constitution of the State to exercise the elective franchise." Cooley, *Constitutional Limitations*, 6 Ed. 40.

Mr. Hallett claimed "the right of sovereignty" by the negative argument that the Constitution of the United States nowhere recognized the right of revolution; but it may be answered that the constitution was formed in order to perpetuate a government without revolutions, to give a permanent and legal basis for the new order of things. The difficulty is in the word "right;" it is a moral right to revolt when the evils of a government are so great that revolution is less to be feared than the existing evils; but this is accomplished only by the breaking up of the whole legal system: it is idle to talk of a "constitutional right" to ignore the constitution. Mr. Hallett's affirmative argument, like that put forward by the Rhode Island suffragists, is that such right is granted by the Declaration of Independence and various State Bills of Rights.

It would seem to be fair to conclude that the proposed People's Convention could not be legal or legitimate; it would not be a regular exercise of the sovereignty, because it was to be held without law and in antagonism to the legal government of the State. Yet this conclusion does not exclude the possibility that the people of Rhode Island might be justified if it came to be shown that they supported the convention: it is not denied that they had the right of revolution. The suffragists could be justified in their action only through the claim that they were inaugurating a peaceful revolution, such as that made by the United States when it overthrew the Articles of Confederation and adopted the constitution in 1787–89. The Rhode Island movement in 1841 was plainly illegal and illegitimate.

The question remains whether it was justifiable, as was the change in the revolution of 1776 and the virtual, though peaceful, revolution in 1789. Many subsequent events must be described before a properly considered conclusion can be reached, but it cannot be gainsaid that the issue was between legality and revolution and the ethics of the question turn upon the query how far a revolution was justifiable in this particular case.

A peculiar difficulty must here again be noticed: Rhode Island had no legal means of amending the constitution. Hence, the question arose whether the General Assembly had any more legal right to summon a convention than had any other body. The suffrage committee declared that there was "no constitutional mode of amending the government except by the people at large."(19) But the general and self-justifying method to initiate a constitutional convention is by the legally appointed officials of the government and in Rhode Island, while the charter did not directly ordain that the legislature should summon a convention to propose a constitution, yet it did indirectly grant the power, by authorizing the General Assembly to make "new forms of government."

Again, the general implied powers of a legislative body, if no clause is found forbidding it, would include the right to call a convention, perhaps even to submit amendments for ratification. The practically uniform custom in the various States of the Union ought to have had its influence in Rhode Island; the precedents in the State itself had always upheld this legislative right of initiation of changes in the fundamental law; the action of the legislature in submitting the question of a convention to the people in 1821 and 1822, and even more the calls for a convention in 1824 and 1834 were at least indications of the general belief that this power belonged to the General Assembly.

This question might be examined from a different point of view Conditions had changed since the colonial charter was granted in 1663; then the colonists asserted that it was not amendable by the royal authority which gave it, and the crown would permit no amendment by the people of the colony. When, however, the colony became the State and the authority of royalty over the people of Rhode Island was overthrown, the Charter of 1663 lost its charter characteristics and only continued to be a form of government; it was, after 1776, the fundamental law—the constitution of the State—and therefore could be amended or superseded in the usual way. That method was the initiatory action of the State legislature. The fact that the charter contained no provision for its own amendment did not render the course of the suffrage party any the less illegitimate.

AUTHORITIES.—**1** *Burke's Report*, 403–404. **2** *Burke's Report*, 263, 414. **3** *Burke's Report*, 852. **4** Turner, *Trial of Dorr*, 55; *Burke's Report*, 946. **5** *New Englander*, I, 86. **6** Wayland, *Affairs of Rhode Island*, 7. **7** Pitman, *Reply to Morton*, 19. **8** Wayland, *Affairs of Rhode Island*, 21. **9** Channing, *On the Duty of the Free State*, II, 65, 69. **10** Pitman, *Reply to Morton*, 20, 21. **11** Henry Y. Cranston, *Congressional Globe*, I Sess., 28 Cong., 1843–44, XII, 364. **12** Wilson, *Works*, I, 17. **13** Wilson, *Works*, III, 293. **14** *Elliott's Debates*, IV, 9; *Story*, 4 Ed., I, 250. **15** Poore's *Charters and Constitutions*; see, also, Jameson, *Constitutional Conventions*, § 245; *Burke's Report*, 36–38. **16** Wilson, *Works*, I, 20–21. **17** Pitman, *Reply to Morton*, 20. **18** Jameson, *Constitutional Conventions*, § 109. **19** *Burke's Report*, 270.

CHAPTER VIII.

THE CONVENTIONS.

AS the suffragists had decided to bring to an issue the right of the people to express their will, without regard to the sanction of the State authorities, the State Suffrage Committee sent out its own summons for the People's Convention, setting Saturday, August 28, 1841, as the day for the holding of meetings to elect delegates: this would be three days before the official semi-annual election of Representatives, at which, under the vote of the Assembly, the freemen were to choose delegates to the Freemen's Convention. The suffragists thus plainly declared their intention to anticipate the action of the freemen. The interest in the proposed People's Convention declined during the summer months, a natural result of the season; but hand-bills were posted in the various towns, calling attention to the approaching day, and the suffrage leaders used every means to bring out the voters. The anti-suffragists showed a remarkable inability to realize the importance of the agitation; not until the day of the vote did the leading Newport newspaper note the call for the People's Convention, and then it gave expression to its lack of interest by remarking: "It is stated that the Constitution about to be framed by this convention will be presented to the General Assembly at their October session, with a petition for its adoption as the supreme law of the State."[1]

The 28th of August was a rainy day; but 7,512 votes were cast, and all the towns chose delegates except Westerly, West Greenwich, and East Greenwich.[2] In Newport 584 votes were reported to have been cast, of which number 198 were given by freemen:[3] if this rate held good throughout the State, about 2,500 freemen had voted, or one-quarter of the legal voters, and about 4,600 non-freemen registered their desires for a convention, or less than half the number of non-freemen in the State. While the result suggested that it would not need much further agitation to prevail upon the freemen to grant a liberal constitution, the election had not the hoped-for presumption of expressing the will of the people, inasmuch as it did not show a clear majority, either of freemen or of non-freemen.

The persons nominated by the suffrage party, in the various towns, met with no opposition, so far as is known. Of the eighteen delegates from Providence, more than two-thirds were freemen, and at least five of the eight delegates from Newport were legal voters, and the proportion probably held good throughout the State. Five of these eighteen delegates from Providence were also chosen, on the following Tuesday, to represent the city in the Freemen's Convention. The six "Independent" candidates who were defeated by the suffragists were leading citizens of the city, such as Nehemiah R. Knight, governor from 1817 to 1820, and United States Senator from 1823 until 1841; William G. Goddard, and William R. Staples. A spirited canvass took place in Providence over the choice of Representatives. Two had been nominated by both parties for the contested places. John H. Clarke and Walter S. Burges received 512 and 504 votes respectively, while their opponents polled but 430 and 383.[(4)] The success of the suffrage freemen in Providence indicated the effects of the "Campaign of Education."

The People's Convention met as directed, Monday, October 4th, 1841, and was organized for business by four o'clock on Tuesday afternoon. By the following Saturday they had completed a constitution, and adjourned to meet again after the people had had time to examine the document and recommend changes.[(5)] The leading men in the convention were: Thomas W. Dorr, of Providence; Dutee J. Pearce, of Newport; Ariel Ballou, of Cumberland; John R. Waterman, of Warwick; Joshua B. Rathbun, of Tiverton; Perez Simmons, of Providence; Palemon Walcott, of Smithfield; Dr. J. A. Brown, of Providence; and Samuel H. Wales, of Providence.[(6)] Interest in the sessions was slight, and the number of spectators was few; and Mr. Dorr is quoted as saying that he was afraid that the adjournment would prove the death-blow to the constitution. In closing an editorial, the *Providence Journal* said: "It must be considered a curious spectacle, and one which no other country, if any other State, can present—a number of men assembled for the avowed purpose of overthrowing the government, under which they live, without any authority from the legislative or executive powers, and yet proceeding without opposition and without hindrance. The monstrous tyranny of the State government, which was so loudly denounced, was not displayed on that occasion."

The convention met again, by adjournment, on November 15th, and entirely completed its labors on the 18th. A few alterations in the text of the constitution were made, and it was ordered to be submitted to the people.[(7)] Perhaps the most notable feature of this session was the carefully prepared address of 8,000 words delivered by Mr. Dorr, on the right of the people of Rhode Island to form a constitution. Ostensibly offered in response to a query whether a majority of the qualified freeholders was deemed requisite

THOMAS W. DORR.

(FROM AN ENGRAVING OF A DAGUERREOTYPE MINIATURE BY A. L. DICK.)

for the adoption of the People's Constitution, the speech reviewed the whole question, brought up all the arguments for the right of the people to make a constitution at will, without the request or consent of the legislature, and closed by answering the query as follows: "The freeholders are a part of the people, though not the whole people; and we are happy to find the liberal portion of them going along with us in this good work. Our ticket is so formed that every voter will respond to the question whether he be qualified under the existing laws or not. A majority of the freeholders is not necessary to our success; but it will be gratifying to find them on the right side."[8]

Leaving the discussion of the constitution framed by the People's Convention until it may be compared with the Freemen's Constitution, which was promulgated a few days later, it is necessary here to note the controversy over the limitation of the right of suffrage to "every *white* male citizen."[9] The questions of abolition and of the privileges that should be granted to free negroes caused much trouble both in and out of the convention, and as early as the middle of September, communications began to appear in the newspapers concerning the right of the negroes to vote.[10] Before the convention acted, a remonstrance was presented by a "committee in behalf of the people of color," holding that disfranchisement simply from "the existence of the fact color" was unjustifiable; but no attention was paid to the remonstrance, and a few days later a proposition to strike out the word "white" received but eighteen votes out of a total of about a hundred.[11] At the November session of the convention, a communication was received from the Rhode Island Anti-Slavery Society asking permission to be heard in opposition to the insertion of the word "white." The convention laid the letter on the table, and though permission was accorded to "any citizen of the State" to address them on the propriety of striking it out, the word remained in the constitution.[12]

The leaders of both parties were very careful not to permit themselves to lose any votes by a pronounced adherence to abolitionist principles, and doubtless felt that it would be better to postpone the question of negro suffrage until after the adoption of the constitution. Hence the word "white" remained in the second article; but, near the close of the constitution, a section was inserted, which read as follows: "The General Assembly shall, at their first session after the adoption of this constitution, propose to the electors the question whether the word 'white,' in the first line of the first section of article 2 of the constitution, shall be stricken out. The question shall be voted upon at the succeeding annual election; and if a majority of the electors voting shall vote to strike out the word aforesaid, it shall be stricken from the contitution; otherwise not."[(13)] The suffrage party thus permitted an early vote upon it, without the complicated method of adoption which other amendments to the constitution must undergo; and, as a further concession to the negroes and the abolitionists, the constitution exempted those who were excluded from voting, because of their color, from taxation and military duty.[(14)]

The official Freemen's Convention met, in accordance with the call, Monday, November 1st, 1841. It proceeded with its work slowly and with deliberation, and was not hastened by the action of the People's Convention. The *Providence Journal* said: "The Convention was called before that of the Suffrage Associations, and without any reference to that movement; we think it is clearly the duty of the members to ascertain in good faith the objects for which they were chosen, to make as good a Constitution as they can, and to submit it to the people. The views and wishes of the suffrage party should be regarded precisely as the views and wishes of any other respectable portion of our fellow citizens. Their *opin-*

ions deserve all the consideration to which their weight may entitle them; their *threats* (of such as threaten) deserve none at all."[15] The convention remained in session two weeks: with regard to the suffrage, it had in mind only the desires and interests of the freemen, but apparently the delegates did not feel very clear as to what the freemen desired. Adjournment was secured to February, 1842, with several sections undecided upon: the reasons for postponement were evidently to obtain further instructions or ideas from their constituents, and to ascertain what the People's Convention would do at its second session. The delegates left the matter of suffrage quite open, merely suggesting for future consideration a scheme of property qualification, excluding sons of freemen.[16]

The two conventions had met, and as a result two constitutions were before the people. As the two instruments are compared, it will be seen that each of them devoted its first article to a declaration of rights and privileges; the only sections in the Bill of Rights of the Freemen's Constitution not found in nearly identical terms in the People's Constitution are the freedom from imprisonment of debtors who had turned over their property; the privilege of the people to keep and bear arms; and the prohibition of slavery. Each constitution contained a clause relating to the suspension of the privilege of *habeas corpus*, the Freemen's adding that the authority of the General Assembly should be required for this purpose. On the other hand, we find in the People's Constitution declarations of democracy, representative government, and "soul liberty;" a full statement of the "self-evident truths" of the Declaration of Independence; a protest against the use of "favor or disfavor in legislation toward any man, party, society or religious denomination;" the right of "fugitive slaves" to a trial by jury; and a rule forbidding calling in question the religious belief of any witness. The more notable variation was the declaration, by the People's Constitution, of the right of the people to ordain and alter their government, and of the right of the jury, in criminal cases, to judge the law as well as the fact. The absence of the clause forbidding slavery, and the attack upon the Fugitive Slave law, in the same document, are noteworthy.

In the suffrage article of the People's Constitution the right to vote was granted to "every white male citizen of the United States, of the age of twenty-one years, who had resided in this State for one year, and in any town, city, or district of the same for six months, next preceding the election at which he offers his vote."(17) By the preliminary suggestion of the Freemen's Convention, suffrage was limited to the possessors of $134 worth of land, or of $500 worth of taxable personal property. By each constitution persons in the military, naval, or marine service of the United States were not considered as having acquired residence; and paupers, lunatics, criminals, etc., were excluded. The People's Constitution also limited voting on questions of taxation to payers of a property tax. Each instrument required a strict regulation of voters, and exempted electors from arrest on days of election.

In the classification of the departments of government and the grant of legislative power there were few important points of divergence: the Freemen's Constitution retained for the General Assembly some judicial powers, and forbade lotteries in the State; the People's described the process by which a bill might become a law.(18)

Naturally the two constitutions differed materially in their apportionment of the Representatives.(19) By the People's a fixed apportionment was made, granting two Representatives each to twenty-one towns; one each to Jamestown, Middletown, and Barrington;

three each to Cumberland, North Providence, and Scituate; four to Warwick, and five each to Smithfield and Newport; while each of the six wards of Providence might send two Representatives. Power was given to the General Assembly, whenever necessary, to redetermine the bounds of the wards of Providence. By the Freemen's Constitution the apportionment was variable and based on population: it allowed to each town at least two Representatives, and not more than eight; 4,000 inhabitants were sufficient for three Representatives; 6,500 for four; 10,000 for five; 14,000 for six; 18,000 for seven; and 22,000 for eight.[a] In brief, according to the census of 1840, the immediate differences in the two proposals were that by the People's Constitution Providence would have twelve Representatives instead of eight; Smithfield and Newport five instead of four; and Jamestown, Middletown, and Barrington one instead of two; but neither made sufficient allowance for future disturbances of population.

In organization the Senate would be identical, except that by the People's Constitution the presiding officer was the Lieutenant Governor, and by the Freemen's the Governor, but the Lieutenant Governor was *ex-officio* a member.[20] The radical difference was in the apportionment of the Senators. By the People's Constitution there were to be twelve districts and twelve Senators; by the Freemen's, sixteen districts and nineteen Senators. Providence would have in either case two Senators, and Smithfield one, while Newport was allowed two by the Freemen's and but one by the People's Constitution.

---

[a] This would have allowed, until the census of 1850, three Representatives each from Cumberland, North Providence, and Scituate; four each from Smithfield, Warwick, and Newport; and eight from Providence.

The sections relating to impeachments were identical in the two constitutions.[21] The rights and duties of the executive power were substantially the same.[22] The People's Constitution forbade the commander-in-chief to march the militia out of the State, without their consent, or that of the General Assembly, and provided that the Governor should send messages to the General Assembly and require information from military and executive officers; it also arranged for an annual election of a sheriff in each county. The Freemen's Constitution kept the power of pardons and reprieves in the hands of the General Assembly, granting the Governor the right to reprieve only to the end of the next session of the legislature; while the People's placed the entire power over pardons and reprieves in the control of the Governor, except in cases of impeachment.

The Freemen's Constitution provided for elections in a manner closely resembling that of the People's;[23] and the sections in the Freemen's Constitution relating to qualifications for office nearly all appear also in the People's.[24] The articles referring to the judiciary were practically identical; the only important divergence being the provision in the Freemen's Constitution that the judges of the Supreme Judicial Court shall in all cases instruct the jury in the law.[25] The articles relating to constitutional amendments did not materially vary;[26] the Freemen's Constitution required a three-fifths vote of the people to ratify amendments, and the People's but a majority.[27] Each constitution provided the means by which the people might vote on the ratification.[28] Most of the "General Provisions" are common to the two instruments: the most important sections not in the Freemen's are those removing from the General Assembly jurisdiction over cases of insolvency, divorce, etc.;[29] providing for the referendum on the passage of bills creating banks of issue;[30] and affirming the power of the General Assembly to amend or repeal all acts of incorporation thereafter granted.[31]

In summarizing these constitutions, it is seen that the People's was not only much more liberal, but also more carefully and thoroughly framed; and it was more in accord with modern ideas of government and the constitutions of other States. It is only necessary to read the Freemen's Constitution in order to realize that it was prepared by those who would turn from the beaten track only so far as they were compelled to go. In the Bill of Rights the People's Constitution was, on the whole, superior to its rival. In its removal of the judicial power and the power of pardon from the General Assembly, and in its attempt to place the regulation of banks of issue and other incorporated bodies in the hands of the people, it tended to limit the "omnipotent power" of the legislature. The suffragists took a very peculiar position, however, in their claim that in criminal cases the jury should judge the law as well as the fact.

While on the general question of apportionment and in comparatively minor points the People's Constitution responded to the complaints that had been made against the charter government, a new question arose which created new divergences. Instead of choosing the ten Assistants, or Senators, at large, by each constitution the Senators were to be elected by districts; but in size and character these systems of districts differed. Neither apportionment could be considered satisfactory, with reference to the population of that time;[32] and both the constitutions showed a lack of appreciation of the evils of a fixed representation, unchangeable except by amendments to the constitution. The twelve senatorial districts of the People's Constitution averaged 9,092 inhabitants, and ranged from 11,586 to 6,476. These divergences from the average population might have been obviated.[b]

Not so much can be said for the Senate apportionment of the Freemen's Constitution. Providence, with its 23,172 inhabitants, was assigned two Senators; while Newport town and District Two, outside of Newport, each of which had less than 8,600, were also granted two.[c] The average population for a Senator, by the census of 1840, was 5,728; the actual figures ranged from 11,586 to 2,835.

Between the two apportionments of Representatives there was not much choice: though that of the People's Constitution was fixed, it was more in accord with the population of the time, giving Providence twelve instead of eight, and Smithfield and Newport five instead of four; the three very small towns might perhaps deserve the two Representatives each allotted by the Freemen's Constitution if the proposition be accepted that a town, as a town, had some rights.

Leaving the burning question of the suffrage out of account, the People's Constitution seems in most respects preferable to its rival, though its upholders had no reason to scorn the Freemen's Constitution; the general provisions of the latter were fairly acceptable to the ordinary citizen, and seem, except in a few points, to have been unobjectionable even to the suffragists themselves; hence they were practically compelled to fall back upon the main issue of the suffrage qualifications.

(b) Newport, with 8,333 population, might have made a district by itself; and, if Jamestown and New Shoreham had been annexed to District Nine, its number of inhabitants would have been increased from 7,107 to 8,541.

(c) Smithfield's 9,543 and District Five's 9,532 were granted but one Senator each.

It is not necessary to restate these qualifications or to discuss them: the People's Constitution gave almost universal suffrage; the Freemen's Convention had not decided what to do. They talked of a tax qualification, and referred the matter to the people for advice; what would be the final decision, no one could tell. The suffragists seemed warranted in assuming that but little increase of the franchise would be obtainable from the Freemen's Convention. They therefore took immediate steps for referring their constitution to the people.

AUTHORITIES.—**1** *Newport Mercury*, Aug. 28, 1841. **2** *New Age*, Sept. 3, 1841. **3** *Newport Mercury*, Sept. 4, 1841. **4** *Providence Journal*, Sept. 1, 1841. **5** *New Age*, Oct. 15, 1841. **6** *Providence Journal*, Oct 12, 1841. **7** *Providence Journal*, Nov. 19. 1841. **8** *Burke's Report*, 857–864. **9** Art. II, People's Constitution; *see Appendix*. **10** *Providence Journal*, Sept. 17, Sept. 18, Sept. 27, Oct. 1, Oct. 14, Oct. 25, 1841. **11** *Burke's Report*, 111: Testimony of John S. Harris. **12** *Burke's Report*, 113; *Idem*. **13** Art. XIV, Sec. 22, People's Constitution. **14** Art. II, Sec. 3, People's Constitution. **15** *Providence Journal*, Nov. 2, 1841. **16** *Republican Herald*, Nov. 17, 1841. **17** Art. II, People's Constitution. **18** Art. III and Art. IV, of both Constitutions. **19** Art. V, of both Constitutions. **20** Art. VI, of both Constitutions. **21** Art. VII, of both Constitutions. **22** Art. VIII, of both Constitutions. **23** Art. IX, Freemen's Constitution; Art. X, People's Constitution. **24** Art. X, Freemen's Constitution; Art. II, Sec. 10, Art. IX, Sec. 3, Art. IV, Secs. 3 and 4, People's Constitution. **25** Art. XI, of both Constitutions. **26** Art. XII, of both Constitutions. **27** Art. XIII, of both Constitutions. **28** Art. XIV, People's Constitution; unnumbered Article, Freemen's Constitution. **29** Art. IX, Sec. 4, People's Constitution. **30** Art. IX, Sec. 9, People's Constitution. **31** Art. IX, Sec. 10, People's Constitution.

CHAPTER IX.

THE PEOPLE'S CONSTITUTION.

EVEN if it were conceded that the people have the right, at any time, and without the request or consent of the existing government, to frame a constitution for a State, the adoption of such constitution by the people would need to be closely scrutinized. The method provided by the People's Constitution for its adoption was as follows:

"1. This constitution shall be submitted to the people, for their adoption or rejection, on Monday, the 27th day of December next, and on the two succeeding days; and all persons voting are requested to deposit in the ballot-boxes printed or written tickets in the following form: I am an American citizen, of the age of twenty-one years, and have my permanent residence, or home, in this State. I am (or not) qualified to vote under the existing laws of this State. I vote for (or against) the constitution formed by the convention of the people, assembled at Providence, and which was proposed to the people by said convention on the 18th day of November, 1841.[a]

---

[a] In some of the printed ballots which the suffragists prepared, after the word "I" a blank was left, and a star referred the voter to the bottom of the ballot to the direction: "Write your name in this place." In most cases there was no blank space, and the name was signed at the

"2. Every voter is requested to write his name on the face of his ticket; and every person entitled to vote as aforesaid, who, from sickness or other cause, may be unable to attend and vote in the town or ward meetings assembled for voting upon said constitution, on the days aforesaid, is requested to write his name upon a ticket, and to obtain the signature, upon the back of the same, of a person who has given in his vote, as a witness thereto. And the moderator or clerk of any town or ward meeting convened for the purpose aforesaid, shall receive such vote, on either of the three days next succeeding the three days before named for voting on said constitution.[(b)]

"3. The citizens of the several towns in this State, and of the several wards in the city of Providence, are requested to hold town and ward meetings on the days appointed, and for the purpose aforesaid; and also to choose, in each town and ward, a moderator and clerk, to conduct said meetings, and receive the votes.

"4. The moderators and clerks are required to receive, and carefully to keep, the votes of all persons qualified to vote as aforesaid, and to make registers of all the persons voting; which, together with the tickets given in by the voters, shall be sealed up and returned by said moderators and clerks, with certificates signed and sealed by them, to the clerks of the convention of the people, to be by them safely deposited and kept, and laid before said convention, to be counted and declared at their next adjourned meeting, on the 12th day of January, 1842."[(1)]

---

bottom of the ballot. After the words "I am," in the third line, a space was left, and on some of the ballots a reference to the foot-note, "Write the word *not*, if you are not a voter." In the next line, space was reserved for the insertion of the words "for" or "against." A sample ballot read as follows:

1776. [EAGLE] 1841.

Adoption of the Constitution of Rhode Island.

PEOPLE'S TICKET.

—*Burke's Report*, 354-355.

(b) The unique method of proxy-voting is not difficult of comprehension; in brief, any friends of the constitution had the privilege of bringing to the meetings the names of any who were willing to sign their names merely, without troubling themselves further.

The voting was held on the appointed days, at these unofficial ward and town meetings, in all the towns of the State. The character of the meetings may be judged from the testimony of a few of those especially interested. One witness said: "I acted as moderator in the sixth ward of the city of Providence at the time the vote was taken on the adoption of the people's constitution; and, as such, endeavored to have the voting conducted with as much fairness, and with as great a desire to prevent fraudulent or illegal voting, as ever was done in any other similar ward meeting. Great care was taken by me, as the presiding officer of that meeting, that no one should vote but such as had the right by the provisions of said constitution. Votes were rejected by me on that occasion; and I do not now know of a single vote remaining on the register, or among the ballots, which is not a good vote."(2) The testimony of another prominent suffragist was to the point: "I was present at the meetings for voting for the people's constitution in the town where I resided (Smithfield), and which cast more than 1,300 votes for that constitution. Although not an officer of said meetings, I took an active part therein, and can unhesitatingly say that the voting was carried on with the utmost good faith, and with a determination not to receive the votes of any persons not competent by the provisions under which they were voting. . . . From all my knowledge of the voting at the time, with all I have since learned, I am very fully of opinion that a less number of illegal votes were polled for that constitution than in any contested election held in the State for many years."(3) A former suffragist, after he had abandoned his fellow-workers, testified as follows: "Of the manner in which these meetings and the voting were conducted, (except at the 3d ward polls in the city of Providence, where I attended myself,) I can say nothing; though it was then, and has been since, supposed that uniformity prevailed, in a great measure, in mo parts of the State. In the above-named ward, no evidence w required . . . of the qualification to vote of any one who offere except his own yea or nay; and even of foreigners, strangers, otherwise, no naturalization papers, or other evidence of citizenshi was required. During the last three days, or days of proxy-votin I was informed by the warden or moderator, and clerk, that a lar number of votes were deposited in the ballot-box, which had bee received from seamen and others, then absent, previous to their d parture."[4]

The result of the vote was duly announced by the People Convention, which met again January 12, 1842, and appointed committee of twenty-five to examine and count the votes cast the 27th day of December and the five subsequent days.[c] Th committee canvassed the returns, and reported, January 13, as fo lows:

	Freemen.	Non-Freemen.	Total.
Providence County, ...	2,933	5,734	8,667
Newport County, ...	639	1,200	1,839
Washington County, ...	572	735	1,307
Kent County, ...	533	970	1,503
Bristol County, ...	283	345	628
	4,960	8,984	13,944

[c] As the officers of this convention, together with this committee, must have been among leading men of the party, a list of their names seems important. President: Joseph Joslin, of Ne port. Vice-Presidents: Wager Weeden, of South Kingstown; and Samuel H. Wales, of Providen Secretaries: William H. Smith and John S. Harris. Committee: William James (chairman), John Waterman, Dutee J. Pearce, David Daniels, Oliver Chace, Jr., Robert R. Carr, Ariel Ballou, Thom W. Dorr, Samuel T. Hopkins, Alfred Reed, William C. Barker, Abner Haskell, Alexander All Willard Hazard, Welcome B. Sayles, Sylvester Himes, Israel Wilson, Jonathan Remington, Christop Smith, Elisha G. Smith, Samuel Luther, Erasmus D. Campbell, Nathan Bardin, Joshua B. Rathb and Nathan A. Brown.

The committee added to the table the following explanatory statement: "The whole number of males in this State, over the age of twenty-one years, as nearly as can be ascertained . . . is 26,142. Deducting at a moderate computation 3,000 persons who are not citizens of the United States, etc., . . . the remainder is 23,142, of whom a majority is 11,572. The constitution has received 873 votes more than one-half of all the adult males in the State, and 2,372 more than half of all those qualified to vote for said constitution by citizenship, age, and residence, and an actual majority of 4,746. . . . Of the persons who voted, 4,960 are qualified voters under the existing laws of the State. The greatest number of votes ever polled by said voters was 8,622; . . . of this number, a majority of 1,298 have voted for the constitution,—making, also, as your committee believe, a majority of all the freemen of the State. The committee have found all the returns of votes from the several towns and wards to have been regularly made, and accompanied with lists of all the persons voting, which lists enumerate the qualified voters, and those who are not. Every voter has signed his name upon his ticket; and the committee believe that both the voting and the returns have been as regular and accurate as at any election ever held in this State. . . . The committee report to the convention, as the result of their examination and count of the votes, that the constitution proposed to the people by said convention on the 18th day of November last, has been adopted by a large majority of the citizens over the age of twenty-one years, having their permanent residence in the State."(5)

The committee's report was accepted and the following resolutions were adopted by the convention: "Whereas, by the return of the votes upon the constitution, proposed to the citizens of this State by this convention on the 18th day of November, 1841, it satisfactorily appears that the citizens of this State, in their original and sovereign capacity, have ratified and adopted said constitution by a large majority; and the will of the people, thus decisively made known, ought to be implicitly obeyed and faithfully executed: We do, therefore, resolve and declare that said constitution rightfully ought to be, and is, the paramount law and constitution of the State of Rhode Island and Providence Plantations. And we do further resolve and declare, for ourselves, and in behalf of the people whom we represent, that we will establish said constitution and sustain and defend the same by all necessary means. *Resolved*, That the officers of this convention make proclamation of the return of the votes upon the constitution; and that the same has been adopted, and has become the constitution of this State; and that they cause said proclamation to be published in the newspapers of the same. *Resolved*, That a certified copy of the report of the committee appointed to count the votes upon the constitution, and of these resolutions, and of the constitution, be sent to his excellency the Governor, with a request that he communicate the same to the two Houses of the General Assembly."[(6)]

The suffrage leaders had now carried their plan through, and had declared their constitution the fundamental law of the State, in place of the charter. In a previous chapter it was stated that a legal adoption of a constitution ordinarily required other methods than those which were used by the supporters of this constitution. Even if the claim of the suffragists was legitimate, we should expect to find a constitution, prepared by a convention whose delegates had been elected by a majority of the people, and then adopted by a majority of the people, so that both proposition and ratification of the fundamental law of the State might at least represent the will of the people. It is clear that the delegates were not chosen by a majority of the freemen nor of the non-freemen; it is necessary now to consider whether the constitution was ratified by an affirmative vote of more than half the so-called qualified voters.

The convention declared the constitution adopted, because ratified "by a majority of the people." Of what people? According to the committee, of the males, over twenty-one years, who are citizens of the United States, and have a permanent residence within the State. Accepting their estimate, and their exclusion of those under guardianship, insane, and criminals, and ignoring the 80,000 or more women and children in the State, the number of "the people" was very likely not far from their figure of 23,142. The suffragists then claimed that the constitution was adopted on the ground that 13,944 of these 23,142—a majority of 4,746—had ratified it. Then, according to the convention, we must conclude that the constitution would not have been adopted if there had been, in this list of 13,944, as many as 2,373 improper votes; for then the remaining 11,571 votes would have been a minority of the 23,142 qualified voters.

What is the historic probability that the elections were so carefully conducted that there were not two or three thousand votes cast contrary to the limitations formulated by the People's Constitution itself? Were the opportunities for intentional or unintentional errors many or few? How honest were the intentions of the men who were behind this movement? To answer all these questions there is not sufficient evidence. On one point, however, it is safe to make an assertion: many of the leaders were honest in their intentions and in their acts; they had a thorough belief in their theory of the rights of the people; and, in the case of many of them, there can be no question that they would have dropped the matter if they had felt that the number of votes reached only about 11,000 instead of 14,000.

Nevertheless, no one can suppose that among the seventy-two moderators and clerks of these town-meetings, entirely isolated in the thirty-six polling places,[d] there would be no attempt to use deceit to aid their cause. A very important piece of evidence was the votes themselves, with the names of the voters written upon them, as well as the lists of the voters; these were carefully preserved and examined by the "select committee," and the list of names was printed,[7] but after a short time no one was permitted to examine it. It is very certain that this list included some names absolutely fictitious; some names of sailors then, and for at least two months previous, at sea; some names of dead persons; some unnaturalized aliens; and some persons in the employ of the United States.[e] The accuracy of the list, as well as of the votes, depends upon the integrity of the election officers. They were not under oath, but oaths were not required of the regular officials in the legal town-meetings;[8] official party inspectors or supervisors at the polls were not then customary. The principal reason for distrust is that the usual individual watchfulness of interested opponents was lacking; those opposed to the constitution, almost without exception, remained away from the polls, so that, according to the returns, but 46 votes out of nearly 14,000 were cast against the constitution, and these in but six of the thirty-one towns.

Another usual check was absent; there could be no legal punishment for any person who stated a falsehood upon his ballot. He might not be an American citizen; he might have failed, intentionally or from carelessness, to insert the word "not" before "a free-

---

[d] There were thirty-six towns, and six wards in the city of Providence.

[e] As, for example, the soldiers at Fort Adams.

man;" he might have been less than twenty-one years of age; and yet his statement, on his ballot, would be all the proof required that he possessed the necessary qualifications of a voter. Even the honest people might have been unintentional participants in a fraud. In an election designed to show that the people of Rhode Island had made a change of government, the ordinary precautions and checks were here lacking.

Since 2,400 out of the 14,000 votes cast would vitiate the result, on the theory of the suffragists themselves, more than five votes out of six must be undoubted in order to give assurance. According to the convention report, only about 10,200 persons voted for the constitutions on the first three days; then came a proxy vote of over 3,800.[9] The opportunities for fraud were thus increased many fold. Perhaps, had the question been sifted at the time, it might have been once for all decided before the lists of names were withdrawn from investigation;[f] but the General Assembly took the ground that the whole movement was extra-legal, and that they would have nothing to do with it, and refused to make any investigation of the vote. Charges of fraud at the time bore mainly on the question of the number of freemen voting;[g] they are of little value as evidence, and have almost no bearing upon the question of the total vote cast.

One reason why claims of illegality were few, in the first months of 1842, was that the anti-suffragists speedily took the ground of

---

[f] As early as January 22, 1842, the *Providence Journal* requested permission to copy the list for publication, but was refused *Providence Journal*, Jan. 28, 1842. This is not surprising, for who could trust the list in the hands of most bitter opponents of the constitution?

[g] "In Providence, of the 1,059 Freemen's votes, 375 were not on the ward lists;" "in Coventry, of the 157 Freemen's votes, 40 never were Freemen;" "of the 17 Freemen's votes in West Greenwich, 10 were not Freemen;" "in Cumberland, some of the votes were cast by citizens of Massachusetts;" "of the 309 Freemen's votes in Warwick, but 185 were on the town clerk's list." *Providence Journal*, Jan. 28, 1842.

the General Assembly, viz.: that the presence or absence of fraudulent voting had no effect upon the question, since the whole movement was illegal. An examination was, however, later made of the votes cast in Newport, and a list of the fraudulent votes was published in the leading opposition newspaper; this showed 562 unauthorized ballots out of the 1,203 votes cast;[h] that there were frauds in Newport is undeniable, though the degree of them may have been exaggerated. Even the suffrage party could not deny the possibility of fraud in all the elections, and in the case of Newport, they made only a lame attempt to show that no fraud was intended;[10] but a witness before the "select committee" testified: "I am aware that charges of fraudulent voting, on the question of the adoption of the people's constitution, have been made by the charter party; but I never have seen anything but general and vague assertions, except with regard to the town of Newport. That party made charges of that character against that town, and published a list of those who, they say, had no right to vote. I, at the time, sought information from our friends with regard to the fact; and it is but just to say that there were votes received in that town, as I have been informed, which ought not to have been; but the reason given at the time for receiving them was, that they were included in the census, and, if not taken, *our side* would be counted *against us* by our opponents. The list

---

[h] The *Providence Journal*, Feb. 7, 1843, is responsible for the following table of fraudulent votes in Newport:

Unnaturalized foreigners,	251	Fancy names,	61
United States soldiers,	53	Without consent of parties,	13
Residents of other towns,	40	Colored persons,	5
At sea,	56	Pauper,	1
Minors,	16	Insane,	1
Other persons absent,	30		
Voted twice,	19	Making in all,	552
Variations on names of residents,	6		

published as bad voters by the charter party, I *know* is not true; but how many of those that I have spoken of there were I cannot say. My informant estimated them at less than 200."[11]

Both *a priori* reasoning and positive evidence, therefore, cast doubt on the tabulated results of the election; the chances of fraud were great; the protection slight; and the temptation large. If, as admitted, there were frauds in Newport, to the number of 200 out of 1,203, then many of the 13,944 were not properly cast. That there were 2,373 wrongful votes can neither be proved or disproved; but where so much depended on getting a decisive result, to show public opinion, the suffragists had not made out a clear case.

Some light is thrown upon this all-important question by popular votes subsequently taken. In March, 1842, the people were called upon to vote on the adoption of the Freemen's Constitution. The number of votes cast at that time was 16,702; then two classes of persons qualified to vote for the People's Constitution were excluded from voting on this occasion;[1] 8,689 votes only were cast against that constitution, though the suffrage leaders were opposed to it and had publicly advised their adherents to vote against it. The 8,013 affirmative votes must have been cast almost altogether by people who did not vote for the People's Constitution. There were not, in any computation, enough qualified citizens to cast 14,000 votes in December, and 8,000 voters in March. And what had become of over 5,000 voters who favored the People's Constitution in December, but would not come out against the Freemen's Constitution in March? In April, 1842, upon the election of officers under the People's Constitution, there

---

(1) Naturalized citizens, who did not own $134 worth of land, and persons who had not resided in the State two years. These two classes did not include a large number.

was a total of only 6,004 votes cast; in this case, however, every such voter was making himself liable to punishment for a breach of laws passed by the charter government, forbidding the holding of these elections by the suffragists, whom their opponents had begun to style the upholders of "Suvveriñitiy." This comparison of votes appears to have affected the mind of one of the ablest of the suffrage leaders, Samuel Y. Atwell, of Glocester. "He had never spoken or written anything, which said, implied, or included the assertion, that the People's Constitution is the paramount law of the land. That opinion would depend on the fact, whether a majority of the people of this State had voted for that constitution. Of this he had never been satisfied. Many things had led him to doubt it, and especially the vote upon the last constitution. That result had made it a great matter of doubt, whether a majority of the people of the State were in favor of that constitution, and of course whether it had ever been adopted."(12) And thus we must leave the question: "It is a matter of doubt."(j)

(j) Too much credit should not be given to the *Reminiscences of a Journalist*, the volume written by Charles T. Congdon, the editor of the *Express;* but his statement should at least be noted: "The People's Constitution was never fairly adopted by a majority of the people. Whatever deficiency was anticipated was supplied by proxy votes, and by the managers of the movement, in the name of the dead, the absent, the non-existent everywhere." Congdon, 115.

AUTHORITIES.—**1** Art. XIV, People's Constitution. Other details are omitted here, as not essential to this discussion. **2** *Burke's Report*, 104: Testimony of John S. Harris. **3** *Burke's Report*, 253–254: Testimony of Welcome B. Sayles. **4** *Burke's Report*, 664: Testimony of Jacob Frieze. **5** *Burke's Report*, 438–439. **6** *Burke's Report*, 436–437. **7** *Burke's Report*, 476–622. **8** *Review of Wayland*, 23 (foot-note). **9** *Burke's Report*, 353. **10** *Republican Herald*, Dec. 31, 1842. **11** *Burke's Report*, 104: Testimony of John S. Harris. **12** Apr. 2, 1842, in the General Assembly, Mr. Atwell is thus reported. *Providence Express*, Apr. 4, 1842; *New Age*, Apr. 9, 1842; *Providence Journal*, Apr. 4, 1842; Potter, *Considerations*, 5 (foot-note).

CHAPTER X.

THE FREEMEN'S CONSTITUTION.

THAT the formation and declared adoption of the People's Constitution had its effect upon the conservative party is plainly shown, by the action taken by the General Assembly in January as well as by the Freemen's Convention in February. The demand of public opinion for increased suffrage had finally become so strong that the General Assembly saw the necessity of granting a larger measure of relief. Since it was evident that the Freemen's Convention would considerably enlarge the franchise, it seemed best to almost the entire membership of the legislature to permit a larger number of citizens to vote on the adoption of the constitution than the existing laws allowed. Perhaps the strongly-urged claim of the suffrage party that a constitution should be adopted by a majority of the people—which expression meant, in their minds, a majority of the male residents—may have had its influence on the General Assembly.

An extension of the suffrage, therefore, came near being made by the Assembly: a motion in the House to grant the suffrage, on all questions, "to all male citizens, of lawful age, natives of the United States, resident two years in the State and six months in the town,"[(1)] was only defeated by a vote of 37 to 30,[(2)] in order to substitute in its place the following provision, which would throw the responsibility upon the convention: "Whereas the good people of this State having elected delegates to a convention to form a constitution, which constitution, if ratified by the people, will be the supreme law of the State: therefore, be it enacted by the General Assembly as follows: All persons now qualified to vote, and those who may be qualified to vote under the existing laws previous to the time of such their voting, and all persons who shall be qualified to vote under the provisions of such constitution, shall be qualified to vote upon the question of the adoption of said constitution."[3]

All eyes were now turned upon the approaching adjourned meeting of the Freemen's Convention. In January, Joseph Veazie, a delegate from Providence, resigned, on the ground that the people had already adopted a constitution;[4] whereupon the General Assembly passed an act requesting the freemen of the various towns to fill any vacancies in the delegations from such towns;[5] and a special election was held in Providence, early in February, at which the noticeably small total of 136 votes was cast, and J. H. Clarke elected. The other five pro-suffrage delegates, in spite of their dual membership in both conventions, did not resign, even though repeatedly urged by the newspapers to define their position. In the adjourned session of the Freemen's Convention a proposition to ratify the People's Constitution, and another to adjourn because its work was unnecessary, was rejected. With regard to the troublesome franchise problem, while it did not go as far toward universal suffrage as the People's Convention, its liberality seems remarkable in view of its carefully guarded suggestion in November. The revised suffrage article of the Freemen's Constitution, as definitely determined by the convention in February, was a close approximation to that of the People's Constitution. It differed from the latter in denying the suffrage to naturalized citizens of less than three years' residence and not possessing the freehold qualification; and in demanding at least two years' residence of all voters.[6]

Meanwhile the People's Constitution had been brought before the General Assembly. January 11, 1842, Mr. Atwell presented a bill to alter the day of annual election, to dissolve the constitutional convention, and to adjourn the General Assembly in May *sine die.*[7] This was the day before the adjourned meeting of the People's Convention, and therefore before the official announcement made by that convention of the adoption of their constitution. It is not strange to find expressions of surprise in the newspapers. "Waiving all discussion upon the right of revolution, as exercised, or, at least, attempted to be exercised, in the overthrow of the State government, there has as yet been presented no legal evidence of the number of votes cast, during the week's voting, of the manner in which they were given, or of the qualifications of the persons voting. Nay, before the votes have been counted by the convention, much less examined by the public, with no other evidence than a bare newspaper report, these resolutions are brought forward, proposing to abandon the entire government of the State into the hands of men who have not yet even demanded it. Allowing the proceedings of the suffrage party to have been perfectly legal, it must be shown that the 14,000 votes are the votes of citizens of the State, of lawful age, and the burden of proof rests with those who claim the government. The right of possession is valid until the party claiming brings forward his proof."[8]

Three days later, January 14, the Assembly received from the Governor a set of documents called "papers from the 'People's Convention.'"[9] Six days later, January 20, Mr. Atwell called up his bill and moved that, with the papers communicated by the

Governor, it be referred to a committee of fifteen, who should b authorized to examine the whole subject, and investigate the ele tions and the returns.[10] Debate on this motion consumed all th sessions to mid-day of the 22d of January.[11] When the vote wa taken, Mr. Atwell was able to carry ten other members with hin against fifty-seven who refused to investigate the affair "becaus there was nothing in it."[a] February 5, Mr. Atwell's bill and th papers from the People's Convention were indefinitely postponed.(

Not satisfied with this negative expression of opposition to th People's Constitution, the General Assembly passed, at this sam session, the following resolutions:

"Whereas a portion of the people of this State, without th form of law, have undertaken to form and establish a constitutio of government for the people of this State; and have declared suc constitution to be the supreme law; and have communicated suc constitution unto this General Assembly; and whereas many the good people of this State are in danger of being misled b the informal proceedings; therefore,

"*It is hereby resolved by this General Assembly*, That all ac done by the persons aforesaid for the purpose of imposing upo this State a constitution, are an assumption of the powers of go ernment, in violation of the rights of the existing government, an of the rights of the people at large.

"*Resolved*, That the convention called and organized in purs ance of an act of this General Assembly, for the purpose of forr ing a constitution to be submitted to the people of this State, the only body which we can recognize as authorized to form suc a constitution; and to this constitution the whole people have

---

[a] *Burke's Report*, 443. One of these ten is recorded as having voted in favor of Mr. Atwel motion of the previous June, proposing a new call for a reapportioned convention, with almost u limited suffrage. Six of his associates, at this time, actually voted against him on the earlier occasio

right to look, and we are assured they will not look in vain, for such a form of government as will promote their peace, security and happiness.

"*Resolved*, That this General Assembly will maintain its own proper authority, and protect and defend the legal and constitutional rights of the people."[13]

Meanwhile the Freemen's Convention had continued its existence, and on the last day of its session, February 19, 1842, passed a resolution appointing March 21, 22, and 23 as the days upon which the voters might approve or reject the constitution.

The people of Rhode Island might now be comprised in at least four classes or parties. At one extreme we find the advocates of the People's Constitution, who intended to live up to their resolution to uphold that instrument whatever happened. At the other extreme were the charter advocates, who were opposed to any change, and therefore objected to the Freemen's Constitution. Midway stood two moderate parties who voted for the Freemen's Constitution: first those who were in favor of a liberal instrument, formed and adopted in accordance with the legal methods provided by the existing government; second, those—doubtless very few—who voted for one constitution, and who were also willing to vote for the other.[b]

We might suppose that the extreme suffragists would ignore

---

[b] In *Burke's Report*, 354–355, are printed copies of four ballots (selected out of the fourteen thousand) cast by: William Sprague, of Warwick; George B. Holmes, Henry G. Mumford, and Stephen Branch, of Providence. These men were stigmatized as traitors to the cause, because, after having voted for the People's Constitution, they became "among the most violent persecutors of the suffrage party." They were not the only "traitors" who voted for the Freemen's Constitution, for to them must be added some, at least, who voted for the People's Constitution only to influence public opinion, and could have felt no objection to voting on the second expression of choice. See Wayland, *Affairs of Rhode Island*, 15; Letter from "Fifth Ward," *Providence Journal*, Feb. 28, 1842.

the Freemen's Constitution and decline to vote for or against it. But this would have been inconsistent with their views of sovereignty. Even if they had, in December and January, adopted one constitution, another, adopted in March, might supersede the first, even before it went into operation. The *Republican Herald* briefly stated the position of this party, as follows: "A sort of feeling appears to have taken possession of many persons who voted for the People's Constitution that because they did so it would not be right for them to take any part at the polls for or against any other. For our own part we do not so regard the matter. It is our opinion that the people have not, by voting for that constitution, parted with their original sovereignty."[(14)]

The two cohorts on the day of the vote on the Freemen's Constitution were, then: the law and order party, in favor; and the charter advocates, voting with their enemies, the suffragists, against it. When the vote was counted, the Freemen's Constitution was found to be defeated by the small majority of 676; 8,013 yes to 8,689 no.[(15)] It is evident that the vote of the suffragists would not have been sufficient to defeat it, but for the aid of the ultra-charter men.

Why did the suffrage party decide to vote against the Freemen's Constitution? Mr. Dorr, in his inaugural address, explained that "this constitution was voted against by a large majority of the friends of the people's constitution—not because it was made by the freemen, and not by themselves, but because its leading provisions were unjust and anti-republican, and tended to prolong, under a different guise, some of the greatest of those evils which had been the occasion of so much complaint under the old charter system."[(16)] Mr. Dorr mentions no specific cause of complaint, but we find a list of four criticisms, which a contemporary writer gave as "the chief grounds on which the suffrage party opposed this constitution."[17] (1) The retention of the property qualification for naturalized citizens, a provision retained until 1888;[18] (2) the unequal apportionment in both branches of the General Assembly: in the preceding chapter it has been shown that on this point the difference between the two constitutions was scarcely worth considering; (3) the provision in relation to amendments: this was only a question of requiring a three-fifths vote as against a majority vote; (4) the people had already adopted a different and a better constitution. Analyzing these complaints, the last seems the real and effectual reason for the opposition, and not the content of the Freemen's Constitution, an instrument brought about through the agitation of the suffragists but killed by their hostility.

In coming to this decision, the basis of the conclusion here stated is not entirely *a priori* reasoning, but testimony before the select committee which brought out the true position of the suffragists. "The landholder's constitution, in itself, would have been, so far as it concerned suffrage, I think, acceptable; and its adoption would have given peace to the State, and power, as was generally believed, to the suffrage party in Rhode Island for some years to come; but coming forth as it did, coupled with an implied surrender of an invaluable right, the suffrage men freely (and, I believe, from a clear and strong sense of duty), omitted all present, personal, and local advantages, rejected the offered constitution, and, by so doing, incurred calamities too numerous to be here related."[19] This position seems unreasonably stiff. The right to frame and adopt a constitution, irrespective of the forms of law, would not have been waived by accepting the Freemen's Constitution to supersede the People's. A large minority, at least, of the people of Rhode Island were opposed to the principles of the suffragists concerning constitution-making: the existing government and the existing "people" of the State, the freemen, were evidently determined to prevent the People's Constitution from going into operation; instead, they offered the suffragists a constitution nearly as satisfactory to them as their own. By this constitution the suffrage was opened to about as many non-freemen as freemen; and at once the suffragists would obtain control of the government and doubtless might have made amendments, still further extending the suffrage. The suffragists had really obtained, at their first organized agitation, nearly all for which they asked.

Against an acceptance of this practical victory was set an abstract doctrine of "sovereignty:" no matter what civil disturbances might follow, the People's Constitution was to be the law of the land, and should be upheld through thick and thin. Here was the vital mistake of the suffragists; therefore their cause had been one constantly, even rapidly, gaining; from the mere handful of agitators in the autumn of 1840 they had become a large minority, if not a majority, of the people. From this time on their cause waned; there were daily defections from their ranks; and by the first of May the ebb-tide was plainly noticeable. The rejection of the Freemen's Constitution was an error of great moment. Had but three hundred and fifty suffragists changed their votes from no to yes, the Freemen's Constitution would have been adopted, the Dorr rebellion would not have occurred, the community would never have been disturbed, the suffrage party would have taken the reins of government, the sovereign right of the people would not have been injured, and peace and quiet would have reigned supreme in the State.

AUTHORITIES.—1 *Rhode Island House Journals*, Feb. 1, 1842; *Providence Journal*, Feb. 7, 1842. 2 *Rhode Island House Journals*, Feb. 4, 1842. 3 *Rhode Island Acts and Resolves*, Jan., 1842, p. 58;

Burke's Report, 646. **4** *Providence Journal*, Jan. 26, 1842. **5** *Rhode Island House Journals*, Feb. 1, 1842; *Burke's Report*, 646. **6** Art. II, Freemen's Constitution. *See Appendix*. **7** *Rhode Island House Journals*, Jan. 11, 1842; *Burke's Report*, 443. **8** *Providence Journal*, Jan. 12, 1842. **9** *Rhode Island House Journals*, Jan. 14, 1842; *Burke's Report*, 443. **10** *Rhode Island House Journals*, Jan 20, 1842. **11** *Rhode Island House Journals*, Jan. 20, 21, 22, 1842. **12** *Rhode Island House Journals*, Jan. 22, 1842. **13** *Rhode Island Acts and Resolves*, Jan., 1842, p. 45. **14** *Republican Herald*, Mar. 2, 1842. **15** *Rhode Island House Journals*, Mar. 30, 1842; *New Age*, Apr. 2, 1842; *Providence Express*, Mar. 31, 1842; *Burke's Report*, 119; *Rhode Island Manual, 1696–97*, 128. **16** *Burke's Report*, 725. **17** *Democratic Review*, X, 604 (foot-note). **18** *Rhode Island Manual, 1896–97*, 46. **19** *Burke's Report*, 278: Testimony of Aaron White.

CHAPTER XI.

THE ELECTIONS.

UNEASINESS in the rank and file of the suffrage party began to be shown before the date of the vote on the Freemen's Constitution. Many of the advocates of a new constitution were not convinced of the legal status of the instrument which had been voted upon in December and January. Accordingly, at the beginning of March, a private request was made to the justices of the Supreme Court of the State to express their opinion upon the validity of the People's Constitution. In reply they said: "We have ever held it our duty, as Justices of the Supreme Judicial Court, not to intermeddle with party politics, nor to volunteer our opinion on questions of law which might be presented to us officially. The questions submitted to us, in your note, do not seem to us to be of such class, nor are they such, under all the circumstances of the case, as we feel at liberty to decline answering. We state then, as our opinion, that the convention which formed the 'People's Constitution' assembled without law; that in forming it they proceeded without law; that the votes, given in favor of it, were given without law, and however strong an expression of public opinion they may present, that said constitution, instead of being the paramount law of the land, is of no binding force whatever; that obedience to it will form no justification or excuse for any act done in pursuance of it; and that any attempt to carry it into effect by force will be treason against this State, if not against the United States."[(a)]

It was at once evident to the suffrage leaders that a counter opinion was necessary, to strengthen the wavering. Accordingly, twelve days later, a week before the voting upon the Freemen's Constitution, one of the newspapers published the so-called "Nine Lawyers' Opinion,"[(b)] or "Right of the People to Form a Constitution. Statement of Reasons." It added nothing to the regular suffragist arguments; in brief, it held that the sovereign power of a State is the power which prescribes the form of government; in Rhode Island, at the Revolution, it passed to the whole people; for, if to a part, the owners of land, then it really passed to the soil itself; the sovereign power should be used but rarely; the people should judge time, necessity, and mode; the convention need not be called by the General Assembly; no mode of obtaining a constitution is established in the State; the General Assembly has no power; it can only request; in fine, the two conventions were alike in constitutional authority, one being requested by the people, the other by the General Assembly. The expression so commonly used, "without law," meant merely without the request of the legislature, a servant of the people.[(c)] In conclusion, the nine lawyers

(a) *Providence Journal*, March 3, 1842. This reply was signed by Job Durfee, Levi Haile, and W. R. Staples, the three Supreme Court Justices.

(b) These nine lawyers were Samuel Y. Atwell, Joseph K. Angell, Thomas F. Carpenter, David Daniels, Thomas W. Dorr, Levi C. Eaton, John P. Knowles, Dutee J. Pearce, and Aaron White, Jr. The "Nine Lawyers' Opinion" has been republished by Sidney S. Rider, in *Rhode Island Historical Tracts*, XI, 65–92.

(c) Then followed a long list of quotations prepared by George F. Man. This is evidently the foundation upon which the majority of the select committee, in *Burke's Report*, and Mr. Hallett, in his plea, based their quotations.

said: "We respectfully submit to you, fellow citizens, that the *People's Constitution* is a 'republican form of government,' as required by the Constitution of the United States, and that the people of this State, in forming and voting for the same, proceeded without any defect of law, and without violation of any law." This opinion was drawn up by Thomas W. Dorr, and signed by the nine lawyers, March 14, 1842.(1) The opinion does not explicitly, nor perhaps by implication even, hold that the People's Constitution had become the fundamental law of Rhode Island; nevertheless it was effective in holding many votes against the Freemen's Constitution.

At the very time that the suffragist lawyers were formulating their ideas in opposition to the opinion of the State Supreme Court, the grand jury was in session at Bristol. Here, March 25, 1842, Chief Justice Durfee addressed the jury in a charge that is worthy of careful study, and is injured by any summary, however full.(2) He declared allegiance to be the first duty of every person, a duty due to an implied contract—on one side receiving protection from the State; on the other demeaning oneself faithfully and unhesitatingly to support the State. Movements like those of the suffragists can find no justification in law, for they violate allegiance to the government. The State is a self-subsistent body politic and corporate, designed to continue its existence, by succession and accession, through all time. The corporate people are the sovereign people, and the forms of government but the instruments of its will. The moment that the corporate people ceases to exist as such, everything is resolved into its natural elements, and the State is gone. The State has also to regard its status in the federal system: if, by revolution, the State is overthrown, and a new State is established, on what legal or constitutional principles can it hold, or be readmitted to, its place in the Union? If the question of the existence of the new State is presented to the Supreme Court of the United States, then will be asked, not who voted for it, or how many; but what right had anybody to vote for it at all as the supreme law of Rhode Island? This pretended constitution is without legal authority, and of no more value in the courts of the Union than so much blank parchment. What are the consequences? When corporate Rhode Island ceases to exist, what becomes of her delegation to Congress; of her bill in chancery, claiming through her charter a portion of the territory now held by Massachusetts; of the public property; the court-houses; the jails; the public records; the public treasury, bonds and securities; the actions pending in the courts of the State; corporations? but enough— "I dare go no further. And all this for what?" For an extension of suffrage and an equalization of representation. "Revolution in Rhode Island means a conflict among the very elements of society. Neighbor against neighbor, friend against friend, brother against brother, father against son, and son against father—and all this for what?" . . . "And as to that instrument called the 'people's constitution,' . . . standing, as it does, alone and without any legal authority to support it, it is not the supreme law of this State; and those who may attempt to carry it into effect by force of arms will, in the opinion of the court, commit treason." Thus, even before the defeat of the Freemen's Constitution, the judiciary of the State had fully declared itself.

When the Freemen's Constitution had been defeated, the contest reverted to one between the old charter and the People's Constitution; and the latter had a new point of vantage. In the adjourned session of the legislature, beginning March 30, 1842, another attempt was made to bring the General Assembly into line with "the people:" on the second day of the session, Mr. Atwell introduced a bill to resubmit the People's Constitution to the people of the State,[3] proposing that all those who had been allowed to vote on the adoption of the Freemen's Constitution should vote upon this resubmission. "If adopted," said he, "it would be the law of the land; if rejected, there would be an end to the matter, according to the principles claimed by the suffrage party."[4] Mr. Keech, of Burrillville, offered another bill, providing for the repeal of the existing election law, and the holding of the next election of officers according to the provisions of the People's Constitution,[5] but Mr. Atwell opposed this bill as not being the "best mode of quieting the State." It was lost by a vote of 2 to 52, and then Mr. Atwell's motion was defeated, 3 to 59.[6]

The General Assembly, however, appointed a committee "to obtain all the facts relating to the rejection of the late constitution, and to enquire what legislation is now necessary."[7] Mr. Atwell wished the committee to investigate "what improper means, if any, were used, and by whom, to influence the people in voting for or against the constitution,"[8] but he was promptly ruled out of order. The committee reported that in its judgment the following reasons had influenced the vote against the constitution: first, the false representation that the government was an aristocracy, while in fact a democracy; secondly, dissatisfaction with the apportionment in a portion of the State.[9] The report continued with a discussion of the history of the conventions and the constitutions, and stated that the "People's Constitution was considered merely as indicating the wishes of the people for an extension of suffrage. It was expected that the people would have received the constitution in the same spirit in which it was offered. But misrepresentations were used to defeat it." The report criticised the motives of the suffragists, and characterized them as "deluded men."

Mr. Atwell criticised the report as *ex parte*, and entered into a long speech upon the inequality of the representation in the State Senate as proposed by the Freemen's Constitution.[10] Mr. Randolph answered by stating that the constitution was a matter of compromise, by which Providence was granted increased representation in the House and the farmers were given a preponderance in the Senate. The report was accepted without further discussion.

The General Assembly accepted also a law proposed by the committee, declaring elections under the People's Constitution to be criminal, in an act entitled "An Act in Relation to Offenses against the Sovereign Power of the State."[11] After a preamble declaring that "certain designing persons [had] framed and [were] endeavoring to carry through a plan for the subversion of the government, under assumed forms of law, but in plain violation of the first principles of constitutional right," the statute enacted that all meetings for the election of State officers, other than in accordance with the State laws, were illegal and void; that moderators, wardens, and clerks of such meetings would be deemed guilty of misdemeanor and subject to six months' imprisonment and a fine of from $500 to $1,000; that any person accepting any office by virtue of such elections, or allowing his name to be used as a candidate, would be deemed guilty of high crime and subject to a year's imprisonment and $2,000 fine; and that any person assuming a State office because of such election would be deemed guilty of treason and subject to imprisonment for life; trials of such cases were to come before the Supreme Judicial Court, and might be held in any county of the State, irrespective of the county in which the offense was committed.

Upon this statute there was very little discussion in the House, and it was passed by a vote of 60 to 6.[(12)] It was immediately dubbed the "Algerine Law," for a reason suggested by one of the suffrage newspapers: "The *Dey* of Algiers has had his *day;* and Rhode Island is the last place in which the arbitrary doctrines of this ex-potentate can be revived with success or impunity."[(13)] The severity of this act has been strongly criticised, not only by the suffragists of that day, but by more unprejudiced men since. From the standpoint of the law and order party, however, the General Assembly could scarcely do less than protect the people of the State from the illegal proceedings of the suffragists. In Virginia a law had existed for years declaring such actions treason, and prescribing the penalty of death.[(14)]

In spite of legislature and judiciary, the suffragists continued their preparations for an election under their constitution. The first step had been taken before the publication of the Freemen's Constitution, when, February 16, 1842, "the friends of the Suffrage Constitution" held a convention, and nominated a ticket for their April election consisting of General Thomas F. Carpenter for Governor, Judge Wager Weeden for Lieutenant-Governor, William H. Smith for Secretary of State, Walter S. Burges for Attorney-General, and John Sterne for General Treasurer.[(15)] Of these men, three were Whigs and two Democrats—the convention thus trying to keep national party issues out of the election. General Carpenter declined, on the ground that it would be wiser to head the ticket with a Whig than a Democrat; Mr. Burges also declined. The convention then nominated Judge Weeden for Governor, and authorized a committee to fill any vacancies.[(d)] The three leading

---

[(d)] This committee consisted of: Thomas W. Dorr, chairman; Benjamin Arnold, Jr., Nathaniel Mowry, Dutee J. Pearce, Joseph Gavit, John R. Waterman, and Nathan Bardin.

men on this committee, and henceforth in the suffrage movement, were Dorr, Pearce, and Waterman.

February 22, it was announced that Judge Weeden had positively declined;[16] but three days later the committee's revised ticket was announced, with Weeden for Governor, William C. Barker for Lieutenant-Governor, Burges for Secretary of State, John P. Knowles for Attorney-General, and Sterne for General Treasurer;[17] again there was a nearly equal division between the parties. This ticket stood in a prominent place in the suffrage organ until about the first of April, when the so-called "Algerine Law" was passed; it then disappeared, and Chairman Dorr announced that the publication of the ticket for State officers and Senators was suspended in consequence of vacancies, and that it would be republished the next week with the vacancies filled.[18] A few days later, the State committee (the chairman not included) announced that the ticket was not yet complete,[19] and it became known that all the five nominees for general office had resigned. On April 11 the finally-revised list was published: Thomas W. Dorr for Governor, Amasa Eddy, Jr., for Lieutenant-Governor, William H. Smith for Secretary of State, Joseph Joslin for General Treasurer, and Jonah Titus for Attorney-General.[20] No other ticket or nominations were made.

Under the provisions of the People's Constitution the election for officers was held April 18; and later the "People's House of Representatives" counted the votes through a committee appointed for that purpose.[21] In every case but one the candidates for general officer and for Senators were chosen unanimously; the general officers averaged 6,360 votes each—or about 7,500 less than the alleged vote on the constitution itself. The Senators elected received an average vote of 538, the extremes being 1,315 and 119;

showing either a poor apportionment, or great variations of interest in the election.[e]

Two days after the "People's Election" occurred the regular charter election. The law and order party renominated four Whigs; for Governor, Samuel Ward King; for Secretary of State, Henry Bowen; for Attorney-General, Albert C. Greene; and for General Treasurer, Stephen Cahoone. Nathaniel Ballou, the candidate for Lieutenant-Governor, the only new one on the ticket, had been Speaker of the House as far back as 1825, and his nomination was evidently a bid for Democratic votes. In opposition to Governor King a ticket was prepared headed by General Carpenter, who had been the original candidate on the "People's ticket." The ground upon which he stood is not very plain: as a Democrat he would claim the party vote, but as an upholder of the People's Constitution he did not show consistency in being a candidate for any office at this "needless" election. General Carpenter received 2,211 votes, and Governor King 4,864, with 5 scattering.[22]

SAMUEL WARD KING.

In comparing the votes at these elections, a few points should be remembered. Every person who voted on April 18 came under

[e] The twelve Senators elected, with the votes received, were: (1) Eli Brown, 820; (2) Hezekiah Willard, 1,315; (3) John Paine, 652; (4) Abner Haskell, 907; (5) Solomon Smith, 856; (6) Benjamin Nichols, 648; (7) John Wood, 237; (8) Benjamin Chace, 324; (9) John B. Cook, 119; (10) Joseph Spink, 234; (11) William James, 135; and (12) Christopher Smith, 210.

the penalties of the "Algerine Law;" although the advocates of this election claimed that a few days later it would infallibly be repealed by the "People's General Assembly." At the charter election, of course none but freemen were allowed to vote; and large numbers of these legal voters were suffragists who would naturally decline to vote on the ground that, under the circumstances, the charter election was a farce; even the opposition candidate was a suffragist; but the entire freemen opposition vote, including the suffragists, was barely 2,200, while those of the freemen who were opposed to the People's Constitution, and were willing to vote for the re-election of the Whig Governor, turned out at the polls to the number of 4,864. It will be remembered that the committee of the People's Convention computed that there were 9,590 freemen in all, of whom 4,960 voted for the People's Constitution, thus giving it a majority of the freemen of the State. That was only an estimate; and it is certain that 4,864 freemen—also a majority of 9,590—voted for a continuance of the charter government in voting for Governor King, even after the People's Constitution had been nominally adopted, and Thomas W. Dorr had been elected Governor in accordance with its terms. The people's government was in a minority of freemen, if not of adult male citizens.

The elections over, there was nothing for the suffragists to do but to wait for inauguration day; while the charter government might, if it chose, occupy itself with preparing criminal cases. Something like 36 moderators, 36 clerks, 5 candidates for general offices, 12 senatorial candidates, 86 candidates for the House, and 5 shrievalty candidates had laid themselves liable to arrest for the misdemeanors of holding elections and running for office under an unreal constitution. Now was the time for the government to put down the anticipated revolution. The period before the first of

May was short, it is true, but sufficiently long to so cripple the suffragists that the new charter government could easily complete the suppression, and the people's government could not organize. This would seem now to have been the right step for the law and order party, if they were sure of their position. But not an arrest was made, under the "Algerine Law," in the whole month of April, and the various officers-elect of the people's government went about their daily business unmolested.

AUTHORITIES.—**1** *Rhode Island Historical Tracts*, XI, 65. **2** *Burke's Report*, 706-717. This address was published by the grand jury, with the permission of Judge Durfee **3** *Rhode Island House Journals*. Mar 30, 1842. **4** *Providence Express*, Mar 31, 1842; *New Age*, Apr. 2, 1842. **5** *Rhode Island House Journals*, Mar. 30, 1842; *Providence Express*, Apr. 2, 1842; *New Age*, Apr. 2, 1842. **6** *Rhode Island House Journals*, Apr. 1, 1842. **7** *Rhode Island House Journals*, Mar. 31, 1842; *Rhode Island Acts and Resolves*, March, 1842, pp. 3-4. **8** *Providence Express*, Mar. 31, 1842; *New Age*, Apr. 2, 1842. **9** *Rhode Island House Journals*, Apr. 1, 1842; *Rhode Island Acts and Resolves*, March, 1842, p. 3. **10** *Providence Express*, Apr. 2, 1842; *New Age*, Apr. 2, 1842. **11** *Rhode Island House Journals*, Apr. 1, 1842; *Rhode Island Acts and Resolves*, March, 1842, pp. 16-18; *Burke's Report*, 133-135. **12** *Rhode Island House Journals*, Apr. 2, 1842; *Providence Express*, Apr. 4, 1842. The six were: Atwell, Burges, Gavitt, Keech, Thurston, and Walling. **13** *Providence Express*, Apr. 5, 1842. **14** See page 89. **15** *Providence Journal*, Feb. 17, 1842; *New Age*, Feb. 18, 1842. **16** *Providence Journal*, Feb. 22, 1842. **17** *New Age*, Feb. 25, 1842. **18** *New Age*, Apr. 2, 1842; *Providence Express*, Apr. 1, 1842. **19** *New Age*, Apr. 9, 1842. **20** *Providence Journal*, Apr. 11, 1842. **21** *Burke's Report*, 452-454. **22** *Rhode Island Manual*, *1896-97*, 102.

CHAPTER XII.

APPEAL TO THE NATION.

THE old charter government and both the newly elected governments realized that the chances of a peaceful settlement of the controversy were small. Apparently the adherents of the two parties — the upholders and opponents of the People's Constitution — were nearly equal in numbers. The legislature had passed the "Algerine Law," and found itself confronted with a stupendous task if it attempted to enforce it. A half-hearted enforcement of the statute would avail nothing: it would be necessary to thoroughly carry out its provisions. The one hundred and eighty persons guilty of a breach of this act were among the most prominent citizens, and behind them stood at least a large minority of the citizens of the State. The sheriffs of the five counties would have found it quite difficult to make arrests without the support of some strong military force.

Neither the punitive statute of the Charter General Assembly nor the opinion of the Supreme Court had deterred the people's party from holding its election, and now the regular executive power did not dare to act against it. Enforcement of the law, in all probability, could be obtained only by the calling out of the State militia; but, since the citizens of the State were so evenly divided, the Charter government felt no certainty that it would find the citizen soldiery ready to come to its aid. Indeed, the suffragists expected that many, perhaps a majority, of the military companies would be found arrayed with them; and the "Constitutional State Committee" went so far as to invite the "Chartered Companies, the Military Companies, and the Volunteer Companies, who are in favor of the People's cause and constitution," to be present as an escort to the newly elected Governor Dorr and the "People's General Assembly."(1)

Though the law and order newspapers persistently belittled the exigency, yet the official acts of the government show that the State authorities realized the gravity of the situation: they had private evidence that made them even more doubtful of their ability to cope with the difficulty, and fearful of civil war. As early as February 5, 1842, Samuel Currey testified to a conversation which he had held with Franklin Cooley, who had informed him that a messenger had gone to Boston "to procure 2,000 stand of arms, and that this supply of arms was for the use of those who were about to enforce the people's constitution against the authority, civil military, of the existing government."(2)

Martin Stoddard, president of the mass convention at Newport, May 5, 1841, gave an account of the proceedings of the suffragists, and closed by stating that he believed that "without some interference on the part of the Executive of these United States, the peace and quiet of this State *cannot* be preserved, and that all the horrors of a civil war will, and must, be suffered by our people."(3) Jacob Frieze, from his intimate acquaintance with the leaders of the suffrage party, testified that they had been "extremely anxious that the legal convention should not form a constitution that would be acceptable to the people; and that, let what would come, they would carry their constitution into effect, and organize and establish a government on it, by force, if necessary." He claimed to be "fully persuaded that a firm resolve pervaded their ranks never to give back from their purpose if they can perceive a probability of its execution by any means in their power."(4) Other testimony was obtained of a similar nature, that the suffragists were arming themselves and that military companies from outside the State had promised aid.(5) The charter government was also furnished with copies of resolutions passed in the town of Cumberland, "That the people's constitution we will maintain *at all and every hazard*," and "as one man, *we will, by every means in our power*, oppose the adoption of this spurious constitution, nor abate our efforts until it shall be one of the things that were. . . . We stand ready at a moment's warning, with our lives and honor, to carry into full effect the people's constitution, according to the conditions of the same, unless otherwise ordered by the General Government of this nation."(6)

The General Assembly had scarcely adjourned when the executive authority therefor decided that it was necessary to appeal to the general government. April 4, 1842, Governor King sent two letters to President Tyler, asking for help. The first letter was a formal call for the aid promised in the Federal Constitution: "The State of Rhode Island is threatened with domestic violence. Apprehending that the legislature cannot be convened in sufficient season to apply to the Government of the United States for effectual protection in this case, I hereby apply to you, as the Executive of the State of Rhode Island, for the protection which is required by the constitution of the United States."(7) Nothing important had occurred since the adjournment of the legislature; only a day or two would have been needed to bring the members of the Assembly together; and no domestic violence could have been expected to occur before April 18, the people's election day. The charter government blundered, evidently, in thus depending on a petition from the Governor rather than from the legislature.

In the other letter of the same date, the Governor wrote: "For nearly a year last past, the State of Rhode Island has been agitated by revolutionary movements, and is now threatened with domestic violence. . . . There is but little doubt but that a proclamation from the President of the United States, and the presence here of a military officer to act under the authority of the United States, would destroy the delusion which is now so prevalent, and convince the deluded that, in a conflict with the government of this State, they would be involved in a contest with the Government of the United States, which could only eventuate in their destruction."(7)

Governor King sent John Whipple, John Brown Francis, and Elisha R. Potter to carry these letters and also copies of the acts of the General Assembly, and other documents relating to the conditions in the State, including the affidavits just cited. The commission fully laid the matter before the President, and remained in Washington several days, doing whatever they could to influence both the executive and legislative branches in favor of the law and order party.(8)

April 11, 1842, President Tyler sent a reply to Governor King, in which he regretted "the unhappy condition of things in Rhode Island." He, however, looked upon the controversies as "questions of municipal regulation . . . with which this Government can have nothing to do." The President then carefully defined what he believed to be his powers under the Constitution and laws of the United States.[a] The reason urged for refusing aid was that he nowhere found authority to anticipate a revolutionary movement.

He did, however, clearly commit himself to two propositions which put him on the side of the law and order party in their adherence to the old charter. The first was to give the important assurance that if an insurrection should "actually exist against the government of Rhode Island, and a requisition [be then] made upon the Executive of the United States," the President would "not be found to shrink from the performance of a duty, which, while it would be the most painful, is, at the same time, the most imperative." In the second place, he denied that he had any right to look into the "real or supposed defects of the government," or to be the "armed arbitrator between the people of the different States and their constituted authorities." He added: "It will be my duty, on the contrary, to respect the requisitions of that government which has been recognized as the existing government of the State through all time past, until I am advised, in regular manner, that it has been altered and abolished, and another substituted in its place, by legal and peaceable proceedings, adopted and pursued by the authorities and people of the State."

The effect of the letter of the President, which was published immediately upon its arrival, can be readily judged. The govern-

---

[a] First, he quoted the provision of the constitution providing that "the United States shall guaranty to every State in this Union a republican form of government . . . and, on application of the legislature, or of the executive (when the legislative cannot be convened) against domestic violence." Next was cited the act of Congress, February 28, 1795, "that in case of an insurrection in any State against the government thereof, it shall be lawful for the President of the United States, upon application of the legislature of such State, or of the executive (when the legislature cannot be convened) to call forth such numbers of the militia of any other State or States as may be applied for, as he may judge sufficient to suppress such insurrection." Additional authority existed, under the act of March 3, 1807, granting the President the right, in such cases as those enumerated above, to use the land and naval forces of the United States as well as the militia. *Burke's Report*, 658–659: Letter of President Tyler.

ment of the State was strengthened by the assurance that the President would recognize the charter government until its successor had been legally chosen by the authorities as well as the people of the State. The law and order party was stimulated to resist the establishment of an usurping government, trusting that, in case an insurrection should arise, they could depend upon the aid of the United States. The letter from the President, together with the "Algerine Act" of the legislature, caused many of the rank and file of the suffragists to weaken, and even played havoc, as has been seen, with the ticket which the party had prepared for the first election under the People's Constitution. Those who were undecided quickly joined the law and order party; but the leaders of the suffragists continued their preparations for the election and inauguration.

One reason for this confidence is found in the letters written by Dr. J. A. Brown, the president of the Rhode Island Suffrage Association,[(9)] who had gone on a mission to Washington in the hope to counteract the efforts of Whipple, Francis, and Potter, and to obtain promises of assistance to the people's party, or at least to prevent the giving of aid to the charter government. In these letters, Dr. Brown assured his friends that he had met Senator Allen of Ohio, who was heart and soul with the suffragists; that he had conversed with Wright, Benton, Buchanan, and a host of others. He had even had an interview with the President, and he wrote: "The President will never send an armed force to Rhode Island, or in any other way attempt to prevent the people from obtaining and enjoying their just rights."

However much Dr. Brown may have been deceived or may have deceived himself, in his interview with President Tyler, it is certain that he succeeded in obtaining the sympathies, political or otherwise, of some of the Democratic leaders at Washington. On the day of the people's election, April 18, 1842, Allen submitted a resolution to the Senate, requesting the President to give Congress all the information that he had "relative to proceedings which have taken place, or are in contemplation in that State [Rhode Island], with a view to the establishment of a constitutional republican form of government for the people thereof, in the place of the land company Charter granted by King Charles II of England;" and, with this information, to communicate to Congress "all correspondence, proclamations, orders and proceedings," which had been taken by the President "touching the matter."[(10)] The resolution was read, ordered to be printed, taken up again two days later and passed over informally.[(11)] April 22, 1842, the resolution was laid on the table by a vote of 24 to 13, the negative vote being cast by: Allen, of Ohio; Benton, of Missouri; Buchanan, of Pennsylvania; Fulton, of Arkansas; Henderson, of Mississippi; Linn, of Missouri; McRoberts, of Illinois; Smith, of Connecticut; Sturgeon, of Pennsylvania; Tappan, of Ohio; Wilcox, of New Hampshire; Wright, of New York; and Young, of Illinois.[(12)] Five days later a motion to consider the resolution failed of passage, by 18 to 20: Archer, of Virginia; Bagly, of Alabama; and Calhoun, of South Carolina, had changed sides and voted for the consideration, as did also Sevier, of Arkansas; Williams, of Maine; and Woodbury, of New Hampshire; who did not vote on the former occasion.[(13)] April 28, consideration was again refused by 9 to 28;[(14)] and April 30, a motion to take up the resolution was also negatived.[(15)] Two more attempts were made to consider the resolutions, but both were defeated: one May 2, by a vote of 15 to 28;[(16)] the other May 17, by 15 to 23.[(17)]

Meanwhile the President took no further important steps with regard to the difficulties in Rhode Island. May 2, the garrison at Fort Adams was raised from 10 officers and 109 men to 21 officers and 281 men,[18] a change which, it is reasonable to suppose, would not have been considered necessary had there been no trouble in the State. The orders issued from the Headquarters of the Army at Washington contain no statement of reasons for the large increase in the garrison at Fort Adams;[19] and it must be noticed, also, that the entire garrison consisted of artillery, and was quite remote from the probable scene of any conflict that might occur. The only other step taken was the direction to Major Payne, the commander at the fort, to use his best efforts to "obtain accurate information as to the probability of a conflict between the two political parties now understood to be ready to resort to arms for the possession of the government of Rhode Island." The major was also directed to report daily to the Secretary of War and to Major-General Scott.[20] Whether or no the executive or the military authorities of the United States had any intention to take the part of either of the contesting parties, this attempt to obtain information shows a distinct interest.

As neither Congress nor the President was likely to take any immediate steps for or against either party in Rhode Island, all eyes were turned within the little commonwealth during the last week in April and the first week in May. No overt act was probable, on the part of the suffragists, before their inauguration day, May 3; but the charter officers-elect did not come into possession of the government until May 4: hence, the old government must deal with the beginning of the insurrection, and then turn the difficulty over to their successors. To be sure, the personnel of the two sets of officials was but slightly different, but the charter government was in great doubt of its status; the leaders were perfectly certain of the wisdom of their position, but by no means sure what had been the effect upon their followers of the cries of "sovereignty," of "the people," of the "right to frame a constitution." There was a general feeling of dread and expectancy. The government knew that even peaceful revolutions frequently carried with them persons who desired to obtain a personal benefit from a disturbed state of affairs. About this time the rumor became current that the suffragists had promised, if force was needed, that their followers might do what they would with "Beauty and the banks."[(21)] This baseless slander upon the suffrage leaders had sufficient circulation to increase the feeling of hesitation and fear. To the other troubles of the law and order party were also added threats of outside interference.[(b)]

Without waiting to meet the shock of a contest between rival governments, Governor King, toward the end of April, set in motion the legislature by calling a special session of the General Assembly; and then took the unusual step of recommending a Board of Councillors to advise and counsel with the Governor; he also suggested applying to the President for aid; and advised an organization of additional military force.[(22)] The message was referred to a committee of ten—two from each county.[(23)] In accordance with the report of this committee, the Board of Councillors was appointed by the General Assembly "to advise with the Governor as to the

---

[(b)] The *Providence Journal*, April 7, 1842, editorially spoke as follows: "THE GENERAL GOVERNMENT DEFIED. Hitherto, although we have been accustomed to hear the State government defied, and the General Assembly threatened, even the Town House orators have professed to respect the General Government. But as the certainty grows more apparent that the General Government will interfere if called upon, as it is constitutionally bound to do, it becomes necessary for even that to be defied. The *Express* of yesterday therefore openly defies the General Government, and solicits '*aid from abroad*' to assist in putting down the legal government, and to force upon the people of Rhode Island a constitution which they do not want."

executive measures proper to be taken in the present emergency of the State." This Governor's Council consisted of: Richard K. Randolph, James Fenner, Edward Carrington, Lemuel H. Arnold, Nathan F. Dixon, Peleg Wilbur, and Byron Diman,[24] seven of the most noted political leaders in the State.[c] The appointment of this council seems entirely in accord with the charter; for such a body had once existed in the Board of Assistants, but its successor was the Senate, which had since become merely a legislative body. To create a new part of the government, with powers of its own, would have been a piece of constitution-making; but there was nothing in the charter forbidding an advisory council, and its appointment seems an act of wisdom. Another preparation for the crisis was the enactment of a statute which indicated fear of the disorders that accompany revolution: the riot act was amended by repealing the clause which required the delay of an hour before using military force after making or attempting to make proclamation of the riot act.[25]

Having thus shown its determination to stand by the charter, the law and order party was willing to yield to the feeling, prevalent in this session, that the troubles could not be quieted until a new constitution had been adopted. Accordingly a proposition was made, April 27, to call a third convention to frame a constitution. This proposition caused a short, but vigorous, discussion, but gave place to a motion to postpone the question until the next session

---

[c] James Fenner was one of the most popular Democrats in the State; he had been Governor many times, and was again elected to the chair in 1843. The six other councillors were Whigs, and were prominent lights in their party councils. R. K. Randolph was the leader in the House, and was, the next month, chosen Speaker. Byron Diman was the Lieutenant-Governor of the State. Nathan F. Dixon was later a Representative to Congress, and was the son of a United States Senator, as well as the father of another United States Senator--all three bearing the same name. Peleg Wilbur was a presidential elector in 1832, casting his vote for Henry Clay. Edward Carrington, though less prominently chosen to office, was well known in Rhode Island politics.

and to refer it to the government-elect (which would mean a delay of only a week): this was carried by a vote of 45 to 12.[26] The session was nearly at an end; nothing was sacrificed by the delay.

We have now come to the first of May, 1842; the two parties were drawn up, ready for the struggle; the two governments-elect were ready to meet and organize; the two governors-elect were waiting for the day when they could deliver their inaugural addresses; the people of Rhode Island were all on the *qui vive*, and there was a hush that precedes the storm. The people's legislature awaited the third day of May for its first session at Providence;[d] the charter General Assembly would not meet until the next day, at Newport.[e]

---

[d] By the terms of the People's Constitution two sessions yearly of the General Assembly were provided. The session for the election of officers was appointed for the first Monday of June, at Newport, except the introductory session of the new government, which was to be at Providence on the first Tuesday of May. The Assembly was required to hold its winter session alternately at Providence and at some place in the counties of Washington, Kent, or Bristol, as determined by the Assembly in June.

[e] By the terms of the charter, the General Assembly was required to meet at least twice a year. The session for the election and inauguration of officers was appointed for Newport, on the first Wednesday of May. The other session might be held anywhere in the State, but was set for the last Wednesday in October. The principal meeting-places for the legislature, in the history of the charter government, had been—besides Newport—Providence, South Kingstown, East Greenwich, and Bristol, the shire towns of each county. The headquarters of the government had, by 1842, come to be Providence—the principal offices being in the Court House or State House in that city. The Freemen's Constitution would have introduced a still more complicated political geography: one session must be held at Newport, on the last Tuesday of May; another annual session, on the last Monday of October, was appointed for South Kingstown once in two years; at Bristol and East Greenwich, alternately in the intermediate years; the adjournment from the October session must be at Providence.

AUTHORITIES.—**1** *New York Courier and Enquirer*, Apr. 27, 1842. **2** *Burke's Report*, 655–656: Affidavit of Samuel Currey. **3** *Burke's Report*, 660–662: Affidavit of Martin Stoddard. **4** *Burke's Report*, 663–665: Affidavit of Jacob Frieze. **5** *Burke's Report*, 662: Affidavit of Hamilton Hoppin. **6** *Burke's Report*, 665–667: Affidavit of Christopher Robinson. **7** *Burke's Report*, 656–657: Governor King's Letters to President Tyler. **8** *New York Evening Post*, Apr. 15, 1842: Letter from Washington. **9** *New Age*, Apr. 16, 1842. **10** *Congressional Globe*, II Sess., 27 Cong., 1841–42, p. 430; *Senate Journal*, II Sess., 27 Cong., 1841–42, p. 299; *Senate Documents*, II Sess.,

27 Cong., 1841–42, IV, 244. **11** *Congressional Globe*, II Sess., 27 Cong., 1841–42, p. 432. **12** *Congressional Globe*, II Sess., 27 Cong., 1841–42, p. 438; *Senate Journal*, II Sess., 27 Cong., 1841–42, p. 309. **13** *Congressional Globe*, II Sess., 27 Cong., 1841–42, p. 446; *Senate Journal*, II Sess., 27 Cong., 1841–42, p. 315. **14** *Congressional Globe*, II Sess., 27 Cong., 1841–42, p. 449; *Senate Journal*, II Sess., 27 Cong., 1841–42, p. 317. **15** *Congressional Globe*, II Sess., 27 Cong., 1841–42, p. 459. **16** *Congressional Globe*, II Sess., 27 Cong., 1841–42 p. 462; *Senate Journal*, II Sess., 27 Cong., 1841–42, p. 323. **17** *Congressional Globe*, II Sess., 27 Cong., 1841–42, p. 506; *Senate Journal*, II Sess., 27 Cong., 1841–42, p. 347. **18** *Burke's Report*, 699: Report of Assistant Adjutant-General Thomas, Apr. 8, 1844. **19** *Burke's Report*, 700: Letter from Assistant Adjutant-General Freeman to Colonel A. C. W. Fanning, commanding Fort Monroe, Va., dated Apr. 25, 1842. **20** *Burke's Report*, 701: Letters from General Freeman to Major Payne, dated Apr. 25 and 26, 1842. **21** *Burke's Report*, 69–70. **22** *Rhode Island House Journals*, Apr. 25, 1842; *Rhode Island Acts and Resolves*, Apr., 1842, pp. 3–9; *National Intelligencer*, Apr. 28, 1842. **23** *Providence Journal*, Apr. 26, 1842; *Republican Herald*, Apr. 27, 1842. **24** *Rhode Island Acts and Resolves*, Apr., 1842, p. 10. **25** *Rhode Island House Journals*, Apr. 27, 1842; *Rhode Island Acts and Resolves*, Apr., 1842, pp. 9–10. **26** *Rhode Island House Journals*, Apr. 26 and 27, 1842; *Providence Express*, Apr. 28, 1842.

CHAPTER XIII.

RIVAL GOVERNMENTS.

TUESDAY, May 3, 1842, was a day remarkably full of interest to the citizens of Providence and the vicinity. Though it was not a legal holiday, the streets of the city were crowded, not merely with the people of Providence, but with visitors from all parts of the State. A procession to escort the Governor-elect and the General Assembly was formed in the square in front of the Hoyle Tavern, at the junction of Westminster and Cranston streets, and numbered perhaps 2,000 men, including some companies of militia, the Independent Company of Volunteers, with the Providence Brass Band, heading the line. The march was down Westminster street, across Weybosset bridge, through Benefit and Main streets, and back across the bridge.[1] The State House, as was to be expected, was closed, and the suffrage leaders had secured for the occasion an unfinished building intended to be used as a foundry: hence the term "Foundry Legislature" used in taunting the people's government. To this building, on or near Eddy and Dorrance streets, the procession escorted the Government-elect.

The military escort, before being dismissed, passed resolutions that the People's Constitution was the supreme law of the State, and that it ought to be obeyed by all good citizens thereof; and that, "as a component part of the militia of this State, we are bound to respect Thomas Wilson Dorr as our 'commander-in-chief' under said constitution and that we will obey all lawful orders coming from him as commander-in-chief of this State, for the defence of said constitution, the laws of this State, and the laws of the United States, when called upon so to do." The companies present thus definitely arrayed themselves on the side of the new government, which might reasonably expect, therefore, to be upheld by them in case a necessity for military intervention presented itself. Few companies, however, had offered to form a part of the escort, and fewer still had presented themselves; in fact, the majority of the State militia had, up to this time, given little sign of attachment either to Governor Dorr or to Governor King.[2]

The House of Representatives duly met, and organized by choosing Dutee J. Pearce, of Newport, temporary presiding officer, and Welcome B. Sayles, of Smithfield, Speaker. Sixty-six of the eighty Representatives presented their credentials; five towns were unrepresented. The Speaker took the oath of office and administered it to the Representatives-elect. John S. Harris and Levi Salisbury were elected clerks. A committee of sixteen was appointed to count the votes for State officers, and, after a recess, reported the officers-elect, with their respective votes.[a] The Gov-

---

[a] As usual, the size of the procession can only be estimated by noting the reports in the newspapers of the day. The *New Age* claimed that 3,000 persons were present in line, while the *Providence Journal* declared that, by actual count, the procession numbered 1,630 persons. The *New Age* speaks of the Independent Company of Volunteers, "several militia companies and volunteer corps, and then butchers on horseback in white frocks." The *Journal* counted 467 persons that carried guns, 127 with swords, and 54 men on horseback but not armed.

ernor, the Lieutenant-Governor, the Secretary of State, the Attorney-General, and nine of the twelve Senators appeared and were sworn into office; the General Treasurer took the oath on the following day. It will thus be seen that seventy-nine of the ninety-seven officers and members of the Assembly showed the courage of their convictions by their presence and their oaths of office.

The Governor then delivered his inaugural address in the presence of the two Houses of the legislature.(3) This address, like all the documents coming from the pen of Thomas W. Dorr, was remarkably well prepared and appropriate for the occasion: reviewing the circumstances under which the new constitution had been prepared, and presenting a brief account of the previous attempts made in Rhode Island for a change in the form of government, Governor Dorr clearly and succinctly set forth the position of the people's party. Necessarily most of the address was given to these preliminary subjects, and the recommendations to the legislature were brief and to the point. He advised the repeal of the "force law" and recent kindred acts of the previous Assembly, and suggested that immediate attention be paid to the organization of the militia. He also recommended prompt action with regard to the provisions of the constitution "relating to the security of the right of suffrage against fraud, and to the registration of voters." He closed by quoting the constitutional provision that "The laws should be made, not for the good of the few, but of the many; and the burdens of the State ought to be fairly distributed among its citizens."

The General Assembly remained in session two days, and, before adjourning to meet in Providence on the first Monday in July, passed certain resolutions and general laws.(4) They requested the Governor to make known to the President of the United States, the Houses of Congress, and the Governors of the various States, the facts concerning the adoption of the constitution and the establishment of the new government. They requested the Governor to make proclamation to the people of the State that the government was duly organized, calling upon them to obey the constitution and the laws enacted under it. They repealed the "Algerine Law," passed an act providing for the registration of electors and the manner of voting, abolished the Governor's Council, repealed the amendment to the riot act, chartered a new company of militia, amended the corporation license act, revived the charter of an artillery company, and arranged the method of electing officers of militia companies. A committee was appointed to "demand, receive and transfer the records, books and papers appertaining to the office of Secretary of State," and another committee "to demand, receive and transfer all the moneys, lands, securities, records, books and papers, and every other article appertaining to the office of the General Treasurer." The final resolution of the session continued in office until the adjourned session all officers not re-elected or replaced, and postponed all unfinished business to the same time. With these acts of legislation the General Assembly adjourned, never to meet again.

In reviewing the proceedings of the People's Legislature, we are struck both by the boldness and the timidity which were displayed. It required no ordinary courage for these eighty or more men to come together and organize a legislature and a government in direct antagonism to the existing State government, for by these acts they laid themselves liable to arrest for treason, and they knew that the National Executive had plainly declared against them. They must now either carry things with a high hand, and completely establish themselves in full possession of the entire government, or suffer the punishment of defeated rebels.

Having thus assumed all the executive and legislative functions of the State, the people's government showed a fatal hesitation; the State House in Providence and the State archives were in its power, but the Assembly was too timid to stretch forth its hand and take them. A proposition was made, in the House of Representatives, to instruct the Sheriff to take possession of the State House for the use of the Assembly, "but there was a difference of opinion; three-fourths of the members being opposed to such a step, and in favor of a simple request only for the opening of the building."[5] The Assembly thus placed itself in opposition to the Governor, whose intention it was to take possession of the State House,[6] yet refrained from pushing its opposition to an effectual point.

Governor Dorr always declared that "this ill-judged omission was of fatal consequences. The day was thus lost, and ultimately the cause itself, through the vacillating and retreating disposition of its friends. They held, on that day, every thing in their own hands. All might then have been accomplished without loss or injury to any one."[7] In the light of subsequent events we can see that this was the turning point. To obtain possession of the State House would have been a peaceful, as well as an easy, task: the old charter government had lost its force, and could accomplish little; the new charter government had yet to organize; and the charter officials were at Newport. The timidity of the charter government during the last two weeks of April was more than counterbalanced by the timidity of the People's Assembly on May 3 and 4.

Another singular step taken by the People's Legislature was the retention of the charter courts of law and their officials. Governor Dorr called this "a remarkable oversight,"(8) while an opponent sarcastically suggested that it was "an extraordinary act of legislative courtesy."(9) This continuation of the charter courts in the full exercise of their powers, especially the Supreme Judicial Court, consisting of men so opposed to the People's Constitution as were Chief Justice Durfee and Justices Haile and Staples, seems almost incredible.

A still stronger proof of the timidity of the People's General Assembly is shown by the hasty adjournment. A legislature chosen in accordance with the provisions of a new constitution would be supposed to have an extra amount of business to undertake. A reform Assembly, chosen to rearrange many of the important concerns of the State, might well have kept busy for weeks. A legislative body, elected under the unusual circumstances which surrounded the Foundry General Assembly, adjourning for two months, on the second day of its first session, presents a perplexing problem. Whatever the reasons for the adjournment, the consequences are evident. Every one must have expected some sort of conflict with the charter government, and perhaps with the military power of the nation: by its adjournment the Assembly threw the whole brunt of the battle upon Governor Dorr. When, later, he left the State, he was openly charged with cowardice; but the legislature gave the first example of lack of courage. The only assignable reason for the hasty adjournment was the request of the Assembly that the Governor send a commission to the President of the United States.

The charter government-elect met as usual, at Newport, May 4, and went through a short session in the usual routine of legislative work. The House organized by the choice of Richard K. Randolph, of Newport, as Speaker.[10] The only important measure was the following resolutions:[11]

"Whereas a portion of the people of this State, for the purpose of subverting the laws and the existing government thereof, have framed a pretended constitution, and for the same unlawful purpose have met in lawless assemblages, and elected officers for the future government of this State; and whereas the people so elected, in violation of law, but in conformity to the said pretended constitution, have on the third day of May instant, organized themselves into executive and legislative departments of government, and, under oath, assumed the duties and exercise of said powers; and whereas, in order to prevent the due execution of the laws, a strong military force has been called out, and did array themselves to protect the said unlawful organization of government, and to set at defiance the due enforcement of law; Therefore,

"*Resolved by the General Assembly,* That there now exists in this State an insurrection against the laws and constituted authorities thereof; and that, in pursuance of the constitution and laws of the United States, a requisition be, and hereby is, made by the legislature upon the President of the United States, forthwith to interpose the authority and power of the United States to suppress such insurrectionary and lawless assemblages, to support the existing government and laws, and protect the State from domestic violence.

"*Resolved,* That his excellency the Governor be requested immediately to transmit a copy of these resolutions to the President of the United States."

Henry Bowen, Secretary of State, certified the seal of the State to a copy of these resolutions on that day, May 4;[12] and Governor King sent Speaker Randolph and State Senator Elisha R. Potter, afterwards Representative to Congress, to carry the resolutions to the President, and give a personal letter to the President, expressing the hope that speedy assistance would be furnished.(13) On the same day Governor Dorr transmitted to President Tyler the resolutions of the People's Assembly, with the accompanying note:—(14) "Sir: as requested by the General Assembly, I have the honor of transmitting to you, under the seal of the State, the accompanying resolutions; and I am, very respectfully, your obedient servant, Thomas W. Dorr, Governor of the State of Rhode Island and Providence Plantations. To John Tyler, President of the United States."(b)

Each of the two governments thus sought to obtain the support of the national government, which was likely to be decisive. President Tyler, on the other hand, was anxious to see the matter settled without his interference. Governor King, representing the long-established government, and fortified by the previous promises of the President, was put off with good advice for the present. May 7, Tyler replied to his letter of the fourth, stating that his opinion as to the President's duty had not changed, but that later information caused him to believe that "the danger of domestic violence is hourly diminishing, if it has not wholly disappeared."(c) He concluded with another promise to uphold the charter government, if the necessity presented itself.(15) Two days later the President wrote a confidential letter to King, and entrusted it to Speaker Randolph, advising a proclamation of amnesty and a call for a new convention.(16) May 12, King answered that the General

(b) The *Providence Journal*, May 6, 1842, calls attention to the duplicating of the State seal. "It will be seen by the proclamation of Thomas W. Dorr, calling himself Governor of Rhode Island, that the seal of the State has probably been forged, as he speaks of affixing it to his proclamation. Whoever has done this has committed a very serious offence."

(c) What this "later information" was is not apparent, unless it may have been the news of the adjournment of the People's Legislature.

By his Excellency Thomas W. Dorr

Governor, Captain-General and Commander in Chief, of the State of Rhode Island and Providence Plantations.

To Charles S. Landers of Smithfield — **Greeting.**

YOU, the said Charles S. Landers — **being chosen and appointed** Captain **of the** Artillery ***Company*** **in the County of** Providence **in the State aforesaid, named the** "First Woonsocket Artillery Company" —

and duly approved of, are hereby, in the name of the said State, authorized, empowered and commissioned to have, take and exercise the office of Captain — of the Company aforesaid, with the rank of Captain and the privileges to which you are entitled by the Laws of the said State: and to command, guide, and conduct the same, or any part thereof. And in case of an invasion or assault of a common enemy, to molest or disturb this State, you are to alarm and gather together the Company under your command, or any part thereof you shall deem sufficient, and with them, to the utmost of your skill and ability, you are to resist, expel, kill and destroy the same, in order to preserve the interest of the good people in these parts. You are also to follow such other instructions, directions and orders, as shall from time to time be given forth, either by the General Assembly, or the Governor ~~and Council~~ of this State, or other your superior officers. And for your so doing, this Commission shall be your sufficient warrant and discharge.

GIVEN under my hand, and the seal of the said State, this Fifth *day of May in the year of our Lord one thousand eight hundred and forty* — two *and of Independence the sixty*- sixth

BY HIS EXCELLENCY'S COMMAND:

William H. Smith Sec'ry.

Thomas W. Dorr.

Assembly, at its June session, would doubtless organize a convention, and that it had "already been announced as the opinion[(d)] of the executive that" pardons for past "designs against the State" would be granted to those who would "withdraw themselves from such enterprise, and signify their return to their allegiance to the government."[(17)]

On the day of Tyler's letter to King, Dorr was on his way to Washington to plead the cause of the People's Government in person. In accordance with the directions of his General Assembly, he had appointed Dutee J. Pearce and Burrington Anthony, the people's sheriff of Providence county, to bear the legislative resolutions,[(18)] but almost before the commission had started[(e)] the People's Governor set out for the same purpose. This hurried departure of the Governor naturally gave rise to the report that he had fled from the State for safety. Roger W. Potter, the charter sheriff of Providence county, had been provided with a warrant for the arrest of the Governor, on Thursday (May 5). He afterwards testified that he could not find the man, although he acknowledged that he did not make any very systematic search for him.[(f)] Later movements leave no room for doubt that the Governor intended to return to Rhode Island, and that the resolutions passed by an assemblage of suffrage sympathizers, urging him to

(d) Under the charter government in Rhode Island, the power of pardons was held by the Assembly and not by the Governor.

(e) "Mr. Dorr arrived in New York on Saturday (May 7), on his way, it is said, to this city." *National Intelligencer*, May 10, 1842. "I left the State on the Saturday after the Legislature adjourned." Testimony of Dutee J. Pearce, in Pitman, *Trial of Dorr*, 26.

(f) "Witness was first directed to go to Burrington Anthony's house for Dorr; but, after dinner, was directed not to go there, but to arrest Dorr if he should find him down street in the city. Did not know what might be considered his place of residence, as he had removed from his former home to the Franklin House, and afterwards left the house. Did not know that his residence was at B. Anthony's. Did not inquire for him there. Was told that he might be found at the printing office personally represent his government at Washington, had considerable influence in leading him to make the journey. It is certain, however, that the secrecy pursued did not help the cause of the people's government, at least within the State itself.[g] Not until Monday did the suffrage organ deign to allude to the question of the Governor's movements, and then it merely stated that he was not in Rhode Island, but was away for a few days on important public business, and that it was presumed that he was at Washington.[19]

The two commissioners and the Governor joined forces in Philadelphia on Monday (May 9),[20] and proceeded at once to Washington. Their stay at the Capital was brief, inasmuch as Dorr and Pearce started for home on Wednesday (May 11),[21] and Anthony arrived in Providence on the morning of Thursday (May 12).[22] The steps which Governor Dorr and his associates took while in Washington have been most carefully kept secret. No account of

---

of the *Herald* or *Express*." Testimony of Potter, in Turner, *Trial of Dorr*, 12; see Pitman, *Trial of Dorr*, 25. "Our opponents are at their wits end to know what has become of Gov. Dorr. They say that they wish to arrest him, but can't find him. Why did they not do it when he was daily in the street? As soon as they knew that he was absent on business, they pretended to be on the lookout, and sent a troop of officers down to the Steam boat, for a sham to take him *in transitu*, when it was well known that he was beyond their jurisdiction." *Providence Express*, May 10, 1842.

[g] "The warrant against Mr. Dorr has not been served, owing to the impossibility of finding him.. He is either concealed or has left the city. We are inclined to the opinion that he has gone off, that he went across the country and met the railroad train at one of the country depots. In order to cover his retreat and give an air of dignity to his flight, the meeting at the Court House parade passed a resolution requesting him to go to Washington and represent the interests of his party at the seat of government. People who go abroad, on honorable missions, generally go in the broad light of day and by the most convenient and customary routes." *Providence Journal*, May 9, 1842. "Shortly after the session of the People's Assembly, having attended to the necessary executive business, I set out for the city of New York, with the intention of proceeding to Washington. I was strongly urged to visit the capital by many of the best friends of our cause, and a vote to the same effect was adopted at a large meeting of the citizens of Providence. They were desirous that I should ascertain, on the spot, what were the springs of the movement against us at Washington, and whether there was a final determination to suppress our constitution by force." Dorr, in "Address to the People of Rhode Island," August, 1843, in *Burke's Report*, 750.

their movements while in the city has been preserved. However, they had no success in prevailing upon the executive authorities to take any different ground from their position already described. Doubtless individual Senators and Representatives may have spoken cheering words to the deputies from the new government, but no official action was taken by Congress either during or immediately subsequent to their visit to Washington. The communication from Governor Dorr, informing the United States that the State government under the new constitution had been duly established, was received by the Senate and immediately laid upon the table.[(23)]

Meanwhile the issuance by the charter government of the warrant for the arrest of Governor Dorr was merely a forerunner of the conflict which had already begun between the rival governments. In less than a week after the adjournment of the Assembly, the people's government was in a state of collapse. The first arrest was that of Daniel Brown, a Representative from Newport, on a warrant issued and served May 4:[(24)] he was admitted to bail in the sum of $5,000. The next day came the arrest of Dutee J. Pearce, two days before he started for Washington:[(25)] he was granted the same bail. Many warrants were issued on this day, and the next day Burrington Anthony was arraigned, and admitted to bail in season to proceed to the national capital.[(26)] Other arrests followed as the days went by, among the most important being those of the General Treasurer, Joseph Joslin; Representative Benjamin Arnold, of Providence; Speaker Sayles, of Woonsocket; and Senator Hezekiah Willard, of Providence.[(27)] Mr. Arnold was reported to have refused to give the $2,000 bail, and to have been taken to prison.[(28)]

These wholesale arrests were naturally followed by numerous withdrawals from office. May 5, the resignation of Nathaniel C.

Smith, Representative from Newport, was announced;[29] the next day that of George Niles, of Richmond;[30] and on the following day that of William L. Thornton, of Providence.[31] Before the return of Governor Dorr to the State, the resignations of many others had been publicly announced, among them being those of James Yeaw, of Scituate; T. G. Haszard, of Westerly; Sydney S. Tillinghast, of East Greenwich; William P. Arnold, of Westerly; and Jonah Titus, the Attorney-General.[32] The *Providence Journal* exultantly summarized the state of the people's government as follows: "The revolution is in a state of suspended animation. Governor Dorr had hid or run away. Pearce is missing. Sheriff Anthony has absquatulated. The Secretary of State's office is over the line, and their headquarters nobody knows of. Their General Assembly has evaporated."[33]

To resist these arrests and to prevent further resignations, the suffragists were at their wit's end, and their organ, the *Providence Express* (the daily edition of the *New Age*), made a dangerous blunder in the minatory method which it adopted. In its issue of May 9, appeared the following:

"PARTICULAR NOTICE.

"The following is the order of Proceedings under the 'Algerine Act' to the present time, according to their respective dates:

"No. 1, May 4th.—MR. DANIEL BROWN of Newport arrested for Treason, on complaint of

"☞ WILLIAM PECKHAM of S. Kingstown.

"The warrant was issued by ☞ JOB DURFEE of Tiverton, resident citizen on Quawket Neck.

"Mr. Brown was held to bail in the amount of $5000, with two sureties to the same amount.

"2d.—The HON. DUTEE J. PEARCE of Newport was arrested, May 5th, for Treason, on complaint of ☞ —— CRANDALL of Newport ☜ by ☞ WM. H. DOUGLAS of Newport. ☜ The warrant was issued by ☞ JOB DURFEE ☜ aforesaid. Mr. Pearce was held to bail with two sureties, in the sum of $5000 each.

"3d, May 6th.—BURRINGTON ANTHONY, Esq. late Marshal of the United States for this District, was arrested for Treason by ☞ DANIEL K. CHAFFEE of this city, No. 40, High Street. On complaint of ☞ HENRY G. MUMFORD of this city, No. —, Bowen Street. ☜ The Warrant was Issued by ☞ HENRY L. BOWEN, of this city, No. —, George Street. ☜ Mr. Anthony was held in bail in the sum of $4000."

Well might the *Journal* ask: "Do the men of the suffrage party approve of this? Do they agree that their fellow citizens, the judicial and executive officers of the State, shall be marked for the torch of the incendiary or the dagger of the assassin? If the wretched and unprincipled leaders of this foul conspiracy think that they can, in this manner, intimidate men from the discharge of their duty, they will find themselves greatly mistaken."[34]

AUTHORITIES.—**1** *Providence Journal*, May 4, 1842; *New Age*, May 7, 1842; reprinted in *Burke's Report*, 717–719. **2** The Journals of the Senate and the House of Representatives of the People's Government are given in *Burke's Report*, 448–461. **3** This address may be found in the *New Age*, May 7, 1842; reprinted in *Burke's Report*, 720–731. **4** The Acts and Resolves of this General Assembly are reprinted in *Burke's Report*, 461–469. **5** Testimony of Dorr, in Turner, *Trial of Dorr*, 73. **6** Testimony of Carter and Pearce, in Turner, *Trial of Dorr*, 31 and 13. **7** Testimony of Dorr, in Turner, *Trial of Dorr*, 73. **8** Turner, *Trial of Dorr*, 73. **9** Prosecuting Attorney Bosworth, in Pitman, *Trial of Dorr*, 63. **10** *Rhode Island Manual, 1896–1897*, p. 95. **11** *Rhode Island House Journals*, May 4, 1842; *Rhode Island Acts and Resolves*, May, 1842, p. 17; *Burke's Report*, 673. **12** *Burke's Report*, 673–674. **13** *Burke's Report*, 672–673. **14** *Burke's Report*, 675. **15** *Rhode Island House Journals*, May 11, 1842; *Burke's Report*, 674. **16** *Burke's*

Report, 676. **17** *Burke's Report*, 676–677. **18** *New Age*, May 14, 1842. **19** *Providence Express*, May 9, 1842. **20** Testimony of Pearce, in Pitman, *Trial of Dorr*, 26. **21** *New York American*, May 13, 1842. **22** *Providence Express*, May 13, 1842. **23** *Congressional Globe*, II Sess., 27 Cong., 1841–42, p. 479. **24** *Providence Journal*, May 5, 1842; *Providence Express*, May 9, 1842. **25** *Providence Journal*, May 6, 1842; *Providence Express*, May 9, 1842. **26** *Providence Journal*, May 7, 1842; *Providence Express*, May 9, 1842. **27** See the Providence newspapers from May 9 to May 14, inclusive. **28** *National Intelligencer*, May 12, 1842, taken from the *New York Commercial Advertiser*. **29** *Providence Journal*, May 5, 1842. **30** *Providence Journal*, May 6, 1842. **31** *Providence Journal*, May 7, 1842. **32** See the Providence newspapers from May 9 to May 14, inclusive. **33** *Providence Journal*, May 9, 1842. **34** *Providence Journal*, May 10, 1842.

CHAPTER XIV.

TAMMANY HALL.

NINE days had now passed since the organization of the people's government: beyond Governor Dorr's proclamation and official communications to Washington, no executive action had been taken. The legislature had been in session two days, but none of the statutes which it enacted had, as yet, gone into effect, in any sense of the term. The Governor himself was absent from the State, and a veil of secrecy surrounded all his actions; and many of the officials and representatives had withdrawn from the government. The rank and file of the people's party felt that they were leaderless; they realized that their government was practically non-existent; they were ready to acknowledge that their cause was lost. The former leaders of the party had placed the burden upon the chief executive, and he had apparently deserted them. Something ought to be done, and that at once.

At this juncture Sheriff Anthony arrived in Providence, bringing report of the mission to Washington. Immediately notice was issued to the friends of suffrage to assemble in the afternoon, in front of the State House, to hear the report and to take action accordingly.(1) Benjamin Arnold, Jr., presided, and after a few remarks introduced the commissioner, who—realizing the importance of the moment—spoke most encouragingly. Interviews had been obtained with President Tyler, Secretary of State Webster, and with several Senators and Representatives; and he declared that the cause was rapidly gaining friends, and would soon win the day. He urged the party to continue in its course, and spoke of the general condemnation of the "Algerine Law" which he had found wherever he had been. Dr. Brown then presented a series of bold resolutions, which showed that the inflammatory publications of the party organ had not been without effect.(2) At the same time, these resolutions were, for the most part, mere bravado. Though bravely standing up for their fundamental constitutional principle, though vehemently attacking the "Algerine Law," and though honestly promising to support the Governor, they did not endorse the people's government, they did not propose to attempt to overthrow the charter authorities, and they contained no clause which would prevent the people's party from yielding to the *de facto* government, if it would treat them leniently and give them a liberal constitution. That such a result was desired by the leaders at this meeting is shown by Anthony's statement, a few days later, that he had been informed by President Tyler that he proposed to write Governor King a private letter, advising that some advances should be made to the people and that no more arrests should be made under the "Algerine Law."(3) This letter, as has been shown, had been written by the President on the very day of the arrival of the commissioners in Washington.

Governor Dorr and his faithful friend, Pearce, were no more certain of the future than their leaderless followers in Providence. On their arrival in New York, May 12, no plans for future action had been matured.(4) Dorr himself did not hesitate to state to friends whom he met in that city that he could do no more; that he must now trust to the promise of the President that he would procure an act of amnesty for all past offences.[5] But the Governor met with a welcome from these New York friends which cheered his drooping spirits and urged him on to further action. He had yielded to what seemed the inevitable because he knew that he and his followers could not overthrow the charter authorities, who had retained possession of the government, if, as he felt certain, they should be upheld by the national power. Now it was suggested to him that he might depend upon the assistance of friends from other States, if the President should send forces to Rhode Island. As will be seen, the forty-eight hours spent in New York had great influence upon the history of Rhode Island during the next two months.

Dorr's New York friends were leaders of Tammany Hall, an organization which had already twice shown its interest in the popular movement in Rhode Island. Before the middle of April, a memorial was prepared and circulated for signatures in New York city, requesting the National House of Representatives to impeach the President for his "armed interference, or threatened coercive measures, against the people of Rhode Island, in their struggle to cast off the authority claimed over them under King Charles Second's charter."[6] Nothing further is heard of this memorial, but April 27 a meeting was held at Tammany Hall to awaken interest in the movement in Rhode Island.[7] Aaron Vanderpool presided, and the assembled braves were addressed by A. W. Parmenter, of Rhode Island, one of the subordinate leaders of the people's party.[a]

---

[a] A mistake was made by the suffrage leaders when they brought into prominence a man like Parmenter, who had spent eighteen years in the Massachusetts State Prison. See Potter, *Considerations*, 7.

The arrival of Governor Dorr was the signal for immediate action. First came social amenities: the Tammany organ semi-officially announced that "His Excellency, Governor T. W. Dorr, of Rhode Island, has consented to attend the performance at the Bowery Theatre this evening, accompanied by the Rhode Island Delegation and several other distinguished personages."[8] The "delegation" consisted of Dorr and Pearce, and the escort was led by E. F. Purdy, late President of the Board of Aldermen.[9]

During the day (Friday, May 13) the Governor met many of the chief personages of Tammany at his headquarters, Howard's Hotel,[10] and the next morning was accorded a reception at Tammany Hall. Many citizens called upon him, and the Governor made an address which was received with applause. Pearce had already left for home, but Speaker Sayles, who came to Dorr's assistance, earnestly seconded the Governor's remarks.[11] A crowd collected in the park near the Hall, and when it became necessary for Dorr to leave in order to catch the Stonington steamboat, an impressive escort was formed, under the lead of William H. Cornell as grand marshal, consisting of a brass band, a number of firemen drawing a "brass 12-pounder," and perhaps five hundred citizens. The barouche, following the escort, was decorated with the American flag and contained Governor Dorr and Speaker Sayles, together with Alderman Purdy and Levi D. Slamm, editor of the *New York New Era*.[b]

---

[b] *New York New Era*, quoted by the *New York Evening Post*, May 16, 1842; *New York American*, May 18, 1842. According to the *New Era*, the escort was a "vast civic procession which numbered thousands of our most worthy, industrious and respectable citizens." The *American* says of it: "We never, in our lives, saw a worse looking set than the Governor's escort—the Five Points could not have beaten it at an election. The Governor sat bareheaded, looking as grave as an owl. He is a man of nerve and no mistake— Any, but such a person, would have broken down in a fit of laughter, at the absurdity of the thing."

Up to this point the movement in New York City may be said to have been that of a few men, who were desirous of starting an agitation. The next step was the calling of a mass meeting to be held at "The Park," on Tuesday evening (May 17) to "adopt such action as may be needful in view of the threatened interference of the United States Government to put down the free people of Rhode Island."(12) Among the thirty-six names appended to this call were: Vanderpool, Purdy, and Slamm, already mentioned, and William C. Bryant, Samuel J. Tilden, Walter Bowne, Alexander Stewart, Ely Moore, Stephen Allen, and John I. Morgan.(c) The meeting was called to order by Vanderpool; C. C. Cambreleng was chosen president; and twenty-six vice-presidents, nominated by Purdy, were appointed.(d) The meeting was addressed by Vanderpool, Cambreleng, Moore, and others;(13) and adopted resolutions criticising President Tyler for forcible interference in the affairs of Rhode Island. A "corresponding committee" of twelve was appointed, containing such names as Vanderpool, Purdy, Slamm, and Tilden.(e) The news-

(c) *New York American*, June 9, 1842. The call was signed by A. Vanderpool, Campbell P. White, William C. Bryant, C. C. Cambreleng, Ely Moore, J. W. Edmonds, Daniel Stanton, Walter Bowne, David Bryson, Hezekiah W. Bonnel, Thomas W. Tucker, Daniel Ward, John Pettigrew, Samuel J. Tilden, Nelson J. Waterbury, William McMurray, Theodore Sedgwick, J. Sherman Brownell, Elijah F. Purdy, Abraham Hatfield, S. Cambreleng, John V. Greenfield, Henry J. Anderson, Alexander Stewart, Stephen Allen, Nicholas Schureman, John I. Morgan, Gideon Ostrander, Frederick R. Lee, Levi D. Slamm, Josiah Hopkins, Auguste Davezac, J. L. O'Sullivan, John H. Bowie, L. Bonnefaux, and Clement Guion.

(d) *New York Observer*, May 21, 1842; *New York American*, June 9, 1842. The vice-presidents were: Henry Yates, Campbell P. White, David Bryson, John M. Bradhurst, Josiah Rich, Levi D. Slamm, George Paulding, A. V. Williams, Hezekiah W. Bonnel, Andrew Surre, John I. Morgan, Daniel Winship, Daniel Jackson, Walter Bowne, Henry J. Anderson, James R. Manley, Wm. O. Shiels, Freeman Campbell, A. G. Crasto, George S. Mann, Rufus Prime, Alex. Stewart, Stephen Allen, Alex. F. Vache, Alex. Hamilton, and Frederick R. Lee.

(e) *New York American*, June 9, 1842. The "corresponding committee" consisted of: Aaron Vanderpool, Elijah F. Purdy, Samuel J. Tilden, Joseph Hopkins, Auguste Devezac, Chas. A. Secor, Ely Moore, Levi D. Slamm, Alex. F. Vache, Nelson J. Waterbury, John H. Bowie, and James B. Greenman.

papers of the day placed the attendance at from 4,000 to 12,000—the estimate varying in accordance with the political principles of the papers.[14]

Such were the public steps taken in New York City, between May 12 and May 17, to show sympathy for Governor Dorr and the people's party in Rhode Island. All this was legitimate enough: but behind and partly concealed were plans of the Tammany leaders and advice and encouragement to the semi-fugitive executive which can only be inferred from hints and from later developments. The Governor is reported to have stated in his Tammany Hall address that all the aid which his government desired from other States was assistance to prevent the government of the United States from forcibly keeping the charter authorities in possession of the State.[15] Editor Slamm was the most energetic of these *quasi* friends of Dorr; at "The Park" meeting he made the significant announcement[16] that he had already chartered a steamboat to carry 1,000 fighting men to Rhode Island whenever the General Government should dare to attempt to interfere in that State. An editorial in the *New York Evening Post* still further shows the position of Tammany Hall: "Is the Chief Magistrate aware of the danger of attempting to wield the military force of the federal government in a local controversy, which may be settled without it? . . . We fear that Mr. Tyler had not pondered maturely, when he assented to the advice—Mr. Webster's, probably—which led him to promise the assistance of the federal troops to the landholders. . . . We would point out the danger—not the danger merely, but the certainty of shameful failure and defeat, bloody perhaps, but total and inevitable—if the Executive persists in the design to uphold the obsolete charter and abrogated government of Rhode Island, by force of arms."[17]

The position of Governor Dorr and the Tammany men is even more plainly set forth in letters to Governor Cleaveland, of Connecticut, and Governor Fairfield, of Maine, May 13 and May 17.[18] The latter letter contained the following assurances: "The People of Rhode Island are now threatened with a military intervention, unless they abandon their Constitution, and surrender all the rights which are so justly estimated by those who are worthy to be the descendants of venerated ancestors, or to be the citizens of a democratic Republic. In behalf of the People, whom I have the honor to represent, I respectfully request you to bring the proceedings at Washington and the question of our rights to the attention of the Legislature of the State of Maine, now, or soon to be, in session. Being unable to contend singly against the forces of the United States, we invoke the aid of your State in this contest, which involves the great principles of American Freedom, and the dearest privileges of a Sovereign People."

While in New York, Dorr received a communication,[19] which must be quoted in full:

"NEW YORK, May 13, 1842.

"*To Thomas W. Dorr, Governor of the State of Rhode Island:*

"SIR:—Several military companies of this city and vicinity having tendered their services to form a military escort to accompany you to Providence, we have the honor to apprise your Excellency of the fact. This distinction which they so much admire, we hope will meet with your cheerful acceptance.

"With sentiments of the highest respect,

"We are, very respectfully yours,

"ALEXANDER WING, JR., *Colonel 13 Reg't, N. Y. A.*
"ABRAHAM J. CRASTO, *Lt. Colonel, 236 Reg't, N. Y. S. I.*"

The next day, the Governor returned the following reply:

"NEW YORK, May 14, 1842.

"*To Colonels Wing and Crasto:*

"GENTLEMEN:—I return to you my most sincere thanks for the offer, contained in your letter of yesterday, of an escort of several military companies to accompany me to the city of Providence. It is impossible to mistake the spirit in which this offer is made. It is an indication of the fraternal interest with which you regard the present struggle for their just rights of the people of Rhode Island, whom I have the honor to represent. While I should not feel justified at the present moment in withdrawing you from your homes and business, on the expedition contemplated, allow me to say that the time may not be far distant, when I may be obliged to call upon you for your services in that cause to which you would so promptly render the most efficient aid—the cause of American citizens contending for their sovereign right to make and maintain a republican Constitution and opposed by the hired soldiers of the General Government. In this unequal contest, I invoke your aid and that of your associates in arms. We appeal from the Government to the people, and rely upon them in the last resort to defend our rights from every arbitrary aggression. Be pleased to make my cordial acknowledgments to the officers and privates, who have so kindly united with you in the honor which has been proffered me; and accept the regards of your friend and fellow-citizen,

"THOMAS W. DORR."

A proclamation which Governor Dorr issued soon after his return to Rhode Island merely repeated his position as given above;[20] after stating some facts concerning his trip to Washington, the Governor declared that the President had intimated "an intention of resorting to the forces of the United States to check the movements of the people of this State in support of their republican constitution recently adopted. From a decision which conflicts with the right of sovereignty inherent in the people of this State, and with the principles which lie at the foundation of a democratic republic, an appeal has been taken to the people of our country. They understand our cause; they sympathize in the injuries which have been inflicted upon us; they disapprove the course which the national Executive has adopted towards this State; and they assure us of their disposition and intention to interpose a barrier between the supporters of the people's constitution and the hired soldiery of the United States. . . . As your representative, I have been everywhere received with the utmost kindness and cordiality. To the people of the City of New York, who have extended to us the hand of a generous fraternity, it is impossible to overrate our obligation at this most important crisis. It has become my duty to say, that, as soon as a soldier of the United States shall be set in motion, by whatever direction, to act against the people of this State, in aid of the charter government, I shall call for that aid to oppose all such force, which, I am fully authorized to say, will be immediately and most cheerfully tendered to the services of the people of Rhode Island from the City of New York and from other places. The contest will then become national, and our State the battle ground of American freedom. As a Rhode Island man, I regret that the constitutional question in this State cannot be adjusted among our own citizens. . . . They who have been the first to ask assistance from abroad, can have no reason to complain of any consequences which may ensue."

Governor Dorr returned to the State with much less secrecy than he left it. In the interim he had learned that amnesty would, in all probability, be granted him and his friends, if they proceeded no further with their movement; but that, in case of necessity, the national forces would be arrayed against him. He had, however, been brought to believe that, in this emergency, the citizens of other States, especially those of New York, would come to his rescue. His mind was made up, therefore, to proceed with the attempt to obtain control of the State. He realized that, at first, he would be opposed only by the charter authorities; he believed that the "majority" of the people of the State would support him; and he hoped to defeat the *de facto* government before it could receive outside assistance. If, after that, the United States forces should be sent into the State, he relied upon the promises of assistance which had been so freely offered him in New York, being assured that the "people" of the entire country were with him. How self-deceived he was, both as to the feeling in Rhode Island and the assistance "from abroad," will soon be seen.

Dorr arrived in Stonington, Connecticut, Sunday morning, May 15, where he found a small delegation from Providence, which had come down Friday evening to meet him. The news of his arrival reached the city, and at 2 o'clock, Sunday afternoon, a special train was sent to Stonington, carrying perhaps 200 men, a portion of whom were armed.(21) On Monday morning, May 16, at about 10 o'clock, the Stonington train arrived back in Providence, and the People's Governor was welcomed by a crowd of perhaps 3,000 persons.(22) A procession was formed of about 1,200 men; 300 of these were armed, about 100 of whom belonged to the militia; and some 75 were mounted.(23) Perhaps, under these circumstances, it is not surprising that no attempt was made by the charter sheriff to serve the warrant in his possession.

The procession moved quietly through the principal streets of the city, escorting the Governor to the residence of Burrington Anthony, on Atwell's avenue, which was to be, for the time, his headquarters. Before dismissing his escort, Dorr seized the opportunity to appeal to his followers to support him in his future movements. Rising in his carriage he made an address, at once "well timed and eloquent"[(24)] and "furious and inflammatory."[(25)] He spoke especially in reference to his reception in New York, which had been highly gratifying to him. He referred to the rumor that he had procured the aid of 500 men from abroad, which he denied. He announced, however, that he had been promised the aid of 5,000 men, and that he could have them at any time.[(26)] He declared that he was sure of aid enough from New York to cope with any force which the United States might use against his party.[(27)] The speech was of three-quarters of an hour's length, and in the midst of it the orator drew his sword, which he said "had been presented to him in New York by the brother of an officer who had been slain in Florida," and made some remark about using it again. Though his exact words might be useful in forming an estimate of the speaker's character, yet they are hard to ascertain, for the various reports illustrate how differently the same statement may be heard by different people. One of the witnesses for the prosecution, in the trial of Dorr for treason, swore that the prisoner stated that the sword had been "dipped in blood once, and rather than yield the rights of the people of Rhode Island, it should be buried in gore to its hilt."[(28)] A second witness modified the statement into "the sword had been dyed in blood," and that "he should use it again in the same way in defence of the rights of the people of this State."[(29)] A third heard merely that the sword had been "dyed in blood."[(30)] On the other hand, a witness for the defence declared that he was in the barouche with Governor Dorr; that he sat within three feet of him when he spoke; and that his remark about the sword was that "it had never been dishonored, and never should be while in his hands."(31) Another witness stood very near the carriage, and swore that Mr. Dorr added "that it had never been dishonored in battle, and he hoped it never would be;" that "he was willing to die with that sword in his hand, if need be, to sustain the Constitution of the State."(32) The reporter for the charter organ saw him "draw his sword, brandish and flourish it around, and declare his readiness to die in the cause in which he had sacrificed everything but his life."(33) The suffrage organ, however, heard the more violent declaration that "its ensanguined blade should be again embued with blood, should the people's cause require it."(34) It seems fair to

Dorr flourishing the Sword which he received in New York makes great professions of what he would do

(COLLECTION BROWN UNIVERSITY LIBRARY.)

conclude that the remark — however worded — was of a kind to inflame the passions of many of the assembled crowd.[f]

The military remained to guard the house, and preparations were begun to reëstablish the people's government. The suffrage organ had published that morning the proclamation of Governor Dorr, already quoted. The day following — May 17 — was full of suspense and dread. For several days the people of Providence had been disturbed in their business; many stores were closed; shops were without operatives; the streets were filled with groups of people feverishly discussing the latest news. Some crisis was surely approaching, but no one knew what form it would take. Governor King might succeed in obtaining the arrest of his rival on the warrant which had been prepared but not served; Governor Dorr might be able to obtain possession of the government by some bold stroke. No one could tell what companies of the State militia would support the charter and what the people's government. A few only had declared themselves on either side. Governor Dorr, in his proclamation, had called upon the militia to elect officers, and upon volunteers to organize.

The charter government was not at all decided concerning the steps which it ought to take. Some members were anxious for the immediate summons of a convention; others did not wish to do anything under threats. All granted that concessions must be made, but different opinions were held as to the proper time. Until the actual return of Governor Dorr, hopes had been enter-

---

(f) As an indication of the general plan pursued by the charter people to deride Governor Dorr and the people's party, the following is significant: "Mr. Dorr made a great flourish, last Monday, about his sword, which he drew and brandished in a most fearful manner, and told a great story about its having belonged to an officer who fell fighting for his country. This sword belonged to a Lieutenant named Reill, who died of dysentery on the passage from St. Marks to Providence, and all the blood that was ever upon it would not wet the point." *Providence Journal*, May 18, 1842.

tained that he might permit his own arrest; then a general amnesty and a new convention would easily follow.(35) But the resolutions of May 12, followed by the report of the proceedings in New York City and by the Governor's proclamation, showed that this could not be easily accomplished. President Tyler earnestly desired a peaceful settlement of the trouble, but saw clearly the difficulties. After receiving a copy of the proclamation, he wrote: "Mr. Dorr's recent proceedings have been of so extravagant a character as almost to extinguish the last hope of a peaceable result; and yet I cannot but believe that much is meant for effect and for purposes of intimidation merely. I certainly hope that such may be the case, though the recent proceedings in New York may have excited new feelings and new desires."(36) The charter government, divided in opinion, accomplished nothing. They made no attempt to arrest Governor Dorr, either on the 16th or the 17th. Apparently they did not expect any immediate movement on his part, and were accordingly caught napping when he made his next strike.

AUTHORITIES.—**1** *Providence Express*, May 13, 1842. **2** *Providence Journal*, May 13, 1842. **3** *Providence Express*, May 25, 1842; *Providence Journal*, May 26, 1842; *Republican Herald*, May 28, 1842. **4** *Burke's Report*, 876; *Trial of Dorr*: Testimony of Pearce. **5** *New York Courier and Enquirer*; copied by *National Intelligencer*, May 24, 1842. *Journal of Commerce*; copied by *New York Observer*, June 4, 1842. **6** *New York Evening Post*, April 16, 1842. **7** *New York Evening Post*, April 28, 1842; *New York American*, May 4, 1842. **8** *New York Evening Post*, May 13, 1842. **9** *New York American*, May 16, 1842. **10** *New York Courier and Enquirer*, May 13, 1842. **11** *New York Evening Post*, May 16, 1842. **12** *New York American*, May 16, 1842; quoted by the *National Intelligencer*, May 17, 1842. **13** *New York Observer*, May 21, 1842. **14** The *New York American*, May 18, 1842, states the number as 4,000 or 5,000. The *New York Evening Post*, May 18, 1842, states that a Whig paper placed it at 5,000 or 6,000, and a Democratic paper at 12,000. **15** *National Intelligencer*, May 17, 1842. **16** *New York Courier and Enquirer*, May 18, 1842. **17** *New York Evening Post*, May 14, 1842. **18** *New York Observer*, June 4, 1842. **19** *Providence Journal*, May 19, 1842. **20** *Providence Express*, May 16, 1842; *Burke's Report*, 679–680. **21** *Providence Journal*, May 16, 1842. **22** *Providence Express*, May 17, 1842. **23** *Providence Journal*, May 17, 1842; *Providence Express*, May 17, 1842. **24** *Providence Express*, May 17, 1842. **25** *Providence Journal*, May 17, 1842. **26** Pitman, *Trial of Dorr*, 26–27: Testimony of Wm. P Blodget. **27** Turner, *Trial of Dorr*, 35: Testimony of Sam. H. Wales. **28** Pitman, *Trial of Dorr*, 26–27: Testimony of Wm. P. Blodget. **29** *Burke's*

Report: Trial of Dorr, 878: Testimony of Edward H. Hazard. **30** *Burke's Report: Trial of Dorr*, 879: Testimony of Orson Moffit. **31** Pitman, *Trial of Dorr*, 72: Testimony of Benj. M. Darling. **32** Turner, *Trial of Dorr*, 35: Testimony of Sam. H. Wales. **33** *Providence Journal*, May 17, 1842. **34** *Providence Express*, May 17, 1842. **35** *Burke's Report*, 677: Letter of E. R. Potter to the President, May 15, 1842. **36** *Burke's Report*, 678: Letter of President Tyler to Mr. Potter, May 20, 1842.

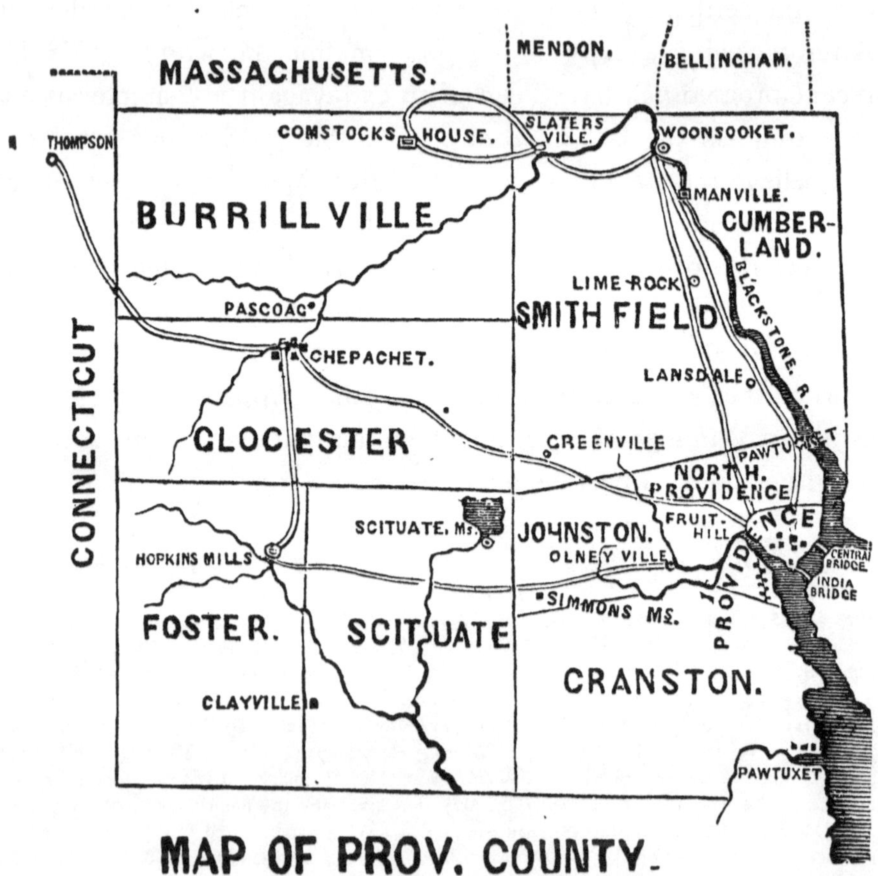

CONTEMPORARY NEWSPAPER MAP.

(COLLECTION RHODE ISLAND HISTORICAL SOCIETY.)

CHAPTER XV.

THE ARSENAL.

WHILE the charter authorities were waiting and doing nothing, the People's Governor was not spending the day in inaction. Within thirty-six hours after his arrival in Providence, he had made sufficient preparation, as he thought, to warrant him in beginning his attack on the *de facto* government. Most of the time was spent in quiet movements that did not reach the ears of Governor King or his subordinates. The first public act occurred near the close of the afternoon of Tuesday, May 17, and clearly foreshadowed his course. A portion of the militia and other armed men that had remained to guard Governor Dorr's headquarters were sent to the "Town House Lot," with directions to take the field pieces in the possession of the artillery company.[1] Although the demand for the surrender of the guns was not complied with, no resistance was offered, and two pieces were seized.[a] The movement was made so hurriedly that balls and shot were forgotten; and the authorities recovered their wits in

[a] These guns did not belong to the State. They had been taken at the surrender of Burgoyne and had been sent to the artillery company by Washington, to replace some that had been borrowed from them and lost. Turner, *Trial of Dorr,* 36: testimony of Capt. Josiah Reed.

time to remove these useful munitions to a place of safety before the company returned after them. These guns, together with four or five others, were placed in front of Anthony's house, and pointed directly down the steep hill toward the center of the city.[(2)]

This bold stroke seemed to awaken the charter government, for the time being. The militia of Providence was called upon to be in readiness, and the companies outside the city were ordered to report in the city, armed and equipped for service.[(b)] Early in the evening, guns and ammunition were given to citizens, by official orders, and a steamboat was sent down the bay to be ready to bring up companies of militia. At Governor Dorr's headquarters all was activity: a council of war was held early in the evening, but many of his friends, including several of his immediate relatives and members of the people's legislature, attempted to persuade the Governor that his designs could never be accomplished and to prevail upon him to refrain from a useless shedding of blood. Some of his chief counsellors agreed that the employment of force was inadvisable, but nothing that could be said influenced him. After these friendly advisers had retired, he presented to the few faithful followers plans, which, it was said, were first to seize the arsenal, and then to establish barracks in the college. He considered that, when he had effected so much, he would be strong enough to seize the cadet and infantry armories, and the market house.[(4)] Whether he made these propositions or not, it is certain that he attempted

---

(b) *Providence Journal*, May 18, 1842.

"Orders No. 5.

"Adjutant-General's Office, Providence, May 17, 1842.

"SIR:—You are hereby ordered to report yourself, with the men under your command, armed and equipped for service, forthwith, to this department, for further orders. By order of his Excellency,

"SAM. W. KING, *Governor and Commander-in-Chief.*

"E. DYER, JR., *Adjutant-General of Rhode Island.*"

TO THE CITIZENS

OF PROVIDENCE!!!

You are reqested FORTHWITH to repair to the

State Arsenal

and TAKE ARMS.

SAMUEL W. KING.

Governor of the State of Rhode Island.

***Providence,* May 17, 1842, 6 o'clock P. M.**

WALL PLACARD USED TO NOTIFY CITIZENS.

(COLLECTION RHODE ISLAND HISTORICAL SOCIETY.)

to carry out the first of them; failing in this, the whole campaign was lost.

About midnight a force arrived from Woonsocket, and joined the guard around the headquarters.(5) Orders were issued for an attack upon the arsenal, and at midnight a gun was fired as a signal. Before two o'clock the little army, accompanied by Dorr himself, set out for the arsenal.(6) The city bells rang in an alarm, and militia and citizens began to fill the streets. The charter government was unprepared, and was, at this moment, practically leaderless. No one knew where the enemy were. The night was dark, and a dense fog had set in. Each citizen felt that his nearest companion might be an enemy.

By instinct, almost, the throng pushed for the arsenal, a stone building, situated on Cranston street, next to the Dexter Training Ground. The building and the State armament were in the charge of Quartermaster-General Samuel Ames, a near relative of Governor Dorr. Colonel Leonard Blodget was commandant of the arsenal, and under him, that night, was a guard of about 200 men, many of them volunteers.(7) Preparation had here been made to resist an attack, and, when the enemy approached, Blodget was in charge of the upper story, and Ames had posted himself below, with the regular arsenal guard.(8)

The Governor's party proceeded out Atwell's avenue, through Love's lane, or Knight street, and approached the arsenal on the northeast side. Their number has been variously estimated: the testimony of Colonel Carter, that he counted them before they started and found 234 in all, may be accepted as fairly correct.(9) At first they took position in a grove, but soon they approached within short range, halted, and adjusted their field pieces.(10) A flag of truce was sent to the arsenal, and demand was made for its

The attempt on the Arsenal on the night of May 17th

Upper room of the Arsenal, on the night of the 17th of May.

(COLLECTION BROWN UNIVERSITY LIBRARY.)

surrender. Colonel Blodget asked, "In whose name?" On receiving the reply, "On the part of Colonel Wheeler, and in the name of Governor Dorr," the commandant retorted that he knew no Colonel Wheeler nor Governor Dorr.[(11)]

During the march from the headquarters to the arsenal, the small army had lost several of its soldiers and received no recruits. Colonel Wheeler vanished on receiving the reply of Colonel Blodget, and Dorr placed the cannons in charge of Colonel Carter. A peaceful surrender having been refused, Dorr ordered that the cannon be fired. The audacity of this order is almost inexplicable. In a dense fog, with less than 200 men, with two cannon, almost without ammunition, the order is given to fire upon a building, built of stone, stocked with guns, powder, and ball, and fully guarded. If a gun had been fired, the cannons in the arsenal might have ploughed down the unprotected attacking force. But the guns flashed twice without result: they were either plugged, or the touch-holes filled with wet or dissolved powder.[(c)] A report was circulated the next day, on the authority of Orsen Moffitt, that Dorr himself, after the first failure, was seen vainly to "apply the torch to the cannon."[(12)] We have, however, the direct testimony of Colonel Carter that he did not;[(13)] and of four other persons who stated that they did not see Dorr with a torch, and that they did not think that he himself touched a gun.[(d)] In a dark night, and in dense fog, the testimony of one man is hardly enough to

(c) Colonel Carter's testimony (Turner, *Trial of Dorr*, 32), that, when the guns were bored out, the following morning, the openings were filled with dissolved powder, which had hardened and become solid, is probably a true statement of the cause of the failure of the guns. Hiram Chappell's testimony (Pitman, *Trial of Dorr*, 37), that he plugged the cannon, is fully offset by that of John S. Dispeau (Pitman, *Trial of Dorr*. 48), that Chappell confessed to him, while they were in jail together, that he had made up the story in order to obtain his discharge.

(d) These were Laban Wade, W. H. Potter, Horace A. Pierce, and Henry A. Kimball. Pitman, *Trial of Dorr*, 55, 75. Turner, *Trial of Dorr*, 18, 20.

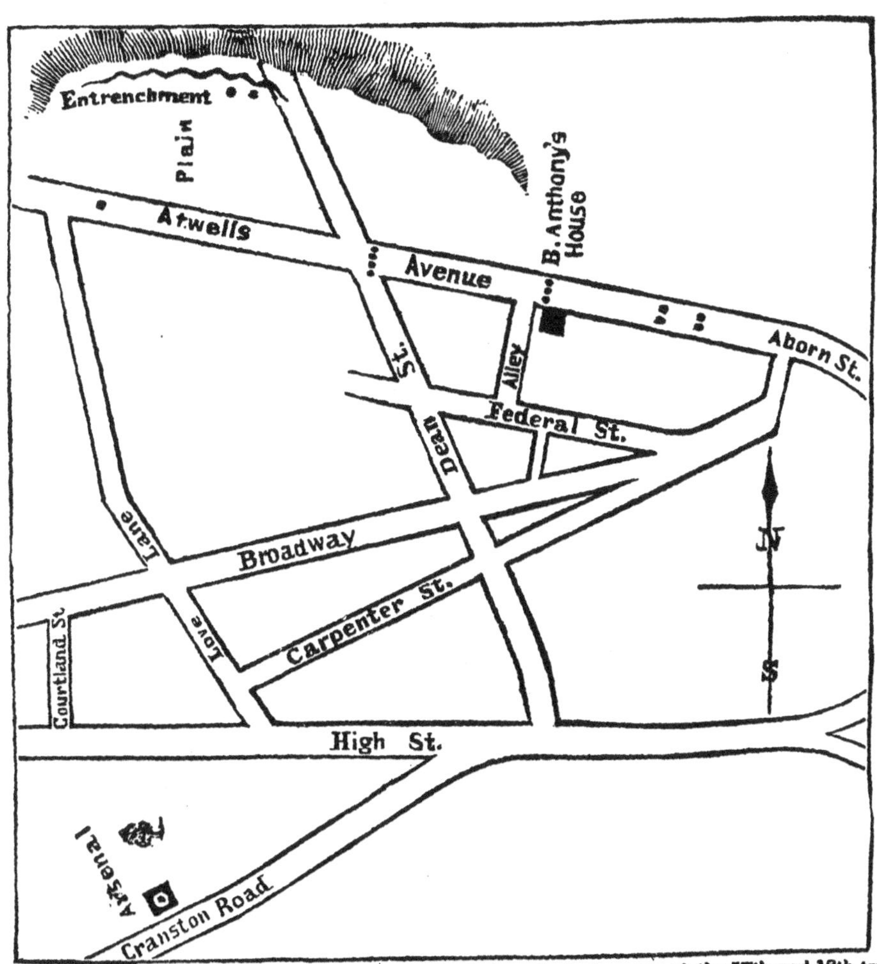

The above map represents the ground upon which the principal events of the 17th and 18th transpired The house of Burrington Anthony, where Dorr's headquarters were established, is situated on a hill 76 feet above high-water mark. The hill rises from the foot of Atwell's Avenue, where it joins Aborn street, Anthony's house is on the level just upon the top of it. The ascent is steep. The dots in front of the house mark the first position of the insurgents' guns. The four dots below, towards Aborn street, mark the spot where the column halted, under the brow of the hill, to unlimber the guns. The dot on Atwell's Avenue, near Love Lane, marks the spot to which one of the insurgents' guns was removed, under cover of which the others were carried out upon the plain to the north, near Dean street; their position is marked on the map by two dots. The guns of the Bristol Artillery and Marine Artillery were then carried near the junction of Dean street and Atwell's Avenue, and those of the Newport Artillery were placed upon the plain on the other side of Dean street, so as to command the flank of the insurgents' guns. At the same time, the Marine Artillery were ordered to march up Atwell's Avenue, and the Bristol Artillery, supported by the Warren Artillery, to march up Dean street While they were executing this order, the insurgents agreed to the surrender of the guns, as detailed below

(COLLECTION RHODE ISLAND HISTORICAL SOCIETY.)

counterbalance the opposing witnesses, though it would not have been inconsistent with the Governor's character to have attempted to fire: the essential is that he gave the order to fire; he was near the cannon; his courage or foolhardiness was displayed, whether he personally used the torch or not.

The attack upon the arsenal was a failure; that it was a bloodless failure was due only to the condition of the cannon: the sound of the first gun would have caused blind attack and counter attack, and great loss of life might easily have followed. The honest people of Rhode Island must have heard with thankful hearts of the "flashes in the pan."

Desertions continued, and when daylight approached not more than fifty men were left on the field.[(14)] Dorr himself vainly strove to keep some kind of order among his forces, but succeeded only in bringing his cannon from the field.[(15)] Soon after daylight, about fifty men, under the lead of the Governor, returned to the headquarters; where, in front of Anthony's house, they again placed the guns, commanding the hill down Atwell's avenue, and prepared them for use. Signals were given for the troops to collect, but the number of armed men diminished rather than increased.[(16)]

About eight o'clock a letter was handed Governor Dorr, informing him that all the officers of his government, living in Providence, had resigned.[(e)] His friends, who were at the headquarters, advised him to leave at once, and to return when a fitting opportunity occurred.[(16)] Dorr followed the advice, though he afterwards said that he strongly regretted the action,[(17)] and before nine o'clock was rapidly driving towards Woonsocket.[(18)] Soon after his flight, Gov-

---

(e) The facts hardly warranted this statement in the letter. Two Senators and nine Representatives had resigned, the entire Assembly delegation from the city, except those who had previously resigned; but none of the officers of the people's government resigned at this time.

DORR'S HEADQUARTERS—BURRINGTON ANTHONY HOUSE.

ernor King and Sheriff Potter arrived at Anthony's, demanded Thomas W. Dorr, and made a thorough search of the house.[19] Meanwhile a portion of the charter militia attempted to follow the fugitive, but were misled and soon gave up the pursuit. Another portion marched in the direction of Dorr's headquarters, but were stopped on Atwell's avenue by the cannon. The Newport Artillery had begun preparations to clear the hill, when the Dorr cannon were withdrawn, attended by about thirty men,[20] who took up a position on the summit of the hill north of Atwell's avenue and overlooking the cove.[21] Under the orders of "General" DeWolf[22] a slight intrenchment was thrown up and signal guns were fired, without success, to attract the adherents of the people's government to the hill.[23] Early in the afternoon they sent a proposition to surrender the guns, but coupled with a request that the Newport Artillery should be withdrawn. Trusting to their word, the charter authorities withdrew the artillery; but the few desperadoes failed to keep the promise, and more firmly entrenched themselves upon the brow of the hill. They were so situated, however, that they were unable to do any injury, and by Thursday morning the guns had been abandoned,[24] and were shortly after returned to the arsenal. The war, for the present, was over.

The charter militia had been kept under arms during the entire day (Wednesday, May 18), and business was at a standstill. Stores were closed, and numbers of citizens enrolled themselves as volunteers.[f] The greatest excitement pervaded every part of the city,

---

[f] *Providence Journal*, May 19, 1842. The following proclamation was issued early in the morning:

"City of Providence, Mayor's Office, May 18, 1842,

"All citizens friendly to maintaining the peace and good order of the city are urged to lay aside their business for this day and assemble at 7½ o'clock A. M., with arms, at the Cadet Alarm Post. If any have not arms, they will be provided.

"THOS. M. BURGESS, *Mayor*."

and a general and intense alarm existed. "A speedy and most sanguinary conflict seemed inevitable; and the public mind, which on the day previous had been tossed to and fro by every idle rumor, now dwelt with the most intense and painful anxiety upon one dread object, a civil war."[(25)] That such a conflict did not occur may be due to the early report that Governor Dorr had fled, to the resignation of the people's government officials, and to the rumor of a compromise which was industriously circulated and which was publicly announced from the people's headquarters.

The resignation was prepared by John A. Howland, and handbills were printed, by his order, early in the morning after the attack on the arsenal. Eleven members of the People's Assembly from Providence protested against the position of the President in interfering "between the old and the new government of the State as being against the fundamental rights of the people," but they declared that they could not carry on a contest with the general government; and, therefore, they declined to act further, and resigned. They added that they could not countenance and had not countenanced, "in any manner, the late movement of the Governor elected under the People's Constitution, but in every way had endeavored to counteract and prevent so deplorable an act and one so destructive to the cause" in which they were engaged. The names appended were those of the two Senators and nine Representatives from Providence.[(26)] It is true that some of these names were appended by friends, but they were afterwards approved by the men themselves.[(g)] Within a few days, at least seven other resignations appeared in the public prints.

(g) *Providence Journal*, May 20, 21, and 23, 1842. Senator Hezekiah Willard wrote a letter, giving his "unqualified sanction;" and Representative Benjamin Arnold, though in New York, approved the signing of his name.

First section of Cadets in pursuit of Dorr.

(COLLECTION OF SAMUEL W. BROWN.)

The rumor of a compromise held the attention of the public for many days. Its first appearance followed soon after the report that Dorr had fled, and therefore gained the more credence. That the Governor would again abandon the cause, so soon after his return, seemed inexplicable unless on the theory that he had agreed to an armistice until the proposed compromise could be concluded. Though no one was able to give the nature or the terms of the compromise, yet the belief that one was pending which would be "honorable to both parties" was strong enough to quiet the city.(27) Interest in the matter was kept up by daily references in the suffrage organ. No one, however, knew whether the arrangement was temporary or permanent; whether Dorr had actually abdicated or not, when he retired from the city; nor whether the resignations of the Providence members of the Assembly were final, or depending upon some action of the charter government.(28) On Saturday the suffrage organ contained another long editorial on the rumored compromise, "so generally admitted as correct," but acknowledged that it had been able to ascertain only that Burrington Anthony was primarily responsible for the rumor, and that he had promised, early Wednesday morning, that it would be ratified in the course of the day and would be published the next morning. He also declared that no further arrests would be made, and directed the adherents of the people's government peaceably to return to their homes.(29) On the other hand, the charter organ, on Monday, declared: "This story (of the compromise) the *Express* knows to be wholly and utterly false and without the slightest foundation or pretense whatever."(30)

A few days later letters appeared in the Providence newspapers from Burrington Anthony, John S. Harris, and John Whipple, giving the following facts with regard to the so-called compromise.(31)

When Anthony reached Providence, on his return from Washington, he brought a letter from Secretary Webster to John Whipple, urging concessions to the people's party, provided that their government should be abandoned.[32] Not finding Whipple in Providence, Anthony immediately returned to New York, and together with Harris and Pearce held a conference with Whipple. A proposition was made that a case be prepared for the Supreme Court of the United States; its decision would settle the controversy; meanwhile the people's government would remain quiescent. Another proposition was suggested—that both legislatures should pass identical bills calling a new convention. Whipple declined to carry either proposition to Governor King. He finally agreed to advise his government to cease further prosecutions while the people's government remained inactive. This, Whipple declared, was "no compromise." Whipple met Anthony on the street, in Providence, on Monday (May 16), and told him that he did not believe that King and his council would accept the proposition when they met on Wednesday. In the morning, after the return of Dorr from the arsenal, Harris met Samuel H. Wales, who reported that King had said that if Dorr should leave the city the business might be arranged. Thereupon Wales and others wrote advising Dorr to retire, but he had already gone. Anthony and Harris addressed the crowd from the window, announcing a compromise, but were met with demands for King. Harris and Wales went to see the Charter Governor, and were told that they might assure the people that "he would do all in his power to have the differences settled satisfactorily to both parties."

The alleged "compromise" had no stronger foundation than the conversations just detailed, and it is evident from them that Dorr did not leave the city to carry out any arrangements, especially as he declared, in a public letter, that he had repeatedly refused to agree to any compromise which should involve the surrender of the constitution. Neither Anthony nor Harris had any official authority to announce a compromise, nor had they any reason for considering that any proposition which they had made would be accepted by the charter government. Dorr expressly repudiated every action taken by Anthony, after his return to Providence; and all knew that Whipple had no official position and could only advise King and his council. True, the charter government had shown confidence in Whipple, entrusting to him the embassy to the President, and his recent return from Washington, as well as the favor of the letter from Webster, would seem to indicate that his advice would probably be followed. The only basis of the compromise seemed to lie in the desire of all parties, on the fateful morning, to go to any lengths in order to prevent further trouble.(33)

The farcical failure at the arsenal, the resignations of members of the legislature, and their repudiation of the military movements, together with the flight of the Governor, would seem to have freed the charter government from any accusation of acting under threats. No opposition to the *de facto* authorities apparently remained, and the way was open for a new convention which would furnish "a liberal extension of the suffrage." Even the charter organ declared: "We take the earliest opportunity, after the establishment of law and the manifestation of the determination of the people to stand by the government, to record our opinion that such an extension should be made."(34)

The collapse of the military movement had its legitimate effect in New York City also. Daily editorials had appeared in the *New York New Era* after the departure of Governor Dorr for Rhode

Island, and Editor Slamm did not hesitate to avow that all that had been asked and all that was contemplated in New York was to raise men enough to resist the United States soldiers.[35] These editorials, together with the reports of the Park Meeting and the publication of the correspondence between Colonels Wing and Crasto and Governor Dorr, created great excitement in New York, and even led the *Tribune* to say: "We fear the firebrands thrown into Rhode Island by reckless demagogues in this city, to subserve their own personal ends, will have caused a general conflagration within forty-eight hours hence."

The agitation continued until the news from Rhode Island suddenly brought it, outwardly, at least, to an end. Friday (May 20), an official bulletin from Tammany Hall appeared in the *New Era*, entitled, "Enrollment of Volunteers."[36] After sundry *whereases*, including one that expressed the fear that the President would send "mercenary soldiers" into the "territory of our sister State of Rhode Island," it was declared that the undersigned, "appealing to Divine Providence for the purity of our motives, do pledge our 'sacred honor' to hold ourselves in readiness, to be organized into companies of 'Patriotic Volunteers,' under such officers as shall by ourselves be elected, and upon the requisition of Governor Dorr, to march at the shortest notice to the aid of our Republican brethren of Rhode Island, in the event that any *armed interference* be made by the Federal Government to the jeopardy of their *inalienable* and *indefeasible* rights." Scarcely had the bulletin appeared when the story of Wednesday's doings in Providence showed that, for the present, at least, the national government would not need to send troops to that city.[h]

[h] "Judging from their looks, never did a set of people feel before quite so foolish and forlorn, as did the leaders of the Park Meeting of insurgent sympathizers on the receipt of the news from Rhode

The national Senate felt the effect of the change in the situation in Rhode Island. Up to this time, the friends of the President and of the charter government in the Senate had been satisfied merely to oppose the resolutions of Senator Allen and his associates. On May 13, Senator Buchanan presented the proceedings at a meeting of citizens held in Philadelphia, on the subject of the formation of a new constitution by the people of the State of Rhode Island, which were laid on the table.(37) May 17, Senator Allen moved to take up the resolutions which he had presented a month before, but was defeated, 15 to 23.(38) He had then presented new resolutions against the interference of the President,(39) and endorsed them in a long speech, in which he declared that there were two governments in operation in Rhode Island, and criticised Tyler for assuming to himself the power of deciding between them. Senator Simmons, of Rhode Island, upheld the position of the charter government, claimed that it was supported by a majority of the citizens, declared that the franchise in the State was liberal, and denied the legality of the People's Constitution.(37) The matter was passed over informally, and the resolutions were printed. The next day, the resolutions, on motion of Senator Talmadge, were laid on the table, by a vote of 28 to 18.(40)

May 23, however, Senator Talmadge introduced resolutions declaring that a "recognized State is republican," and entitled to the protection pledged by the Constitution of the United States; that a government cannot be superseded except in the prescribed way;

Island yesterday. They tried to whistle their courage up for a while, and even attempted to deceive themselves by the miserable lie that it was Governor King who had fled and not the puissant Dorr. But it was no go. The flag which had been kept flying for several days at Tammany Hall, in honor of Dorr and his proceedings, was struck, and all looked as sad as though 'melancholy had marked them for her own.'" *New York Commercial Advertiser*; copied in the *National Intelligencer*, May 24, 1842.

that an attempt to overthrow the regular State government is an act of domestic violence; that Rhode Island should be properly protected in the present crisis; and that it was the duty of the President to take preparatory steps and to adopt efficient measures for this purpose.(41) The resolutions were printed, and here the matter rested for nearly a month. June 21st, 1842, Senator Allen's resolution was assigned, by a vote of 21 to 15, to Monday week.(42) That day fell upon the Fourth of July, and nothing further was heard of the matter. The Rhode Island controversy was settled, as far as any intelligent eye could see, and, not only in Rhode Island, but also in Washington, and even in New York, all was quiet.

AUTHORITIES.—**1** *Providence Journal*, May 18, 1842. **2** *Providence Express*, May 18, 1842. **3** *Providence Journal*, May 19, 1842; Wayland, *Affairs of Rhode Island*, II. **4** *Providence Journal*, May 21, 1842. **5** *Providence Express*, May 18, 1842. **6** *Providence Journal*, May 19, 1842. **7** Turner, *Trial of Dorr*, 16: Testimony of Col. Blodget. **8** *Providence Journal*, May 27, 1842: Letter of Sam. Ames. **9** Turner, *Trial of Dorr*, 31. **10** *Providence Journal*, May 19, 1842 **11** *Providence Journal*, May 18, 1842. **12** Pitman, *Trial of Dorr*, 33 **13** Turner, *Trial of Dorr*, 32. **14** Turner, *Trial of Dorr*, 21: Testimony of Benjamin M. Darling. **15** Turner, *Trial of Dorr*, 26: Testimony of Laban Wade. **16** Turner, *Trial of Dorr*, 32: Testimony of Charles W. Carter. **17** *Letter of Dorr*, May 21, 1842: Published in *Providence Express*, May 28, 1842; *New York Evening Post*, May 28, 1842; *Providence Journal*, May 30, 1842; *Boston Post*, May 30, 1842; *Republican Herald*, June 1, 1842. **18** Turner, *Trial of Dorr*, 23: Testimony of George B. Aldrich. **19** Turner, *Trial of Dorr*, 14: Testimony of Roger W. Potter; *Providence Journal*, May 19, 1842. **20** Turner, *Trial of Dorr*, 13 and 32: Testimonies of William P. Blodget and Charles W. Carter. **21** *Providence Journal*, May 19, 1842. **22** A resident of Uxbridge, Massachusetts. **23** *Providence Journal*, May 21, 1842. **24** *Providence Journal*, May 20, 1842. **25** *Providence Express*, May 19, 1842. **26** *Providence Journal*, May 19, 1842; *Republican Herald*, May 21, 1842; *New York Courier and Enquirer*, May 20, 1842. **27** *Providence Express*, May 19, 1842. **28** *Providence Express*, May 20, 1842. **29** *Providence Express*, May 21, 1842. **30** *Providence Journal*, May 23, 1842. **31** Anthony's letter was published in the *Providence Express*, May 25, 1842, and was copied by the *Providence Journal*, May 26, 1842, and the *Republican Herald*, May 28, 1842. Harris's letter appeared in the *Providence Express*, May 26, 1842, and in the *Providence Journal*, May 18, 1842. Whipple's letter was published in the *Providence Journal*, May 26, 1842, and was copied by the *Providence Express*, May 27, 1842, and the *Republican Herald*, May 28, 1842. **32** *Providence Journal*, May 26, 1842. **33** *New York Evening Post*, May 28, 1842. **34** *Providence Journal*, May 19, 1842. **35** *National Intelligencer*, May 19, 1842. **36** *New York Courier and Enquirer*, May 21, 1842; *National Intelligencer*, May 24, 1842. **37** *Senate Journal*, II Sess., 27 Cong., 1841–42, p. 339. **38** *Congressional Globe*, II Sess., 27 Cong., 1841–42, p. 506. **39** *Senate Documents*, II

Sess., 27 Cong., 1841-42, IV, 303. **40** *Congressional Globe*, II Sess., 27 Cong., 1841-42, p 510. **41** *Congressional Globe*, II Sess., 27 Cong., 1841-42, p. 523; *Senate Documents*, II Sess., 27 Cong., 1841-42, IV, 304 "*Resolved*, That, by the Constitution, the United States are bound not only to guaranty to every State in the Union a republican form of government, but also to protect each one of them against invasion and, upon proper application, against domestic violence. *Resolved*, That the form of government with which a State came into the Union and has been recognized and represented as a member of the Union, must be taken and regarded as republican; and that such State is entitled to all that protection against invasion and domestic violence which is pledged by the Constitution of the United States. *Resolved*, That the Government of a State so coming into and recognized as a member of the Union, can only be changed or superseded, consistently with the principles of our American Republics, when it is done in pursuance of, and in the mode prescribed by the laws of such State; and that any attempt by force to overthrow that Government is disorderly and revolutionary, tending to anarchy and bloodshed, and, in the end, to the destruction of public liberty, and is such a domestic violence, as entitles that State, by her Legislature (or Executive, when the Legislature cannot be convened), to apply for, and obtain from the United States protection against the same. *Resolved*, That the application made by the Legislature of Rhode Island, one of the 'Old Thirteen,' to the President of the United States, for protection against domestic violence, was within the meaning and terms of the Constitution; and that it was the duty of the President to take such preparatory steps as a wise and prudent forecast demanded, and to adopt such efficient measures as are contemplated by the Constitution, and the laws made in pursuance of it, for giving such protection." **42** *Congressional Globe*, II Sess., 27 Cong., 1841-42, p. 659.

CHAPTER XVI.

THE INTERIM.

THE people's government had utterly collapsed: the Governor had fled from the State; the legislature had lost its quorum of members; not an officer of the government was attending to his duties—many had been arrested and many had vanished from sight. Even Governor Dorr himself afterwards acknowledged that the situation was disheartening, when he spoke of the lack of support and the unpromising result of the attack upon the arsenal. We may well ask, as he did, why further attempts were not abandoned as impracticable and hopeless;[1] why, "after such a demonstration as has been described, all thoughts of any further proceeding to carry into effect the people's constitution were not abandoned, and the cause was not left to expire in the hands of those who had brought it into existence?"[2]

We are compelled to take Governor Dorr's own answer to this question, as no one else has ever attempted to answer it, and at least he was logical to the bitter end: "The rights of the case were not taken away by a failure of arms."[2] "Rights and duties are not to be measured by degrees of success or failure. The Constitution was valid and subsisting. The People could not abandon it by their votes or by their acts."(3) "Nor could I be permitted to believe that the cause was surrendered by its friends."(2) "This misadventure in the city of Providence was attributed to unforeseen circumstances, to accident, to the want of a more general notice in the country towns for a general rally at the headquarters of the State, to a temporary panic in the city, to the pusillanimity of leading friends of the cause in that place, from whom better things were expected, and whose hearts had failed them in the moment of trial."(4)

Here is found another side of the character of the People's Governor—he did not know when he was beaten. He could accept reasons, without end, for the temporary defeat of the 18th of May, but he could not see that these men, whose "hearts had failed them," were the only ones upon whom he had ever been able to rely for any real assistance, whether in action or advice. Very few of the officers of the people's government were present at the attack on the arsenal, or approved of the movement. After the failure of that attack, scarcely a prominent supporter of the government accepted Dorr's lead.

In spite of the desertions, Governor Dorr was easily deceived by expressions of sympathy and promises of aid, and he wrote that "Encouraging reports and statements were received, through letters and by visitors, from various parts of the State, all indicating an earnest desire to retrieve the late disaster, to regain the position that had been lost, and to carry into complete effect the Constitution and government of the People. The quotas of men in the several towns, including Providence, who were pledged to support [me], whenever [I] should call upon them, amounted to 1,300."(5) We shall soon see how terribly disappointed he must have been in the result of his next attempt.

Now that it was seen that Dorr alone was responsible for the acts of the people's government, his flight and the uncertainty of his whereabouts or his plans naturally began to give rise to rumors of all descriptions. The thirty days following the collapse of the attack on the arsenal were not lacking in excitement. Governor King and his council, weak and vacillating though they had been, now saw the future more clearly than the majority of Rhode Island citizens, and determined to make another attempt to secure aid from the national government. President Tyler's promise of future aid, if it should prove necessary, gave hope that perhaps he might consider that the time had now come.

Seven days after the arsenal fiasco, the Governor sent a letter to the President, setting forth the situation as it appeared to him:(6) he feared the approach of another crisis; he had been informed by "messengers" that Dorr "and his agents" were raising troops in neighboring States; he had no hesitation in affirming that the law and order militia was sufficient to meet any force of Rhode Islanders which the people's government could collect, but from evidence that forces were organizing in Massachusetts, Connecticut, and New York, he felt that his troops could repel them only with "the loss of many valuable lives." For this reason he appealed to the President; suggesting that a sufficient body of troops at Fort Adams, subject to the requisitions of the executive of the State, would "insure peace and respect for the laws, and deter invasions."

President Tyler cautiously replied, May 28th, that he had taken steps to "ascertain the extent of the dangers of any armed invasion, by the citizens of other States." While he considered that there was no apparent probability of a "violation so flagrant and unprecedented of all our laws and institutions," yet he promised that "should the necessity of the case require the interposition of the authority of the United States, it will be rendered in the manner prescribed by the laws."[7] The Secretary of War, J. C. Spencer, dispatched letters to Colonel Bankhead, at Fort Adams,[8] and to General Eustis, at Boston,[9] asking them to take all necessary means to obtain information concerning the "movements made in other States," and especially concerning the rumored preparation of war material at Boston.

On the request of President Tyler,[10] Daniel Webster, the Secretary of State, sent a personal friend to visit Rhode Island and report to him the situation there. In a letter dated June 3, 1842, this friend informed the Secretary that all was quiet; that a large majority of the members of the people's government had resigned their places and renounced allegiance to their constitution; and that, except Governor King and his council, all "intelligent persons" feared no "irruption upon them of an armed force to be collected in other States."[11] Mr. Webster at once forwarded this letter to the President, and no further steps were taken for the time being. It was doubtless this private information which prevented the public appearance of a proclamation, commanding all persons connected with the insurrection to disperse, which was prepared but never issued.[a]

Meanwhile the rumors in Rhode Island gradually became more consistent with each other. Any movement now of the advocates

---

(a) *Burke's Report*, 684.

"BY THE PRESIDENT OF THE UNITED STATES OF AMERICA.

"A PROCLAMATION.

"Whereas the legislature of the State of Rhode Island has applied to the President of the United States, setting forth the existence of a dangerous insurrection in that State, composed partly of deluded citizens of the State, but chiefly of intruders of dangerous and abandoned character coming from other States, and requiring the immediate interposition of the constitutional power vested in him to be exercised in such cases, I do issue this my proclamation, according to law, hereby commanding all insurgents, of the people's constitution must clearly be a movement of force, and must begin on the borders of the State, and there could be no question but that it would be in the northern portion. June 2d, rumors of an intended encampment at Woonsocket were current.(12) The next day came reports of meetings of agitators at Scituate, Chepachet, and Woonsocket.(13) It was reported that a lot of land in Smithfield, "about a mile from Woonsocket, at a place called Daily Hole, near the Friend's Meeting House," had been hired for an encampment, which was to be fortified. At this time the *Express* said: "There seems to be considerable excitement *abroad*, about Governor Dorr's movements at Woonsocket, without sufficient reason. There is little or no excitement at *home*, and there are no known grounds for any."(14)

Rumors of a depot of arms on the Connecticut side of the line next appeared.(15) Perhaps the friendly attitude of Governor Cleaveland of that State toward Governor Dorr may have given rise to this story. Meetings at Diamond Hill Plain, and armed men on the Douglas turnpike, were next reported.(16) June 18th an attempt was made to obtain cannon and ammunition in the possession of the artillery company of the little town of Warren, in Bristol county.(17) This was unsuccessful, but it had the effect of thoroughly awaking

---

and all persons connected with said insurrection, to disperse and retire peaceably to their respective abodes within twenty-four hours from the time when this proclamation shall be made public in Rhode Island.

"In testimony whereof, I have caused the seal of the United States to be hereunto affixed, and signed the same with my hand.

"Done at the city of Washington, this —— day of ——, in the year of our Lord one thousand eight hundred and forty-two, and of the independence of the United States the sixty-sixth.

"JOHN TYLER.

"By the President:

"DANIEL WEBSTER,

"*Secretary of State.*"

the charter government to the feeling that danger was threatening them. The *Journal* editorially expressed the feelings of the law and order party thus:[18] "At this time, when nearly all the leading men profess to be opposed to forcible measures, and when most of them have publicly resigned their treasonable offices, the natural enquiry is, what are all these preparations for? Why is this constant commotion kept up? Why are military companies banded to act against the government? Why are meetings held for military exercises? Why are cannon stolen? Why do the insurgents refuse to surrender the arms of the State yet illegally in their possession? One reason of all this may be a disposition to keep up an organization without any definite object, but ready to take advantage of any favorable turn that the tide of affairs may take; but another and more important object, we imagine, is to influence the General Assembly, now in session."

HENRY Y. CRANSTON.

The legislature met for its June session at Newport, Monday, the twentieth.[19] No quorum appeared until the next day, and then the Assembly devoted most of its time to the allied subjects of constitutional conventions and the suffrage. Nearly a score of petitions and resolutions of town meetings were received bearing on these matters. On motion of Henry Y. Cranston, of Newport, all these petitions were referred to a select committee of two from each county. A resolution calling for a convention was presented by David Daniels, and also referred to the committee.[20] Two days later the committee rendered its report in the form of a resolution calling for a convention to frame a constitution for the State. After a short consideration the resolution was adopted, sent to the Senate, and there amended; the amendments were concurred in by the House. The legislature then adjourned, to meet in Providence the following Saturday.[21]

The call for the constitutional convention of 1842 was patterned after that for the convention of 1841, and is of interest only in two or three respects.[22] The apportionment of delegates, in accordance with its provisions, was practically the same as that of the year before. The city of Providence was allowed but six delegates; Smithfield, Newport, and Warwick were given four each; and the remaining towns were granted two or three each. The delegates to the 1841 convention were chosen by the freemen of the State, that is, by those citizens who had the right of suffrage in accordance with the existing laws. The delegates to the 1842 convention were to be elected by the votes of all "native male citizens of the United States, of the age of twenty-one years and upwards," who had lived in the State for three years. It will be noted that the word "native" appears in this call, and that the length of residence is put at three years instead of one. Otherwise the franchise for the election of delegates varied little from that proposed by the people's party. The call also provided that those persons who, by the provisions of the constitution to be framed by the proposed convention, should have the right to vote for the State officers, should have the privilege of voting for or against the constitution itself. Evidently the law and order people had had their eyes opened; they conceded to the suffragists almost as much as the reformers had asked.

When the General Assembly met again, on Saturday, at Providence, the situation had begun to be serious. The first step taken by the legislature was to repeal the charters of two militia organizations that were thought untrustworthy, and to grant charters to several new companies.[23] A resolution was then proposed, by Mr. Whipple, offering amnesty to those who had made themselves liable to arrest under the terms of the "Algerine Law." This resolution was laid on the table for the time and hastily withdrawn on Monday, when affairs had taken an even more serious appearance. The Assembly then adjourned to Monday, after passing an "Act establishing martial law."[24] The next day Governor King issued a proclamation "to make known the same unto the good people of this State, and all others, that they may govern themselves accordingly."[25] When Monday came, the General Assembly met at 10 o'clock, and immediately adjourned until the next Thursday afternoon.[26]

AUTHORITIES.—**1** Turner, *Trial of Dorr*, 75. **2** *Burke's Report*, 755: Address of Dorr, August, 1843. **3** Turner, *Trial of Dorr*, 75. **4** Turner, *Trial of Dorr*, 75. **5** Turner, *Trial of Dorr*, 75. **6** *Burke's Report*, 681 **7** *Burke's Report*, 682. **8** *Burke's Report*, 682. **9** *Burke's Report*, 683. **10** *Burke's Report*, 685: Letter from Daniel Webster to President Tyler, June 3, 1842. **11** *Burke's Report*, 685: Letter to Daniel Webster, June 3, 1842. **12** *Providence Journal*, June 2, 1842. **13** *Providence Journal*, June 3, 1842. **14** *Providence Express*, June 4, 1842. **15** *Providence Journal*, June 6, 1842. **16** *Providence Journal*, June 14, 1842 **17** *Providence Journal*, June 20, 1842. **18** *Providence Journal*, June 21, 1842. **19** *Rhode Island House Journal*, June 20, 1842 **20** *Rhode Island House Journal*, June 21, 1842. **21** *Rhode Island House Journal* June 23, 1842; *Providence Journal*, June 25, 1842. **22** *Burke's Report*, 444–446. **23** *Rhode Island House Journal*, June 25, 1842; *Burke's Report*, 819 **24** *Rhode Island House Journal*, June 25, 1842; *Rhode Island Acts and Resolves*, June, 1842, p. 7; *Providence Journal*, June 25, 1842. **25** *Burke's Report*, 373. See page [229]. **26** *Rhode Island House Journal*, June 27, 1842.

CHAPTER XVII.

ACOTE'S HILL.

THE month of June had two-thirds passed before the people of Rhode Island awoke to the fact that further danger actually threatened them. It was not easy to believe that another attempt to establish the people's government by force could be proposed by the fugitive or his friends. The *Boston Post* expressed truthfully the prevailing opinion in Rhode Island; this was that no resort to violence was intended, but that the friends of suffrage desired to give a warning to the legislature to do its duty and take the first steps toward a new and liberal constitution.[(a)]

In this, however, the people were mistaken. Governor Dorr planned to try once more. Having spent some time in New York, where he received much sympathy, though little material assistance, he left that city on Tuesday, the twenty-first, to return to Rhode Island.[(1)] The next morning he arrived in Norwich, Connecticut, on the steamboat *New Haven*.[(2)] With him was the "Spartan

---

(a) "We are confident that, if the suffrage men are taking the measures stated, they are but precautionary, and that there will be no resort to violence if the legislature, which is now in session, does its duty, by surrendering to the people at once, and without any onerous conditions, the long withheld right of self-government." *Boston Post*, June 22, 1842. See also *Providence Journal*, June 23, 1842.

IN THE SPARTAN RANKS

Band," a small number of men from the metropolis, not more than twenty, probably, under the command of Michael Walsh.[3] At Norwich, the Governor was met by his Secretary of State, William H. Smith, as well as by a few other friends.[4] As a result of this interview, an order was sent to convene a council of military officers at Chepachet, to determine whether any step should be taken at this time or not.[5] This place was chosen, since it would probably be the base of operations if the council favored immediate action.

In one respect Chepachet was well adapted for this purpose. It was a little village in the town of Glocester, in the northwest part of the State. This town bordered upon Connecticut, and extended about half the distance across Rhode Island. Chepachet was five miles east of the Connecticut line, perhaps eight south of the Massachusetts border, and sixteen northwest of the city of Providence. On the other hand, the village was in the center of a small farming community, which attempted little more than to raise sufficient crops for its own support. The month was June, and harvest time was far in the future. The charter forces would cut off supplies from Providence, and in the opposite direction cities and large towns were few and far between. A force of any size must make a movement quickly, from such a base, or lack of provisions would quickly prove its ruin.

Before the council of military officers had had time to meet, the rank and file had already taken possession of Chepachet. Governor Dorr was informed, at North Killingly, Connecticut, to which place he had proceeded from Norwich,[6] that five hundred men had "assembled at Chepachet without orders," and that an attack upon them by the charter forces was momentarily expected. At once the fugitive commander-in-chief hastened to the spot, to "share with them the fortunes of the cause."[7] He arrived at two o'clock on Saturday morning (the 25th), and found that he or some other leader was imperatively needed.[8]

The village of Chepachet had been the center of exciting scenes for three days. Early Wednesday morning a cannon had been brought to the village by a half dozen men, from Woonsocket Falls.[9] Other cannon arrived during the day, and men began to collect in the neighborhood. By Thursday it was reported that four hundred men had arrived, with some field pieces, plenty of ammunition, and more muskets than men.[10] On Friday the number was said to have increased—the *Journal* stating that six hundred men were in the village,[11] the *Express* admitting the number to be seven hundred.[12]

Governor Dorr, on his arrival, did not find even six hundred men. In the morning, by his own account, there were less than two hundred, and some of these left that afternoon; that night there were not more than fifty on the spot, the remainder being scattered throughout the neighborhood; the largest number present, at any one time, during Saturday, Sunday, and Monday, was less than two hundred and fifty.[13] The discrepancy in these estimates of the number of persons present may not seem so great if it is realized that the Governor counted only the men under proper orders, while the newspapers counted spectators, stragglers, and "hangers on."

Governor Dorr found that his small band had begun to fortify Acote's Hill, an eminence about eighty feet in height, a short distance from the center of the village. The Providence turnpike passed along the southern side of this hill, entering the main street of the village at the southwest corner of the hill.

Immediately east of it was a lower hill, separated from it by a sandy, rocky ravine. Next east, on the same side of the road, was a pond, Across the turnpike, to the south, was a stretch of table-land, gradually rising to a height of a hundred and thirty feet, completely commanding Acote's Hill. No fort had been built, but slight breastworks had been thrown up on the south and west sides, the other sides being entirely unprotected.[14]

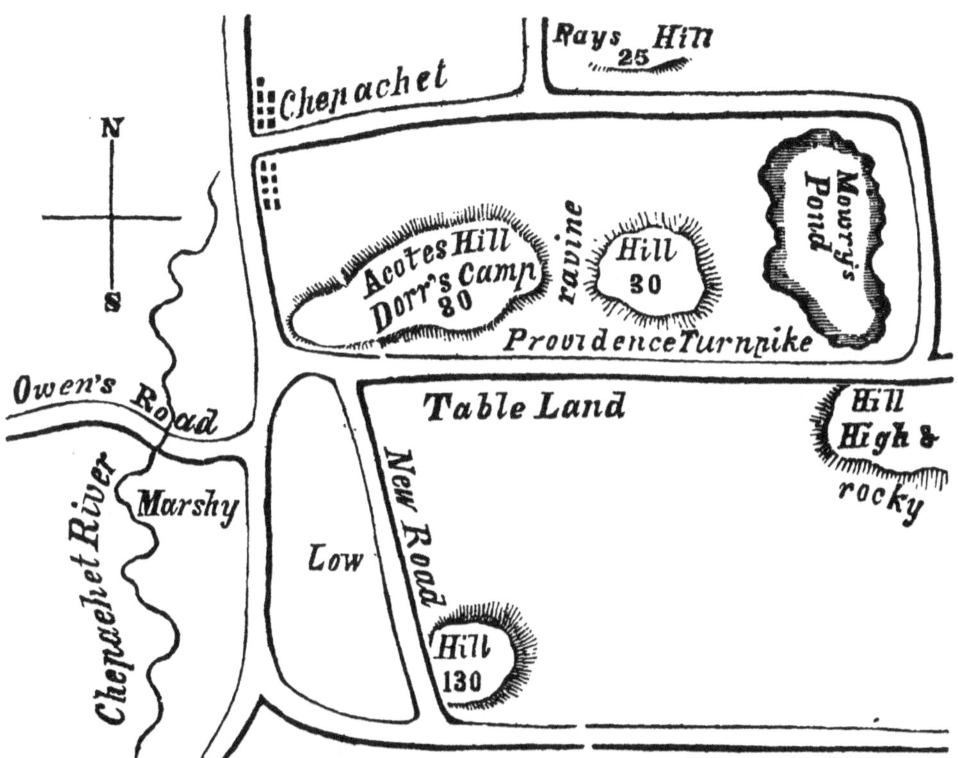

Above is a rough, but we believe a pretty accurate map of the position of the insurgent camp, and of the surrounding country They were entrenched upon Acote s Hill, which is 80 feet high. The hill on the south is 130 feet high, and of course commands the entrenchment It is three quarters of a mile distant. From Chepachet to the most eastern point on the map, is two miles. The entrenchment was on the western part of the hill, facing the east and south The descent towards Chepachet is very steep, and was not protected by any embankments. There are no embrasures, but open spaces are left in the entrenchment in which the cannon were placed.

MAP OF CHEPACHET SHOWING DORR'S CAMP.

(COLLECTION RHODE ISLAND HISTORICAL SOCIETY.)

Governor Dorr made the claim afterwards that he was greatly surprised to find the men "posted in an untenable position."[15] However, he took no steps to find or obtain a more tenable position. A little more work was done on the fortifications, several cannon were mounted, and then the men apparently settled down to wait the turn of events. Saturday passed, and nothing further was done but to send orders to all the towns in the county for the people's militia to "repair forthwith to headquarters for its defence." Sunday passed, and as many men departed as arrived; for until Monday morning, there was no attempt made to enforce discipline among the troops.[16]

Scarcely had the armed men begun to collect at Chepachet when they also were troubled with rumors. The fear that the charter government would send a large force against them was uppermost in the minds of all.[17] When the report came, late in the evening of Wednesday, June 22, that a body of men had been seen approaching the village along the turnpike, guards were posted at the entrance to the village; and one or two hours after midnight the entire hostile force, consisting of four men, was arrested and lodged in a barn. Two were travelling from Providence to Killingly, Connecticut;[b] the other two had been sent out by the executive council to see what movements were being made at Chepachet.[c] The four men were bound together and, between the files of a company of soldiers, were compelled at once to walk the twelve miles to Woonsocket Falls. Throughout the march they were harshly treated, and one became so exhausted that he had to be carried. Reaching Woonsocket at six in the morning, the four

---

[b] These men were Charles J. Shelley and John C. Keep, both of Providence.

[c] Samuel W. Peckham and Charles F. Harris, both of Providence.

men were taken to a hill which seemed to be the headquarters of the so-called suffragists. After a couple of hours delay, the men were permitted to go, no reason being found for holding them.[18]

Hastily returning to Providence, the four men presented themselves before a justice of the peace and swore to the truth of the story which they related. They had had considerable conversation with the insurgents, both at Chepachet and Woonsocket, and had learned that the two bands were preparing to unite immediately at Chepachet. The insurgents claimed that they cared nothing about the General Assembly nor any of its acts—they were pledged to uphold *their* constitution. Before sunset, they said, at least two thousand men would have assembled, and aid was on the way from New York; then they would march to Providence and demand its surrender; if refused, they would bombard the city.[19]

This was of course merely the talk of a rabble, yet the story spread like wildfire throughout the city and thoroughly awakened the charter authorities. Governor King wrote a beseeching letter to President Tyler, stating his grounds for fearing that open violence was again ready to break out,[20] and describing the theft of cannon and powder, the gathering of armed men in the northern part of the State, and the establishment of a kind of martial law in Woonsocket and Chepachet. He enclosed the depositions of the four citizens of Providence who "were cruelly treated under pretense of being spies," and sent the letter by the hands of Senator William Sprague, directing him personally to present the case to the President.[21]

Perhaps Mr. Tyler cannot be criticised very severely if he felt like saying, "Wolf, wolf, when there is no wolf." In April Governor King had asked aid; in May he had twice begged for assistance; now, in June, he again sent a beseeching letter. At any rate, the President deferred a direct reply to the request by again calling the Governor's attention to the fact that the Rhode Island legislature was in session, and that the communication should have come from it.[22] Governor King might well have answered that this session of the Assembly was legally the same as that of May 4, when it did officially call upon the President. However, though Colonel Bankhead wrote to Washington, advising the sending of troops;[23] though Postmaster Hallett, of Providence, sent to the Postmaster-General an account of the situation;[24] though Senators Simmons and Sprague and Representative Tillinghast called upon the President, and also sent him an urgent letter,[25] John Tyler did not yield. Two days after the fiasco of Acote's Hill, he requested the Secretary of War to go to Providence and take what steps were necessary.[26] No steps were necessary, and the President had done well to keep his head.

GOVERNOR KING RESIDENCE.

After sending his messages to President Tyler, Governor King began to take steps to make use of the entire militia to repel the "invasion." Orders were at once sent out to all parts of the State, directing the military companies to put themselves in readiness for service and to be prepared to march to the scene of action within two or three days. Saturday morning, three hundred and fifty men arrived in Providence—the artillery companies from Newport, Bristol, and Warren—and the steamboat at once returned to Newport for the remainder of the militia of that town; a body of four hundred men arrived on the railroad, from the southern part of the State;[27] the militia of Providence and the neighboring towns were mustered and held under arms, ready to move at a moment's warning. In the afternoon a review of the troops in Providence was held at Smith's Hill, when sixteen hundred men passed the reviewing officers,[28] while two or three hundred more were on duty in the city. On the arrival of the third and fourth brigades, later in the day, it was estimated that the force in Providence numbered twenty-five hundred men.[29]

Sunday was comparatively a quiet day in Providence. Martial law was declared, guards were stationed in all parts of the city, and the statutes were enforced with unusual severity. About thirteen hundred men were under arms on Jefferson Plains, and the rest of the army, now numbering three thousand, was quartered in private families or at the college, from which the students had been turned out.[29] A portion of the fourth brigade was ordered to march direct to Foster, a town south of Glocester and bordering on Connecticut. From this point as a base, the retreat from Chepachet to Connecticut might easily be cut off. William Gibbs McNeill was appointed Major-General and given command of the entire force. He made his headquarters at the Tockwotten House, at India Point.[30]

Hour after hour passed, on Monday, and no move was made. The troops were kept in readiness, but for what? Were they simply collected in Providence to act in defense of that city? Did they not dare to take the offensive and attack the insurgents on

Acote's Hill? Were Governor King and General McNeill, with 3,000 or 4,000 men, afraid to attack the hill defended by a few cannon and a force of a thousand men, at the highest estimate? Perhaps they feared disloyalty in their own ranks; but would a delay make the men more loyal? Or were the charter authorities waiting in the hope of obtaining a favorable reply from President Tyler?

COL. W. W. BROWN.

WHO "STORMED" THE FORT ON ACOTE'S HILL.

A remarkable change in the appearance of affairs came Monday night. All was activity at the charter headquarters, and orders were issued to begin the march. A sudden confidence seemed to have taken possession of those high in authority. The advance guard which had been sent forward to Greenville was ordered to proceed at once to Chepachet. Apparently this new confidence did not pervade the entire army. The officers in command of the various divisions of the charter forces obeyed these new orders slowly, using great caution.

A
PART
OF THE
STATE
OF
RHODE-ISLAND
BURRILLVILLE
CUMBERLAND
SMITHFIELD
GLOCESTER
CHEPACHET
GREENVILLE
SCITUATE MILLS
JOHNSTON
FRUIT HILL
SCITUATE
FOSTER
CLAYVILLE
CITY OF PROVIDENCE

Not until nearly eight o'clock on Tuesday morning (June 28), did the advance guard reach the neighborhood of the hill.[31] The result of the attack was soon announced to the people of Providence by the Military Orders, Number 54.

"The village of Chepachet and fort of the insurgents were stormed at quarter before 8 o'clock this morning, and taken with about one hundred prisoners by Colonel William W. Brown; none killed and no one wounded."[32]

The *Providence Journal* issued an extra edition in the afternoon, telling the story thus:

"*Dorr Fled and His Fort Taken.*

"News has this moment arrived that the force under command of Colonel Brown has taken the insurgent fortification. Dorr has fled but large numbers of his men have been captured."[33]

The true facts seem to be that no fort was taken, for the rude fortifications need not be dignified by that name; that no fort was stormed, for Acote's Hill was without a defender; that none of the charter forces were killed nor even wounded, because there was no fighting; and that the prisoners reported as captured were taken from places of hiding or were non-combatants who were guilty only of being found on the spot. Governor Dorr had left, and his troops had disbanded more than twelve hours earlier; and the poor, deluded men, thus practically deserted, were trying to obey their last orders and escape to their homes.[34]

Dorr's flight was known to the charter authorities early Monday evening, and was the cause of the confidence so suddenly displayed. Walter S. Burges, one of Governor Dorr's personal friends and former adherents, received a letter from Chepachet[d] about seven o'clock on Monday evening. It was handed to him, with the seal unbroken, by Colonel Edwin H. Hazard, for it had been intercepted by the charter authorities. Mr. Burges, at Colonel Hazard's request and in his presence, opened the letter, and found a line directed to himself and an enclosure directed to the publishers of the *Providence Express.* The letter to Mr. Burges was signed "T. W. Dorr," and was a request that the enclosure be delivered as directed. Governor Dorr also wrote: "Believing that a majority of the people who voted for the constitution are opposed to its further support by military means, I have directed that the military here assembled be dismissed." He added that he hoped that "no impediments" would be "thrown in the way of the return of [the] men to their homes." Colonel Hazard carried the letter directed to the *Express* to General McNeill, who immediately opened and read it. A few moments later a general council was held, at which were present, among others, Governor King, several members of the executive council, General McNeill, Colonel Bankhead, and Mayor Thomas S. Burgess.[35]

The decision as to the state of affairs in Rhode Island for the next few days now rested wholly with the charter authorities; so they might publish the letter, and quiet the excitement so generally prevalent; they might keep their forces where they were, and permit the misguided insurgents to return to their homes without

---

(d) "Glocester, R. I., June 27, 1842.

"*To the Publishers of the 'Express,' Providence, R. I.*

"Having received such information as induces me to believe that a majority of the friends of the people's constitution disapprove of any further forcible measures for its support; and believing that a conflict of arms would therefore, under existing circumstances, be but a personal controversy among different portions of our citizens, I hereby direct that the military here assembled be dismissed by their respective officers.

"T. W. DORR, *Commander-in-Chief.*"

THE CAPTURE OF ACOTE'S HILL.

Drawn by Henry Lord, who "was taken near Acote's Hill, marched with other prisoners, with arms pinioned, to Providence, and there confined in the State prison, with thirteen others, in a cell 7 feet by 10, in which he was kept twenty-one days."—*Burke's Report*, 80.

molestation; or they might delay the publication of the letter, make a brave show of force, capture the abandoned fort, take as many prisoners as possible, and prove themselves so energetic that even the persistent Dorr would not dare to try again. They chose the latter course. The letter to Mr. Burges was handed to him at about seven in the evening of Monday, and must have been sent from Chepachet at least two hours earlier. Not until the next morning was the letter given to the *Express*, which had already suspended publication, fearing a riotous attack on the establishment. However, Mr. Burges obtained permission from the Governor for the publishers to print an extra edition, containing the letter, which did not appear until after noon.[36] A few hours later, the *Journal* copied the letter and printed it in the same edition with the news of the "Capture of Dorr's Fort."[37]

The decision to abandon the movement was made by a military council held by Dorr in the afternoon, but the order for dismissal was not, however, promulgated to the men until seven o'clock, and an hour later Governor Dorr and the officers had deserted the spot.[38] The men were left to return home or flee from the State as best they could. What were the grounds upon which the decision to abandon the movement was made? Was it because the conflict was evidently so unequal? A meagre five hundred or a thousand men were arrayed to withstand the three thousand or four thousand charter soldiers. For a time Governor Dorr anticipated that his followers in Providence would follow the charter army, harass it from the rear, and thus render it less effective.[39] But he was undeceived in this matter when he was told the names of many former suffragists who were in the charter ranks.[40] The little band on Acote's Hill was in an "untenable position." Not only was the hill ill fortified, but the artillery ammunition would

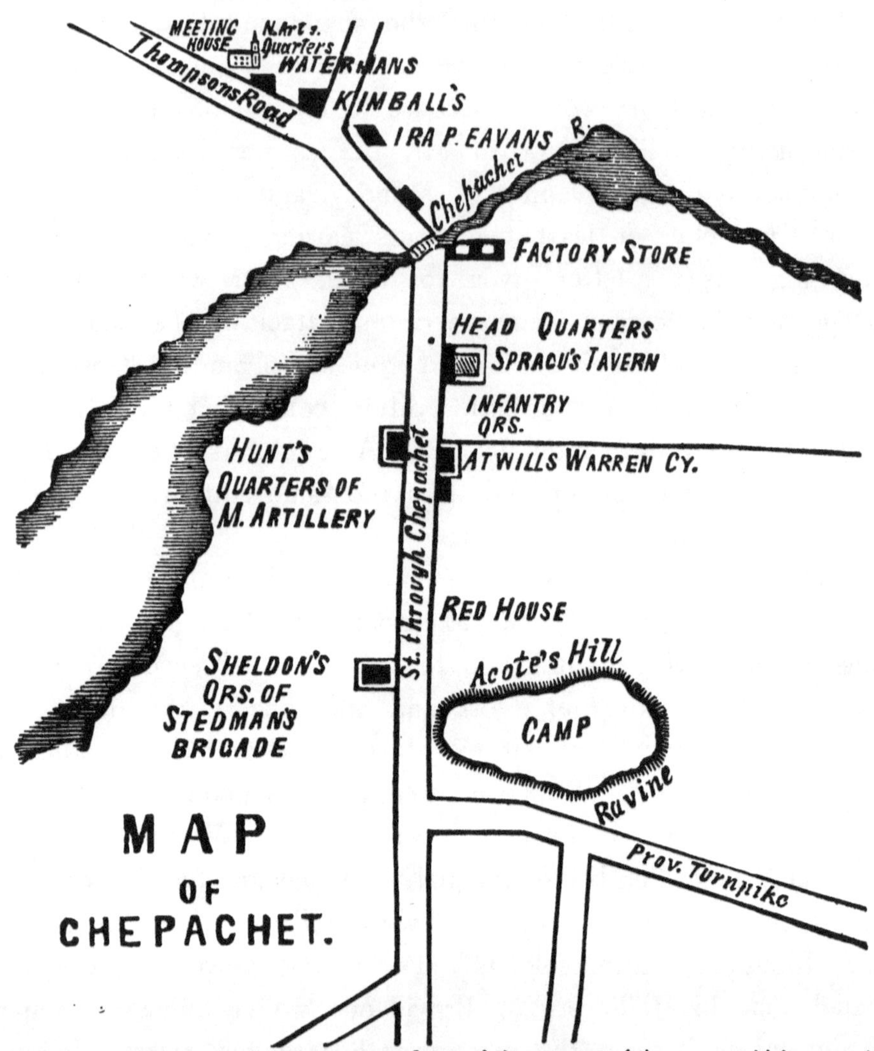

The above map shows the village of Chepachet, and the quarters of the troops which were stationed there Col. Brown's headquarters were at Sprague's tavern, the Newport Artillery, were quartered in the meeting house; the Light Infantry at Sprague's tavern, the Warren Artillery and Infantry at Samuel Y. Atwell's house, the Marine Artillery at Mr Hunt's the Third Brigade at Mr Sheldon's, and a portion of it at Mr. Atwell's, after the Warren companies had left The Bristol Artillery, Newport Volunteers, Middletown Volunteers, Bristol Neck Infantry, and Barrington Volteers. left Chepachet and quartered at Greenville for the night.

(COLLECTION RHODE ISLAND HISTORICAL SOCIETY.)

be exhausted in fifteen minutes.[41] "There was a scarcity of provisions," testified the "Acting Adjutant-General at Chepachet," "though a few barrels of flour and beef remained when the camp broke up."[42] There was no water on the hill, nor was there an abundant supply in the neighborhood.[43] Well might the military officers hesitate.

Nevertheless, the military reasons, though evidently sufficiently strong, were not given by Governor Dorr or his officers as the true cause for the disbanding. Dorr, inconsistent as he was in many ways, was always consistent in his intention to abide by the will of "the people." Nothing could have moved him but the belief that a "majority of the friends of the people's constitution disapproved of any further forcible measures for its support." When he had come to this conclusion, Governor Dorr gave up the fight.

The People's Governor required many proofs before he was led to the belief that the people were no longer with him; and even his former associate refused him further support. Perhaps the first light that broke upon the Governor came from a card that appeared in the *Newport Mercury* of Saturday, and was copied far and wide;[e] it was signed by Dutee J. Pearce and five others, and

---

[e] *Newport Mercury*, June 25, 1842; *Providence Journal*, June 27, 1842; *Republican Herald*, June 28, 1842; *Massachusetts Spy*, June 29, 1842.

"We were opposed to the hostile movements recently made in this State—some of us labored hard to prevent them—we are now opposed to any movements of the kind, and are willing to do what can well be required of us to suppress them. The late Act of the Legislature, providing for calling a Convention of the People, in most of its provisions meets our cordial approbation, and taken as a whole will receive our support. We hope our political friends will give it theirs. We who are members of the Legislature under the people's Constitution, long since relinquished all idea of ever again taking our seats in the same—some of us have made public avowals of our determination upon this subject. We are of opinion that under existing circumstances, it would be the height of folly for that legislature to attempt again to organize.

"(*Signed*), Dutee J. Pearce, Rober R. Carr, Daniel Brown, George C. Shaw, Sanford Bell, Benj. Chase.

"NEWPORT, June 24, 1842."

stated that the undersigned were opposed to any hostile movement and were willing to do what they could in opposition to it. On the whole, they approved the act of the Assembly calling for a convention. The light was strengthened by another card which appeared in Monday's *Journal*, to the same purport, signed by David Daniels, W. S. Burges, and more than a dozen others.[f] Even the *Express* disapproved of his proceedings.[44]

Furthermore, the number of men that came to his support was lamentably small. Fourteen thousand had voted for the constitution, it was claimed, but only a few hundred would take up arms for it. Thirty-five hundred Providence citizens had cast their ballots in favor of the new organic law: ten officers and thirty-five men came from that city to uphold their Governor at Chepachet.[45] "Since the people have deserted us, whether from cowardice or otherwise, and gone over to the enemy, giving them the majority,

---

[f] *Providence Journal*, June 27, 1842; *Republican Herald*, June 28, 1842.

"Monday morning, June 27, 1842.

"*To the Editor of the Journal:*

"DEAR SIR:—Will you have the goodness to insert in your extra *Journal*, the enclosed circular, and call upon all who have advocated the suffrage cause, as a matter of principle, to manifest their devotion to the same, by sustaining the government of the State, against all force, domestic or foreign, which may be found arrayed against it. The path to success in this cause is *now*, at least, the path of law and order.

"Yours in haste,

"W. S. BURGES.

"'TO THE SUFFRAGE MEN OF RHODE ISLAND.

"'The late law of the General Assembly, containing in our opinions, the substance of what we have ever contended for, we heartily recommend its provisions to the candor of our friends, and trust that they will render it their undivided support. The use of force in opposition to the Government is NOT to be tolerated—And we hope that the feelings, wishes, and opinions of the undersigned, may be well considered by those who would now oppose the present existing government of the State.'"

Signed by David Daniels, W. S. Burges, Hezekiah Willard, Adnah Sacket, A. V. Potter, Silas Weston, George W. Ham, J. W. Anthony, E. Montgomery, Wm. Blanding, Wm. Wentworth, Harvey Chaffee, Leonard A. Stalley, and a great many others.

we ought not to contend longer; it would be a faction against the majority."[46]

For the time, Dorr's letter was kept secret by the charter authorities; although in the city and throughout the entire vicinity the excitement was intense.[47] Perhaps, had the people understood that all danger was at an end, Tuesday would have been a quieter day; and the charter government would have saved itself much criticism. The truth was that the charter authorities greatly feared that troops were preparing to come from other States to assist the People's Governor. To be sure, probably as many non-residents of Rhode Island were enrolled among the charter troops as came to the assistance of the suffrage army; and even Major-General McNeill did not claim to be a resident of the State.[48] Yet Governor King was much afraid of the insurgents "from abroad," and Rhode Island was almost surrounded by other States; hence the military authorities thought it wise to station guards at various points along the border, especially at the Pawtucket bridge over the Seekonk river, in the village of Pawtucket. There the Kentish Guards were stationed in the late afternoon of Tuesday, and travel across the bridge was seriously interrupted during the evening, as every passer-by was halted and challenged. Some of the malcontents, who had not shown the courage of their convictions by betaking themselves to Chepachet, were ready to hoot the soldiers, and, perhaps, threw stones at them. Naturally, and yet inexcusably, the soldiers were goaded on to fire. Who fired, or why they fired, has never been legally ascertained; but, inasmuch as the guns were all loaded with ball, and these must hit somewhere, three people were shot, all of them on the Massachusetts side of the bridge, and one, Alexander Kelby, was instantly killed. There is no evidence that any of these men had given any cause for the firing, and it is certain that Mr. Kelby had but just come from his home to look after his oldest son, who had been called out by the commotion. Had the letter from Governor Dorr been published Tuesday morning, the only real fatality of the Dorr rebellion might have been avoided.[49]

AUTHORITIES —**1** *Burke's Report*, 756: Address of Dorr, August, 1843. **2** *Providence Journal*, June 23, 1842. **3** Pitman, *Trial of Dorr*, 45: Testimony of Silas A. Comstock; Turner, *Trial of Dorr*, 18; also Pitman, *Trial of Dorr*, 35: Testimony of Hiram Chappel. **4** *Providence Journal*, June 25, 1842. **5** *Burke's Report*, 756: Address of Dorr, August, 1843. **6** *Providence Journal*. June 27, 1842. **7** *Burke's Report*, 756: Address of Dorr, August, 1843. **8** *Boston Saturday Evening Gazette*, June 25, 1842. **9** *Providence Journal*, June 23, 1842. **10** *Providence Journal*, June 24, 1842. **11** *Providence Journal*, June 25, 1842. **12** *Providence Express*, June 25, 1842. **13** *Burke's Report*, 756: Address of Dorr, August, 1843 **14** *Providence Journal*, June 27, 1842. **15** *Burke's Report*, 757: Address of Dorr, August, 1843 **16** *Burke's Report*, 759: Address of Dorr, August, 1843. **17** *Burke's Report*, 341: Deposition of Jedediah Sprague. **18** *Burke's Report*, 690: Depositions of Peckham, Harris, and Shelley; *Providence Journal*, June 24, 1842. **19** *Burke's Report*, 692: Deposition of Keep. **20** *Burke's Report*, 688. **21** *Burke's Report*, 688: Letter of Thomas M. Burgess, Mayor of Providence, to the President; *Burke's Report*, 689. **22** *Burke's Report*, 694: Letter of Colonel Bankhead to the Adjutant-General of the United States. **23** *Burke's Report*, 688. **24** *Burke's Report*, 695. **25** *Burke's Report*, 697. **26** *Boston Saturday Evening Gazette*, June 25, 1842. **27** *Providence Journal*, June 27, 1842. **28** *Boston Saturday Evening Gazette*, June 25, 1842. **29** *Providence Express*, June 27, 1842. **30** *Providence Journal*, June 27, 1842. **31** *Burke's Report*, 760: Address of Dorr, August, 1843. **32** *Burke's Report*, 761: Address of Dorr, August, 1843. **33** *Providence Journal*, June 29, 1842. **34** *Burke's Report*, 760: Address of Dorr, August, 1843. **35** *Burke's Report*, 307: Deposition of Walter S Burges. **36** *Burke's Report*, 309: Deposition of Samuel Low. **37** *Providence Journal*, June 29, 1842. **38** *Burke's Report*, 758: Address of Dorr, August, 1843. **39** Turner, *Trial of Dorr*, 25: Testimony of Dutee J. Pearce. **40** Pitman, *Trial of Dorr*, 53: Testimony of Dutee J. Pearce. **41** *Burke's Report*, 759: Address of Dorr, August, 1843. **42** Turner, *Trial of Dorr*, 27: Testimony of William H. Potter. **43** *Burke's Report*, 759: Address of Dorr, August, 1843. **44** *Providence Express*, June 23, 1842; Pitman, *Trial of Dorr*, 70: Testimony of Charles W. Carter. **45** *Burke's Report*, 757: Address of Dorr, August, 1843. **46** Pitman, *Trial of Dorr*, 70: Testimony of Carter. **47** *Providence Journal*, June 29, 1842. **48** Turner, *Trial of Dorr*, 28: Testimony of General William Gibbs McNeill. **49** *Burke's Report*, 292–307: Depositions of fifteen persons; *Providence Journal*, June 29, 1842; *Evening Chronicle*, July 2, 1842.

CHAPTER XVIII.

MARTIAL LAW.

"THAT old fool has taken away more lives in that naked country than I for the murder of my father." So said the king of England, Charles II, of Sir William Berkeley, after the suppression of Bacon's Rebellion, in 1677. One might reasonably hope that the charter authorities would have more political wisdom or a greater humanitarian spirit than the bigoted governor of Virginia colony. Unfortunately the historian can find little to praise among the happenings of the month following the fiasco at Acote's Hill. Martial law ruled the State, and personal passions governed those who enforced the military law. From June 26th until August 8th no resident of Rhode Island might consider himself or his property safe if he belonged to the supposed majority, the fourteen thousand who were said to have voted for the People's Constitution. Under martial law, not only those present at the attack on the arsenal and those with Dorr at Chepachet were liable to sudden arrest, but all those who had arms in their possession, or who had held aloof from the task of marching against their neighbors at Acote's Hill. Under the Algerine law, not only the men who had attempted to "exercise any of the legislative, executive or ministerial functions" of any office in the State, but also all those who had in any manner signified "that they accepted any executive, legislative, judicial or ministerial office," as well as the moderators, wardens, and clerks of all meetings, to elect such officers, other than those held "in the manner, for the purposes, at the times, and by the freemen, by law prescribed," were liable to fine and imprisonment.

The "war," however, was over. The charter government knew positively that it no longer had any danger to fear. Governor Dorr had not only fled again from the State and had ordered his men to return to their homes, but he had also publicly announced that he was convinced that the people were no longer with him. There existed no possibility of further attempts to obtain control of the government by force. Dorr's followers at Acote's Hill were too incensed against him to follow his lead again, even if he were foolish enough to inaugurate another movement. Harsh action by the charter government, after June 28, 1842, could not be justified on the ground of political danger. Nevertheless, as a legal justification for all it did, the charter government referred to the act declaring martial law, which had been proclaimed by the Governor on Sunday, in the following proclamation:

"By his excellency Samuel Ward King, governor, captain-general, and commander-in-chief of the State of Rhode Island and Providence Plantations.

"A PROCLAMATION.

"Whereas the General Assembly of the said State of Rhode Island and Providence Plantations did, on the 25th day of June, A. D. 1842, pass the act following, to wit:

State of Rhode-Island and Providence Plantations.

In General Assembly, June Session, 1842.

An Act establishing Martial Law in this State.

Be it enacted by the General Assembly as follows:

*S*ec. 1. The *S*tate of Rhode-Island and Providence Plantations, is hereby placed under Martial Law; and the same is declared to be in full force, until otherwise ordered by the General Assembly. or suspended by Proclamation of his Excellency the Governor of the *S*tate.

True copy---witness,

HENRY BOWEN, *S*ec'ry.

WALL PLACARD.

(FROM COLLECTION, RHODE ISLAND HISTORICAL SOCIETY.)

"'AN ACT ESTABLISHING MARTIAL LAW IN THIS STATE.

"'*Be it enacted by the General Assembly as follows:*

"'SECTION I. The State of Rhode Island and Providence Plantations is hereby placed under martial law, and the same is declared to be in full force until otherwise ordered by the General Assembly, or suspended by proclamation of his excellency the governor of the State:'

"I do therefore issue this my proclamation, to make known the same unto the good people of this State, and all others, that they may govern themselves accordingly. And I do warn all persons against any intercourse or connexion with the traitor Thomas Wilson Dorr, or his deluded adherents, now assembled in arms against the laws and authorities of this State, and admonish and command the said Thomas Wilson Dorr and his adherents immediately to throw down their arms and disperse, that peace and order may be restored to our suffering community, and as they will answer to the contrary at their peril. Further, I exhort the good people of this State to aid and support, by example and by arms, the civil and military authorities thereof in pursuing and bringing to condign punishment all engaged in said unholy and criminal enterprise against the peace and dignity of the State.

"In testimony whereof, I have caused the seal of said State to be affixed to these presents, and have signed the same with my hand. Given at the city of Providence, on the 26th day of June, A. D. 1842, and of the independence of the United States the sixty-sixth.

"SAMUEL WARD KING.

"By his excellency's command:

"HENRY BOWEN, *Secretary*."[a]

---

[a] *Burke's Report*, 373. It will be noted that martial law was declared, not by the military government, but by the civil; not by the commander-in-chief, not by the Governor of the State, but by its

From the 25th of June until the 8th of August, the act declaring martial law remained in force; on that day its operation was suspended by the Governor until the first of September; and on the 30th of August, the Governor indefinitely suspended the act, though it continued on the statutes unrepealed.[1] During the forty days that martial law was in full operation, the people of Rhode Island had an unexcelled opportunity to ascertain which was preferable, civil or military rule. Hundreds of men were arrested and held in "durance vile;" hundreds of houses were searched for hidden weapons, or men.

The number of persons arrested was out of all proportion to the necessities of the case. Granting that there were two hundred men present at the attack upon the arsenal, and five hundred, all told, at Acote's Hill, we can count but six hundred in all as in "armed rebellion," for at least one-half of the two hundred were among the five hundred; but the number of arrests recorded by the partisan *Journal* counted up to more than half this number.[b]

---

legislature; not over the section of the State alone in which the civil power was in danger of being unable to cope with the insurgents, but in all sections of the State; and that, though it might be suspended by the Governor, it would even then hang over the people as a threat until repealed by the General Assembly. These facts show plainly that the Governor of Rhode Island practically possessed only ministerial functions; and that the General Assembly was all powerful, being bound by no "Bill of Rights." It is of interest to note that both the Freemen's and the People's Constitutions contained in their "Declarations of Rights" a section declaring that "The military shall *always* be held in strict subordination to the civil authority" (see Appendixes B and C); while the constitution adopted after the long experience of martial law, and which has remained the organic law for more than fifty years, omitted the word "always," and added a clause, so that the section reads: "The military shall be held in strict subordination to the civil authority. And the law martial shall be used and exercised in such cases only *as occasion shall necessarily require*." (See Appendix D.)

[b] *Providence Journal*, July 2, 4, 6, 7, 8, 9, 12, 13, 14, 16, 20, 23, and 30, 1842. The *Journal*, on the 14th, stated that two-thirds of the prisoners had been discharged. The paper had printed lists, perhaps incomplete, of about one hundred and seventy persons who had been discharged; therefore there were left eighty-five still in confinement. The *Journal* proceeded to state that some were discharged before the examination commenced, and it therefore supposed that "not a quarter of those who had been taken remained in confinement." A simple example in arithmetic: four times eighty-five is three hundred and forty.

The men arrested were almost entirely from the northern part of the State. In one group of thirty-three prisoners, twenty-seven were from Providence County, five from the adjoining county of Kent, and one from Boston.[2] Nearly all of the arrests occurred within a week after the march to Acote's Hill, though martial law continued in force more than a month after the last arrest. The examination of the prisoners was begun early in July, by a board of three commissioners, appointed for this special purpose by the military government.[3] The number was later increased to five,[4] consisting then of Elisha Harris, Stephen Branch, Alfred Bosworth, Henry L. Bowen, and Joseph M. Blake.[c] Some of the prisoners were discharged before the regular examinations began, which lasted about a fortnight. On the second of July, forty-nine were discharged, and twenty-eight committed for trial. Three days later, fourteen were discharged and fifteen remanded. The next day, twenty-eight were examined, and all but two discharged. This process continued until July 13th, when one hundred and sixty-nine had been released, leaving about eighty in confinement. During the next ten days, at least half of these were also discharged. The rest awaited the meeting of the grand jury.

The charter government is censurable, not only for the exceedingly large number of arrests, but for the indiscriminate character of the arrests, the methods of making them, and the treatment of the prisoners by the military, and for the sufferings of their families, thus suddenly deprived of bread winners. A few illustrations may be given: A Providence blacksmith was arrested, at his home,

---

[c] One of these commissioners, a Whig, was a member of the State Senate. One, a Democrat, was elected Representative at the August town meeting and afterwards served eight years as Attorney-General. Another, a Whig, was a Representative at the time, and, in October, was chosen Speaker of the House. Another, a Democrat, was also a member of the State House of Representatives.

on Saturday, July 2d, marched through the streets of the city by a band of twelve men, nine of whom were negroes, and confined in the armory over night; Sunday he was released by the colonel, as no charges were made against him.(5) A farm employee, of Warren, was arrested at the house of his employer, at four o'clock on the morning of the 29th of June, kept in jail seven days, examined by one of the commissioners, and discharged three days later, there being no accusation against him, unless it was that of being employed by a moderator of a people's town-meeting.(6) A minister in the town of Cumberland was eating his dinner, on Thursday, June 30th, when three soldiers burst into the room and searched the house; though they found no concealed weapons, they made the clergyman a prisoner and marched him to a tavern. These soldiers belonged to a company of the State militia, which was returning from Woonsocket to Providence with twenty-one prisoners. These were driven the twelve miles to Providence, in front of the militia, with soldiers in each wagon guarding the prisoners with muskets.(7) At another time, more than a hundred prisoners were marched from Chepachet to Providence, tied together with large bed-cords. "The rope was passed in a clove hitch around each man's arm, passing behind his back, and fastening him close up to his neighbor; there being eight thus tied together in each platoon."(8)

Naturally, the jail and prison accommodations in Rhode Island were found too small on this occasion. It causes no surprise to find that sixteen persons were confined for three days in one cell, twelve feet by nine.(7) In another cell, seven by ten, fourteen men were confined.(8) A third, containing eight persons, gave room enough for the men to lie down.(9) The prisons of those days were none too cleanly, nor were the cells provided with too much fresh air during that month of July. It is true, as William H. Smith, the People's Secretary of State, was assured,[10] that prison cells are much alike; but he was discontented with rooms "about nine feet square, with immense blocks of rough-hewn granite for walls, and with many bolts, bars, rivits, and iron doors of sufficient strength to secure the most ferocious ruffian that ever lived."[11]

The period of arrest under martial law finally passed, the civil law again became supreme, and the grand juries met. Indictments were brought in against some of the leaders in the insurrection,

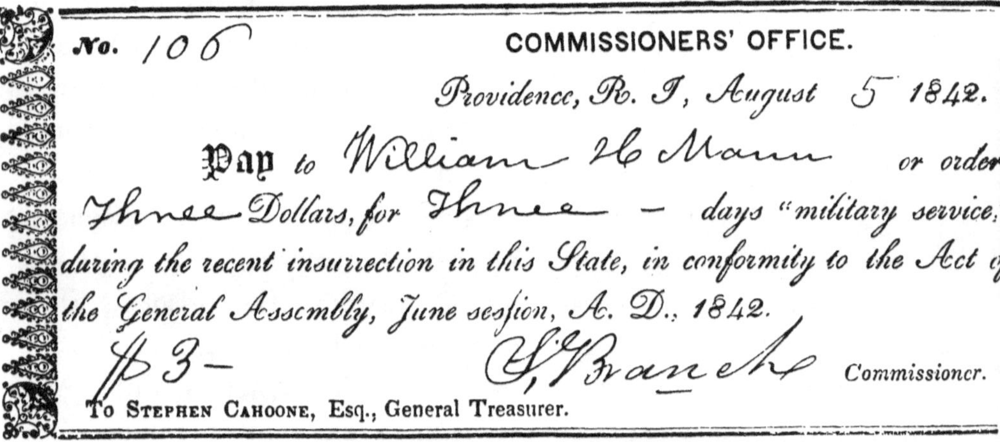

No. 106 COMMISSIONERS' OFFICE.

Providence, R. I, August 5 1842.

Pay to William H Mann or order

Three Dollars, for Three – days "military service," during the recent insurrection in this State, in conformity to the Act of the General Assembly, June session, A. D., 1842.

$3 – S. Branch Commissioner.

To Stephen Cahoone, Esq., General Treasurer.

ORDER FOR PAY FOR MILITARY SERVICE.

(COLLECTION OF CHARLES GORTON.)

and trials were at last held. The case of Joseph Gavit, of Charlestown, in the county of Washington, may be taken as a sample of many cases. The grand jury brought in a true bill against Mr. Gavit, because he, "wickedly devising and intending the subversion and overthrow of the government, being moved and seduced by the instigation of the devil, did unlawfully, maliciously, and traitorously assume to exercise, and did exercise, the functions of the office of member of the House of Representatives," etc. He was at once arraigned and pleaded "not guilty." His case was continued until the November term, when it was again continued. After the lapse of more than a year from the third day of May, 1842, the day of the meeting of the foundry legislature, the newly-elected Attorney-General decided not to prosecute the case further.[(12)]

The cases of William H. Smith,[(13)] of Dutee J. Pearce,[(14)] of Burrington Anthony,[(15)] of Benjamin Arnold, Jr.,[(16)] as well as of many others, would provide much interesting matter; but two trials are of such vital importance in the history of the State, and the nation as well, that they must be selected for special consideration. When Luther M. Borden and eight other men broke into the house of Martin Luther, of Warren, early in the morning of the twenty-ninth of June, they little thought that within a few years the whole country would become interested in the great case before the United States Supreme Court, entitled Luther *versus* Borden.[(17)]

Martin Luther, a shoemaker, was chosen moderator of the town meeting, held in Warren, April 18th, under the People's Constitution. Of whatever other illegal acts he may have been guilty, serving as moderator and receiving votes contrary to the "Algerine Law" were the only crimes for which he was indicted.[(18)] However, when martial law was declared, Luther, on the advice of friends, quietly crossed the border to Fall River.[(19)] While he was away from home, nine men, headed by Luther Borden, armed with an order from Quartermaster John T. Child, broke into Luther's house in order to arrest hin. Unable to find the man they were after, they arrested two employees, discourteously treated Luther's mother and other members of the household, and threw the house and its contents into general confusion. Luther remained in Massachusetts until after the election of April, 1843, and then returned home. Within a few days he was arrested and held in $2,000 bail.

He was duly indicted for the crime of acting as moderator, tried, convicted, and sentenced to pay a fine of $500 and costs, and to be confined in jail for six months.

Claiming a residence in Massachusetts, Luther had brought an action for trespass against Borden *et al.*, in the United States Circuit Court, in November, 1842. The plaintiff presented a statement of the trespass, which the defendants did not deny, but which they justified under martial law. The plaintiff then presented evidence to prove that martial law had been illegally declared, as the charter government had expired on May 3d, when the People's Constitution went into effect; and he asked the court to instruct the jury that the People's Constitution was in full force in June, 1842, and that "a majority of the free white male citizens of Rhode Island, of twenty-one years and upwards, had a right to reassume the powers of government and establish a written constitution; and that, having so exercised such right, the pre-existing charter government became null and void." Judge Story, "*pro forma*, upon the understanding of the parties, and to carry up the rulings and exceptions of the said court to the Supreme Court of the United States, refused to give the said instruction, and ruled that the government and laws under which" the defendants acted justified their action. Accordingly the jury found "the defendants not guilty in manner and form as the plaintiff had declared against them."

The famous case of Luther *vs.* Borden came up before the Supreme Court of the United States at the 1848 term. The counsel for the plaintiff were Benjamin F. Hallett, of Boston, and ex-Attorney-General Nathan Clifford, of Maine; the attorneys for the defense were John Whipple, of Rhode Island, and Daniel Webster, of Massachusetts. The case was argued before six members of the bench, Justices Catron, Daniel, and Mackinley being absent. The questions at issue easily resolved themselves into the one point, namely, the determination of the legal government in Rhode Island in June, 1842.

Mr. Hallett presented three questions for the court to answer: "Had the people of Rhode Island, in the month of December, 1841, without the sanction of the Legislature, a right to adopt a State constitution for themselves, that constitution establishing a government republican in form, within the meaning of the Constitution of the United States? Was the evidence of the adoption by the people of Rhode Island of such a constitution, offered in the court below by the plaintiff in this cause, competent to prove the fact of the adoption of such constitution? Upon the issuing of the proclamation of the convention, by which it had been declared duly adopted, namely on the thirteenth day of January, 1842, and the acts under it, did not that constitution become the supreme law of the State of Rhode Island?"

Supposing these questions answered in the affirmative, then the charter government was, *ipso facto*, dissolved by the adoption of the People's Constitution and by the organization and proceedings of the new government under the same. Consequently the act of March, 1842, "in relation to offences against the sovereign power of the State," and the act "declaring martial law" passed in June, were both void. The act of June, being void, afforded no justification for the acts complained of in the plaintiff's declaration, and those acts, by common law, amount to trespass.

The arguments presented by Mr. Hallett, in support of these positions, have been frequently referred to, earlier in this work. The speech lasted three days, and covered such a variety of topics that even the official Supreme Court Reporter declared himself "much at a loss how to give even a skeleton of the argument."

Mr. Hallett answered the questions as to "What is a State?" "Who are the people?" and "Where resides the ultimate power of sovereignty?" He upheld the right of the people to establish governments. He declared that in the United States no definite or uniform mode had ever been established for initiating or changing a form of State government; that State legislatures had no power or authority over the subject and could interfere no further than to recommend; that the great body of people may change their form of government at any time, in any peaceful way, and by any mode that they for themselves determine to be expedient; that even when a subsisting government points out a particular mode of change, the people are not bound to follow that mode; and that where no constitution exists, and no fundamental law prescribes a mode of amendment, they must adopt the mode for themselves; and that the mode they select, when adopted, ratified, or acquiesced in by a majority of the people, is binding upon all. Mr. Hallett also answered the question as to when a constitution takes effect, discussed in full the difference between a change of government and a revolution, and affirmed that a revolution to change the form of a State government was impossible.

Mr. Whipple declared the question to be decided to be "whether a portion of the voters of a State, either the majority or the minority, whenever they chose, assembling in mass meeting, without any law, or by voting where there is no opportunity of challenging voters, may overthrow the constitution and set up a new one." Mr. Webster devoted his attention principally to an examination of one question: whether the Supreme Court could take judicial cognizance of the questions presented in the record. Mr. Clifford spoke solely on the issue whether a State had a right to declare martial law or not.

The next year Chief Justice Taney read the opinion of the Court. On the new and grave issue presented, the existence and authority of the government under which the defendant acted was called into question. The Court was asked to review the action of the Circuit Court in instructing the jury that the charter government and laws were in full force. The Chief Justice held that "Judicial power presupposes an established government, capable of enacting laws and enforcing their execution and of appointing judges to expound and administer them," and that "the acceptance of the judicial office is a recognition of the authority of the government from which it is derived." He thus upheld the position of the Supreme Court of Rhode Island, that it could not traverse judicially the authority of the government under which it acted. The Court then approved the instructions of the Circuit Court, on the ground that the power to determine that a State government has been lawfully established is not one of the powers which the courts of the United States possess.

Thus the Supreme Court of the United States positively refused to decide the political question, but held that whatever State government was *de facto* in power, its decisions and the decisions of its courts were authoritative in the courts of the United States. Had the People's Constitution prevailed; had the government organized under it become established; had the parties opposed to it risen in rebellion; had martial law been proclaimed by it; and had plaintiff and defendant in this cause occupied each other's places—Chief Justice Taney must have decided in the same way and thrown out the case as not within the authority of the Court. The judicial branch of the national government thus left the case to Rhode Island itself, just as the legislative department had practically done, and as the executive power had, fortunately, been compelled to do by the adverse fortune of the People's Governor.

A point argued strongly by Attorney-General Clifford against the right of the State government to declare martial law received small consideration in Taney's opinion. The brief space devoted to the question contained little else than the decision that a State may unquestionably use its military power to put down an armed insurrection which is too strong to be controlled by the civil government. Mr. Justice Woodbury, of New Hampshire, considered that this matter deserved a fuller treatment than the Chief Justice had given it, and, therefore, filed a strong dissenting opinion. He agreed with the Court in the decision of the political question, but could not justify to himself the ruling that martial law in Rhode Island, at the time and under the existing circumstances, was justifiable. The opinion of Mr. Justice Woodbury in the case of Luther *vs.* Borden is so well known and has become so valuable an authority in all matters relating to the law martial, that but a brief mention is needed here. After producing evidence to show that the Rhode Island government did not practically differ from that of other States in its powers over martial law, the judge affirmed that it was bold doctrine to abolish all constitutional restrictions even in time of war; but that it was much bolder to remove them in time of peace. He declared that, at the farthest, martial law could only be declared in that part of the State in which there was an insurrection and not over the whole State.[d] In his opinion, the act of the legislature was unjustifiable from all points of view.

---

[d] This would exempt the town of Warren.

AUTHORITIES.—1 *Burke's Report*, 472; *Providence Journal*, August 9 and 31, 1842; *Evening Chronicle*, August 9, 1842; *Republican Herald*, August 10. 1842; *National Intelligencer*, August 13, 1842. 2 *Providence Journal*, July 2, 1842. 3 *Providence Journal*, July 4, 1842. 4 *Providence*

Journal, July 12, 1842. **5** *Burke's Report*, 318: Deposition of Nathaniel Knight. **6** *Burke's Report*, 324: Deposition of Stafford Healy. **7** *Burke's Report*, 313: Deposition of Leonard Wakefield. **8** *Burke's Report*, 316: Deposition of Henry Lord. **9** *Burke's Report*, 321: Deposition of Otis Holmes. **10** *Providence Journal*, June 9, 1842. **11** *Providence Express*, June 18, 1842. **12** *Burke's Report*, 792; *Providence Journal*, June 2, July 8, 1842. **13** *Burke's Report*, 771; *Providence Journal*, June 4, 9, and 15, 1842. **14** *Providence Journal*, June 2, 1842, and subsequently. **15** *Burke's Report*, 776. **16** *Burke's Report*, 786. **17** 7 *Howard*, 1; *Burke's Report*, 357–473. **18** *Burke's Report*, 800: Indictment of Martin Luther. **19** *Burke's Report*, 322: Deposition of Martin Luther.

BY HIS EXCELLENCY,

SAMUEL WARD KING,

GOVERNOR, CAPTAIN-GENERAL, AND COMMANDER-IN-CHIEF OF THE STATE OF RHODE-ISLAND AND PROVIDENCE PLANTATIONS.

A PROCLAMATION.

WHEREAS on the eighth day of June instant, I issued a Proclamation, offering a reward of one thousand dollars for the delivery of the fugitive Traitor, THOMAS WILSON DORR, to the proper civil authority: and whereas the said Thomas Wilson Dorr having returned to this State and assumed the command of a numerous body of armed men, in open rebellion against the Government thereof, has again *fled* the summary justice which awaited him; I do therefore, by virtue of authority in me vested, and by advice of the Council, hereby offer an additional reward of four thousand dollars for the apprehension and delivery of the said Thomas Wilson Dorr to the Sheriff of the County of Newport or Providence, within three months from the date hereof.

L. S.

GIVEN under my hand and the seal of said State, at the City of Providence, this twenty-ninth day of June, in the year of our Lord one thousand eight hundred and forty-two, and of the Independence of the United States of America the sixty-sixth.

SAMUEL WARD KING.

BY HIS EXCELLENCY'S COMMAND:

HENRY BOWEN, Secretary of State.

PROCLAMATION OFFERING REWARD FOR DORR.

(BROWN UNIVERSITY LIBRARY.)

CHAPTER XIX.

TREASON AGAINST A STATE.

BY the Algerine Act, Thomas Wilson Dorr and the other executive and legislative members of the people's government were guilty of treason. By the ordinary "Treason Act" of the State, Dorr, Anthony, and others were guilty of high treason, because of the events of the seventeenth of May. Warrants for the arrest of these "traitors" followed quickly after the session of the foundry legislature, and rewards were offered for their capture. A high price was put upon Dorr's head, and requisitions for his return were sent to the Governors of the neighboring States.[1] But the twenty-seventh of June showed Governor Dorr to be the arch-traitor, if there was treason at all, and every effort was put forth to obtain his capture. Though he was "broken down, deserted by the faithless followers of a faithless leader, and apparently without a chance of recovering," yet it was strongly felt that "the peace of the State would not be secure" until he had been placed under arrest.[2]

But neither the thousand-dollar nor the five-thousand-dollar rewards accomplished the desired result. Governor Davis, of Massachusetts, near the end of May, honored the requisition and agreed to return the fugitive, if found within the commonwealth. Governor Seward, of New York, took the same ground.[3] Governor Cleaveland, of Connecticut, refused to honor the requisition. Quoting the clause of the Constitution of the United States, under which the requisition had been made: "A person charged in any State with treason, felony, or other crime, who shall flee from justice and be found in another State, shall, on demand of the executive authority of the State from which he fled, be delivered up, to be removed to the State having jurisdiction of the crime,"[4] he made the claim that this provision of the constitution "was intended to facilitate the ordinary administration of criminal justice in the several States by reclaiming fugitives from the justice of one State to another; but it was never designed to affect political rights or attain political objects."[5]

The refuge in Connecticut was, as has been seen, a boon to Dorr in his preparations for the battle of Acote's Hill. But again he fled, and again rewards were offered and requisitions prepared. In August it was positively announced that Governor Dorr was in Westmoreland, New Hampshire,[6] and a requisition was made upon Governor Hubbard, of that State, for the surrender of the fugitive from justice.[7] But the New Hampshire executive was of a like mind with Governor Cleaveland, and declined to observe the explicit provision of the Constitution of the United States.[8] He sent a letter of explanation through the mails, addressed to "His Excellency Sam. W. King, acting as Governor of Rhode Island," which was immediately returned unopened.[9] When this letter saw the light, it was found to contain three reasons for the refusal: such a requisition should come from the *real* Governor; political offences are not referred to in the constitutional provision; and the "treason" of the clause means treason against the United States.[10] In the light of later events we can but wonder whether Governor Hubbard conferred with Governor Dorr before giving this third reason.

More than a year passed before Governor Dorr returned to Rhode Island. During this period a constitutional convention adopted a new constitution, which was ratified by the people.[11] In April, 1843, sixteen thousand five hundred and twenty votes were cast for Governor,[12] and in May the new constitution went into effect. August 10th, 1843, the People's Governor wrote from Boston an open letter, an "Address to the People of Rhode Island."[13] This long paper, from which copious extracts have been already made, reviewed, in Dorr's masterly style, the entire controversy from the proposed constitution of 1824 through the April election of 1843, and threw the failure of the movement upon the suffragists themselves, and announced that he proposed to return to Rhode Island soon after the August elections.[14]

October 31st, 1843, Thomas Wilson Dorr quietly entered the City Hotel, in Providence, where he was unable to obtain accommodations. He stepped across the street, to the office of the *Republican Herald*, where he was immediately arrested by Jabez J. Potter, Deputy Sheriff of Providence county,[15] under an indictment for high treason made by the grand jury of Newport county on the twenty-fifth of August, 1842.[a]

Mr. Dorr was lodged in the Providence jail, where he remained until the twenty-ninth of February, 1844, when he was taken before the Supreme Judicial Court, sitting at Newport.[b] He was at

[a] *Providence Journal*, August 26, 1842. At the same time, indictments for high treason were returned against Dutee J. Pearce, Joseph Joslin, Daniel Brown, Seth Luther, Nathan N. Carpenter, John Plain, and George Frizzell.

[b] Lawyer Turner prepared and published a pamphlet of 116 pages, entitled "Report of the Trial of Thomas Wilson Dorr for Treason. From Notes taken at the time." Joseph H. Pitman also wrote an account of the trial, in a pamphlet of 132 pages. Mr. Turner's account also forms a

once arraigned, whereupon he denied the jurisdiction of the court: the offense was charged to have been committed in the county of Providence, and the case should therefore be tried there; the prisoner thereby claiming that the clause of the Algerine Act permitting indictment and trial in a different county from the one in which the crime was committed was "against common right, unconstitutional and void." Five days later, Mr. Dorr waived the question of jurisdiction, being desirous of avoiding delay. Without entering here into the legal point raised by this plea as to the jurisdiction, it may be said that Mr. Dorr's prosecution would doubtless not have found it so easy a matter to obtain a jury in Providence county to convict the People's Governor as they did in Newport county.

Governor Dorr plead not guilty, and the trial was set for April 26th, 1844. The case came before the entire Supreme Court, consisting of Chief Justice Job Durfee and Associate Justices Levi Haile, William R. Staples, and George A. Brayton.[c] The first step in order was the selection of a jury. In all, one hundred and fifteen men were examined before the jury of twelve was obtained.

---

portion of *Burke's Report*, pages 865 to 1048. Turner and Pitman's reports of the trial contain no important inconsistencies Turner is especially complete in his report of the arguments of the defense; therefore his account is by far the more valuable and is here the more frequently quoted.

[c] Judge Durfee will be remembered as having given the famous charge to the grand jury at Bristol, in March, 1842. He was first appointed to the bench in 1833, and was made Chief Justice in 1835, which position he held until 1848. Judge Haile had been on the bench since 1835, and remained a judge until his death, in 1854. Judge Staples, well known as a local historian, had served since 1835, and continued in service until 1856, being Chief Justice the last two years before he resigned. It will be noted that these three men also formed the Supreme Court under the People's Constitution, by the act of the Foundry Legislature, in May, 1842. Judge Brayton had been added to the court on the inauguration of the government under the new constitution, in June, 1843; he remained on the bench until his resignation, in 1874, having served the last six years as Chief Justice. Under the charter, the judges were elected annually by the legislature; under the new constitution they were chosen for life, being removable only by majority of the members of each house or by impeachment.

The defendant was allowed twenty peremptory challenges, all of which he used; and eighty-three men were set aside because they had formed and expressed an opinion of the guilt or innocence of the prisoner.

Among the questions proposed by the Attorney-General to be asked of the panel, two were objected to by the defendant. The first was "Did you vote for the said Thomas Wilson Dorr for Governor, at the election on the 18th of April, 1842?" The other was "Have you formed the opinion or do you believe that said Dorr was the Governor of this State, or authorized to exercise the duties of Governor, at any time between the 16th day of May, 1842, and the 28th of June, 1842?" Counsel for the defendant claimed that these questions would insure "a partial jury of political opponents." The court took the matter under deliberation and, being equally divided in their opinion, did not permit the questions to be put. It may be well to add here, however, that the twelve jurymen were to a man Algerines and Whigs, and that but three of the entire panel of 118 belonged to the Democratic party, which at this time was practically a Dorrite party.

Joseph W. Blake, Attorney-General, appeared for the State, assisted by Alfred Bosworth, of Warren. Samuel Y. Atwell, the principal counsel for the defense, was absent on account of illness; therefore Mr. Dorr conducted his own case, assisted by George Turner, of Newport, and Walter S. Burges, of Providence. The first witness was examined on Tuesday, April 30th, and the last on May 3d; Mr. Turner occupied Friday afternoon, the entire day Saturday, and Monday forenoon in his address to the jury, though some of his time was yielded to the defendant. Mr. Dorr's closing argument, the pleading of the Attorney-General, and the charge to the jury by Chief Justice Durfee completed the day:

the jury brought in its verdict at two o'clock, Tuesday morning. The testimony of the witnesses is valuable only in clearing up certain points in the narrative of the "war," and has been freely drawn upon for this purpose. There was no attempt on the part of the defense to deny any of the facts; it merely sought to show justification.

The counsel for the defense proposed five points upon which the prisoner would rest his case. Two of the points related to the Algerine Act. One claimed that indictments must be found in the county in which the crime was committed: the court declined to hear arguments on this point, inasmuch as they had already expressed an adverse opinion in a previous case. The other point was that such indictment must at least be tried in such county: this the court also set aside as having been previously decided.

A third point made was that the defendant committed no treason, inasmuch as he performed the acts in his capacity as Governor of the State. The court asked for testimony to this fact. Mr. Turner first proposed to prove by authorities that a constitution was adopted and a Governor duly elected, and he offered the votes of the people in proof of the adoption. Mr. Dorr offered to call each of the fourteen thousand voters separately before the court in proof. Chief Justice Durfee refused to permit such testimony to go to the jury: the point had already been decided in a previous case; the court could recognize no other constitution than that under which it held its existence; numbers were nothing; the legality only of the proceeding must be examined; and, "if the prisoner was governor of the State, the evidence of it is a certificate of record from the proper officer." In this connection the defense asked permission to argue the question before the jury. This was in accordance with the idea in the People's Constitution that "in all criminal cases, the jury shall judge both of the law and the facts."[16] The court could hardly do otherwise than refuse such a request, especially as the new constitution, under which the Court existed, expressly provided that the "judges of the Supreme Court shall, in all trials, instruct the jury in the law."[17]

A fourth point insisted upon by Governor Dorr and his counsel was evidently the most important one. It was, in substance, the third reason given by Governor Hubbard, of New Hampshire, for not honoring the requisition of Governor King. "In this country," Mr. Turner claimed, "treason is an offense against the United States only and cannot be committed against an individual State." The prisoner stated it thus: "The argument is that treason, which is defined by the Constitution, and punished by the laws, of the United States, excludes all separate State treasons, even if the exclusion be not in express terms."

Mr. Turner, in his plea, entered into an elaborate examination of the authorities relating to treason; he quoted from Coke, Hale, Hawkins, Foster, Blackstone, Burlamaqui, Tucker, Patterson, Burgh, Locke, Story, Hamilton, Iredell, Wilson, Jay, Marshall, and Madison, to show that treason was an offense committed against the "*jura summa imperii*," or the rights of sovereignty, and that, in the United States, sovereignty resided in the people of the United States—not in the people of any individual State. He admitted that each State was, for certain purposes, sovereign within itself; but he affirmed that, in other matters, the several States had yielded their sovereignty to the United States. Rhode Island could not declare war or contract alliances; she could not send ministers abroad or receive foreign ministers; she could not raise nor maintain armies; she could not coin money nor regulate the currency; neither could she, constitutionally, punish as treason any act done toward herself as a State. The Constitution of the United States distinctly defines treason against the United States, and grants to Congress the power to declare the punishment for treason; therefore, by implication, the States gave up their right to try citizens for treason.

Mr. Turner next discussed the question whether the State constitutions contained clauses concerning treason against the individual State or not. He announced that such a clause was not inserted in any State constitution adopted prior to 1812; and that in 1842 it was to be found in but nine of the fundamental laws of the twenty-six States then forming the Union. When asked if there were no treason-statutes in any of the other States, he answered that he did not know. Finally Mr. Turner turned his attention to the provision in the Constitution upon which State Governors have based their demand upon other executives for a return of a fugitive from justice. He claimed that this clause was borrowed from the Articles of Confederation: it was then proper, since the States still retained their sovereignty; and necessary for their security against offenders. "Under the Constitution, treason against the United States, over which the courts of the United States had jurisdiction, might be committed in one State and the person charged might flee into another, as before; but there is no provision in the Constitution for the arrest of the person so escaping and his return to the State where the act was committed, and where alone he must be tried, unless it be the clause in question. So that the construction of this clause is not necessarily limited, by terms, to State offences as distinguished from United States offences."

Governor Dorr presented another view of the meaning and *raison d'être* of this provision. In his view, at the time of the adoption of the Constitution of the United States, treason could be committed against the individual States. "Now, as the Constitution contemplated no such apparatus of circuits and districts as was afterwards provided by Congress, and as the offense could only be punished in the State where it was committed, the Constitution could not otherwise provide than for the return of the fugitive to that State. Does it involve an inconsistency to suppose that the framers of the Constitution then had in view the punishment, in and by a State, of the offense of treason, which they had established and which had been so punishable before? When the courts of the United States were afterwards established, a mode was provided, through the warrant of a United States judge, for transferring a person so charged to the State where the offense had been committed." Therefore, Mr. Dorr implies, though not in distinct words, that the word "treason" in this clause under discussion meant "treason against the United States," now punishable by the federal government.

Mr. Bosworth, for the prosecution, very briefly presented the arguments for the State. He admitted the position taken by Mr. Turner as to the nature of treason and sovereignty in the United States. He denied, however, that the whole people of the United States were sovereign in Rhode Island, contending that each State was still sovereign in every matter which had not been distinctly yielded to the United States. Without the power to punish acts which amount to treason, a State cannot protect itself. "Treason may as well be committed against a State as against the United States; and the power of punishing it has not been surrendered to the United States." Swift, Story, Dane, Tucker, Rawle, and Johnson all regard treason against a State as possible. Attorney-General Blake was prepared to argue the matter still further, but was informed by Chief Justice Durfee that it was unnecessary to take more time; the Court was unanimous on that point.

The Chief Justice, in giving his charge to the jury, did not permit them to misunderstand the position of the Court. The question whether the crime of treason could be committed against one of the States of the Union was one of mere constitutional law, and one for the Court alone to decide. "As the organ of the court, I say to you, gentlemen, that wherever allegiance is due there treason may be committed. Allegiance is due to a State and treason may be committed against a State of this Union." Chief Justice Durfee called attention to the "fugitive from justice" provision of the Constitution of the United States, and claimed that it recognized the possibility of treason against a State "by an implication too strong to be resisted." The organized sovereign people of Rhode Island, in the opinion of the Court, had, through its legislative body, declared what treason against the State should mean; "this law is constitutional and binding on all; the sovereign authority of this State is such that treason can be committed against it."

As has been seen, Governor Dorr and his counsel based their arguments primarily on the impossibility that a person should be guilty of treason against two governments at the same time. In the Federal Convention discussion over the treason provision of the proposed constitution brought out similar ideas. Dr. Johnson contended that treason could not be both against the United States and individual States, "being an offence against the sovereignty, which can be but one in the same community." Mr. Madison also feared that to leave the individual State "in possession of a concurrent power might involve double punishment." Gouverneur Morris proposed that the United States be given exclusive power to declare what should be treason. On the other hand, Colonel Mason suggested that the United States would have a qualified sovereignty, and the individual States would retain a part of their sovereignty, so that an act might be treason against a particular State which would not be treason against the United States. When Mr. King asserted that no line could be drawn against levying war against the United States and against an individual State, Mr. Sherman answered that resistance against the laws of a particular State might be different from resistance against the laws of the United States; and Mr. Ellsworth added that the Union and the individual States ought each to have power to defend their respective sovereignties. Though Madison and Morris persisted in declaring their fear of a double punishment if the provision was left as proposed, the convention voted that the clause should read, "Treason against the United States shall consist only in levying war against them," etc.[(18)] A candid reading of the discussion can lead only to the conclusion that though some of the members of the convention did not believe that a man could be guilty of two treasons at the same time, yet that the convention did not consider that the clause which they discussed, as finally worded, excluded the possibility of treason against a State.

Mr. Turner's argument that the individual States had, by implication at least, yielded their sovereignty in the matter of treason, just as they had yielded it in other points, meets with another difficulty. Not only does the Constitution of the United States give the power to make treaties to Congress, but in another place it distinctly takes it away from the States: not only does it place the laying of import duties in the hands of the national legislature, but it directly denies to each State the power to levy such duties. On the other hand, in defining treason and authorizing Congress to declare its punishment, it distinctly speaks of treason "against the United States," and nowhere intimates that the power to punish treason against a State did not still belong to such State.

Mr. Turner's point that the original State constitutions did not contain a treason clause, and that but nine of the twenty-six State constitutions did contain such clause, was of but little account.[d] Though it is true that sixteen State constitutions did not contain the clause in 1842 (one of these being the Rhode Island charter), it is also true that most, if not all, of these States, Rhode Island included, did contain a statutory provision defining treason.[e] Moreover, it was the consensus of opinion among the constitutional authorities that treason was a common-law offense in each State, and therefore no constitutional or statutory enactment was needed. Dr. Wharton upholds Judge Story's charge to the grand jury in Rhode Island, in 1842, in which the proposition was advanced that treason must be an offense against a State unless the object of levying war be manifestly for some matter of a general concern to the United States; and he quoted Judge Tucker to the same effect.[19] Dr. Wharton also declared that "the course of practice adopted at the time of the formation of the Federal Constitution, when the attention of the judiciary was closely called to the boundaries of national and State sovereignties, and pursued to the present day, is to recognize levying war against a State as forming a State offense, cognizable in a State court, and punishable by State authority."[20]

---

[d] Mr. Turner was usually quite correct in his statements of facts, but he was in error here, for he omitted the constitution of Maine from his list.

[e] In ascertaining these facts, all the constitutions of every State have been examined and the statutes of ten of the States which, in 1842, did not contain a treason clause in their constitutions.

Sergeant, in his Constitutional Law, published in 1822, holds that treason against a State may be committed by an open and armed resistance to the laws of a State or a combination and forcible attempt to overturn or usurp the government.[21] Rawle's View of the Constitution, published in 1829, took the same ground: "Similar acts committed against the laws or government of a particular State, are punishable according to the laws of that State, but do not amount to treason against the United States."[22]

The lawyers in this case of Rhode Island *versus* Thomas Wilson Dorr had but few precedents upon which to base their arguments. During the course of the second war with England, an attempt was made to try a citizen of New York for treason against that State. The Supreme Court quashed the indictment on the ground that, in case of war between the United States and a foreign nation, giving aid and comfort to the enemy was treason against the United States and not against the State of which the party was a citizen. At the same time the Court declared that treason might be committed against a State by an open opposition to its laws.[23] As far as has been ascertained, after careful investigation, this case of Lynch in New York alone preceded the case of Dorr in Rhode Island: the third known case was that of John Brown, in Virginia.

Had President Tyler sent military assistance to Governor King, and had Governor Dorr in his armed resistance to the charter government come into opposition to the federal soldiers, the case would have been different. The crimes alleged, under such circumstances, would have been treason against the United States and not treason against the State of Rhode Island.[24] President Tyler's conservatism saved Governor Dorr from this issue, but it ought not to have saved him from all accountability for his course. Trial for treason against the State properly followed acts in opposition to the government of the State. The plea that he committed no treason against the United States should not exempt him from the natural consequences of his movements in Rhode Island. Besides, treason against a State "is recognized as having a substantive and independent existence in that clause of the federal constitution which provides" for the return of the fugitive from the justice of a State, charged with treason against that State.[25] The attempt of Turner and Dorr to explain away the word "treason" in that clause as not meaning treason against a State was pettifoggery.

The four points so far discussed were legal questions which the Court promptly ruled out, and which therefore did not go to the jury. A fifth point of defense was that the evidence did not support the charge of treasonable and criminal intent on the part of the defendant. Mr. Turner argued that Governor Dorr proceeded justifiably and from a high sense of duty; that the whole evidence showed that throughout he acted without traitorous intent, believing himself to be in the right. It need hardly be added that this was undoubtedly true. However, in the charge to the jury, the Court removed whatever hope the prisoner might have had, by saying: "It may be that he really believed himself to be the Governor of the State and that he acted throughout under this delusion; however this may go to extenuate the offense, it does not take from it its legal guilt." Finally the court simplified the whole matter for the jury by stating that if they believed, "by the testimony of two or more witnesses, or by confession in open court," that the prisoner made a military demonstration at Providence against the arsenal, or that he commanded an armed force at Chepachet with the avowed object of overturning the existing government, then it was their duty to return a verdict of guilty.

Evidently there was but one thing for the jury to do. "The court made everything plain for us," said one of the jurymen afterwards. The jury agreed upon the verdict at once. They retired at eleven on Monday evening, and, "waiting for the crowd to disperse," brought in the verdict of guilty at two o'clock, Tuesday morning, May 7th. Eight days later counsel Turner brought in a bill of eighteen exceptions and a motion for a new trial. The exceptions were, some of them, trivial or technical, such as the usual charges of misconduct in obtaining the jury, and of improper admission of evidence, and errors in the rulings of the Court on the legal questions presented: more important was the claim for the admission of testimony to show that the prisoner was legally entitled to do what he did; that treason was an offense against the United States only; that the Algerine Act was unconstitutional; and that the jury must consider the question of intent on the part of the prisoner.

June 10th the Court met to hear arguments on the motion for a new trial. For three days Mr. Turner argued at length, taking up each exception in order; the Attorney-General briefly replied, and the Court took the matter under advisement. On the fourteenth the Court stated that the motion for a new trial was denied. Mr. Turner then read a motion in arrest of judgment on the ground that the trial was held in Newport county. He argued the point fully; the Attorney-General answered in brief; and Mr. Atwell, present for the first time, made a final plea in behalf of his client. June 24th the Court denied the motion in arrest of judgment, and the next morning the Attorney-General demanded the sentence. The prisoner was permitted to address the Court, when asked why sentence should not be pronounced upon him, and made an able reply, bringing out in brief but telling paragraphs his criticisms of the fairness of the trial. In conclusion he said: "I am bound, in duty to myself, to express to you my deep and solemn conviction that I have not received at your hands the fair trial by an impartial jury to which by law and justice I was entitled."

At once Chief Justice Durfee pronounced sentence: "that the said Thomas Wilson Dorr be imprisoned in the State prison at Providence, for the term of his natural life, and there kept at hard labor in separate confinement." Two days later, June 22d, Mr. Dorr was removed to Providence and duly placed in the State prison in that city.[26]

AUTHORITIES.—**1** *Providence Journal*, May 28 and June 9, 1842; *Providence Express*, May 28, 1842. **2** *Providence Journal*, July 2, 1842. **3** *Providence Journal*, May 28, 1842. **4** Constitution of the United States, Art. IV, Sect. 2, Clause 2. **5** *Cleaveland to King*, 5; *New York Courier and Enquirer*, June 2, 1842; *National Intelligencer*, June 11, 1842. **6** *Republican Herald*, August 13, 1842; *Boston Saturday Gazette*, August 13, 1842. **7** *Providence Journal*, August 20, 1842. **8** *Providence Journal*, August 23, 1842. **9** *Providence Journal*, August 26, 1842; *Boston Saturday Evening Gazette*, August 27, 1842. **10** *Providence Journal*, September 5, 1842. **11** *Rhode Island Manual*, 1896-1897, 129. **12** *Rhode Island Manual*, 1896-1897, 102. **13** *Burke's Report*, 731. **14** *Burke's Report*, 764. **15** *Providence Journal*, November 1, 1843. **16** People's Constitution, Appendix. **17** Constitution of 1842, Appendix. **18** *Eliot's Debates*, V, 447. **19** Wharton, *Criminal Law*, § 2769. **20** Wharton, *Criminal Law*, § 2772. **21** Sergeant, *Constitutional Law*, 371. **22** Rawle, *View of the Constitution*, 142. **23** 11 *Johnson*, 553; see also *Kent*, 403 note; *Wharton*, 2772; *Sergeant*, 371 note; *Rawle*, 143 note. **24** Wharton, *Criminal Law*, § 2771. **25** Wharton, *Criminal Law*, § 2766. **26** *Republican Herald*, June 29, 1844.

CHAPTER XX.

THOMAS WILSON DORR.

THE natural reaction soon set in. At the time of Governor Dorr's conviction, Governor Fenner had but recently been placed again in the gubernatorial chair. The law and order party was in full power throughout the State, having a firm grasp upon the General Assembly. The summary trial of Governor Dorr, however, was not acceptable even to the law and order faithful, and the appearance of unfairness made it unacceptable to the mass of the people, Sympathy for the martyr Governor grew with remarkable rapidity. The General Assembly even showed signs of weakness; it could not be held strictly to the course laid out for it. Finally, when Governor Dorr's aged parents petitioned the legislature for an act of amnesty, the General Assembly, in January, 1845, voted that "the prayer be so far granted that Thomas W. Dorr be liberated from his confinement in the State prison upon his taking the following oath or affirmation:

"'I do solemnly swear that I will bear true faith and allegiance to the State of Rhode Island and Providence Plantations; and that I will support the constitution and laws of this State and of the United States: So help me God.'"(1)

The imprisoned Governor could not bring himself to obtain his liberty by what seemed to him an act of inconsistency. Undoubtedly he believed that he was the legal Governor of the State; he considered that the People's Constitution was still binding, and that the constitution to which he was asked to swear allegiance was null and void. Declining to take the oath, he remained in prison. The agitation for his release continued, however. The Democratic party became fully identified with his cause, and the fight at the April election was between the law and order party and the "Liberationists." Liberation societies were formed throughout the State; liberation sentiment was stimulated by every means possible. As a result, Governor Fenner was defeated for re-election by the "liberation" candidate, Charles Jackson, by a vote of 8,010 to 7,800.[2] The rest of the law and order State ticket was elected, though the "liberationists" had a majority in the General Assembly.

JAMES FENNER.

June 27, 1845, exactly one year after the prison doors closed upon Governor Dorr, they opened again to permit him to go free. On that same day the General Assembly had passed "an act to pardon certain offences against the sovereign power of this State and to quiet the minds of the good people thereof." This law provided for the discharge from prison merely of "any person who has been convicted of the crime of treason against the State and is now in prison under the sentence of the law."(3) Governor Dorr quietly retired to the home of friends, broken down in health and spirits, barely more than a wreck of his former self.

CHARLES JACKSON,
THE "LIBERATION" GOVERNOR.

The "liberation" issue alone elevated Mr. Jackson to the governorship, and the next year he was defeated for re-election.(4) After that the terms "Law and Order" and "Liberation" went out of use, and the normal Whig majority regularly defeated the Democratic minority until 1851. In that year the minority became the majority, and Philip Allen was chosen Governor, while the other State officers were replaced by Democrats.(5) Scarcely had the General Assembly organized, in May, 1851, when it passed a resolution restoring Mr. Dorr to his civil and political rights.(6)

Governor Allen's majority, in 1851, was less than nine hundred. The next year he was re-elected by a majority of four hundred in a total vote of eighteen thousand: this was the year that Rhode Island gave its electoral vote to a Democratic candidate for President, the only time since 1836. The next year Governor Allen polled more than ten thousand votes as against eight thousand for William W. Hoppin, the Whig candidate. The strong Democratic wave, this year also carried the General Assembly, which, in February, 1854, proceeded to take a step that must have appalled even

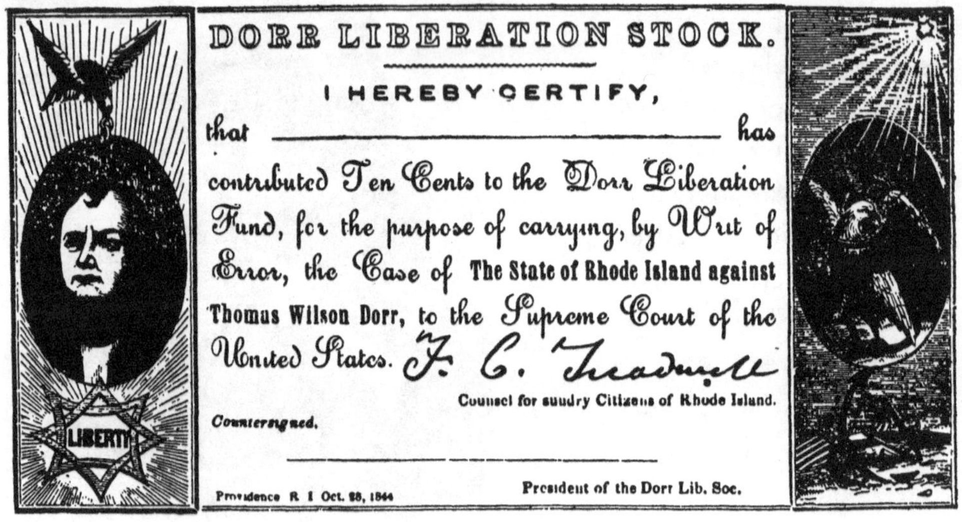
DORR LIBERATION STOCK.

I HEREBY CERTIFY,

that ______________ has contributed Ten Cents to the Dorr Liberation Fund, for the purpose of carrying, by Writ of Error, the Case of The State of Rhode Island against Thomas Wilson Dorr, to the Supreme Court of the United States. F. C. Treadwell

Counsel for sundry Citizens of Rhode Island.

Countersigned.

____

Providence R I Oct. 28, 1844 President of the Dorr Lib. Soc.

CERTIFICATE DORR LIBERATION STOCK.

(COLLECTION OF CHARLES GORTON.)

Governor Dorr. It passed an act reversing and annulling the judgment of the Supreme Court of Rhode Island rendered against Thomas W. Dorr.[7]

This act was unique: it was an illustration of what Governor Dorr called the "Omnipotence of the Legislature." Criticising certain features in the trial of Thomas W. Dorr, it affirmed that he had been wrongfully convicted, and that these wrongs should be redressed. Since the English forefathers had been in the habit

The Four Traitors,*

Who most infamously sold themselves to the Dorrites, for Office and Political Power.

Let us not reward Traitors, but with just indignation abandon them as "Scape- Goats," to their destiny—forever.

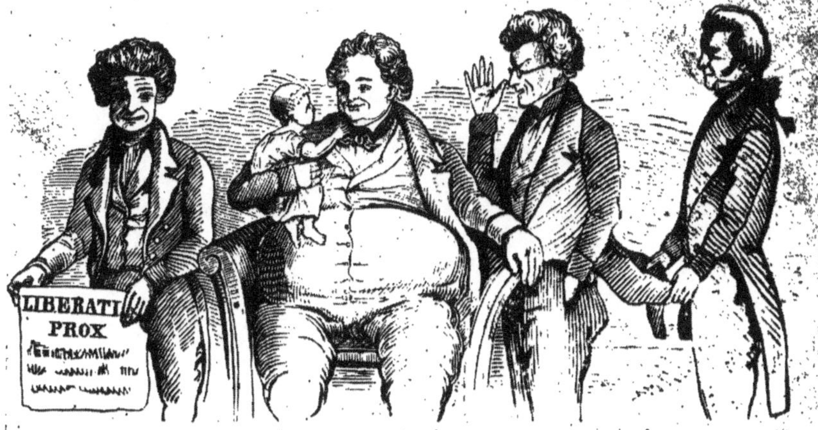

Charles Jackson.	**Samuel F. Man.**	**James F. Simmons.**	**Lemuel H. Arnold.**
Providence.	*Cumberland.*	*Johnston.*	*South Kingston.*

"O, heaven, that such companions thou'dst unfold;
And put in every honest hand a whip
To lash the rascals naked through the world"

"APOLOGETIC NOTE. At the present, dark, dismal and degenerate period of our history—when a man regardless of himself and his God, will sell his birthright for a mess of pottage — when an obscure individual like Polk, is elected to the Presidency, and a pompous, self - conceited man like Jackson. to the Gubernatorial chair — and other Dorrites, too contemptible to mention among men, are appointed to fill different offices under the general government — when Foreigners, ignorant, barbarous and uncivilised, as the wild ass of the wilderness, pour in upon us like the plagues of Egypt, scourging and desolating the land — when the murderer, with brazen front and seared conscience, his hands still dropping with human blood, stalks abroad, at noonday, unpunished — when there seems to manifest itself (among a certain, ignorant, low - bred Class of radicals, disorganisers, abolitionists assuming to be jurists, conscientiously afraid of the gallows, and vile, illiterate and decayed priests, a nuisance in society,) such a criminal and unhallowed sympathy for felons of every description, when we would do something for the public good, and attempt to stay the torrent of moral and political profligacy, which sapping the foundation, seems to threaten the overthrow of our most valuable institutions — when the law is trampled under foot with impunity — and every thing around is anarchy and confusion — to those who are disposed to cavil or criticise, and it is very easy to do so, we would say, that as the Originals could not be induced to sit for their portraits, without large sums of gold or pledges of high political trust, they were necessarily, with much difficulty, sketched from recollection ; it cannot therefore be reasonably supposed, that their features are precisely exact ; but if they had sat to the artist, the expression of their faces, being as variable as their characters, what might seem a good likeness to day, would cease to be so to - morrow ; and this we deem a full and sufficient apology.

* The conduct of these men ; two of them in particular, towards Governor Fenner, who fearlessly and nobly, sustained the State, through all its recent difficulties, is so treacherous, base and execrable, and is so well understood by the intelligent part of the community, that it needs no comment."

of reversing judgments by act of Parliament, and since the charter granted to the General Assembly the right "to alter, revoke, annul, or pardon such fines, mulcts, imprisonments, sentences, judgments, and condemnations as shall be thought fit," and since the new constitution continued to the General Assembly the powers heretofore exercised, therefore it decreed that the judgment against Thomas Wilson Dorr be "Hereby repealed, reversed, annulled, and declared to be as if it had never been rendered." The clerk of the Supreme Court for the county of Newport was ordered to "write across the face of the record of said judgment the words, 'Reversed and Annulled by Order of the General Assembly at their January Session, A. D. 1854.'" This act was passed in the House of Representatives by a vote of thirty-nine to eighteen.[(8)]

No act of any legislature could redress the injury which had been done to Governor Dorr. Worn out in mind and body, without spirit or energy, grown old before his time, the unhappy man dragged out a miserable existence. To him the opening of the prison doors was no vindication: rather, it was equivalent to saying, "You have been punished enough; you may go now." The complimentary vote for United States Senator by the minority of the General Assembly could mean but little to the man who, by his conviction and release, had been made worse than an alien. Six years passed away, and Governor Dorr, no longer young, strong, or energetic, was given his civil rights: what cared the broken-hearted man! Three years more and the "omnipotent" legislature overruled the verdict of the court: does any one believe that such an act brought happiness to the dying man? Ten months later Thomas Wilson Dorr passed away, at the age of forty-nine.

Who was this would-be Governor; this disturber of the peace of Rhode Island; this pleader before Tammany Hall; this military leader; this prisoner at the bar? He was a man "endowed with intellectual powers which, had they been properly directed, would have always secured him a commanding influence. Those powers, too, were disciplined by an education more accomplished perhaps than any other man of his age in Rhode Island had been privileged to obtain. As a man of science and letters, he might have attained honorable distinction, had he chosen to dedicate his time either to science or to letters. As a statesman he might have rendered his native State substantial service. He might have been a true-hearted, private gentleman, honored by the respect and confidence of the community in which he resided."[9] Such was the testimony of his most bitter enemy in the midst of the conflict which he had brought upon his State.

His friends could hardly say more. "Mr. Dorr is an educated gentleman of the most respectable family and connexions. He, personally, has stood high in the confidence and esteem of his fellow-citizens. His whole course of life, his sentiments, and his actions have been such as to free him from the imputation of having, in anything, been governed by other motives than a desire and a zeal for the best interests of his fellow-citizens and of the State."[10] When foes and friends so closely agree, we must accept their verdict as final.

The month of May, 1842, either changed the whole nature of Governor Dorr, or brought out traits that had never before been seen. The month was like a high wall, separating absolutely what preceded from what followed it. Deserted by his friends, true as well as false, he enjoyed the confidence of no one. Aided before the Court by his lawyers, he nevertheless bore the brunt of the trial himself. He was set free from prison and granted his civil rights; but the interest and enthusiasm which eventually brought these favors was interest in the martyr, not in the personality of the martyr; enthusiasm for justice, not for the welfare of the man who had failed. Can such a condition of things be explained? Can the inmost character of such a man be read and understood?

How had Mr. Dorr shown his talents before the crisis in his life? How had the people expressed their confidence in him? What had he accomplished? Before he reached the age of thirty the citizens of Providence chose him as one of their four Representatives in the General Assembly. Here he was active in many ways. A pronounced Whig, and strongly opposed to the national government as then represented by Andrew Jackson,[11] in November, 1834, he brought into the legislature resolutions against the removal of the public funds from the Bank of the United States; against executive control of the national treasury; against the spoils system in national politics; and in favor of rechartering the Bank of the United States.[12] These four resolutions were adopted by practically a two-thirds vote; but the youthful partisan found himself in a hopeless minority when he opposed an amendment proposing the taxation of State banks. Perhaps this predisposition in favor of the State banks shows that the enthusiasm for the national bank was more that of a party leader than of a firm believer in the truth of the cause; and it may help to explain the fact that six years later, in a Democratic caucus, Mr. Dorr presented resolutions praising President Van Buren especially for his "strenuous opposition to the late Bank of the United States."[13]

The young statesman, in his early career in the legislature, showed himself a friend of the debtor class by his fight against a bank law of his day. By obtaining a repeal of this law he deprived the banks of a power over debtors not permitted other creditors; a power which practically made the bank a preferred creditor.[14]

Mr. Dorr again appeared as a reformer in opposing the attempt made in 1836 to enact laws against the abolitionists, thereby incurring great hostility from the Whig leaders of the State. That which forever drove him from the Whig party was his position, early taken, in favor of the extension of the suffrage. From the twelfth of March, 1834, when his famous Address to the People of Rhode Island was issued, he was a suspected man in Whig councils. When the Whigs failed to stand behind the constitutional convention, Mr. Dorr retired from the party. When he ran for Congress, as a Constitutionalist, in 1837, and received seventy-two votes, not quite one per cent. of the entire vote, the break was complete. Two years later he was nearly elected Representative, as a Democrat, running considerably ahead of his companion on the Democratic ticket.(15) Politicians could not use a man of such independence, and he remained politically quiet until he was persuaded to accept the People's nomination for Governor.

Nevertheless, Mr. Dorr was active in the public service outside of the State legislature. For several years he was one of the most valued members of the Providence School Committee. Many reforms in the management and conduct of the schools were carried through by his energy and push, and the present excellent condition of the Providence schools owes much to the fact that sixty years ago they had in him a true friend. When Mayor Brigham died, just as the agitation for a new constitution was begun, in February, 1841, Mr. Dorr received a nearly unanimous vote for President of the Board.(16)

Mr. Dorr was a leading member of the Rhode Island Historical Society. In the list of officers chosen in 1840 we find Chief Justice Durfee, Vice-President; Judge Staples, Secretary; and Thomas Wilson Dorr, Treasurer; and among the trustees: Thomas F. Carpenter, John Pitman, Elisha R. Potter, and Samuel Y. Atwell.[17] Here was complete harmony among political enemies. Mr. Dorr was a commissioner of the Scituate bank, chosen to that position by the legislature of the State.[18] He was also administrator and trustee of the property of several private individuals; and just before the attack on the arsenal he told his friend, Walter S. Burges, where all his papers were, and gave him the keys to use in case of need.[19]

Mr. Dorr is thus shown to have been one of Rhode Island's model citizens. He had the courage of his convictions, politically, even when they resulted in driving him out of his party. His lack of consistency in his views on the United States Bank may surely be pardoned, as due partly to the rupture of party relations and partly to the change in the man himself as he grew from the age of twenty-nine to that of thirty-four. As a public-spirited citizen, we find him earnest and true; in financial, educational, and historical affairs he took strong and energetic positions; and finally, as a neighbor and friend, he was greatly beloved. Surely, "A far nobler destiny he might have achieved."

In what lay his failure? Can we place all the censure, as he himself tried to do, upon the weak and vacillating people who deserted him? Can we hold President Tyler responsible for the disaster, as did many of the Governor's friends? Was Governor Dorr ahead of his times, and unable to bring his followers up to his position? Or was there some quality lacking in his composition, without which failure was inevitable? Did he undertake a task too great for him, but one which the right man might have accomplished? Or was the cause so radically erroneous that it must have failed under any leader? These are questions more easily asked than answered.

Dorr had his faults and idiosyncracies like any other man, and a plain narrative of the movements of the people's Governor, during the two critical months, shows some of them only too plainly. While generally popular, he was not a great leader of men. He had a few very earnest, unselfish friends, but the majority of his followers were place-hunters and "hangers-on." He could map out a plan which might be successful if he personally saw to its execution; but he had not the knack of so directing the work that others could carry it out exactly as it was planned. When the Foundry legislature adjourned, after enacting a few laws, it evidently expected that the executive would carry on the government. But it had failed to provide any of the necessary means. The executive officers had none of the State papers or documents: they had no material of any sort with which to work: above all, they had no funds; no access to the treasury; and no way of collecting taxes. Shall we accuse the timid legislature of being wholly to blame for this condition of affairs? Or should Governor Dorr have had more control over his party? Did he not acknowledge that he advised the immediate taking possession of the State House? He should not have yielded so readily his opinion: as he was situated he was right, and should have compelled the Assembly to follow his bidding. Either he weakly yielded to its judgment, or it had too little confidence in him. As has been seen, the sudden obliteration of the people's government led many people to desert the lost cause.

A second evident characteristic of Thomas W. Dorr was his remarkable credulity; his apparent willingness to believe every report and to accept every suggestion which seemed to favor his cause. We have noticed two especial occasions on which this trait has been apparent. When Tammany Hall, under the lead of such

THE DORR HOUSE, BENEFIT AND BOWEN STREETS.

men as Slamm and Purdy, promised him, or led him to expect, that troops would come from New York to his assistance; when he honestly believed that these proffers came from the hearts of men deeply interested in the suffering non-voters of Rhode Island; when he failed to see that these practical politicians were merely seeking to feather their own nests; then Governor Dorr was foolishly, if not criminally, blind. When, again, he was coaxed to betake himself to Chepachet by the stories of five hundred men there, of the hundreds on the way, of the hundreds more that only awaited his arrival, he ought to have known better. He ought to have realized that when the leaders of the party, the State officers, and the members of the General Assembly, had resigned their places and had repudiated their Governor, the rank and file would not be eager to take the sword for their rights no matter how dear. The fiasco of Acote's Hill was mainly due to Governor Dorr's credulity.

But one more characteristic trait of the People's Governor need be mentioned, and that perhaps the most prominent—his obstinacy; or, as his friends called it, his persistency. Once convinced that he was right, nothing could turn him from his course. When the attack on the arsenal had failed, he was with difficulty persuaded that, for the time at least, his cause was lost. Even though he learned that most of his friends were against him, he repaired to Chepachet. After his third flight from the State, at a time when a heavy reward hung over his head, he wrote from New Hampshire asking if it were not best for him to return to Rhode Island. His persistent obstinacy is especially shown by his refusal to yield one iota—to accept any compromise with the enemy. His constitution, he claimed, was legally adopted—it was adopted by a majority of the people of the State. No later constitution could be legal, unless it superseded the People's Constitution either in the manner therein prescribed or by a majority of the people, just as the People's Constitution had been adopted. Therefore no new constitution, however liberal, however like his own, the people's, was of any interest to him, unless, in his opinion, legally adopted. The People's Constitution was binding still; and he was the true Governor of Rhode Island, even until his death.

In this he but carried his position to the logical end. He was told by such men as ex-President Van Buren, Senator Benton, Governor Morton, and even the historian, George Bancroft, that his proceedings were strictly just and legal. With such authority to uphold him, perhaps we need not wonder that the very fact that Dorr had a clear and logical mind, together with the honesty of his nature, in reality caused his downfall. These commendable traits first drove him out of the party to which he naturally belonged, isolated him from his own family and his best friends, led him to attempt war against his beloved State, placed him in a traitor's cell, and made him, at the end of his short life, a broken-hearted man.

Of whatever failings Thomas Wilson Dorr may be accused, his virtues clearly outrank them. Whatever he did to lose the esteem of his contemporaries is more than offset by the truth of the cause in which he was engaged. His trial and conviction were unnecessary, and his early death might have been postponed. If we call him a rebel, we must call him an honest rebel and one who sought only what seemed to him the true welfare of the people. If we condemn him for what he did, we must praise him for what he meant to do. And, after all, Thomas Wilson Dorr, though he never realized it, did bring a people's government to the people of Rhode Island.

AUTHORITIES.—**1** *Rhode Island Acts and Resolves*, January, 1845, p. 59. **2** *Rhode Island Manual*, 1896–97, 102. **3** *Rhode Island Acts and Resolves*, June, 1845, p. 11. **4** *Rhode Island Manual*, 1896–97, 102. The same year a United States Senator was chosen. Thomas Wilson Dorr was given the complimentary vote of the minority, receiving thirty-four votes out of a total of ninety-eight. *Rhode Island Manual*, 1896–97, 141. **5** *Rhode Island Manual*, 1896–97, 103. **6** *Rhode Island Manual*, 1896–97, 130. **7** *Rhode Island Acts and Resolves*, January, 1854, p. 249. **8** *Providence Journal*, March 1, 1834. **9** *Providence Journal*, May 24, 1842. **10** *Burke's Report: Trial of Dorr*, 967. **11** Potter, *Considerations*, 5, note. **12** *Republican Herald*, November 5, 1834. **13** *Providence Journal*, April 13, 1840. **14** Goodell, *Rights and Wrongs of Rhode Island*, 35. **15** *Rhode Island Manual*, 1896–97, 160. **16** *Providence Journal*, March 1, 1841. **17** *Providence Journal*, July 24, 1840. **18** Pitman, *Trial of Dorr*, 92. **19** Turner, *Trial of Dorr*, 36: Testimony of Walter S. Burges.

CHAPTER XXI.

CONGRESSIONAL INTERFERENCE.

WHEN Senator Allen, of Ohio, permitted his resolutions on Rhode Island matters to be placed on the calendar for "Monday week," which day happened to be July 4th, 1842,[1] the Rhode Island question was dead, so far as the United States Senate was concerned. The House of Representatives apparently cared little about the dual governments, for in neither session of the twenty-seventh Congress do we find any other official reference to the affairs in Rhode Island.

The governments of other States, far as well as near, were, however, greatly concerned. Naturally the most interested States were those of New England. When Governor Dorr sent his begging letter to Governor Fairfield, of Maine,[2] that executive immediately sent a message to the State legislature, as requested by the People's Governor. A caucus of the dominant party was held, in which resolutions were adopted sympathizing with the people's government.[3] However, before the party had an opportunity to put the legislature on record, news arrived of the attack on the arsenal, of Dorr's flight, and of the reported compromise. Accordingly the legislature referred the matter to a committee, which brought in two reports early in June: the majority, believing "that the long-existing difficulties concerning the nature of the State governments were, happily, about to be settled in an amicable manner," declared that it afforded them "lively satisfaction to learn that the contest had ended in the promised establishment of free suffrage;" on the other hand, the minority resolved "that a revolution by force of arms can be justified only by its necessity, as the last resort of the people in their efforts to throw off oppressive and intolerable government, and that no such necessity exists in the free States of this Union."(4)

When the New Hampshire legislature met, early in June, 1842, Governor Hubbard, later known as a friend and protector of Governor Dorr, sent in his annual address. In this he referred to the fact that there had "been, of late, in one of the States of the Union, a controversy of a most extraordinary character, involving the right of the people to self-government."(5) Soon, however, the final flight took place, and the position of the State of New Hampshire is shown only by the attitude of the Governor and the resolution passed by the State convention that renominated Governor Hubbard: "*Resolved* that the General Government has no right to interfere in any political controversy between different portions of the people of a State, in which the question of Sovereignty is in issue; and that John Tyler, the acting President of the United States, by interfering with and deciding the question of sovereignty pending between the two parties in Rhode Island, has been guilty of a wanton and flagrant act of usurpation, for which he deserves impeachment and expulsion from office."(6)

The Vermont Democratic State Convention expressed its views even earlier than that of New Hampshire. It resolved "That we believe in the right of a majority of the people of Rhode Island to change their form of Government from a King's Charter to a

Republican Constitution, and cordially sympathize with them in their attempts to do so; and while we would encourage them to persevere, we cannot but condemn the action of the present Executive and those members of his cabinet who are his advisers in the course he has adopted in ordering an armed force to that State to overawe the people in the exercise of the inalienable rights and privileges guaranteed to them by the Constitution of the United States."(7)

Massachusetts was in the hands of the Whigs in 1842; Governor Davis agreed to honor Governor King's requisition; and, in fact, the Old Bay State practically gave the charter government something more than sympathy. At the next election, however, Governor Davis received one less vote than his opponent, and Governor Morton did not hesitate to uphold the principles upon which the people's party was acting; he did not, however, approve the use of force.

In Connecticut, the legislature showed an interest in her neighbor early in the controversy. On the tenth of May, a resolution was introduced in the House of Representatives to appoint a joint committee of the two houses "to inquire into the expediency of offering the mediation of this State in settling the difficulties existing in our sister State, Rhode Island, under the present 'gestion of affairs.'"(8) This resolution passed the House, but the matter went no farther.

These illustrations show, at least, that the trouble in Rhode Island was attracting general attention. Governor Dorr's failure, and the adoption of the new liberal constitution, however, appeared to end the controversy, and interest in the "Affairs of Rhode Island" quieted down. Some months later, however, the subject was reviewed in the national legislature as a partisan affair, begun with a memorial to Congress from the Democratic members of the Rhode Island General Assembly. To understand the circumstances, we must note the condition of politics in the State during the year 1843.

In October, 1842, the *Journal* showed that the Democrats were beginning to take up the suffrage movement as a party measure, by a labored article designed to prove that that party did not uphold Dorr. It stated that a majority of the State Senate, elected in accordance with the charter in April, 1842, were Democrats; that but four towns gave a majority against King for Governor, at the same election, two of these being Whig and two Democratic; and that while eleven towns voted for the Freemen's Constitution and eight against it, nine Democratic towns voted for it to three against.[9] In November, the *Journal* again tried to show that the Rhode Island Democrats were not Dorrites, by claiming that the call, just issued, for a Democratic convention was made without the approval of the Democratic party; that the most prominent men in that party knew nothing of it and would have nothing to do with it.[10] While there is a measure of truth in this statement, it is only partially true. Many of the leading Democrats had joined the law and order party, and therefore had no interest in this convention; while some others, seeing the strong movement in the party towards Dorrism, held aloof for the time. Yet the names of the delegates to this convention were well known in Democratic annals, and seven of the nine members of the State Central Committee, chosen by this convention, were among the most prominent delegates to the Democratic State convention held in January, 1840.[a]

---

[a] Compare account of the Democratic Republican State Convention in *Republican Herald*, January 18, 1840, with that of the Democratic State Convention, December 20, 1842, given in *Burke's Report*, 239–245. It is interesting to note that at least six members of the committee of nine, and twenty-five of the thirty-six members of the full State committee are recorded as voting for the People's Constitution.

The platform adopted by this convention upheld the national Democratic party, and denounced the Whigs and Henry Clay; but most of the planks referred to domestic matters. The resolutions affirmed "the right of the people" to institute government and to "make or alter the fundamental law at any time" in any way; they criticised the new constitution, but advised the members of the party to register and vote under it; affirming that "in recommending this course and in order to avoid all doubt or misconstruction of [their] purposes, [they] explicitly avowed [their] object to be, to accomplish in a satisfactory manner, and with the least delay, the establishment in fact, as well as in right, of the People's Constitution."(11)

How this result was to be reached was not announced, but it was evident that the upholders of the People's Constitution proposed to make a strong effort to carry the State, under the liberal suffrage of the new constitution. The election took place in April, 1843, and resulted in a good majority for the law and order party. Governor Fenner received 9,100 votes to 7,300 cast for Thomas F. Carpenter.(12) The Senate stood about twenty-two law and order men to seven Democrats (or Dorrites), and the House forty-eight to nineteen.(b) In the words of Governor Dorr, "the suffrage men of Rhode Island seemed to hesitate in employing the ballot-box at the vitally important election of April, 1843, as they had before hesitated to employ the cartridge-box when force had become indispensable to the safety of their cause. Through desertions they

(b) *Providence Journal.* All the Democratic members chosen were from Providence county, the towns of Burrillville, Glocester, Smithfield, Cumberland, North Providence, Cranston, and Johnston giving a majority against the government. From Providence county seven Dorrite Senators were returned to three law and order men, and in the House the county was represented by nineteen Democrats out of thirty-five. The county gave seven hundred more votes to Carpenter than to Fenner, though Providence city furnished a majority of four hundred the other way.

were overthrown at this election."[13] However strong the suffrage party had been, however many desertions occurred at this time, one fact is fixed—the party did not poll a majority of the votes cast, much less of "The People."

Another winter came, and the people of Rhode Island were evidently becoming satisfied with the new constitution. The Democratic minority had been able to accomplish nothing in the General Assembly; everything foretold an easy victory for the law and order party in April, 1844. In fact, the Democratic case seemed so desperate that no State ticket was nominated,[14] and when the election came, but two hundred scattering votes were cast against the reelection of Governor Fenner,[15] while the law and order majority in joint session of the two houses was sixty.[16] With this prospect before them the Democratic members of the legislature appealed to Congress.

THOMAS F. CARPENTER.

This Democratic minority consisted of the seven Senators and eighteen Representatives from seven towns in Providence county, and the Senator from Jamestown, in Newport county. Each of these Representatives is recorded as having voted for the People's Constitution, and the names of five of the Senators are also found in the printed lists.[c] The minority of the legislature, therefore, was nearly, if not quite, unanimously Dorrite from the beginning.

The memorial dated February 1, 1844, after affirming the adoption of the People's Constitution, declared the belief of the signers that the President of the United States, by his interference in the affairs of Rhode Island, caused the overthrow of the People's Constitution and government. The request was made that the National House of Representatives inquire whether the President had any such power of interfering in the "internal affairs of a sovereign State;" and whether the present members of the House from Rhode Island were entitled to their seats. The memorial finally requested "the Congress of the United States to execute to [Rhode Island] the guaranty in the National Constitution, of a Republican Constitution, *in favor of that which was rightfully and duly adopted in [Rhode Island] in December, 1841, and established and carried into effect by the organization of a government under it in May, 1842.*[17]

Representative Burke, of New Hampshire, presented the memorial to the House of Representatives, February 19.[18] It was ordered printed, and, by a vote of 103 to 69, referred to a select committee of five, consisting of Burke, Rathbun, of New York; Causin, of Maryland; McClernand, of Illinois; and Preston, of Maryland. The Rhode Island Representatives, Henry Y. Cranston and Elisha R. Potter, demanded an opportunity for discussion, as they claimed that the memorial was full of misrepresentations, but debate was refused by a vote of 144 to 35.

After two fruitless sessions, the committee, March 7, voted to ask authority to send for persons and papers, and to recommend to

---

[c] The Senators from Burrillville, Johnston, and Cranston are not so recorded.

the House of Representatives to request the President of the United States to furnish copies of all papers and documents in his possession relating to the Rhode Island controversy.[19] The same day, in the House, Mr. Burke requested power to send for persons and papers, and was met by an amendment, offered by Mr. Causin, a member of the select committee, discharging the committee from further service.[20] After eleven days consumed in speeches by Representatives Cranston, of Rhode Island; Rathbun, of New York; Potter, of Rhode Island; Kennedy, of Indiana; Caleb Smith, of Indiana; McClernand, of Illinois; and Stetson, of New York, Causin's amendment was defeated by a vote of 70 to 86, and Burke's resolution was adopted, 78 to 71.[21] March 23d, the resolution requesting information from the President was passed.[d]

The committee held seventeen sessions,[22] the last six of which were spent in listening to the report drawn up by the chairman. At the other sessions, Welcome B. Sayles, John S. Harris, Aaron White, Colonel Bankhead, and Captain Vinton were examined, and

[d] *Congressional Globe*, I Sess., 28 Cong., 1843-44, Vol. XIII, p. 426. In these resolutions the President was requested to lay before the House "the authority and the true copies of all requests and applications upon which he deemed it his duty to interfere with the naval and military forces of the United States, on the occasion of the recent attempt of the people of Rhode Island to establish a free constitution in the place of the old charter government of that State; also, copies of the correspondence between the Executive of the United States and the charter government of the State of Rhode Island, and all the papers and documents connected with the same; also, copies of the instructions to, and statements of, the charter commissioners sent to him by the then existing authorities of State of Rhode Island; also, copies of the correspondence, if any, between the heads of departments and said charter government, or any person or persons connected with said government, and of any accompanying papers and documents; also, copies of all orders issued by the Executive of the United States, or any of the departments, to military officers, for the movement or employment of troops to or in Rhode Island; also, copies of all orders to naval officers to prepare steam or other vessels of the United States for service in the waters of Rhode Island; also, copies of all orders to the officers of revenue cutters for the same service; also, copies of any instructions borne by the Secretary of War to Rhode Island, on his visit in 1842, to review the troops of the charter government; also, copies of any order or orders to any officer or officers of the army or navy to report themselves to the charter government; and that he be requested to lay before this House copies of any other papers or documents in the possession of the Executive connected with this subject, not above specifically enumerated."

the votes cast for the People's Constitution were counted. Benjamin F. Hallett was authorized to obtain depositions of witnesses examined in relation to the trouble in Rhode Island. June 3, 1844, the report, as prepared by Mr. Burke, was adopted, Burke, Rathbun, and McClernand voting for it; Causin and Preston were absent. Later, Mr. Causin presented to the House a minority report.

Meanwhile, April 10, the House received the reply of the President and referred it to the select committee.[(e)] Mr. Burke presented to the House the petition of Henry J. Duff and 175 others, naturalized citizens of Rhode Island, representing that they were deprived of their proper privileges as citizens of the United States,[(23)] and also the petition of certain citizens of Indiana, praying Congress to inquire into alleged abuses practiced by the Rhode Island charter party.[(24)] Mr. Cranston presented a protest from the General Assembly of Rhode Island against the right of the Congress to inquire whether the late charter government of the State had been republican in form or not; against the right of Congress to inquire whether the People's Constitution or the existing constitution was the lawful constitution of the State; and against the doing by Congress of anything that would tend to cause trouble again in Rhode Island.[(25)]

June 7, 1844, Burke's report was read to the House and post-

[(e)] *Congressional Globe*, I Sess., 28 Cong., 1843–44, Vol. XIII, p. 504. In this reply, President Tyler said: "I have to inform the House that the Executive did not 'deem it his duty to interfere with the naval and military forces of the United States,' in the late disturbances in Rhode Island; that no orders were issued by the Executive, or any of the departments, to military officers, for the movement or employment of troops to or in Rhode Island, other than those which accompany this message, and which contemplated the strengthening of the garrison at Fort Adams, which, considering the extent of the agitation in Rhode Island, was esteemed necessary and judicious; that no orders were issued to naval officers to prepare steam or other vessels of the United States for service in the waters of Rhode Island; that no orders were issued 'to the officers of the revenue-cutters for said service;' that no instructions were borne by 'the Secretary of War to Rhode Island, on his visit in 1842 *to review the troops of the charter government;*' that no orders were given to any officer or officers of the army or navy to report themselves to the charter government."

TYRANTS PROSTRATE LIBERTY TRIUMPHANT.

poned until the first Monday in December;[26] and not till January 2, 1845, by a test vote of 102 to 80, was it resolved to print 5,000 extra copies.[27] Then began a discussion on the report, participated in by Burke, Elmer, of New Jersey, and Williams, of Massachusetts, which was completed on the 28th of February.[28] Four days later, the twenty-eighth Congress expired; John Tyler retired to private life, James K. Polk became President, and Rhode Island was at last left to herself.

Burke's Report was elaborate, there being eighty-six pages of formal reports and nearly a thousand more pages of documents, depositions, and other testimony. Unfortunately for the student of Rhode Island history, the evidence herein furnished is not impartial. The testimony of five witnesses, together with the documents which they furnished to the committee, the depositions of fifty persons, copies of the indictments of thirteen men, the documents prepared for the case of Luther *vs.* Borden, the correspondence furnished by the President, and a few other documents, fill the large volume. Not one of the witnesses belonged to the charter party or was an anti-Dorrite; nor was a single document, deposition, or testimony presented on that side of the case. This was due to two things: the committee was interested merely in obtaining a partisan advantage from the publication of the Dorrite side of the struggle; and the law and order authorities, having sure possession of the government, refused to present any testimony, on the ground that Congress had no right to make the investigation.

The brief narrative of the work of the select committee and the proceedings of the House of Representatives given above shows clearly that the investigation was undertaken for purely party reasons. The investigation had barely begun when the nearly unanimous re-election of Governor Fenner occurred in Rhode Island.

Congress knew, beyond a doubt, that the people of Rhode Island, as a whole, were contented with the existing situation; it knew that no result could be obtained from an investigation. The presidential campaign was about to open; the President, whose "interference" the committee was to investigate, had lost favor with his own party and was bidding for a nomination, not by the Whigs, but by his former enemies, the Democrats. What better campaign document could the Democrats ask than a Dorrite account of the Rhode Island controversy. With it they could attack the Whigs everywhere, and President Tyler in particular: they had no love for him.

The whole course of the discussion shows that the party and the select committee had no idea of helping the malcontents in Rhode Island, but rather of promoting their own cause in the coming election. It was Burke himself who moved the postponement of the discussion on the report from June to December. As soon as the House voted to print a second edition, the matter practically dropped; the resolutions which closed the report were under discussion for two days only. That good should come to the people of Rhode Island was a consideration too remote to occur to any one.

Let us briefly summarize the conclusions and proposed resolutions of this report. After an historical review of the happenings in Rhode Island, the committee proceeded to answer in the affirmative the question whether the People's Constitution was adopted by a majority of the adult citizens of Rhode Island. They gave four reasons for coming to this conclusion: first, they had examined the votes and found them as represented, and therefore they were "strong *prima facie* evidence" of the adoption; second, the rejection of the Freemen's Constitution was an indication that a majority of the people were in favor of the People's Constitution;

third, the existing constitution did not receive a majority of the votes of the citizens of Rhode Island; and, fourth, the charter authorities persistently refused to make any investigation into the legality of the vote.

After a long discussion of authorities, the report reached the conclusion that "the sovereign power of the State [resided] in the people of the State," and that the majority of the people could, "in any manner, and at such time as they [deemed] expedient, without the consent of existing authorities, and even against an express provision of a constitution once agreed to by them pointing out the mode," change their form of government. It then debated the question "who are the people?" and decided that the right of suffrage was a *natural* right; that it belonged to all men, though not to women nor to boys under the arbitrary age of twenty-one; and that the "people [included] all *free white male persons* of the age of twenty-one years, who are *citizens* of the State, are of sound mind, and have not forfeited their right by some crime."

The committee next examined into the actions of the President, and showed conclusively, as they seemed to think, that he did intervene with the military power of the Union, and did thereby suppress the People's Constitution. The report, after stating the case against the President, closed the point with the words: "The committee submit to the House and the country to compare the facts with the President's assertion, and to draw the inference." Next the report discussed the power of Congress in respect to the matter of the memorial, and concluded that Congress had the power to set aside a State constitution which did not provide a republican form of government, and to recognize one that did so provide. The committee, however, did not recommend any action by the

House with regard to the constitution of the State of Rhode Island, inasmuch as more than a majority of the *free white male citizens*, etc., of the State, voted at the first election held under the existing constitution. It did recommend that Congress should pass some law, " with a view to meet emergencies like that which [had] occurred in the State of Rhode Island."

The report showed, by reference to a long list of instances, the tyranny and despotism of the charter authorities, and concluded by presenting a set of seven resolutions: affirming the equality of all free men; the right to alter their government at will; the right of the people of Rhode Island to form a constitution in their own way; the adoption of the People's Constitution, and that all acts done under it were legal until the people assented to the new constitution; condemning the President of the United States for his unauthorized interference; and criticising the actions of nine men in Rhode Island for personally entering into the local controversy while holding office under the federal government.

Such was the somewhile famous report and such its fate. No one desired its adoption by the House, and it died with the House that appointed the committee. The printed volume continued to live, however, and the thousands of copies, scattered far and wide, were so many pieces of political capital. The controversies and ill-feelings due to the trouble in Rhode Island have long since passed away, and *Burke's Report* has been forgotten. It is unfortunate, however, that an historical document of so one-sided a nature should be the only original source of record on this subject which is at all accessible to the student of American history to-day.

AUTHORITIES.—**1** See p. 203. **2** *Providence Journal*, June 2, 1842; *Providence Express*, June 2, 1842. **3** *Providence Journal*, May 28, 1842. **4** *Providence Express*, June 15, 1842.

5 *Providence Express*, June 7, 1842; *Republican Herald*, June 8, 1842. **6** *National Intelligencer*, June 18, 1842. **7** *Republican Herald*, May 25, 1842. **8** *New York Courier and Enquirer*, May 10, 1842; *Providence Journal*, May 11, 1842. **9** *Providence Journal*, October 5, 1842. **10** *Providence Journal*, November 15, 1842. **11** *Burke's Report*, 241-244. **12** *Rhode Island Manual*, 1896-97, 102. **13** Turner, *Trial of Dorr*, 77. **14** *Republican Herald*, April 6, 1844. **15** *Rhode Island Manual*, 1896-97, 102. **16** *Providence Journal*, April 5, 1844. **17** This memorial is given in *Burke's Report*, 1-4. **18** *Congressional Globe*, I Sess., 28 Cong., 1843-44, Vol. XII, p. 295; *House Journal*, I Sess., 28 Cong., 1843-44, pp. 419-421. **19** *Burke's Report*, 87. **20** *Congressional Globe*, I Sess., 28 Cong., 1843-44, Vol. XIII, p 356. **21** *Congressional Globe*, I Sess., 28 Cong., 1843-44, Vol. XIII, p. 419. **22** *Burke's Report*, 87-92. **23** *Congressional Globe*, I Sess., 28 Cong., 1843-44, Vol. XIII, p. 464. **24** *Burke's Report*, 91. **25** *Congressional Globe*, I Sess., 28 Cong., 1843-44, Vol. XIII, p. 522; *House Journal*, I Sess., 28 Cong., 1843-44, p. 795; *House Documents*, I Sess., 28 Cong., 1843-44, Vol. V, pp. 4, 5. **26** *Burke's Report*, 1. **27** *Congressional Globe*, II Sess., 28 Cong., 1844-45, Vol. XIV, p. 81. **28** *Congressional Globe*, II Sess., 28 Cong., 1844-45, Vol. XIV, p. 370.

CHAPTER XXII.

THE STRUGGLE ENDED.

STEP by step the conservative party had moved towards a liberal constitution, and the causes and result of their movement may here be briefly sketched. Early in 1841 the Smithfield memorial and the Dillingham petition led the General Assembly to issue a call for a convention to be held ten months later. The mass meetings and conventions in Providence and Newport during the spring of 1841 caused the legislature to rectify the apportionment of delegates to that convention. The continued suffrage agitation, the holding of the People's Convention, and the declared adoption of the People's Constitution resulted in the act of the General Assembly permitting such persons to vote on the adoption of the Freemen's Constitution as would be qualified to vote if that constitution were adopted.

" It may be even more difficult to adopt a constitution than it is to make one."(1) The Freemen's Constitution was defeated, March, 1842. Again the legislature met and discussed the constitutional issue: it decided to let the question go over to the next Assembly, which would meet the following week. The newly-elected body met at Newport, in May, only to find another legislature in session in Providence. This was not the time, evidently, to make any concessions; the contest was on. But the Foundry legislature collapsed; the attack on the arsenal failed. Now was the time to act; now was the time for the existing government to show that it understood the desires of the people. The anti-suffrage organ saw that it must make great concessions. It at once affirmed as its opinion that a new convention must be held, and that a new constitution was an absolute necessity.[2] It even ventured the assertion that a majority of each house of the legislature was of the same opinion; which statement was duly copied in the papers throughout the country.[3]

Accordingly, on the second day of the June session, 1842, a committee was appointed, consisting of two members from each county, to which all matters relating to an extension of the suffrage and the formation of a new constitution might be referred.[4] Petitions and memorials were coming in in great numbers. The committee reported an act calling a constitutional convention, which was adopted just before Governor Dorr appeared at Chepachet.[5] As has been stated, the three important points of this call were the new attempt to apportion the delegates from the various towns; the permission that all native males, of three years' residence, might vote for the delegates; and the direction that the persons qualified by the constitution which would be formed might also vote upon its adoption. At once, certain portions at least of the suffragists accepted the olive branch.[6] A note, signed by Dutee J. Pearce and five other members of the Foundry legislature, appeared, stating that the act, in most of its provisions, met with their cordial approbation, and would, as a whole, receive their support.[7] Other members of the suffrage party appeared in print, recommending the new convention. Even the *Express*, though just about to suspend publication because of martial law, in a leading editorial, advised its friends to render the convention their undivided support. "The late law of the General Assembly, containing in our opinions the substance of what we have even contended for, we heartily recommend its provisions to the candor of our friends."[(8)] This liberal disposition of the suffrage organ did not last, however.

A few days later the *Republican Herald*, which, now that the *Express* was suspended, considered itself the suffrage organ, began to criticise. It acknowledged that "the principles of the Suffrage Party [had] gained a signal triumph over the Charter party," but it advised the adherents of the People's Constitution to refrain from electing delegates, because of the unequal apportionment, the exclusion of naturalized citizens and new-comers from voting, and the "reign of martial law."[(9)] Three days later the *Herald* was emphatic in its condemnation of the act, which it claimed had been "artfully formed to perpetuate power in the hands of the few, to rule with arbitrary sway, over the many." It added that "participating in the approaching election of delegates" would virtually condemn them "for having voted for the suffrage constitution."[(10)]

Martial law was suspended on the eighth of August, 1842; a wise, though late, step of the charter government. It was, however, a mistake merely to suspend it, for it gave the enemies of the government the opportunity to claim that the delegates to the convention, chosen at the regular town meetings in August, were elected under "the duress of military force and the menace of political persecution."[(11)] There were no opposition candidates to the regular law and order tickets, and a very light vote was cast. In the town of Glocester, on motion of Samuel Y. Atwell, who doubtless voiced the suffrage party, the people even voted, 77 to 53, not to elect delegates.[(12)] There is no way of obtaining the exact vote cast, but it was doubtless less than 7,000, or less than the gubernatorial vote at the previous election.[13]

The convention met at Newport, on the twelfth of September, with Henry Y. Cranston chairman and Thomas A. Jenckes clerk.[14] It referred the various subjects of which a constitution treats to sub-committees, and awaited their reports. Naturally the friends of the People's Constitution not only held aloof, but were very free with their criticisms. The *Herald* was rabid in its opposition. It declared that it doubted if an instrument would be framed that could be approved. The delegates, it said, "are not the men to establish the rights of the people on a liberal and permanent foundation."[15] The *Express*, on its re-appearance, began more gently: it even acknowledged that there were "liberal sentiments among many of the members which [were] ably advanced and [were] entitled to the respect even of the suffrage men."[16] The next day the *Express* stated that the committee on suffrage had reported a fair and liberal article; though it had no hope that the convention would not radically change it.[17] Doubtless this did not please the suffrage leaders, for the next day the *Express* reconsidered. "On more carefully perusing the report of the committee on Suffrage we find reason to retract our approbation of its liberality, which was bestowed on a hasty glance."[18]

Before the end of September the convention had finished a draft of a constitution and adjourned to November, to allow the delegates to ascertain whether their constituents desired changes.[19] The proposed constitution was published in the newspapers.[20] The *Express* declared that it printed it in order merely that the people's party might compare its provisions with those of their own existing constitution; they would thereby be confirmed in their opinion that the new plan was inferior and would cling to their own, which was still the fundamental law of the State. The convention re-assembled, adopted the constitution, and submitted it to the people, appointing the twenty-first, twenty-second, and twenty-third days of November, 1842, for the election.

One of the reasons for the adjournment was a clause in the fourth section of the call for the convention, reading: "If said constitution be adopted by a majority of the persons having a right to vote, the same shall go into operation."(21) It was evident that the General Assembly did not literally mean what it said in that clause; therefore the convention, in the following resolution, decided to ask the legislature to interpret it officially:

"Whereas, from the manifest impracticability of ascertaining the precise number of persons that might have a right to vote on the adoption of any constitution to be submitted for adoption under the provisions of the act calling this convention, it is inferrible that it is the true intent of said act that none but those actually voting should be counted; and whereas there is an ambiguity in said act in this particular: Therefore,

"*Resolved*, That the General Assembly be requested to pass such declaratory law as may be deemed necessary for the plainer expression of the intent and meaning of the act aforesaid."(22)

Accordingly a declaratory act was passed, at the October session of the legislature, in accordance with the request of the convention.(23) During the fortnight which elapsed between the day of the adoption of the constitution by the convention and the days set for the voting by the people, the entire community watched the attitude of the suffrage, or Dorrite, leaders. Those voters who upheld the People's Constitution as still the fundamental law of the State must, logically, either refrain from voting on the proposed document or vote against it. The leaders adopted the former course: Governor Dorr wrote from New Hampshire, advising this step, and editorials in the suffrage newspapers recommended such action. The *Express* gave as its opinion that every member of the suffrage party would stay at home on election day.[24]

Why this decision was made is not clear. According to their own doctrines, if this constitution received the votes of a majority of "the people," it would supersede the People's Constitution. They could not deny the right of the people to propose a new constitution, or to vote for or against its adoption. They had defeated one constitution by their votes in the previous spring; might they not expect to accomplish the same result now by voting against this new proposition? No sufficient reason is apparent for bidding the suffragists not to vote, rather than for advising them to vote and to vote "No." One is led to wonder if the *Journal* may not have spoken wisely when it declared that the "Dorr men dare not come out against the constitution, because they know that, by doing so, they would show their own weakness."[25] Is it not possible that they remembered the falling off of their vote from December to March, and that they did not care now to stand up and be counted? At least, we may say that the result proved their decision unwise: they threw away one of the remaining chances of showing themselves to be a majority of the people.

Although the opposition refrained from voting, the constitution was adopted by a vote of 7,032 to 59.[26] January 13th, 1843, the General Assembly counted the votes cast at the November election, and gave official announcement that the constitution was adopted. At the same time the legislature passed an act, carefully regulating the election laws so as to adapt them to the new regime.[27]

The constitution of 1842, as it has been called, was closely patterned after the Freemen's Constitution. One-half of the sections in the two constitutions were identical, even in the wording. One-half of the remaining sections convey practically the same ideas, though slightly changed in form or words. Two sections of the Freemen's Constitution are not to be found in that of 1842: one ordering that a sixth part of every direct tax should be laid upon polls; the other continuing the Court of Probate until provided for by the legislature. Three sections appear in the later constitution that are doubtless due to the agitation of the summer of 1842: one of these provided for referring all acts creating corporations or military and fire companies to the next legislature; the other two expressed the conservative view of governments and constitutions, as opposed to the opinions of the upholders of the People's Constitution.(28) Slight changes were made in six other clauses: martial law was restricted to cases of necessity;(29) the salaries of Senators and Representatives were fixed;(30) a vote of two-thirds of the members of the House was required to impeach the Governor;(31) the Secretary of State should administer the oath to the Governor, instead of the Speaker of the House;(32) members of a school committee need not be qualified electors;(33) and the Supreme Court judges were directed to give their written opinion on any question of law, if requested by the Governor or either House.(34)

The fundamental differences in the two constitutions lay in the sections relating to suffrage and the apportionment of Senators and Representatives. By the later constitution each town was entitled to one Senator, and one only.(35) This was evidently a bid for the vote of the smaller towns, and was an acknowledgment that a town had rights irrespective of its population. The apportionment of Representatives was more nearly in proportion to the population than had been previously proposed by any responsible body. The House was to consist of seventy-two members, divided proportionately among the towns in accordance with the population as shown in each census. There was one limitation on the principle: no city or town was to be allowed more than twelve Representatives, or one-sixth of the entire membership.[36] Considering the jealousy between the city and the rural communities, considering the absolute chaos of views as to apportionment that we have found in Rhode Island in the "forties," we must conclude that the convention of 1842 deserves to be complimented on the happy issue of this dispute, which had been a cause of trouble for several decades.

The suffrage qualifications, by the Freemen's Convention, distinguished naturalized citizens owning the necessary real estate from native-born citizens by requiring three years' residence instead of one; by the new constitution, one year's residence suffices for both classes.[37] The two constitutions agreed in giving the right to vote to native male citizens who did not own real estate, if they had had two years' residence.[38] Herein they were more conservative than the People's Constitution, which placed the necessary residence at one year and opened the suffrage also to naturalized non-property owners. All three constitutions agreed in not permitting any but real estate owners and tax-payers to vote on matters relating to taxation or the expenditure of public moneys. The constitution of 1842 added a new requirement, in the shape of a dollar registry tax, upon all non-tax-payers who should present themselves to be registered, exempting persons who had performed military service during the preceding year.[39]

To what extent had the most radical suffragists, who were content with the People's Constitution, the right to criticise such a constitution? They limited their opposition to the two subjects of apportionment and suffrage. The apportionment would seem to-day to be far more just than that provided in their own constitution. In the matter of suffrage they had some ground for complaint from their point of view: a few persons, those who had been in the State twelve but not twenty-four months, and naturalized citizens not owning real estate, were still deprived of the privilege of voting. The first exclusion was of but little account; the second was calculated to give power to the rural communities, in which the suffragists were strong, inasmuch as foreigners, naturalized or unnaturalized, flocked to the cities and large villages. The suffragists also objected to the registry tax: all that need be said is that the tax was not compulsory, and that opinions still differ upon its advisability.

On only one legitimate ground could the people's party vote against the constitution of 1842 or refrain from voting—on the ground that they should still uphold the People's Constitution, no matter what the result to the State; they had no sufficient objections to the document itself. When the constitution was adopted by an almost unanimous vote of those who went to the polls, the question came, what should the people's party do next? They had ignored the election, and had not put themselves on record against the constitution. They did not hesitate to declare, however, that it did not replace their own constitution, inasmuch as it had not received the votes of a majority of the people.[40]

Yet they saw clearly that the constitution of 1842 was to be the *de facto* fundamental law of the State. They realized that the People's Constitution, whatever it might be *de jure*, was practically null and void. The only possible future for it lay in reviving it in accordance with the ordinary forms of law. They claimed to be a majority of the people; by the provisions of the new constitution, nearly all the people could vote; there was a chance open to them of obtaining control of the government at the polls. Therefore the suffrage leaders advised their followers to register,[41] and the Democratic Convention, as we have seen, fell into line.[42] Perhaps they were inconsistent, but the voters, of all political beliefs, followed the advice, and at the April election 16,520 votes were cast for Governor, nearly twice as many as had been ever given before; and the gubernatorial vote of 1843 was not equalled, in later years, until 1852.[43]

It would be unjust to use these figures as proofs of any one thing, except that a majority of those voting preferred the election of Governor Fenner. The claim that the Fenner vote represented the anti-suffragists, or the anti-Dorrites, and that the Carpenter vote stood for the suffrage, or people's, party, cannot be substantiated. Governor Dorr's suggestion, already quoted,[45] that the people would have won at this election had not some been timid and had deserted at the last moment, is untenable. The nine thousand votes for the law and order candidate cannot be lumped together. Many who cast their votes for Fenner did so because he represented the law and order party and would oppose what they considered the anarchical methods of the opposition; but some were still advocates of the old charter; some had deserted the people's party for the sake of quiet and peace; some were satisfied to continue the administration in power another year; while a large portion were too partisan Whigs to vote a ticket prepared by the Democrats. On the other hand, though many of the seven thousand voters for Carpenter were Dorrites of the ultra stamp, there were also among them many who voted for "the regular Democratic ticket;" some who were constitutionally opposed to the existing government; and some who wished to voice their criticisms of the treatment by the charter government of its enemies after the abandonment of Acote's Hill.

The last General Assembly under the charter was in session on the first day of May, 1843. In grand committee, on that day, it appointed a committee to "be present at and witness the organization of the government under the *constitution* adopted by the people of this State in November last;" and directed them to report as soon as the organization was completed "in conformity to the provisions of said constitution;" in order that they might know when their "functions should have constitutionally passed into the hands of those who have been legally chosen by the people to receive and execute the same."(46) The committee reported on the next day that they had attended to their duty; that the Senate and House of Representatives under the constitution had, that day, been duly organized; and that the "powers of the government as organized under the charter had ceased." Thereupon the grand committee resolved "that the Report be accepted and that the General Assembly be and the same is hereby dissolved."

Thus, on May 2, 1843, after an honored existence of one hundred and eighty years, the charter of King Charles the Second ceased to be the fundamental law of the State of Rhode Island and Providence Plantations. After an intermittent struggle of nearly two-thirds of a century and a violent contest of more than two years, including an armed rebellion of two months, the people of the State replaced the time-worn royal charter by a constitution modeled upon a more modern pattern. Twice the voters had vetoed the call for a constitutional convention; once a convention had labored in vain to prepare a constitution; twice constitutions prepared by conventions had been defeated. Once a constitution, framed in direct opposition to the existing government, declared to be adopted by its framers, under which a full State government had been chosen and a legislature organized, and for the support of which civil war had been undertaken, had failed *de facto* because of the irregular and non-legal method of adoption, the timid character of the revolutionists, and the failure of their arms; and it was destined to be refused the recognition of the legislative and judicial departments, as well as the executive branch, of the national government. After all these failures, a constitution was obtained, which, while it did not receive an affirmative vote of a majority of "the people" upon its adoption, was accepted by a large majority, as is shown by the vote in April, which was cast by fully two-thirds of the possible voters of the State.

Under this constitution the people of Rhode Island have since lived and prospered for more than fifty-five years. Amendments have been adopted, from time to time, slightly modifying its provisions. Since 1854 the General Assembly has been freed from the necessity of counting the votes, and has not been required to hold sessions in more than two places. In the same year an amendment was adopted, giving the power of pardon to the Governor, by and with the advice and consent of the Senate. Forty-six years after the Dorrite suffragists vainly demanded equal suffrage rights for native-born and naturalized citizens, an amendment to that purport was adopted. In 1893 plurality elections were substituted for majority elections in all cases.

Three or four attempts have been made to replace the constitution by a more modern document, but each has failed. In 1853 the voters were twice asked to call a convention to "frame a new constitution," and to "revise the constitution," but they refused by votes of 4,570 to 6,282, and 3,778 to 7,618.[47] After an interval of about forty years the proposition of a new constitution was again broached. The method of amendment provided by the constitution of 1842 seemed too complicated to many citizens of Rhode Island,

and for a time the old question of constitution-making came to the front. Arguments for and against the power of a convention to frame a constitution without regard to the existing fundamental law appeared in the newspapers, and a pamphlet war was begun. Soon, however, the matter quieted down, and the constitution, as a whole, remained undisturbed for a dozen years.

In January, 1897, the General Assembly created a commission of fifteen persons to revise the constitution of the State and report such revision to the Assembly, as a preliminary to its submission to the voters as an amendment.[(48)] In January, 1898, the commission reported a revised constitution, which was unanimously approved by the legislature. A new Assembly was chosen in April, which again approved the document, with few dissenting votes, and submitted it to the people. The electors voted on the adoption at the congressional election, November 8th, 1898, and failed to ratify it: though the affirmative vote greatly exceeded the negative, it fell short of the necessary three-fifths more than a thousand.

The important changes proposed in this revision were few. The required residence of all classes of voters was put at one year; ability to read and write was to be required of all future new voters; the number of Representatives was to be increased from seventy-two to one hundred, and Providence to be allowed one-quarter (twenty-five) instead of one-sixth (twelve); towns and cities were to be divided into representative districts; the Governor was given more power, especially the veto, and was relieved from the duty of presiding over the Senate; biennial elections were to take the place of annual, and new provisions were made for amending the constitution.

In analyzing the vote of 1898, no one reason can be given for the defeat of the constitution. The vote was light, as it came at the relatively unimportant election of congressman. Four of the five cities favored the constitution, though Providence alone gave it the necessary three-fifths vote. This would seem to indicate an opposition, outside of the metropolis, to increasing its power in the Assembly. The southern part of the State showed the greatest opposition, and perhaps this also may be attributed to jealousy of Providence. As a rule, the most thinly-populated towns voted strongly against the proposed constitution: their interests are most unlike those of large cities. Doubtless the educational requirement for future voters was opposed by some, and probably the fact that the constitution was proposed by a Republican legislature made it objectionable to some Democrats. It is generally believed, however, that the principal trouble lay in the proposition for biennial elections. When it is remembered that up to 1843 semi-annual elections were held, and that up to the present time semi-annual sessions of the legislature are required, it is easy to understand why belief in the necessity for frequent elections is so strong. An earlier amendment authorizing biennial elections had been defeated.

One fact is evident from this vote. The old-time geographical divisions had little or no influence upon it. Some towns that persistently upheld Governor Dorr gave large majorities for this new constitution, while others as strongly opposed it. Burrillville gave more than the required three-fifths vote in its favor, while the old Smithfield gave a majority against it,[49] and Glocester was about evenly divided on the question. At any rate, we may accept the vote as showing that the civil war of 1842 is finally ended. The old parties are broken up; the old issues are at an end. The demands of Dorr and his friends are practically all granted, and "The Struggle for a Constitution in Rhode Island" has ended in the adoption of a constitution which, with its amendments, the people refuse to supersede even by one constructed by the leading talent of the State.

AUTHORITIES.—**1** *Providence Journal*, September 27, 1842. **2** See page 200. **3** *National Intelligencer*, June 2, 1842. **4** *Providence Journal*, June 22, 1842. **5** *Rhode Island Acts and Resolves*, June, 1842, pp. 3-5; *Burke's Report*, 444-446. **6** Wayland, *Discourse of July 21, 1842*, pp. 4, 5. **7** *Providence Journal*, June 27, 1842. **8** *Providence Express*, June 27, 1842. **9** *Republican Herald*, August 3, 1842. **10** *Republican Herald*, August 6, 1842. **11** *Burke's Report*, 21. **12** *Providence Journal*, September 1, 1842. **13** *Providence Journal*, September 14, 1842. **14** *Journal of the Constitutional Convention*, 1842. **15** *Republican Herald*, September 17, 1842. **16** *The New Age*, September 19, 1842. **17** *Providence Express*, September 19, 1842. **18** *Providence Express*, September 20, 1842. **19** *Providence Express*, October 1, 1842; *Republican Herald*, October 5, 1842. **20** *Providence Journal*, October 12, 1842; *Providence Express*, October 15, 1842. **21** *Burke's Report*, 445. **22** *Burke's Report*, 647. **23** *Rhode Island Acts and Resolves*, October, 1842, p. 42; *Burke's Report*, 648. **24** *Providence Express*, November 11, 1842. **25** *Providence Journal*, November 14, 1842. **26** *Rhode Island Manual*, 1896-97, p. 129. **27** *Rhode Island House Journals*, January 13, 1843; *Rhode Island Acts and Resolves*, January, 1843, pp. 9 and 36. **28** Article I, Sections 1 and 2: "Section 1. In the words of the Father of his country, we declare that 'the basis of our political systems is the right of the people to make and alter their constitutions of government; but that the constitution which at any time exists, till changed by an explicit and authentic act of the whole people, is sacredly obligatory upon all.' Section 2. All free governments are instituted for the protection, safety, and happiness of the people. All laws, therefore, should be made for the good of the whole; and the burdens of the State ought to be fairly distributed among its citizens." **29** Article I, Section 18. **30** Article IV, Section 11. **31** Article XI, Section 1. **32** Article IX, Section 5. **33** Article IX, Section 1. **34** Article X, Section 3. **35** Article VI, Section 1. **36** Article V, Section 1. **37** Article II, Section 1. **38** Article II, Section 2. **39** Article II, Section 3. **40** *Burke's Report*, 21. **41** *Providence Express*, December 29, 1842. **42** See page 278. **43** *Rhode Island Manual*, 1896-97, p. 102. **44** Though the law and order party was composed mainly of Whigs, it had a large quota of anti-Dorrite Democrats. When, therefore, the party nominated its candidates for general State officers, party lines were practically ignored. Of the five State officers, Governor James Fenner and Attorney-General Joseph M. Blake had been life-long Democrats; Lieutenant-Governor Byron Diman, Secretary of State Henry Bowen, and General Treasurer Stephen Cahoone were Whigs. **45** See page 279. **46** *Rhode Island Acts and Resolves*, May, 1843, pp. 3 and 4. **47** *Rhode Island Manual*, 1896-97, p. 130 **48** This commission, as appointed by Governor Henry Lippitt, consisted of Thomas Durfee, Chairman; Samuel W. K. Allen, Edward L. Freeman, William W. Blodgett, David S. Baker, Samuel Pomroy Colt, John H. Stiness, E. Charles Francis, Robert H. I. Goddard, Charles E. Gorman, Edwin D. McGuinness, Augustus S. Miller, William P. Sheffield, Jr., William B. Weeden, and Nathan F. Dixon. On the death of the last named, Ellery H. Wilson was appointed to take his place. The commission was remarkably representative and could not fail to carry great weight. The different political parties, Senators, Representatives, Mayors, Judges, Attorneys, Merchants, Manufacturers, Bankers, Economists, Historians, were all represented on the Board. The fact that these men could agree on a constitution ought to have had its influence upon the electors. **49** This town has been divided, since 1842, into five parts, but the statement in the text is true.

CHAPTER XXIII.

CONCLUSION.

IT remains to summarize the results of the Dorr rebellion, both in its effect upon the State of Rhode Island and in its relation to national and constitutional issues. Little did Dr. J. A. Brown realize, when he organized the State Suffrage Association and established the *New Age* at his own expense, in 1840, that within three years a civil war would take place in Rhode Island; that many of his friends would be indicted for high treason; and that he himself would be a fugitive from his native State and a resident of Delaware. Much less did he realize that he was inaugurating a strife which would bring to the front constitutional issues of as great import as had appeared at any time during the half century of the United States under the constitution.

What did the agitation accomplish? The end sought by Atwell, Carpenter, Pearce, and Dorr was a new and liberal constitution. Without the agitation, it is fair to say no such constitution could have been obtained. At no time, early in the contest, would the freemen have yielded so much to the suffragists. Whether the form of the movement be approved or not, it must be acknowledged that, almost entirely because of the agitation, the constitution which went into effect in May, 1843, was liberal and well adapted to the needs of the State.

"A revolution is the overthrow of one government and the substitution of another." Therefore the movement in Rhode Island would ordinarily be called an attempted revolution. No one can question the fact that the people's government, inaugurated in May, 1842, was a different government from that under the charter—that it was a new government intended to be substituted for another, which was considered thereby to have been overthrown. The question of importance in this connection is whether the revolution was or was not justifiable,

The change of character at about the middle of May, 1842, should not be overlooked. Before Governor Dorr returned from Washington and New York, the revolution was peaceful; after his return it became military. An armed revolution in Rhode Island in 1842 was manifestly unjustifiable. The people of that State were not oppressed to an extent sufficient to warrant them to take up arms to right their wrongs. From the minute that Governor Dorr appealed to arms the revolution became a mere rebellion. This movement to establish the people's government and to overthrow the existing government by force can have no upholders to-day.

That the peaceful revolution was unjustifiable is not so clearly apparent: a revolution which causes no loss of life and no bloodshed may be proper when an armed movement would be a crime. It may be urged that, inasmuch as the revolution produced a suitable constitution, which it had been impossible to obtain otherwise, the whole movement was defensible and right. But can it be proved that a liberal constitution might not have been obtained without going to such great lengths? Would not an agitation pure and simple have accomplished the purpose as well? Had the history of previous movements been such as to warrant the belief that nothing could be expected from the existing government?

The suffrage agitators, it has been seen, from the very beginning, ignored the charter government. The Smithfield memorial, the Dillingham petition, the various motions of Mr. Atwell in the House, were not the work of the suffrage leaders. They took it for granted that nothing could be obtained from the freemen or their representatives: they would not concede the possibility that agitation alone would accomplish anything. Herein they were in error. The Smithfield memorial started a legitimate movement: the suffrage processions led to a more liberal convention: the expression of opinion, shown by the attendance at the so-called town-meetings of the suffragists in December, caused the Assembly to open the suffrage in the vote on the Freemen's Constitution; and the liberal nature of this constitution was due to the agitation. Agitation, not revolution, was the proper course to take. It is evident that when the freemen saw that the people demanded recognition, and that the demand was something more than a passing desire, they conceded what was asked. Though the Freemen's Constitution was not all that was desired, yet its adoption would have been a long step forward, and all that the suffragists could legitimately expect. Other steps might well follow. The armed revolution was unnecessary: the peaceful revolution led to the use of force, and must inevitably do so. Agitation alone would have served the purpose; and it must be concluded that the peaceful revolution was unnecessary, and, therefore, unjustifiable.

The suffragists claimed, however, that the adoption of their constitution and the establishment of their government was not a revolution. "The people," they declared, "had the right, at any time, in any way, and on any occasion, to change their government."

While the Dorr rebellion cannot be said to have given a final decision on this question, it is certain that this struggle made plain that "the people" are the "organized people;" that a new constitution must be adopted in accordance with the forms of law; and that its adoption, if not strictly legal, must be held to be revolutionary.

"But," said the suffragists, "it would be revolutionary in a monarchical country; but in a democratic country, like the United States, it has become legal. Our declarations and conventions recognize the right of the people outside of all organizations, to act for themselves." The reply that came was clear and distinct: "Revolution is not to be regulated by law. This is an appeal against the law and the government. Allegiance to the government is violated by such non-legal proceedings and such violation is rebellion and treason." The upholders of the "legal right of revolution," if we can couple such words, were unable to make good their claim: the Rhode Island struggle ended by emphasizing the fact that an irregular exercise of sovereignty, like that of the suffrage movement of 1841 and 1842, could not be called legal, and was revolutionary.

Could not the civil strife resulting from this revolutionary movement have been avoided? Was there no authority to which the contesting parties might have appealed? Naturally, the thought turns to the national government. Could it be an arbiter in such State matters? If so, to which branch of the national government should an appeal be made? Having no precedents to guide them, each party appealed to the executive power of the Union, which was centered in an individual, and hence would work more swiftly than the other branches of the government. But the President would not take the position that he was "an armed arbitrator between the people of the different States and their constituted authorities." He could only "respect the requisitions of that government which had been recognized as the existing government of the State," until he had been "advised, in regular manner, that it had been altered and abolished, and another substituted in its place by legal and peaceable proceedings, adopted and pursued by the authorities and people of the State." Should it be necessary, he would use the national army and navy to quell any insurrection against a recognized government.

If the executive branch of the national government failed as an arbiter, could not the legislative branch be called upon? Congress had turned over to the President the power to give aid to the government of any State, and therefore it must be approached from some other side. Let the new government elect Representatives to Congress or choose a United States Senator at a fitting time: then, surely, the contest would be thrown into the national legislature. But the People's Government was too short lived to accomplish this result, and not until 1844 was any attempt made to bring the matter directly before the House of Representatives. The memorial from the minority of the General Assembly asked Congress to determine if the Rhode Island Representatives were entitled to their seats; to inquire if the President of the United States had the power to "interfere" in the affairs of Rhode Island; and to act as arbitrator "in favor" of that constitution and government which had not been in force for nearly two years, if it had ever had any real existence. The contest had become an old story long before this time, and the House of Representatives took no pains to make an official response. Had circumstances been different, it surely would seem as if Congress might easily be the higher authority to which such State disputes might be referred, provided that two sets of Representatives should be chosen by the respective contesting governments.

An appeal was also made to the national judiciary, only to be met by the reply that such matters were not within the province of the courts. "The power to determine that a State government has been lawfully established is not one of the powers which the courts of the United States possess." Neither was it one of the powers of the courts of the State itself. Not only was this doctrine affirmed by the Supreme Court of the State of Rhode Island, but that decision was ratified by the Supreme Court of the United States. The judiciary has no power to deal with political questions as such.

The federal judiciary, as well as the national executive, thus positively refused to act as arbitrator between rival State governments. The courts of the nation recognized the *de facto* government only; the President of the United States was prepared to put down rebellion against the authorities legally in power. The only arbitrator possible was the national legislature, and no proper request was made upon Congress to decide the matter.

Individual States, however, were ready with their advice. Legislatures and party conventions did not hesitate to denounce President and Governor alike. Mass meetings in the great cities hurled their anathemata at the freemen of Rhode Island. To the quiet citizen of to-day such an agitation seems strange. New York might be interested in a political contest in Rhode Island at the present time, but its legislature would hardly feel called upon to place itself on record for or against one of the contesting parties. In the days when the States were more ready than ever to stand up for their own rights as sovereign members of the Union, "interference" of other States in the affairs of Rhode Island was unusual and baneful. Even the editor of the suffrage newspaper, in after years, declared that, in his judgment, the history of the Dorr rebellion "should serve as a perpetual warning against intermeddling. If the Democrats of other States had left Rhode Island to herself, if Governor Morton of Massachusetts, Governor Hubbard of New Hampshire, Governor Cleaveland of Connecticut, if the leading Democrats of New York City had permitted the people of Rhode Island to settle their own disputes, there would have been no serious trouble."

However, we should not be too severe with these "foreigners," as the charter party called them. They did not understand the contest. To them it was a question of liberty battling with tyranny. To them Governor Dorr was fighting for justice, and when he fled he became a martyr. It is not strange that they were unwilling to send him back to Rhode Island, notwithstanding that the Constitution of the United States directed State executives to return fugitives from justice when requested. Though the refusals of Governors Cleaveland and Hubbard to honor Governor King's requisitions were based upon mere subterfuges, still they held good: the Constitution of the United States in no way provides a means to make the "shall" of the provision for returning a fugitive have any imperative value.

Nor can we wonder that friends of Governor Dorr hesitated to return him to Rhode Island and place him in the power of the charter authorities. The course pursued by Governor King and his subordinates, during those six weeks of martial law, was not such as to indicate that justice would be done if Governor Dorr fell into the hands of his enemies. Martial law, declared by a legislature over an entire State, and enforced for a month and a half after the last vestige of the rebellion had disappeared, was so entirely unnecessary and out of place in a democratic republic that it almost defeated and destroyed the victorious government.

The friends of Governor Dorr were not wrong in fearing to return him to Rhode Island. Though twenty-one months intervened between the flight from Acote's Hill and the trial of the People's Governor, yet the animosity of the "powers that were" seemed to be as strong as ever; and the defendant and his counsel had a share in making the trial a successful comedy. To try to prove that treason against a State was an impossibility; to attempt to show that the Constitution of the United States by implication took from the individual States the power to protect themselves from traitors; and to declare that even when the Constitution spoke of a fugitive from justice charged with treason such treason must be treason against the United States, was futile. And yet the country at large could not ignore the issue: if the State of Rhode Island could know no traitors, neither could New York nor Pennsylvania; if Governor Dorr had protected himself by this subterfuge, John Brown might fitly have claimed a like liberation from the State of Virginia in 1859.

The greatest weakness in the whole affair was the last attempt of the legislature to show its omnipotence. We smile at the action of the Rhode Island General Assembly in directing that lines be drawn through the official record of a trial by the Supreme Court, thereby "rendering the sentence null and void and as if it had never been rendered;"—but we smile because we have a fixed notion that there must be three distinct branches of government, each supreme in its own sphere. This final act in the history of Thomas Wilson Dorr is a reminder of the older idea that parliament or the legislature must be supreme in a democracy; and it calls attention to the fact that, in one State, at least, this idea continued even to 1843, and that it cropped out again as late as 1854.

This action of the legislature, a dozen years after the Dorr rebellion, was the result of a sudden effervescence of sympathy for the dying Governor. The entire community was at peace; the constitution was working well and was satisfactory to a large majority of the people. The wounds caused by the civil strife were beginning to heal. The dawn of a new day had come to the State, which was destined to progress steadily and surely towards the prosperous condition of to-day.

APPENDIX A.

THE CHARTER,

GRANTED BY KING CHARLES II.

CHARLES the Second, by the Grace of God, King of England, Scotland, France and Ireland, Defender of the Faith, &c., to all to whom these presents shall come, greeting: Whereas, we have been informed, by the humble petition of our trusty and well-beloved subject, John Clarke, on the behalf of Benjamin[(a)] Arnold, William Brenton, William Codington, Nicholas Easton, William Boulston, John Porter, John Smith, Samuel Gorton, John Weeks, Roger Williams, Thomas Olney, Gregory Dexter, John Coggeshall, Joseph Clarke, Randall Holden, John Greene, John Roome, Samuel Wildbore, William Field, James Barker, Richard Tew, Thomas Harris, and William Dyre, and the rest of the purchasers and free inhabitants of our island, called Rhode Island, and the rest of the colony of Providence Plantations, in the Narragansett Bay, in New England, in America, that they, pursuing, with peaceable and loyal minds, their sober, serious, and religious intentions, of godly edifying themselves, and one another, in the holy Christian faith and worship, as they were persuaded; together with the gaining over and conversion of the poor ignorant Indian natives, in those parts of America to the sincere profession and obedience of the same faith and worship, did, not only by the consent and good encouragement of our royal progenitors, transport themselves out of this kingdom of England into America, but also, since

(a) This is evidently an error for Benedict. This charter is reprinted from the State Manual; is essentially a copy of the original, except capitalization and punctuation.

their arrival there, after their first settlement amongst other our subjects in those parts, for the avoiding of discord, and those many evils which were likely to ensue upon some of those our subjects not being able to bear, in these remote parts, their different apprehensions in religious concernments, and in pursuance of the aforesaid ends, did once again leave their desirable stations and habitations, and with excessive labor and travel, hazard and charge did transplant themselves into the midst of the Indian natives, who as we are informed, are the most potent princes and people of all that country; where, by the good Providence of God, from whom the Plantations have taken their name, upon their labor and industry, they have not only been preserved to admiration, but have increased and prospered, and are seized and possessed, by purchase and consent of the said natives, to their full content, of such lands, islands, rivers, harbors and roads, as are very convenient, both for plantations, and also for building of ships, supply of pipe-staves and other merchandise; and which lie very commodious, in many respects, for commerce, and to accommodate our southern plantations, and may much advance the trade of this our realm, and greatly enlarge the territories thereof; they having, by near neighborhood to and friendly society with the great body of the Narragansett Indians, given them encouragement of their own accord, to subject themselves, their people and lands, unto us; whereby, as is hoped, there may, in time, by the blessing of God upon their endeavors be laid a sure foundation of happiness to all America: And whereas, in their humble address, they have freely declared, that it is much on their hearts (if they may be permitted) to hold forth a lively experiment, that a most flourishing civil state may stand and best be maintained and that among our English subjects, with a full liberty in religious concernments; and that true piety rightly grounded upon gospel principles, will give the best and greatest security to sovereignty, and will lay in the hearts of men the strongest obligations to true loyalty: Now, know ye, that we, being willing to encourage the hopeful undertaking of our said loyal and loving subjects, and to secure them in the free exercise and enjoyment of all their civil and religious rights, appertaining to them, as our loving subjects; and to preserve unto them that liberty, in the true Christian faith and worship of God, which they have sought with so much travail, and with peaceable minds, and loyal subjection to our royal progenitors and ourselves, to enjoy; and because some of the people and inhabitants of the same colony cannot, in their private opinions, conform to the public exercise of religion, according to the liturgy, forms and ceremonies of the Church of England, or take or subscribe the oaths and articles made and established in that behalf; and for that the same, by reason of the remote distances of those places, will (as we hope) be no breach of the unity and uniformity established in this nation: Have therefore thought fit, and do hereby publish, grant, ordain and declare, That our royal will and pleasure is, that no person within the said colony, at any time hereafter, shall be any wise molested, punished, disquieted, or called in question, for any differences in opinion in matters of religion, and do not actually disturb the civil peace of our said colony; but that all and every person and persons may, from time to time and at all times hereafter, freely and fully have and enjoy his and their own judgments and consciences, in matters of religious concernments, throughout the tract of land hereafter mentioned, they behaving themselves peaceably and quietly, and not using this liberty to licentiousness and profaneness, nor to the civil injury or outward disturbance of others, any law, statute, or clause therein contained, or to be contained, usage or custom of this realm, to the contrary hereof, in any wise, notwithstanding. And that they may be in the better capacity to defend themselves, in their just rights and liberties, against all the enemies of the Christian faith, and others, in all respects, we have further thought fit, and at the humble petition of the persons aforesaid are graciously pleased to declare, That they shall have and enjoy the benefit of our late act of indemnity and free pardon as the rest of our subjects in other our dominions and territories have; and to create and make them a body politic or corporate, with the powers and privileges hereinafter mentioned. And accordingly our will and pleasure is, and of our especial grace, certain knowledge, and mere motion, we have ordained, constituted and declared, and by these presents, for us, our heirs and successors, do ordain, constitute and declare, That they, the said William Brenton, William Codington, Nicholas Easton, Benedict Arnold, William Boulston, John Porter, Samuel Gorton, John Smith, John Weeks, Roger Williams, Thomas Olney, Gregory Dexter, John Coggeshall, Joseph Clarke, Randall Holden, John Greene, John Roome, William Dyre, Samuel Wildbore, Richard Tew, William Field, Thomas Harris, James Barker, —— Rainsborrow,

—— Williams, and John Nickson, and all such others as now are, or hereafter shall be, admitted and made free of the company and society of our colony of Providence Plantations, in the Narragansett Bay, in New England, shall be, from time to time, and forever hereafter, a body corporate and politic, in fact and name, by the name of the Governor and Company of the English Colony of Rhode Island and Providence Plantations, in New England, in America; and that, by the same name, they and their successors shall and may have perpetual succession, and shall and may be persons able and capable, in the law, to sue and be sued, to plead and be impleaded, to answer, and be answered unto, to defend and to be defended, in all and singular suits, causes, quarrels, matters, actions and things, of what kind or nature soever; and also to have, take, possess, acquire, and purchase lands, tenements or hereditaments, or any goods or chattels, and the same to lease, grant, demise, aliene, bargain, sell and dispose of, at their own will and pleasure, as other our liege people of this our realm of England, or any corporation or body politic, within the same, may lawfully do. And further, that they the said Governor and Company, and their successors, shall and may, forever hereafter have a common seal, to serve and use for all matters, causes, things, and affairs, whatsoever, of them, and their successors; and the same seal to alter, change, break, and make new, from time to time, at their will and pleasure, as they shall think fit. And further, we will and ordain, and by these presents, for us, our heirs, and successors, do declare and appoint that, for the better ordering and managing of the affairs and business of the said Company, and their successors, there shall be one Governor, one Deputy Governor and ten Assistants, to be from time to time constituted, elected and chosen out of the freemen of the said Company, for the time being, in such manner and form as is hereafter in these presents expressed, which said officers shall apply themselves to take care for the best disposing and ordering of the general business and affairs of and concerning the lands and hereditaments hereinafter mentioned to be granted, and the plantation thereof, and the government of the people there. And, for the better execution of our royal pleasure herein, we do, for us, our heirs and successors, assign, name, constitute, and appoint the aforesaid Benedict Arnold to be the first and present Governor of the said Company, and the said William Brenton to be the

Deputy-Governor, and the said William Boulston, John Porter, Roger Williams, Thomas Olney, John Smith, John Greene, John Coggeshall, James Barker, William Field, and Joseph Clarke, to be the ten present Assistants of the said Company, to continue in the said several offices, respectively, until the first Wednesday which shall be in the month of May now next coming. And further, we will, and by these presents, for us, our heirs and successors, do ordain and grant that the Governor of the said Company, for the time being, or, in his absence, by occasion of sickness, or otherwise, by his leave and permission, the Deputy-Governor, for the time being, shall and may, from time to time, upon all occasions, give order for the assembling of the said Company, and calling them together, to consult and advise of the business and affairs of the said Company. And that forever hereafter, twice in every year that is to say, on every first Wednesday in the month of May, and on every last Wednesday in October, or oftener, in case it shall be requisite, the Assistants and such of the freemen of the said Company, not exceeding six persons for Newport, four persons for each of the respective towns of Providence, Portsmouth and Warwick, and two persons for each other place, town or city, who shall be, from time to time, thereunto elected or deputed by the major part of the freemen of the respective towns or places for which they shall be so elected or deputed, shall have a general meeting or assembly, then and there to consult, advise and determine, in and about the affairs and business of the said Company and Plantations. And, further, we do, of our especial grace, certain knowledge, and mere motion, give and grant unto the said Governor and Company of the English colony of Rhode Island and Providence Plantations, in New England, in America, and their successors, that the Governor, or, in his absence, or, by his permission, the Deputy-Governor of the said Company, for the time being, the Assistants, and such of the freemen of the said Company as shall be so as aforesaid elected or deputed, or so many of them as shall be present at such meeting or assembly, as aforesaid, shall be called the General-Assembly; and that they, or the greatest part of them present, whereof the Governor or Deputy-Governor, and six of the Assistants, at least to be seven, shall have, and have hereby given and granted unto them, full power and authority, from time to time, and at all times hereafter, to appoint, alter and change such days, times and places of meeting and General Assembly, as they shall think fit; and to choose, nominate and appoint, such and so many other persons as they shall think fit, and shall be willing to accept the same, to be free of the said Company and body politic, and them into the same to admit; and to elect and constitute such offices and officers, and to grant such needful commissions, as they shall think fit and requisite, for the ordering, managing, and dispatching of the affairs of the said Governor and Company, and their successors; and from time to time, to make, ordain, constitute or repeal, such laws, statutes, orders and ordinances, forms and ceremonies of government and magistracy, as to them shall seem meet, for the good and welfare of the said Company, and for the government and ordering of the lands and hereditaments, hereinafter mentioned to be granted, and of the people that do, or at any time hereafter shall, inhabit or be within the same; so as such laws, ordinances and constitutions, so made, be not contrary and repugnant unto, but as near as may be, agreeable to the laws of this our realm of England, considering the nature and constitution of the place and people there; and also to appoint, order and direct, erect and settle, such places and courts of jurisdiction, for the hearing and determining of all actions, cases, matters and things, happening within the said colony and plantation, and which shall be in dispute, and depending there, as they shall think fit; and also to distinguish and set forth the several names and titles, duties, powers and limits, of each court, office and officer, superior and inferior; and also to contrive and appoint such forms of oaths and attestations, not repugnant, but as near as may be agreeable, as aforesaid, to the laws and statutes of this our realm, as are convenient and requisite, with respect to the due administration of justice, and due execution and discharge of all offices and places of trust by the persons that shall be therein concerned; and also to regulate and order the way and manner of all elections to offices and places of trust, and to prescribe, limit and distinguish the numbers and bounds of all places, towns or cities, within the limits and bounds hereinafter mentioned, and not herein particularly named, who have, or shall have, the power of electing and sending of freemen to the said General Assembly; and also to order, direct and authorize the imposing of lawful and reasonable fines, mulcts, imprisonments, and executing other punishments, pecuniary and corporal, upon offenders and delinquents, according to the course of other corporations within this our kingdom of England; and again to alter, revoke, annul or pardon, under their common seal, or otherwise, such fines, mulcts, imprisonments, sentences, judgments and condemnations, as shall be thought fit; and to direct, rule, order and dispose of, all other matters and things, and particularly that which relates to the making of purchases of the native Indians, as to them shall seem meet; whereby our said people and inhabitants in the said Plantations, may be so religiously, peaceably and civilly governed, as that by their good life and orderly conversation, they may win and invite the native Indians of the country to the knowledge and obedience of the only true God and Saviour of mankind; willing, commanding and requiring, and by these presents, for us, our heirs and successors, ordaining and appointing, that all such laws, statutes, orders and ordinances instructions impositions and directions, as shall be so made by the Governor, Deputy-Governor, Assistants and freemen, or such number of them as aforesaid, and published in writing, under their common seal, shall be carefully and duly observed, kept, performed and put in execution, according to the true intent and meaning of the same. And these our letters patent, or the duplicate or exemplification thereof, shall be to all and every such officer, superior or inferior, from time to time, for the putting of the same orders, laws, statutes, ordinances, instructions and directions in due execution, against us, our heirs and successors, a sufficient warrant and discharge. And further, our will and pleasure is, and we do hereby, for us, our heirs and successors, establish and ordain, that yearly, once in the year, forever hereafter namely, the aforesaid Wednesday in May, and at the town of Newport, or elsewhere, if urgent occasion do require, the Governor, Deputy-Governor and Assistants of the said Company, and other officers of the said Company, or such of them as the General Assembly shall think fit, shall be, in the said General Court or Assembly to be held from that day or time, newly chosen for the year ensuing, by such greater part of the said Company for the time being, as shall be then and there present; and if it shall happen that the present Governor, Deputy-Governor and Assistants, by these presents appointed, or any such as shall hereafter be newly chosen into their rooms, or any of them, or any other the officers of the said Company, shall die or be removed from his or their several offices or places before the said general day of election, (whom we do hereby declare, for any misdemeanor or default, to be removable by the Governor, Assistants and Company, or such greater part of them, in any of the said public courts, to be assembled as aforesaid,) that then, and in every such case, it shall and may be lawful to and for the said Governor, Deputy-Governor, Assistants and Company aforesaid, or such greater part of them, so to be assembled as is aforesaid, in any their assemblies, to proceed to a new election of one or more of their Company, in the room or place, rooms or places, of such officer or officers, so dying or removed, according to their discretions; and immediately upon and after such election or elections made of such Governor, Deputy-Governor, Assistant or Assistants, or any other officer of the said Company, in manner and form aforesaid, the authority, office and power, before given to the former Governor, Deputy-Governor, and other officer and officers, so removed in whose stead and place new shall be chosen, shall, as to him and them, and every of them, respectively, cease and determine: *Provided always*, and our will and pleasure is, that as well such as are by these presents appointed to be the present Governor, Deputy-Governor and Assistants of the said Company, as those that shall succeed them, and all other officers to be appointed and chosen as aforesaid, shall, before the undertaking the execution of the said offices and places respectively, give their solemn engagement, by oath, or otherwise, for the due and faithful performance of their duties in their several offices and places, before such person or persons as are by these presents hereafter appointed to take and receive the same, that is to say: the said Benedict Arnold, who is hereinbefore nominated and appointed the present Governor of the said Company, shall give the aforesaid engagement before William Brenton, or any two of the said Assistants of the said Company; unto whom we do by these presents give full power and authority to require and receive the same; and the said William Brenton, who is hereby before nominated and ap-appointed the present Deputy-Governor of the said Company, shall give the aforesaid engagement before the said Benedict Arnold, or any two of the Assistants of the said Company; unto whom we do by these presents give full power and authority to require and receive the same; and the said William Boulston, John Porter, Roger Williams, Thomas Olney, John

Smith, John Greene, John Coggeshall, James Barker, William Field, and Joseph Clarke who are herein before nominated and appointed the present Assistants of the said Company, shall give the said engagement to their offices and places respectively belonging, before the said Benedict Arnold and William Brenton, or one of them; to whom respectively we do hereby give full power and authority to require, administer or receive the same: and further, our will and pleasure is, that all and every other future Governor or Deputy-Governor, to be elected and chosen by virtue of these presents, shall give the said engagement before two or more of the said Assistants of the said Company for the time being; unto whom we do by these presents give full power and authority to require, administer or receive the same; and the said Assistants, and every of them, and all and every other officer or officers to be hereafter elected and chosen by virtue of these presents from time to time, shall give the like engagements, to their offices and places respectively belonging, before the Governor or Deputy-Governor, for the time being; unto which said Governor, or Deputy-Governor, we do by these presents give full power and authority to require, administer or receive the same accordingly. And we do likewise, for us, our heirs and successors, give and grant unto the said Governor and Company, and their successors, by these presents, that for the more peaceable and orderly government of the said Plantations, it shall and may be lawful for the Governor, Deputy-Governor, Assistants and all other officers and ministers of the said Company, in the administration of justice, and exercise of government, in the said Plantations, to use, exercise, and put in execution, such methods, rules, orders and directions, not being contrary or repugnant to the laws and statutes of this our realm, as have been heretofore given, used and accustomed, in such cases respectively, to be put in practice, until at the next or some other General Asssembly, special provision shall be made and ordained in the cases aforesaid. And we do further, for us, our heirs, and successors, give and grant unto the said Governor and Company, and their successors, by these presents, that it shall and may be lawful to and for the said Governor, or, in his absence, the Deputy-Governor, and major part of the said Assistants, for the time being, at any time when the said General Assembly is not sitting, to nominate, appoint and constitute, such and so many commanders, governors, and military officers, as to them shall seem requisite, for the leading conducting and training up the inhabitants of the said Plantations in martial affairs, and for the defence and safeguard of the said Plantations; and that it shall and may be lawful to and for all and every such commander, governor, and military officer, that shall be so as aforesaid, or by the Governor, or in his absence, the Deputy-Governor, and six of the said Assistants, and major part of the freemen of the said Company present at any General Assemblies, nominated, appointed and constituted, according to the tenor of his and their respective commissions and directions to assemble, exercise in arms, martial array, and put in warlike posture, the inhabitants of the said colony, for their special defence and safety; and to lead and conduct the said inhabitants, and to encounter, expulse, expel and resist, by force of arms, as well by sea as by land, and also to kill, slay and destroy, by all fitting ways, enterprizes and means, whatsoever, all and every such person or persons as shall, at any time hereafter, attempt or enterprize the destruction, invasion, detriment, or annoyance of the said inhabitants or Plantations; and to use and exercise the law martial in such cases only as occasion shall necessarily require; and to take or surprise, by all ways and means whatsoever, all and every such person and persons, with their ship or ships, armor, ammunition or other goods of such persons as shall, in hostile manner, invade or attempt the defeating of the said Plantation, or the hurt of the said Company and inhabitants; and upon just causes, to invade and destroy the native Indians, or other enemies of the said Colony. Nevertheless, our will and pleasure is, and we do hereby declare to the rest of our Colonies in New England, that it shall not be lawful for this our said Colony of Rhode Island and Providence Plantations, in America, in New England, to invade the natives inhabiting within the bounds and limits of their said Colonies, without the knowledge and consent of the said other Colonies. And it is hereby declared, that it shall not be lawful to or for the rest of the Colonies to invade or molest the native Indians or any other inhabitants inhabiting within the bounds and limits hereafter mentioned, (they having subjected themselves unto us, and being by us taken into our special protection,) without the knowledge and consent of the Governor and Company of our Colony of Rhode-Island and Providence Plantations. Also our will and pleasure is, and we do hereby declare unto all Christian Kings, Princes and States, that if any person, which shall hereafter be of the said Company or Plantations, or any other, by appointment of the said Governor and Company for the time being, shall at any time or times thereafter, rob or spoil, by sea or land, or do any hurt, or unlawful hostility to any of the subjects of us, our heirs or successors, or any of the subjects of any Prince or State, being then in league with us, our heirs or successors, upon complaint of such injury done to any such Prince or State, or their subjects, we, our heirs and successors, will make open proclamation within any parts of our realm of England, fit for that purpose, that the person or persons committing any such robbery or spoil, shall, within the time limited by such proclamation, make full restitution, or satisfaction of all such injuries, done or committed, so as the said Prince, or others so complaining, may be fully satisfied, and contented; and if the said person or persons who shall commit any such robbery or spoil shall not make satisfaction, accordingly, within such time, so to be limited, that then we, our heirs and successors, will put such person or persons out of our allegiance and protection; and that then it shall and may be lawful and free for all Princes or others to prosecute with hostility, such offenders, and every of them, their and every of their procurers, aiders, abettors, and counsellors, in that behalf: *Provided also*, and our express will and pleasure is, and we do, by those presents, for us, our heirs and successors, ordain and appoint that these presents, shall not, in any manner, hinder any of our loving subjects, whatsoever, from using and exercising the trade of fishing upon the coast of New England, in America; but that they, and every or any of them, shall have full and free power and liberty to continue and use the trade of fishing upon the said coast, in any of the seas thereunto adjoining, or any arms of the seas, or salt water, rivers and creeks, where they have been accustomed to fish; and to build and set upon the waste land belonging to the said Colony and Plantations, such wharves, stages and work houses as shall be necessary for the salting, drying and keeping of their fish, to be taken or gotten upon that coast. And further, for the encouragement of the inhabitants of our said Colony of Providence Plantations to set upon the business of taking whales, it shall be lawful for them, or any of them, having struck whale, dubertus, or other great fish, it or them to pursue unto any part of that coast, and into any bay, river, cove, creek, or shore, belonging thereto, and it or them, upon the said coast, or in the said bay, river, cove, creek, or shore, belonging thereto, to kill and order for the best advantage, without molestation, they making no wilful waste or spoil; anything in these presents contained, or any other matter or thing, to the contrary, notwithstanding. And further also, we are graciously pleased, and do hereby declare, that if any of the inhabitants of our said Colony do set upon the planting of vineyards (the soil and climate both seeming naturally to concur to the production of wines) or be industrious in the discovery of fishing banks, in or about the said Colony, we will, from time to time, give and allow all due and fitting encouragement therein, as to others in cases of like nature. And further, of our more ample grace, certain knowledge and mere motion, we have given and granted, and by these presents, for us, our heirs and successors, do give and grant unto the said Governor and Company of the English Colony of Rhode Island and Providence Plantations, in the Narragansett Bay, in New England, in America, and to every inhabitant there, and to every person and persons, trading thither, and to every such person or persons as are or shall be free of the said Colony, full power and authority, from time to time, and at all times hereafter, to take, ship, transport and carry away, out of any of our realms and dominions, for and towards the plantation and defence of the said Colony, such and so many of our loving subjects and strangers as shall or will willingly accompany them in and to their said Colony and Plantation; except such person or persons as are or shall be therein restrained by us, our heirs and successors, or any law or statute of this realm; and also to ship and transport all and all manner of goods, chattels, merchandizes and other things whatsoever, that are or shall be useful or necessary for the said Plantations, and defence thereof, and usually transported, and not prohibited by any law or statute of this our realm; yielding and paying unto us, our heirs and successors, such the duties, customs and subsidies, as are or ought to be paid or payable for the same. And further, our will and pleasure is, and we do, for us, our heirs and successors, ordain, declare, and grant unto the said Governor and Company, and their successors, that all and every the subjects of us, our heirs and successors, which are already planted and settled within our said Colony of Providence Plantations, or which shall hereafter go to inhabit within the said Colony, and all and every of their children, which have been born there, or which shall happen hereafter to be born there, or on the sea, going thither, or returning from thence, shall have and enjoy all liberties and immunities of free and natural subjects within any the dominions of us, our heirs and successors, to all intents, constructions and purposes, whatsoever, as if they, and every of them, were born within the realm of England. And further, know ye, that we, of our more abundant grace, certain knowledge, and mere motion, have given, granted and confirmed, and by these presents, for us, our heirs and successors, do give, grant and confirm, unto the said Governor and Company and their successors, all that part of our dominions in New England, in America, containing the Nahantick and Nanhyganset, alias Narragansett Bay, and countries and parts adjacent, bounded on the west or westerly, to the middle or channel of a river there, commonly called and known by the name of Pawcatuck, alias Pawcawtuck river; and so along the said river, as the greater or middle stream thereof reacheth or lies up into the north country, northward, unto the head thereof, and from thence, by a straight line drawn due north, until it meets with the south line of the Massachusetts Colony: and on the north, or northerly, by the aforesaid south or southerly line of the Massachusetts Colony or Plantation, and extending towards the east, or eastwardly, three English miles, to the east and northeast of the most eastern and northeastern parts of the aforesaid Narragansett Bay, as the said Bay lyeth or extendeth itself from the ocean on the south, or southwardly unto the mouth of the river which runneth towards the town of Providence, and from thence along the easterly side or bank of the said river (higher called by the name of Seacunck river) up to the falls called Patuckett falls, being the most westwardly line of Plymouth Colony, and so from the said falls, in a straight line, due north, until it meet with the aforesaid line of the Massachusetts Colony; and bounded on the south by the ocean; and, in particular, the lands belonging to the towns of Providence, Pawtuxet, Warwick, Misquammacok, alias Pawcatuck, and the rest upon the main land in the tract aforesaid, together with Rhode Island, Block Island, and all the rest of the islands and banks in the Narragansett Bay, and bordering upon the coast of the tract aforesaid, (Fisher's Island only excepted,) together with all firm lands, soils, grounds, havens, ports, rivers, waters, fishings, mines royal, and all other mines, minerals, precious stones, quarries, woods, wood grounds, rocks, slates, and all and singular other commodities, jurisdictions, royalties, privileges, franchises, preheminances, and hereditaments, whatsoever, within the said tract, bounds, lands and islands aforesaid, or to them or any of them belonging, or in any wise appertaining; *to have and to hold* the same, unto the said Governor and Company, and their successors, forever, upon trust, for the use and benefit of themselves and their associates freemen of the said Colony, their heirs and assigns, to be holden of us, our heirs and successors, as of the Manor of East-Greenwich, in our county of Kent, in free and common soccage, and not in capite, nor by knight service; yielding and paying therefor, to us, our heirs and successors, only the fifth part of all the ore of gold and silver which, from time to time, and at all times hereafter, shall be there gotten had or obtained, in lieu and satisfaction of all services, duties, fines, forfeitures, made or to be made claims and demands whatsoever, to be to us, our heirs or successors, therefor or thereout rendered, made or paid; any grant, or clause in a late grant, to the Governor and Company of Connecticut Colony, in America, to the contrary thereof in any wise notwithstanding; the aforesaid Pawcatuck river having been yielded, after much debate, for the fixed and certain bounds between these our said Colonies, by the agents thereof; who have also agreed, that the said Pawcatuck river shall be also called alias Norrogansett or Narrogansett river; and, to prevent future disputes, that otherwise might arise thereby, forever hereafter shall be construed, deemed and taken to be the Narragansett river in our late grant to Connecticut Colony mentioned as the easterly bounds of that Colony. And further, our will and pleasure is, that in all matters of public controversy which may fall out between our Colony of Providence Plantations, and the rest of our Colonies in New England, it shall and may be lawful to and for the Governor and Company of the said Colony of Providence Plantations to make their appeals therein to us, our heirs and successors, for redress in such cases, within this our realm of England: and that it shall be lawful to and for the inhabitants of the said Colony of Providence Plantations, without let or molestation, to pass and repass, with freedom, into and through the rest of the English Colonies, upon their lawful and civil occasions, and to converse, and hold commerce and trade, with such of the inhabitants of our other English Colonies as shall be willing to admit them thereunto, they behaving themselves peaceably among them; any act, clause or sentence, in any of the said Colonies provided, or that shall be provided, to the contrary in any wise notwithstanding. And lastly, we do, for us, our heirs and successors, ordain and grant unto the said Governor and Company, and their successors, by these presents, that these our letters patent shall be firm, good, effectual and available in all things in the law, to all intents, constructions and purposes whatsoever, according to our true intent and meaning hereinbefore declared; and shall be construed, reputed and adjudged in all cases most favorably on the behalf, and for the best benefit and behoof, of the said Governor and Company, and their successors; although express mention of the true yearly value or certainty of the premises, or any of them, or of any other gifts or grants, by us, or by any of our progenitors or predecessors, heretofore made to the said Governor and Company of the English Colony of Rhode Island and Providence Plantations, in the Narragansett Bay, New England, in America, in these presents is not made or any statute, act, ordinance, provision, proclamation or restriction, heretofore had, made, enacted, ordained or provided, or any other matter, cause or thing whatsoever, to the contrary thereof in anywise notwithstanding. In witness whereof, we have caused these our letters to be made patent. Witness ourself at Westminster, the eighth day of July, in the fifteenth year of our reign.

By the King:

HOWARD.

APPENDIX B.

"THE PEOPLE'S CONSTITUTION."

We, the people of the State of Rhode Island and Providence Plantations, grateful to Almighty God for his blessing vouchsafed to the "lively experiment" of religious and political freedom here "held forth" by our venerated ancestors, and earnestly imploring the favor of his gracious providence towards this our attempt to secure upon a permanent foundation the advantages of well ordered and rational liberty, and to enlarge and transmit to our successors the inheritance that we have received, do ordain and establish the following constitution of government for this State.

ARTICLE I.

Declaration of Principles and Rights.

1. In the spirit and in the words of Roger Williams, the illustrious founder of this State, and of his venerated associates, we declare "that this government shall be a democracy," or government of the people, "by the major consent" of the same "only in civil things." The will of the people shall be expressed by representatives freely chosen, and returning at fixed periods to their constituents. This State shall be, and forever remain, as in the design of its founder, sacred to "soul liberty," to the rights of conscience, to freedom of thought, of expression, and of action, as hereinafter set forth and secured.

2. All men are created free and equal, and are endowed by their Creator with certain natural, inherent, and inalienable rights; among which are life, liberty, the acquisition of property, and the pursuit of happiness. Government cannot create or bestow these rights, which are the gift of God; but it is instituted for the stronger and surer defence of the same, that men may safely enjoy the rights of life and liberty, securely possess and transmit property, and, so far as laws avail, may be successful in the pursuit of happiness.

3. All political power and sovereignty are originally vested in, and of right belong to, the people. All free governments are founded in their authority, and are established for the greatest good of the whole number. The people have therefore an unalienable and indefeasible right, in their original, sovereign, and unlimited capacity, to ordain and institute government, and in the same capacity to alter, reform, or totally change the same, whenever their safety or happiness requires.

4. No favor or disfavor ought to be shown in legislation toward any man, or party, or society, or religious denomination. The laws should be made not for the good of the few, but of the many; and the burdens of the State ought to be fairly distributed among its citizens.

5. The diffusion of useful knowledge, and the cultivation of a sound morality in the fear of God, being of the first importance in a republican State, and indispensable to the maintenance of its liberty, it shall be an imperative duty of the legislature to promote the establishment of free schools, and to assist in the support of public education.

6. Every person in this State ought to find a certain remedy, by having recourse to the laws, for all injuries or wrongs which may be done to his rights of person, property, or character. He ought to obtain right and justice freely and without purchase, completely and without denial, promptly and without delay, conformably to the laws.

7. The right of the people to be secure in their persons, houses, papers, and possessions, against unreasonable searches and seizures, shall not be violated; and no warrant shall issue but on complaint in writing upon probable cause, supported by oath or affirmation, and describing as nearly as may be the place to be searched, and the person or things to be seized.

8. No person shall be held to answer to a capital or other infamous charge, unless on indictment by a grand jury, except in cases arising in the land or naval forces, or in the militia, when in actual service, in time of war or public danger. No person shall be tried, after an acquittal, for the same crime or offence.

9. Every man being presumed to be innocent until pronounced guilty by the law, all acts of severity, that are not necessary to secure an accused person, ought to be repressed.

10. Excessive bail shall not be required, nor excessive fines imposed, nor cruel or unusual punishments inflicted; and all punishments ought to be proportioned to the offence.

11. All prisoners shall be bailable upon sufficient surety, unless for capital offences, when the proof is evident or the presumption great. The privilege of the writ of habeas corpus shall not be suspended, unless when, in cases of rebellion or invasion, the public safety shall require it.

12. In all criminal prosecutions, the accused shall have the privilege of a speedy and public trial, by an impartial jury; be informed of the nature and cause of the accusation; be confronted with the witnesses against him; have compulsory process to obtain them in his favor, and at the public expense, when necessary; have the assistance of counsel in his defence, and be at liberty to speak for himself. Nor shall he be deprived of his life, liberty, or property, unless by the judgment of his peers, or the law of the land.

13. The right of trial by jury shall remain inviolate, and in all criminal cases the jury shall judge both of the law and of the facts.

14. Any person in this State, who may be claimed to be held to labor or service, under the laws of any other State, Territory, or District, shall be entitled to a jury trial, to ascertain the validity of such claim.

15. No man in a court of common law shall be required to criminate himself.

16. Retrospective laws, civil and criminal, are unjust and oppressive, and shall not be made.

17. The people have a right to assemble in a peaceable manner without molestation or restraint, to consult upon the public welfare; a right to give

instructions to their Senators and Representatives; and a right to apply to those invested with the powers of government for the redress of grievances, for the repeal of injurious laws, for the correction of faults of administration, and for all other purposes.

18. The liberty of the press being essential to the security of freedom in a State, any citizen may publish his sentiments on any subject, being responsible for the abuse of that liberty; and in all trials for libel, both civil and criminal, the truth, spoken from good motives, and for justifiable ends, shall be a sufficient defence to the person charged.

19. Private property shall not be taken for public uses without just compensation, nor unless the public good require it; nor under any circumstances, until compensation shall have been made, if required.

20. The military shall always be held in strict subordination to the civil authority.

21. No soldier shall, in time of peace, be quartered in any house, without the consent of the owner; nor in time of war, but in manner to be prescribed by law.

22. Whereas Almighty God hath created the mind free, and all attempts to influence it by temporal punishments, or burdens, or by civil incapacitations, tend to beget habits of hypocrisy and meanness: and whereas a principal object of our venerated ancestors in their migration to this country, and their settlement of this State, was, as they expressed it, to hold forth a lively experiment, that a flourishing civil State may stand, and be best maintained, with full liberty in religious concernments: We therefore DECLARE that no man shall be compelled to frequent or support any religious worship, place, or ministry whatsoever, nor be enforced, restrained, molested, or burdened in his body or goods, nor disqualified from holding any office, nor otherwise suffer, on account of his religious belief; and that all men shall be free to profess, and by argument to maintain, their opinions in matters of religion; and that the same shall in nowise diminish, enlarge, or affect their civil capacities; and that all other religious rights and privileges of the people of this State, as now enjoyed, shall remain inviolate and inviolable.

23. No witness shall be called in question before the legislature, nor any court of this State, nor before any magistrate or other person authorized to

administer an oath or affirmation, for his or her religious belief, or opinions, or any part thereof; and no objection to a witness, on the ground of his or her religious opinions, shall be entertained or received.

24. The citizens shall continue to enjoy and freely exercise all the rights of fishery, and privileges of the shore, to which they have been heretofore entitled under the charter and usages of this State.

25. The enumeration of the foregoing rights shall not be construed to impair nor deny others retained by the people.

ARTICLE II.

Of Electors and the Right of Suffrage.

1. Every white male citizen of the United States, of the age of twenty-one years, who has resided in this State for one year, and in any town, city, or district of the same for six months, next preceding the election at which he offers to vote, shall be an elector of all officers who are elected, or may hereafter be made eligible by the people. But persons in the military, naval or marine service of the United States, shall not be considered as having such established residence, by being stationed in any garrison, barrack, or military place in any town or city in this State.

2. Paupers and persons under guardianship, insane, or lunatic, are excluded from the electoral right; and the same shall be forfeited on conviction of bribery, forgery, perjury, theft, or other infamous crime, and shall not be restored unless by an act of the General Assembly.

3. No person who is excluded from voting, for want of the qualification first named in section first of this article, shall be taxed, or be liable to do military duty; provided that nothing in said first article shall be so construed as to exempt from taxation any property or persons now liable to be taxed.

4. No elector who is not possessed of, and assessed for, ratable property in his own right, to the amount of one hundred and fifty dollars, or who shall have neglected or refused to pay any tax assessed upon him, in any town, city, or district, for one year preceding the town, city, ward, or district meeting at which he shall offer to vote, shall be entitled to vote on any question of taxation, or the expenditure of public moneys in such town, city or district, until the same be paid.

5. In the city of Providence, and other cities, no person shall be eligible to the office of mayor, alderman, or common councilman, who is not taxed, or who shall have neglected or refused to pay his tax, as provided in the preceding section.

6. The voting for all officers chosen by the people, except town or city officers, shall be by ballot; that is to say, by depositing a written or printed ticket in the ballot-box, without the name of the voter written thereon. Town or city officers shall be chosen by ballot, on the demand of any two persons entitled to vote for the same.

7. There shall be a strict registration of all qualified voters in the towns and cities of the State; and no person shall be permitted to vote, whose name has not been entered upon the list of voters before the polls are opened.

8. The General Assembly shall pass all necessary laws for the prevention of fraudulent voting by persons not having an actual, permanent residence, or home, in the State, or otherwise disqualified according to this constitution; for the careful registration of all voters, previously to the time of voting; for the prevention of frauds upon the ballot-box; for the preservation of the purity of elections; and for the safe-keeping and accurate counting of votes; to the end that the will of the people may be freely and fully expressed, truly ascertained, and effectually exerted, without intimidation, suppression, or unnecessary delay.

9. The electors shall be exempted from arrest on days of election, and one day before, and one day after the same, except in cases of treason, felony, or breach of the peace.

10. No person shall be eligible to any office by the votes of the people, who does not possess the qualifications of an elector.

ARTICLE III.

Of the Distribution of Powers.

1. The powers of the government shall be distributed into three departments—the legislative, the executive, and the judicial.

2. No person or persons connected with one of these departments shall exercise any of the powers belonging to either of the others, except in cases herein directed or permitted.

ARTICLE IV.

Of the Legislative Department.

1. The legislative power shall be vested in two distinct Houses: the one to be called the House of Representatives, the other the Senate, and both together the General Assembly. The concurrent votes of the two Houses shall be necessary to the enactment of laws; and the style of their laws shall be: Be it enacted by the General Assembly as follows.

2. No member of the General Assembly shall be eligible to any civil office under the authority of the State, during the term for which he shall have been elected.

3. If any Representative, or Senator, in the General Assembly of this State, shall be appointed to any office under the government of the United States, and shall accept the same, after his election as such Senator or Representative, his seat shall thereby become vacant.

4. Any person who holds an office under the government of the United States may be elected a member of the General Assembly, and may hold his seat therein, if, at the time of his taking his seat, he shall have resigned said office, and shall declare the same on oath, or affirmation, if required.

5. No member of the General Assembly shall take any fees, be of counsel or act as advocate in any case pending before either branch of the General Assembly, under penalty of forfeiting his seat, upon due proof thereof.

6. Each House shall judge of the election and qualifications of its members; and a majority of all the members of each House, whom the towns and the Senatorial districts are entitled to elect, shall constitute a quorum to do business; but a smaller number may adjourn from day to day, and may compel the attendance of absent members, in such manner, and under such penalties, as each House may have previously prescribed.

7. Each House may determine the rules of its proceedings, punish its members for disorderly behavior, and, with the concurrence of two-thirds of the members elected, expel a member; but not a second time for the same cause.

8. Each House shall keep a journal of its proceedings, and publish the same when required by one-fifth of its members. The yeas and nays of the

members of either House shall, at the desire of any five members present, be entered on the journal.

9. Neither House shall, without the consent of the other, adjourn for more than two days, nor to any other place than that at which the General Assembly is holding its session.

10. The Senators and Representatives shall, in all cases of civil process, be privileged from arrest during the session of the General Assembly, and for two days before the commencement, and two days after the termination of any session thereof. For any speech in debate in either House, no member shall be called in question in any other place.

11. The civil and military officers, heretofore elected in grand committee, shall hereafter be elected annually by the General Assembly, in joint committee, composed of the two Houses of the General Assembly, excepting as is otherwise provided in this constitution; and excepting the captains and subalterns of the militia, who shall be elected by the ballots of the members composing their respective companies, in such manner as the General Assembly may prescribe; and such officers, so elected, shall be approved of and commissioned by the Governor, who shall determine their rank; and, if said companies shall neglect or refuse to make such elections, after being duly notified, then the Governor shall appoint suitable persons to fill such offices.

12. Every bill and every resolution requiring the concurrence of the two Houses (votes of adjournment excepted), which shall have passed both Houses of the General Assembly, shall be presented to the Governor for his revision. If he approve of it, he shall sign and transmit the same to the Secretary of State; but, if not, he shall return it to the House in which it shall have originated, with his objections thereto, which shall be entered at large on their journal. The House shall then proceed to reconsider the bill; and if, after such reconsideration, that House shall pass it by a majority of all the members elected, it shall be sent with the objections to the other House, which shall also reconsider it; and, if approved by that House, by a majority of all the members elected, it shall become a law. If the bill shall not be returned by the Governor within forty-eight hours (Sundays excepted), after it shall have been presented to him, the same shall become a law, in like

manner as if he had signed it, unless the General Assembly by their adjournment, prevent its return; in which case, it shall not be a law.

13. There shall be two sessions of the General Assembly in every year; one session to be held at Newport, on the first Tuesday of June, for the organization of the government, the election of officers, and for other business; and one other session on the first Tuesday of January, to be held at Providence, in the first year after the adoption of this constitution, and in every second year thereafter. In the intermediate years, the January session shall be forever hereafter held in the counties of Washington, Kent, or Bristol, as the General Assembly may determine before their adjournment in June.

ARTICLE V.

Of the House of Representatives.

1. The House of Representatives shall consist of members chosen by the electors in the several towns and cities, in their respective town and ward meetings, annually.

2. The towns and cities shall severally be entitled to elect members according to the apportionment which follows, viz.: Newport to elect five; Warwick, four; Smithfield, five; Cumberland, North Providence, and Scituate, three; Portsmouth, Westerly, New Shoreham, North Kingstown, South Kingstown, East Greenwich, Glocester, West Greenwich, Coventry, Exeter, Bristol, Tiverton, Little Compton, Warren, Richmond, Cranston, Charlestown, Hopkinton, Johnston, Foster, and Burrillville to elect two; and Jamestown, Middletown, and Barrington to elect one.

3. In the city of Providence there shall be six representative districts, which shall be the six wards of said city; and the electors resident in said districts, for the term of three months next preceding the election at which they offer to vote, shall be entitled to elect two Representatives for each district.

4. The General Assembly, in case of great inequality in the population of the wards of the city of Providence, may cause the boundaries of the six representative districts therein to be so altered as to include in each district, as nearly as may be, an equal number of inhabitants.

5. The House of Representatives shall have authority to elect their own Speaker, clerks, and other officers. The oath of office shall be administered to the Speaker by the Secretary of State, or, in his absence, by the Attorney-General.

6. Whenever the seat of a member of the House of Representatives shall be vacated by death, resignation, or otherwise, the vacancy may be filled by a new election.

ARTICLE VI.

Of the Senate.

1. The State shall be divided into twelve senatorial districts; and each district shall be entitled to one Senator, who shall be annually chosen by the electors in his district.

2. The first, second, and third representative districts in the city of Providence shall constitute the first senatorial district; the fourth, fifth, and sixth representative districts in said city, the second district; the town of Smithfield, the third district; the towns of North Providence and Cumberland, the fourth district; the towns of Scituate, Glocester, Burrillville, and Johnston, the fifth district; the towns of Warwick and Cranston, the sixth district; the towns of East Greenwich, West Greenwich, Coventry, and Foster, the seventh district; the towns of Newport, Jamestown, and New Shoreham, the eighth district; the towns of Portsmouth, Middletown, Tiverton, and Little Compton, the ninth district; the towns of North Kingstown and South Kingstown, the tenth district; the towns of Westerly, Charlestown, Exeter, Richmond, and Hopkinton, the eleventh district; the towns of Bristol, Warren, and Barrington, the twelfth district.

3. The Lieutenant-Governor shall be, by virtue of his office, President of the Senate; and shall have a right, in case of an equal division, to vote in the same; and also to vote in joint committee of the two Houses.

4. When the government shall be administered by the Lieutenant-Governor, or he shall be unable to attend as President of the Senate, the Senate shall elect one of their own members President of the same.

5. Vacancies in the Senate, occasioned by death, resignation, or otherwise, may be filled by a new election.

6. The Secretary of State shall be, by virtue of his office, Secretary of the Senate.

ARTICLE VII.

Of Impeachments.

1. The House of Representatives shall have the sole power of impeachment.

2. All impeachments shall be tried by the Senate; and when sitting for that purpose, they shall be on oath or affirmation. No person shall be convicted, except by a vote of two-thirds of the members elected. When the Governor is impeached, the chief justice of the supreme court shall preside, with a casting vote in all preliminary questions.

3. The Governor, and all other executive and judicial officers, shall be liable to impeachment; but judgments, in such cases, shall not extend further than to removal from office. The party convicted shall, nevertheless, be liable to indictment, trial, and punishment according to law.

ARTICLE VIII.

Of the Executive Department.

1. The chief executive power of this State shall be vested in a Governor, who shall be chosen by the electors, and shall hold his office for one year, and until his successor be duly qualified.

2. No person holding any office or place under the United States, this State, any other of the United States, or any foreign power, shall exercise the office of Governor.

3. He shall take care that the laws are faithfully executed.

4. He shall be commander-in-chief of the military and naval forces of the State, except when called into the actual service of the United States; but he shall not march nor convey any of the citizens out of the State, without their consent, or that of the General Assembly, unless it shall become necessary in order to march or transport them from one part of the State to another, for the defence thereof.

5. He shall appoint all civil and military officers whose appointment is not by this constitution, or shall not by law, be otherwise provided for.

6. He shall, from time to time, inform the General Assembly of the condition of the State, and recommend to their consideration such measures as he may deem expedient.

7. He may require from any military officer, or any officer in the executive department, information upon any subject relating to the duties of his office.

8. He shall have power to remit forfeitures and penalties, and to grant reprieves, commutation of punishments, and pardons after conviction, except in cases of impeachment.

9. The Governor shall, at stated times, receive for his services a compensation which shall not be increased nor diminished during his continuance in office.

10. There shall be elected, in the same manner as is provided for the election of Governor, a Lieutenant-Governor, who shall continue in office for the same term of time. Whenever the office of Governor shall become vacant by death, resignation, removal from office, or otherwise, the Lieutenant-Governor shall exercise the office of Governor until another Governor shall be duly qualified.

11. Whenever the offices of Governor and Lieutenant-Governor shall both become vacant, by death, resignation, removal from office, or otherwise, the President of the Senate shall exercise the office of Governor until a Governor be duly qualified; and should such vacancies occur during a recess of the General Assembly, and there be no President of the Senate, the Secretary of State shall, by proclamation, convene the Senate, that a President may be chosen to exercise the office of Governor.

12. Whenever the Lieutenant-Governor or President of the Senate shall exercise the office of Governor, he shall receive the compensation of Governor only; and his duties as President of the Senate shall cease while he shall continue to act as Governor; and the Senate shall fill the vacancy by an election from their own body.

13. In case of a disagreement between the two Houses of the General Assembly respecting the time or place of adjournment, the person exercis-

ing the office of Governor may adjourn them to such time or place as he shall think proper; provided that the time of adjournment shall not be extended beyond the first day of the next stated session.

14. The person exercising the office of Governor may, in cases of special necessity, convene the General Assembly at any town or city in this State, at any other time than hereinbefore provided. And, in case of danger from the prevalence of epidemic or contagious diseases, or from other circumstances, in the place in which the General Assembly are next to meet, he may, by proclamation, convene the Assembly at any other place within the State.

15. A Secretary of State, a General Treasurer, and an Attorney-General, shall also be chosen annually, in the same manner, and for the same time, as is herein provided respecting the Governor. The duties of these officers shall be the same as now, or may be hereafter be, prescribed by law. Should there be a failure to choose either of them, or should a vacancy occur in either of their offices, the General Assembly shall fill the place by an election in joint committee.

16. The electors in each county shall, at the annual elections, vote for an inhabitant of the county to be sheriff of said county, for one year, and until a successor be duly qualified. In case no person shall have a majority of the electoral votes of his county for sheriff, the General Assembly, in joint committee, shall elect a sheriff from the two candidates who shall have the greatest number of votes in such county.

17. All commissions shall be in the name of the State of Rhode Island and Providence Plantations, sealed with the seal of the State, and attested by the Secretary.

ARTICLE IX.

General Provisions.

1. This constitution shall be the supreme law of the State; and all laws contrary to, or inconsistent with the same, which may be passed by the General Assembly, shall be null and void.

2. The General Assembly shall pass all necessary laws for carrying this constitution into effect.

3. The judges of all the courts, and all other officers, both civil and military, shall be bound by oath or affirmation to the due observance of this constitution, and of the constitution of the United States.

4. No jurisdiction shall, hereafter, be entertained by the General Assembly in cases of insolvency, divorce, sale of real estate of minors, or appeal from judicial decisions, nor in any other matters appertaining to the jurisdiction of judges and courts of law. But the General Assembly shall confer upon the courts of the State all necessary powers for affording relief in the cases herein named; and the General Assembly shall exercise all other jurisdiction and authority which they have heretofore entertained, and which is not prohibited by, nor repugnant to, this constitution.

5. The General Assembly shall, from time to time, cause estimates to be made of the ratable property of the State, in order to the equitable apportionment of State taxes.

6. Whenever a direct tax is laid by the State, one-sixth part thereof shall be assessed on the polls of the qualified electors: provided that the tax upon a poll shall never exceed the sum of fifty cents; and that all persons who actually perform military duty, or duty in the fire department, shall be exempted from said poll tax.

7. The General Assembly shall have no power hereafter to incur State debts to an amount exceeding the sum of fifty thousand dollars, except in time of war, or in case of invasion, without the express consent of the people. Every proposition for such increase shall be submitted to the electors at the next annual election, or on some day to be set apart for that purpose; and shall not be farther entertained by the General Assembly, unless it receive the votes of a majority of all the persons voting. This section shall not be construed to refer to any money that now is, or hereafter may be, deposited with this State by the General Government.

8. The assent of two-thirds of the members elected to each House of the General Assembly shall be requisite to every bill appropriating the public moneys, or property, for local or private purposes; or for creating, continuing, altering, or renewing any body politic or corporate, banking corporations excepted.

9. Hereafter, when any bill creating, continuing, altering, or renewing any banking corporation, authorized to issue its promissory notes for circula-

tion, shall pass the two Houses of the General Assembly, instead of being sent to the Governor, it shall be referred to the electors for their consideration, at the next annual election, or on some day to be set apart for that purpose, with printed tickets containing the question—Shall said bill (with a brief description of it) be approved or not? and if a majority of the electors voting shall vote to approve said bill, it shall become a law; otherwise not.

10. All grants of incorporation shall be subject to future acts of the General Assembly, in amendment or repeal thereof, or in anywise affecting the same; and this provision shall be inserted in all acts of incorporation hereafter granted.

11. The General Assembly shall exercise, as heretofore, a visitatorial power over corporations. Three bank commissioners shall be chosen at the June session for one year, to carry out the powers of the General Assembly in this respect. And commissioners for the visitation of other corporations, as the General Assembly may deem expedient, shall be chosen at the June session, for the same term of office.

12. No city council, or other government, in any city, shall have power to vote any tax upon the inhabitants thereof, excepting the amount necessary to meet the ordinary public expenses of the same, without first submitting the question of an additional tax, or taxes, to the electors of said city; and a majority of all who vote shall determine the question. But no elector shall be entitled to vote, in any city, upon any question of taxation thus submitted, unless he shall be qualified by the possession, in his own right, of ratable property to the amount of one hundred and fifty dollars, and shall have been assessed thereon to pay a city tax, and shall have paid the same, as provided in section fourth of article two. Nothing in that article shall be so construed as to prevent any elector from voting for town officers, and, in the city of Providence, and other cities, for mayor, aldermen, and members of the common council.

13. The General Assembly shall not pass any law, nor cause any act or thing to be done, in any way to disturb any of the owners or occupants of land in any territory now under the jurisdiction of any other State or States, the jurisdiction whereof may be ceded to or decreed to belong to,

this State; and the inhabitants of such territory shall continue in the full, quiet, and undisturbed enjoyment of their titles to the same, without interference in any way on the part of this State.

ARTICLE X.

Of Elections.

1. The election of the Governor, Lieutenant-Governor, Secretary of State, General Treasurer, Attorney-General, and also of Senators and Representatives to the General Assembly, and of sheriffs of the counties, shall be held on the third Wednesday of April annually.

2. The names of the persons voted for as Governor, Lieutenant-Governor, Secretary of State, General Treasurer, Attorney-General, and sheriffs of the respective counties, shall be put upon one ticket; and the tickets shall be deposited by the electors in a box by themselves. The names of the persons voted for as Senators and as Representatives shall be put upon separate tickets, and the tickets shall be deposited in separate boxes. The polls for all the officers named in this section shall be opened at the same time.

3. All the votes given for Governor, Lieutenant-Governor, Secretary of State, General Treasurer, Attorney-General, sheriffs, and also for Senators, shall remain in the ballot-boxes till the polls be closed. These votes shall then, in open town and ward meetings, and in the presence of at least ten qualified voters, be taken out and sealed up, in separate envelopes, by the moderators and town clerks, and by the wardens and ward clerks, who shall certify the same, and forthwith deliver or send them to the Secretary of State, whose duty it shall be securely to keep the same, and to deliver the votes for State officers and sheriffs to the Speaker of the House of Representatives, after the House shall be organized, at the June session of the General Assembly. The votes last named shall, without delay, be opened, counted, and declared, in such manner as the House of Representatives shall direct; and the oath of office shall be administered to the persons who shall be declared to be elected, by the Speaker of the House of Representatives, and in the presence of the House; provided that the sheriffs may take their engagement before a Senator, judge, or justice of the peace. The votes for

Senators shall be counted by the Governor and Secretary of State within seven days from the day of election; and the Governor shall give certificates to the Senators who are elected.

4. The boxes containing the votes for Representatives to the General Assembly in the several towns shall not be opened till the polls for Representatives are declared to be closed. The votes shall then be declared by the moderator and clerk, who shall announce the result, and give certificates to the persons selected. If there be no election, or not an election of the whole number of Representatives to which the town is entitled, the polls for Representatives may be re-opened, and the like proceedings shall be had, until an election shall take place: provided, however, that an adjournment of the election may be made to a time not exceeding seven days from the first meeting.

5. In the city of Providence, and other cities, the polls for Representatives shall be kept open during the whole time of voting for the day; and the votes in the several wards shall be sealed up, at the close of the meeting, by the wardens and ward clerks, in the presence of at least ten qualified electors, and delivered to the city clerks. The mayor and aldermen of said city or cities, shall proceed to count said votes within two days from the day of election; and if no election, or an election of only a portion of the Representatives whom the representative districts are entitled to elect, shall have taken place, the mayor and aldermen shall order a new election to be held, not more than ten days from the day of the first election; and so on, till the election of Representatives shall be completed. Certificates of election shall be furnished to the persons chosen, by the city clerks.

6. If there be no choice of a Senator or Senators at the annual election, the Governor shall issue his warrant to the town and ward clerks of the several towns and cities in the senatorial district or districts that may have failed to elect, requiring them to open town or ward meetings for another election, on a day not more than fifteen days beyond the time of counting the votes for Senators. If, on the second trial, there shall be no choice of a Senator or Senators, the Governor shall certify the result to the Speaker of the House of Representatives; and the House of Representatives, and as many Senators as shall have been chosen, shall forthwith elect, in joint com-

mittee, a Senator or Senators, from the two candidates who may receive the highest number of votes in each district.

7. If there be no choice for Governor at the annual election, the Speaker of the House of Representatives shall issue his warrant to the clerks of the several towns and cities, requiring them to notify town and ward meetings for another election, on a day to be named by him, not more than thirty nor less than twenty days beyond the time of receiving the report of the committee of the House of Representatives who shall count the votes for Governor. If on this second trial there shall be no choice of a Governor, the two Houses of the General Assembly shall, at their next session, in joint committee, elect a Governor from the two candidates having the highest number of votes, to hold his office for the remainder of the political year, and until his successor be duly qualified.

8. If there be no choice of Governor and Lieutenant-Governor at the annual election, the same proceedings for the choice of a Lieutenant-Governor shall be had as directed in the preceding section: provided, that the second trial for the election of Governor and Lieutenant-Governor shall be on the same day; and also provided, that, if the Governor shall be chosen at the annual election, and the Lieutenant-Governor shall not be chosen, then the last-named officer shall be elected in joint committee of the two Houses, from the two candidates having the highest number of votes, without a further appeal to the electors. The Lieutenant-Governor, elected as provided in this section, shall hold his office as is provided in the preceding section respecting the Governor.

9. All town, city, and ward meetings for the choice of Representatives, justices of the peace, sheriffs, Senators, State officers, Representatives to Congress, and electors of President and Vice-President, shall be notified by the town, city, or ward clerks, at least seven days before the same are held.

10. In all elections held by the people under this constitution, a majority of all the electors voting shall be necessary to the choice of the person or persons voted for.

11. The oath, or affirmation, to be taken by all the officers named in this article shall be the following: You, being elected to the place (of Governor, Lieutenant-Governor, Secretary of State, General Treasurer, Attorney-Gen-

eral, or to the places of Senators or Representatives, or to the office of sheriff or justice of the peace), do solemnly swear, or severally solemnly swear, or affirm, that you will be true and faithful to the State of Rhode Island and Providence Plantations, and that you will support the constitution thereof; that you will support the constitution of the United States; and that you will faithfully and impartially discharge the duties of your aforesaid office, to the best of your abilities and understanding: so help you God! or, this affirmation you make and give upon the peril of the penalty of perjury.

ARTICLE XI.

Of the Judiciary.

1. The judicial power of this State shall be vested in one supreme court, and in such other courts, inferior to the supreme court, as the legislature may, from time to time, ordain and establish; and the jurisdiction of the supreme and of all other courts may, from time to time, be regulated by the General Assembly.

2. Chancery power may be conferred on the supreme court; but no other court exercising chancery powers shall be established in this State, except as is now provided by law.

3. The justices of the supreme court shall be elected in joint committee of the two Houses, to hold their offices for one year, and until their places shall be declared vacant by a resolution to that effect, which shall be voted for by a majority of all the members elected to the House in which it may originate, and be concurred in by the same vote of the other House, without revision by the Governor. Such resolution shall not be entertained at any other than the annual session for the election of public officers; and, in default of the passage thereof at the said session, the judge, or judges, shall hold his or their place or places for another year. But a judge of any court shall be removable from office, if, upon impeachment, he shall be found guilty of any official misdemeanor.

4. In case of vacancy by the death, resignation, refusal, or inability to serve, or removal from the State, of a judge of any court, his place may be filled by the joint committee, until the next annual election; when, if elected, he shall hold his office as herein provided.

5. The justices of the supreme court shall receive a compensation, which shall not be diminished during their continuance in office.

6. The judges of the courts inferior to the supreme court shall be annually elected in joint committee of the two Houses, except as herein provided.

7. There shall be annually elected by each town, and by the several wards in the city of Providence, a sufficient number of justices of the peace, or wardens resident therein, with such jurisdiction as the General Assembly may prescribe. And said justices or wardens (except in the towns of New Shoreham and Jamestown) shall be commissioned by the Governor.

8. The General Assembly may provide that justices of the peace, who are not re-elected, may hold their offices for a time not exceeding ten days beyond the day of the annual election of these officers.

9. The courts of probate in this State, except the supreme court, shall remain as at present established by law, until the General Assembly shall otherwise prescribe.

ARTICLE XII.

Of Education.

1. All moneys which now are, or may hereafter be, appropriated, by the authority of the State, to public education, shall be securely invested, and remain a perpetual fund for the maintenance of free schools in this State; and the General Assembly are prohibited from diverting said moneys or fund from this use, and from borrowing, appropriating, or using the same, or any part thereof, for any other purpose, or under any pretence whatsoever. But the income derived from said moneys or fund shall be annually paid over, by the General Treasurer, to the towns and cities of the State, for the support of said schools, in equitable proportions: provided, however, that a portion of said income may, in the discretion of the General Assembly, be added to the principal of said fund.

2. The several towns and cities shall faithfully devote their portions of said annual distribution to the support of free schools; and, in default thereof, shall forfeit their shares of the same to the increase of the fund.

3. All charitable donations for the support of free schools, and other purposes of public education, shall be received by the General Assembly,

and invested and applied agreeably to the terms prescribed by the donors: provided the same be not inconsistent with the constitution, or with sound public policy; in which case the donation shall not be received.

ARTICLE XIII.

Amendments.

The General Assembly may propose amendments to this constitution by the vote of a majority of all the members elected to each House. Such propositions shall be published in the newspapers of the State; and printed copies of such propositions shall be sent by the Secretary of State, with the names of all the members who shall have voted thereon, with the yeas and nays, to all the town and city clerks in the State; and the said propositions shall be, by said clerks, inserted in the notices by them issued for warning the next annual town and ward meetings in April; and the town and ward clerks shall read said propositions to the electors, when thus assembled, with the names of all the Representatives and Senators, who shall have voted thereon, with the yeas and nays, before the election of Representatives and Senators shall be had. If a majority of all the members elected at said annual meetings, present in each House, shall approve any proposition thus made, the same shall be published as before provided, and then sent to the electors in the mode provided in the act of approval; and, if then approved by a majority of the electors who shall vote in town and ward meetings, to be specially convened for that purpose, it shall become a part of the constitution of the State.

ARTICLE XIV.

Of the Adoption of the Constitution.

1. This constitution shall be submitted to the people, for their adoption or rejection, on Monday, the 27th day of December next, and on the two succeeding days; and all persons voting are requested to deposit in the ballot-boxes printed or written tickets in the following form: I am an American citizen, of the age of twenty-one years, and have my permanent residence, or home, in this State. I am (or not) qualified to vote under the existing

laws of this State. I vote for (or against) the constitution formed by the convention of the people, assembled at Providence, and which was proposed to the people by said convention on the 18th day of November, 1841.

2. Every voter is requested to write his name on the face of his ticket; and every person entitled to vote as aforesaid, who, from sickness or other causes, may be unable to attend and vote in the town or ward meetings assembled for voting upon said constitution, on the days aforesaid, is requested to write his name upon a ticket, and to obtain the signature, upon the back of the same, of a person who has given his vote, as a witness thereto. And the moderator, or clerk, of any town or ward meeting convened for the purpose aforesaid, shall receive such vote, on either of the three days next succeeding the three days before named for voting on said constitution.

3. The citizens of the several towns in this State, and of the several wards of the city of Providence, are requested to hold town and ward meetings on the days appointed, and for the purpose aforesaid; and also to choose, in each town and ward, a moderator and clerk, to conduct said meetings, and receive the votes.

4. The moderators and clerks are required to receive, and carefully to keep, the votes of all persons qualified to vote as aforesaid, and to make registers of all the persons voting; which, together with the tickets given in by the voters, shall be sealed up, and returned by said moderators and clerks, with certificates signed and sealed by them, to the clerks of the convention of the people, to be by them safely deposited and kept, and laid before said convention, to be counted and declared at their next adjourned meeting, on the 12th day of January, 1842.

5. This constitution, except so much thereof as relates to the election of the officers named in the sixth section of this article, shall, if adopted, go into operation on the first Tuesday of May, in the year one thousand eight hundred and forty-two.

6. So much of the constitution as relates to the election of the officers named in this section shall go into operation on the Monday before the third Wednesday of April next preceding. The first election under this constitution, of Governor, Lieutenant-Governor, Secretary of State, General Treasurer,

and Attorney-General, of Senators and Representatives, of sheriffs for the several counties, and of justices of the peace for the several towns, and the wards of the city of Providence, shall take place on the Monday aforesaid.

7. The electors of the several towns and wards are authorized to assemble on the day aforesaid, without being notified, as is provided in section 9th of article 10, and without the registration required in section 7th of article 2, and to choose moderators and clerks, and proceed in the election of the officers named in the preceding section.

8. The votes given at the first election for Representatives to the General Assembly, and for justices of the peace, shall be counted by the moderators and clerks of the towns and wards chosen as aforesaid; and certificates of election shall be furnished by them to the Representatives and justices of the peace elected.

9. Said moderators and clerks shall seal up, certify, and transmit to the House of Representatives all the votes that may be given in at said first election for Governor and State officers, and for Senators and sheriffs; and the votes shall be counted as the House of Representatives may direct.

10. The Speaker of the House of Representatives shall, at the first session of the same, qualify himself to administer the oath of office to the members of the House, and to other officers, by taking and subscribing the same oath in the presence of the House.

11. The first session of the General Assembly shall be held in the city of Providence on the first Tuesday of May, in the year one thousand eight hundred and forty-two, with such adjournments as may be necessary; but all other sessions shall be held as is provided in article 4 of this constitution.

12. If any of the Representatives, whom the towns or district are entitled to choose at the first annual election aforesaid, shall not be then elected, or if their places shall become vacant during the year, the same proceedings may be had to complete the election, or to supply vacancies, as are directed concerning elections in the preceding sections of this article.

13. If there shall be no election of Governor or Lieutenant-Governor, or of both of these officers, or of a Senator or Senators, at the first annual election, the House of Representatives, and as many Senators as are chosen, shall forthwith elect, in joint committee, a Governor or Lieutenant-Governor,

or both, or a Senator or Senators, to hold their offices for the remainder of the political year; and, in the case of the two officers first named, until their successors shall be duly qualified.

14. If the number of the justices of the peace determined by the several towns and wards on the day of the first annual election shall not be then chosen, or if vacancies shall occur, the same proceedings shall be had as are provided for in this article in the case of a non-election of Representatives and Senators, or of vacancies in their offices. The justices of the peace thus elected shall hold office for the remainder of the political year, or until the second annual election of justices of the peace, to be held on such day as may be prescribed by the General Assembly.

15. The justices of the peace elected in pursuance of the provisions of this article, may be engaged by the persons acting as moderators of the town and ward meetings, as herein provided; and said justices, after obtaining their certificates of election, may discharge the duties of their office, for a time not exceeding twenty days, without a commission from the Governor.

16. Nothing contained in this article, inconsistent with any of the provisions of other articles of the constitution, shall continue in force for a longer period than the first political year under the same.

17. The present government shall exercise all the powers with which it is now clothed, until the said first Tuesday of May, one thousand eight hundred and forty-two, and until their successors, under this constitution, shall be duly elected and qualified.

18. All civil, judicial, and military officers now elected, or who shall hereafter be elected by the General Assembly, or other competent authority, before the said first Tuesday of May, shall hold their offices, and may exercise their powers, until that time.

19. All laws and statutes, public and private, now in force, and not repugnant to this constitution, shall continue in force until they expire by their own limitation, or are repealed by the General Assembly. All contracts, judgments, actions, and rights of action, shall be as valid as if this constitution had not been made. All debts contracted, and engagements entered into, before the adoption of this constitution, shall be as valid against the State as if this constitution had not been made.

20. The supreme court, established by this constitution, shall have the same jurisdiction as the supreme judicial court at present established; and shall have jurisdiction of all causes which may be appealed to, or pending in the same; and shall be held at the same times and places in each county, as the present supreme judicial court, until the General Assembly shall otherwise prescribe.

21. The citizens of the town of New Shoreham shall be hereafter exempted from military duty, and the duty of serving as jurors in the courts of this State. The citizens of Jamestown shall be forever hereafter exempted from military field duty.

22. The General Assembly shall, at their first session after the adoption of this constitution, propose to the electors the question, whether the word "white," in the first line of the first section of article 2 of the constitution, shall be stricken out. The question shall be voted upon at the succeeding annual election; and if a majority of the electors voting shall vote to strike out the word aforesaid, it shall be stricken from the constitution; otherwise not. If the word aforesaid shall be stricken out, section 3d of article 2 shall cease to be a part of this constitution.

23. The President, Vice-Presidents, and Secretaries shall certify and sign this constitution, and cause the same to be published.

Done in convention, at Providence, on the 18th day of November, in the year one thousand eight hundred and forty-one, and of American independence the sixty-sixth.

JOSEPH JOSLIN, *President of the Convention.*

WAGER WEEDEN,
SAMUEL H. WALES, } *Vice-Presidents.*

Attest:

WILLIAM H. SMITH,
JOHN S. HARRIS, } *Secretaries.*

APPENDIX C.

"THE FREEMEN'S CONSTITUTION."

We, the people of the State of Rhode Island and Providence Plantations, do ordain and establish this constitution for the government thereof.

ARTICLE I.

Declaration of Certain Constitutional Rights and Principles.

In order effectually to secure the religious and political freedom established here by our venerated ancestors, and to preserve the same for their posterity, we do declare that the inherent, essential, and unquestionable rights and principles hereinafter mentioned, among others, shall be established, maintained, and preserved, and shall be of paramount obligation in all legislative, judicial, and executive proceedings.

SECTION 1. Every person within this State ought to find a certain remedy, by having recourse to the laws, for all injuries or wrongs which he may receive in his person, property, or character. He ought to obtain right and justice freely and without being obliged to purchase it, completely and without denial, promptly and without delay, conformably to the laws.

SEC. 2. The right of the people to be secure in their persons, papers, and possessions, against unreasonable searches and seizures, shall not be violated; and no warrant shall issue, but on complaint in writing, upon probable cause, supported by oath or affirmation, and describing, as nearly as may be, the place to be searched, and the persons or things to be seized.

SEC. 3. No person shall be holden to answer for a capital or other infamous crime, unless on presentment or indictment by a grand jury, except in cases of impeachment, or such offences as are usually cognizable by a justice of the peace; or, in cases arising in the land or naval forces, or in the militia, when in actual service, in time of war or public danger. No persons shall be tried after an acquittal, for the same offence.

SEC. 4. Excessive bail shall not be required, nor excessive fines imposed, nor cruel punishments inflicted; and all punishments ought to be proportioned to the offence.

SEC. 5. All persons imprisoned ought to be bailable by sufficient sureties, unless for capital offences, when the proof is evident, or the presumption great. The privilege of the writ of *habeas corpus* shall not be suspended, unless when, in cases of rebellion or invasion, the public safety shall require it; nor ever, without the authority of the General Assembly.

SEC. 6. In all criminal prosecutions, the accused shall enjoy the privilege of a speedy and public trial, by an impartial jury; to be informed of the nature and cause of the accusation; to be confronted with the witnesses against him; to have compulsory process for obtaining them in his favor; and to have the assistance of counsel in his defence, and be at liberty to speak for himself; nor shall he be deprived of life, liberty, or property, unless by the judgment of his peers, or the law of the land.

SEC. 7. The person of a debtor, where there is not strong presumption of fraud, ought not to be continued in prison after he shall have delivered up his property for the benefit of his creditors, in such manner as shall be prescribed by law.

SEC. 8. No *ex post facto* law, or law impairing the obligation of contracts, shall be made.

SEC. 9. No man, in a court of common law, shall be compelled to give evidence criminating himself.

SEC. 10. Every man being presumed innocent until pronounced guilty by the law, all acts of severity that are not necessary to secure an accused person shall be repressed.

SEC. 11. The right of trial by jury shall remain inviolate.

SEC. 12. Private property shall not be taken for public uses, without just compensation.

SEC. 13. The citizens shall continue to enjoy and freely exercise the rights of fishery, and all other rights to which they have heretofore been entitled under the charter of this State, except as is herein otherwise provided.

SEC. 14. The military shall always be held in strict subordination to the civil authority.

SEC. 15. No soldier shall, in time of peace, be quartered in any house, without the consent of the owner; nor in time of war, but in manner to be prescribed by law.

SEC. 16. The liberty of the press being essential to the security of freedom in a State, any person may publish his sentiments on any subject, being responsible for the abuse of that liberty; and in all trials for libel, both civil and criminal, the truth, unless published from malicious motives, shall be a sufficient defence to the person charged.

SEC. 17. The citizens have a right, in a peaceable manner, to assemble for their common good, and to apply to those invested with the powers of government for redress of grievances, or other purposes, by petition, address, or remonstrance.

SEC. 18. The right of the people to keep and bear arms shall not be infringed.

SEC. 19. Slavery shall not be tolerated in this State.

SEC. 20. Whereas Almighty God hath created the mind free, and all attempts to influence it, by temporal punishments or burdens, or by civil incapacitations, tend to beget habits of hypocrisy and meanness; and whereas a principal object of our venerable ancestors, in their migrations to this country, and their settlement of this State, was, as they expressed it, to hold forth a lively experiment, that a flourishing civil State may stand, and be best maintained, with full liberty in religious concernments; we, therefore, declare that no man shall be compelled to frequent or support any religious worship, place, or ministry whatever; nor enforced, restrained, molested, or burdened in his body or goods, nor disqualified from holding any office, nor otherwise suffer, on account of his religious belief; and that all men shall be free to profess, and by argument to maintain, their opinion in matters of religion; and that the same shall in nowise diminish, enlarge, or affect their civil capacities.

SEC. 21. The enumeration of the foregoing rights shall not be construed to impair or deny others retained by the people.

ARTICLE II.

Of the Right of Suffrage.

SECTION 1. Every person who is now a freeman, and qualified voter, shall continue to be so, so long as he retains the qualifications upon which he was admitted.

SEC. 2. Hereafter, every white male native citizen of the United States, or any territory thereof, of the full age of twenty-one years, who shall have had his actual permanent residence and home in this State for the period of one year, and in the town or city in which he may claim a right to vote six months next preceding the time of voting, and shall be seized in his own right of a freehold real estate in such town or city, of the value at least of one hundred and thirty-four dollars over and above all incumbrances, shall, therefrom, have the right to vote in the election of all civil officers, and on all questions in all legal town or ward meetings.

SEC. 3. Every white male native citizen of the United States or any territory thereof, of the full age of twenty-one years, who shall have had his actual permanent residence and home in this State for the period of two years, and in the town or city in which he may claim the right to vote six months next preceding the time of voting, shall have the right to vote in the election of all civil officers, and on all questions in all legal town or ward meetings: *Provided, however,* That no person who is not now a freeman shall be allowed to vote upon any motion to impose a tax, or incur expenditures in any town or city, unless he possess the freehold qualification required by this article, or shall have been taxed upon property valued at least at one hundred and fifty dollars, within one year from the time he may offer to vote, and shall have paid such tax in said town or city.

SEC. 4. Any white male, native of any foreign country, of the full age of twenty-one years, naturalized in the United States according to law, who shall have had his actual permanent residence and home in this State for the period of three years after his naturalization, and in the town or city in which he may claim the right to vote six months next preceding the time of voting, and shall be seized in his own right of a freehold real estate, in such town or city, of the value at least of one hundred and thirty-four dollars over and above all incumbrances, shall, therefrom, have a right to vote in the election of all civil officers, and in all questions in all town or ward meetings. But no person in the military, naval, marine, or any other service of the United States, shall be considered as having the required residence by reason of being employed in any garrison, barrack, or military or naval Station in this State. And no pauper, lunatic, or person *non compos mentis*, or under guardianship, shall be permitted to vote; nor shall any person convicted of any crime deemed infamous at common law, be permitted to exercise that privilege until he be restored thereto by the General Assembly. Persons residing on land ceded by this State to the United States shall not be entitled to exercise the privilege of electors during such residence.

SEC. 5. The General Assembly shall, as soon as may be after the adoption of this constitution, provide for the registration of voters; and shall also have full power generally to enact all laws necessary to carry this article into effect, and to prevent abuse and fraud in voting.

SEC. 6. All persons entitled to vote shall be protected from arrest in civil cases, on the days of election, and on the day preceding and the day following an election.

SEC. 7. In the city of Providence, and all other cities, no person shall be eligible to the office of mayor, alderman, or common councilman, who is not qualified to vote upon a motion to impose a tax or incur expenditures as herein provided.

SEC. 8. The General Assembly shall have power to provide, by special or general laws, for the admission of any native male citizen of the United States, or any territory, who shall have had his permanent residence and home in this State for two years, but who is not otherwise qualified under this article, to vote on such conditions as they may deem proper, except for taxes and expenditures.

ARTICLE III.

Of the Distribution of Powers.

The powers of the government shall be distributed into three distinct branches—the legislative, executive, and judicial.

ARTICLE IV.

Of the Legislative Power.

SECTION 1. This constitution shall be the supreme law of the State; and all laws inconsistent therewith shall be void. The General Assembly shall pass all such laws as are necessary to carry this constitution into effect.

SEC. 2. The legislative power, under this constitution, shall be vested in two distinct houses, or branches, each of which shall have a negative on the other: the one to be styled the Senate, the other the House of Representatives; and both together, the General Assembly. The style of their laws shall be: It is enacted by the General Assembly as follows.

SEC. 3. There shall be one session of the General Assembly holden annually at Newport, on the first Tuesday of May; and one other annual session, to be holden on the last Monday of October, once in two years, at South Kingstown; and the intermediate years, alternately at Bristol and East Greenwich; and the adjournment from the October session shall be holden at Providence.

SEC. 4. No member of the General Assembly shall take any fees, or be of counsel in any case pending before either branch of the General Assembly, under penalty of forfeiting his seat, upon due proof thereof to the satisfaction of the branch of which he is a member.

SEC. 5. The person and estate of every member of the General Assembly shall be free and exempt from any process in any civil action during the session of the General Assembly, and for two days before the commencement and after the termination thereof. And all processes served contrary hereto shall be void. And for any speech in debate, in either House, no member shall be questioned in any other place.

SEC. 6. Each House shall be the judge of the elections and qualifications of its members; and a majority shall constitute a quorum to do business;

but a smaller number may adjourn from day to day, and may compel the attendance of absent members, in such manner, and under such penalties, as each House may prescribe.

SEC. 7. Each House may determine the rules of proceeding, punish contempts, punish its members for disorderly behavior, and, with the concurrence of two-thirds, expel a member; but not a second time for the same cause.

SEC. 8. Each House shall keep a journal of its proceedings. The yeas and nays of the members of either House shall, at the desire of one-fifth of those present, be entered on the journal.

SEC. 9. Neither House shall, during a session, without the consent of the other, adjourn for more than two days, nor to any other place than that in which they may be sitting.

SEC. 10. The General Assembly shall continue to exercise the judicial power, the power of visiting corporations, and all other powers they have heretofore exercised, not inconsistent with this constitution.

SEC. 11. The General Assembly shall regulate the compensation of the Governor and other officers elected by general ticket, or by the General Assembly, and of the members of the General Assembly, subject to the limitations contained in this constitution.

SEC. 12. All lotteries shall hereafter be prohibited in this State, except those already authorized by the General Assembly.

SEC. 13. The General Assembly shall have no power, hereafter, to incur State debts to an amount exceeding fifty thousand dollars, except in time of war, or on case of invasion, without the express consent of the people; nor in any case, without such consent, to pledge the faith of the State for the payment of the obligations of others. This section shall not be construed to refer to any money that may be deposited with this State by the government of the United States.

SEC. 14. The assent of two-thirds of the members elected to each branch of the General Assembly shall be required to every bill appropriating the public moneys, or property, for local or private purposes.

SEC. 15. The General Assembly shall, from time to time, provide for making new valuations of property, for the assessment of taxes, in such manner as they may deem best. No direct State tax shall be assessed upon the ratable property of the State, before a new estimate of such property be taken.

SEC. 16. Whenever a direct tax is laid by the State, one-sixth part thereof shall be assessed on the polls of the qualified electors: provided that the tax on a poll shall never, in any one tax, exceed the sum of fifty cents.

SEC. 17. The General Assembly may provide by law for the continuance in office of any officers of annual appointment, until other persons are qualified to take their places.

ARTICLE V.

Of the House of Representatives.

SECTION 1. The House of Representatives shall consist of members elected by the electors of the several towns and cities in the respective town and ward meetings. Each town or city having four thousand inhabitants, and under six thousand five hundred, shall be entitled to elect three Representatives; each town or city having six thousand five hundred inhabitants, and under ten thousand, shall be entitled to elect four Representatives; each town or city having ten thousand inhabitants, and under fourteen thousand, shall be entitled to elect five Representatives; each town or city having fourteen thousand inhabitants, and under eighteen thousand, shall be entitled to elect six Representatives; each town or city having eighteen thousand inhabitants, and under twenty-two thousand, shall be entitled to elect seven Representatives; each town or city having over twenty-two thousand inhabitants shall be entitled to elect eight Representatives. But no town or city shall be entitled to elect more than eight Representatives, and every town or city shall be entitled to elect two. The representation of the several towns and cities in this State shall be apportioned agreeable to the last census of the people of the United States preceding the election.

SEC. 2. The House of Representatives shall have authority to elect its Speaker, clerks, and other officers. The oath of office shall be administered by the Secretary of State, or, in his absence, by the Attorney-General. The clerks shall be engaged by the Speaker.

SEC. 3. Whenever the seat of a member of the House of Representatives shall be vacated by death, resignation, or otherwise, the vacancy may be filled by a new election.

SEC. 4. The senior member from the town of Newport, present, shall preside at the organization of the House.

ARTICLE VI.

Of the Senate.

SECTION 1. The Senate shall consist of nineteen members, to be chosen annually by the majority of electors, by districts. The State shall be divided into sixteen districts, as follows:

First. The town of Newport shall constitute the first senatorial district, and shall be entitled to elect two Senators.

Second. The towns of Portsmouth, Middletown, Tiverton, Little Compton, New Shoreham, and Jamestown shall constitute the second senatorial district, and shall be entitled to elect two Senators.

Third. The city of Providence shall constitute the third senatorial district, and shall be entitled to elect two Senators.

Fourth. The town of Smithfield shall constitute the fourth senatorial district, and shall be entitled to elect one Senator.

Fifth. The towns of Cumberland and North Providence shall constitute the fifth senatorial district, and shall be entitled to elect one Senator.

Sixth. The towns of Scituate, Cranston, and Johnston shall constitute the sixth senatorial district, and shall be entitled to one Senator.

Seventh. The towns of Glocester, Foster, and Burrillville shall constitute the seventh senatorial district, and shall be entitled to elect one Senator.

Eighth. The town of South Kingstown shall constitute the eighth senatorial district, and shall be entitled to elect one Senator.

Ninth. The towns of Westerly and Charlestown shall constitute the ninth senatorial district, and shall be entitled to elect one Senator.

Tenth. The towns of Hopkinton and Richmond shall constitute the tenth senatorial district, and shall be entitled to elect one Senator.

Eleventh. The towns of North Kingstown and Exeter shall constitute the eleventh senatorial district, and shall be entitled to elect one Senator.

Twelfth. The town of Bristol shall constitute the twelfth senatorial district, and shall be entitled to elect one Senator.

Thirteenth. The towns of Warren and Barrington shall constitute the thirteenth senatorial district, and shall be entitled to elect one Senator.

Fourteenth. The towns of East Greenwich and West Greenwich shall constitute the fourteenth senatorial district, and shall be entitled to elect one Senator.

Fifteenth. The town of Coventry shall constitute the fifteenth senatorial district, and shall be entitled to elect one Senator.

Sixteenth. The town of Warwick shall constitute the sixteenth senatorial district, and shall be entitled to elect one Senator.

And no more than one Senator shall be elected from any town for the same term, in the second senatorial district.

SEC. 2. The Lieutenant-Governor shall *ex-officio* be a member of the Senate.

The Secretary of State shall be, by virtue of his office, Secretary of the Senate, unless otherwise provided by law; and the Senate may elect such other officers as they may deem necessary.

SEC. 3. If, by reason of death, resignation, or absence, there be no Governor or Lieutenant-Governor present, to preside in the Senate, the Senate shall elect one of their own number to preside, until the Governor or Lieutenant-Governor returns, or until one of said offices is filled according to this constitution; and, until such election is made by the Senate, the Secretary of State shall preside.

ARTICLE VII.

Of Impeachments.

SECTION 1. The House of Representatives shall have the sole power of impeachment.

SEC. 2. All impeachments shall be tried by the Senate; and when sitting for that purpose, they shall be under oath or affirmation. No person shall be convicted, except by vote of two-thirds of the members elected. When the Governor is impeached, the chief or presiding justice of the supreme judicial court for the time being, shall preside, with a casting vote in all preliminary questions.

SEC. 3. The Governor, and all other executive and judicial officers, shall be liable to impeachment; but judgment in such cases shall not extend further than to removal from office. The party convicted shall, nevertheless, be liable to indictment, trial and punishment, according to law.

ARTICLE VIII.

Of the Executive Power.

SECTION 1. The chief executive power of this State shall be vested in a Governor.

SEC. 2. The Governor shall take care that the laws be faithfully executed.

SEC. 3. He shall be captain-general and commander-in-chief of the military and naval forces of this State, except when they shall be called into the service of the United States.

SEC. 4. He shall have power to grant reprieves, after conviction, in all cases, except those of impeachment, until the end of the next session of the General Assembly, and no longer.

SEC. 5. The person filling the office of Governor shall preside in the Senate, and in grand committee; and shall have a right, in case of equal division, to vote; not otherwise.

SEC. 6. He may fill vacancies in office not otherwise provided for by this constitution, or by law, until the same shall be filled by the General Assembly, or the people.

SEC. 7. In case of disagreement between the two Houses of the General Assembly, respecting the time or place of adjournment, certified to him by either, he may adjourn them to such time and place as he shall think proper; provided that the time of adjournment shall not be extended beyond the day of the next stated session.

SEC. 8. He may, on special emergencies, convene the General Assembly at any town in this State, at any time not provided for by law; and in case of danger from the prevalence of epidemic or contagious diseases in either of the places in which the General Assembly may by law meet, or to which they may have been adjourned, or from other circumstances, he may, by proclamation, convene said Assembly at any other place within this State.

SEC. 9. All commissions shall be in the name and by the authority of the State of Rhode Island and Providence Plantations, shall be sealed with the State seal, signed by the Governor, and attested by the Secretary.

SEC. 10. In case of the death, resignation, refusal or inability to serve, or removal from office of the Governor, or of his impeachment or absence from the State, the Lieutenant-Governor shall exercise the powers and authority appertaining to the office of Governor, until another shall be chosen at the next annual election for Governor, and be duly qualified, or until the Governor, impeached or absent, shall be acquitted or return.

SEC. 11. If the offices of Governor and Lieutenant-Governor be both vacant by reason of death, resignation, absence or otherwise, the person entitled to preside over the Senate for the time being shall, in like manner, administer the government until he be superseded by a Governor or Lieutenant-Governor.

SEC. 12. The compensation of the Governor and Lieutenant-Governor shall be established by law, and shall not be diminished during the term for which they were elected.

SEC. 13. The duties and powers of the Secretary, Attorney-General, and General Treasurer shall be the same under this constitution as are now established, or from time to time may be prescribed by law.

ARTICLE IX.

Of Elections.

SECTION 1. The Governor, Lieutenant-Governor, Senators, Representatives, Secretary of State, Attorney-General, and General Treasurer shall be elected at the town, city, or ward meetings, to be holden on the third Wednesday of April, annually; and shall severally hold their offices for one year, from the first Tuesday in May next succeeding their election, and until others are legally chosen and duly qualified to fill their places.

SEC. 2. The voting for all officers chosen by the people, except town or city officers, shall be by ballot, in manner to be regulated by law. Town or city officers shall be chosen by ballot, on demand of any two persons entitled to vote for the same.

SEC. 3. The names of the persons voted for as Governor, Lieutenant-Governor, Secretary of State, General Treasurer, and Attorney-General shall be put upon one ticket, and the tickets shall be deposited by the moderator or warden in a box by themselves. The names of the persons voted for as Senators and as Representatives shall be put upon separate tickets, and the tickets shall be deposited by the moderator or warden in separate boxes. The polls for all the officers named in this section shall be opened at the same time.

SEC. 4. All the votes given for Governor, Lieutenant-Governor, Secretary of State, General Treasurer, and Attorney-General, and also for Senators, shall remain in the ballot-boxes till the polls are closed. These votes shall then, in open town and ward meetings, be taken out and sealed in separate envelopes by the moderators and town clerks, and by the wardens and ward clerks, who shall certify the same, and forthwith deliver or send them to the Secretary of State; whose duty it shall be securely to keep the same, and to deliver the votes for general officers to the Speaker of the House of Representatives, after the House shall be organized, at the May session of the General Assembly. The votes last named shall without delay be opened, counted, and declared, in such manner as the House of Representatives shall direct. The votes for Senators shall be counted by the Governor and Secretary of State, within seven days from the day of election, and the Governor shall give certificates to the Senators who are elected.

SEC. 5. The votes for Representatives in the several towns, after the polls are declared to be closed for the same, shall be counted by the moderators and clerks, who shall announce the result, and give certificates to the persons elected. If there be no election, or not an election of the whole number of Representatives to which the town is entitled, the polls for Representatives may be re-opened, and the like proceedings shall be had until an election shall take place: provided, however, that an adjournment or adjournments of the election may be made to a time not exceeding seven days from the first meeting.

SEC. 6. In the city of Providence and other cities, the polls for Representatives shall be kept open during the whole time of voting for the day, and the votes in the several wards shall be sealed up at the close of the meeting by the wardens and the ward clerks in open ward meeting, and delivered to the city clerk. The mayor and aldermen of said city or cities shall proceed to count said votes within two days from the day of election; and if no election, or an election of only a portion of the Representatives, shall have taken place, the mayor and aldermen shall order a new election to be held, not more than ten days from the day of the first election, and so on till the election of Representatives shall be completed. Certificates of election shall be furnished by the city clerks to the persons chosen.

SEC. 7. If no person shall have a majority of votes for the office of Governor or Lieutenant-Governor, the Senate and House of Representatives, in grand committee, may choose one by ballot from the two persons having the highest number of votes.

SEC. 8. In case an election of the Secretary of State, Attorney-General, or General Treasurer should fail to be made by the electors at their annual election, the vacancy or vacancies shall be filled by the General Assembly, in grand committee, from the two candidates for such office having the greatest number of the votes of the electors. Or, in case of a vacancy in either of said offices from other causes, between the sessions of the General Assembly, the Governor shall appoint some person to fill the same until a successor elected by the General Assembly is qualified to act; and in such case, and also in all other cases of vacancies not otherwise provided for, the General Assembly may fill the same in any manner they may deem proper.

SEC. 9. If there be no choice of a Senator or Senators at the annual election, or if a vacancy in the Senate occur from any other cause, the Governor shall issue his warrant to the town and ward clerks of the several towns and cities in the senatorial district or districts that may have failed to elect, or where such vacancy may have occurred, requiring them to open town or ward meetings for another election, on a day to be by him appointed, not more than fifteen days from the time of issuing such warrant; and, in such election, a plurality of votes shall elect.

SEC. 10. All general officers shall take the following engagement before they act in their respective offices, to wit: You, ———, being by the free vote of the freemen of this State of Rhode Island and Providence Plantations, elected unto the place of ———, do solemnly swear (or affirm) to be true and faithful unto this State, and to support the constitution of this State and of the United States; that you will faithfully and impartially discharge all the duties of your aforesaid office, to the best of your abilities, according to law: so help you God. Or, this affirmation you make and give upon the peril of perjury. And the members of the General Assembly shall take an engagement to the same effect.

SEC. 11. In all elections held by the people under this constitution, a majority of all the electors voting shall be necessary to the choice of the persons voted for, except as is herein otherwise provided.

SEC. 12. The officers now elected in grand committee, except justices of the peace, shall continue to be so elected until otherwise prescribed by law.

SEC. 13. The oath or affirmation shall be administered to the Governor, Lieutenant-Governor, and Senators, by the Speaker of the House of Representatives, in presence of the House, or elsewhere, by a justice of the supreme judicial court. The Secretary of State, Attorney-General, and General Treasurer, shall be engaged by the person exercising the office of Governor.

ARTICLE X.

Of Qualifications for Office.

SECTION 1. No person shall be qualified to hold the office of Governor, Lieutenant-Governor, Senator, or Representative in the General Assembly unless he be a duly qualified elector. No person shall be elected a Representative to the General Assembly, or to any town or city office, unless he be a qualified elector, and an inhabitant of the town or city which elects him.

SEC. 2. Every person shall be disqualified from holding any office to which he may have been elected, if he be convicted of having offered, or procured any other person to offer, any bribe to secure his election, or the election of any other person.

SEC. 3. The judges of all the courts, and all other officers, both civil and military, shall be bound by oath or affirmation to support this constitution, and the constitution of the United States.

SEC. 4. No person who holds any office under the government of the

United States, or any other State or foreign country, shall be capable of acting as a general officer, or shall take a seat in the General Assembly, unless, at the time of taking his engagement, he shall have resigned his office under such other government. And if any general officer, Senator, Representative, or judge shall, after his election, accept or hold any office under any other government, he shall not be capable thereafter of acting as a general officer, Senator, Representative, or judge, but the office shall be thereby vacated.

ARTICLE XI.

Of the Judicial Power.

SECTION 1. The judicial power of this State shall be vested in one supreme judicial court, and in such inferior courts as the General Assembly may, from time to time, ordain and establish; and the jurisdiction of the supreme and of all other courts may, from time to time, be regulated by the General Assembly.

SEC. 2. Chancery powers may be conferred by the General Assembly on the supreme judicial court; but no other court exercising chancery powers shall be established in this State, except as is now provided by law.

SEC. 3. The justices of the supreme judicial court shall be elected in grand committee of the two Houses, to hold their offices until their places be declared vacant by a resolution of the General Assembly to that effect, which shall be voted for by a majority of all the members elected to the House in which it may originate, and be concurred in by the same majority of the other House. Such resolution shall not be entertained at any other than the annual session for the election of public officers; and, in default of the passage thereof at said session, the judge, or judges, shall hold his or their places, as is herein provided. But a judge of this, or of any other court inferior to the same, shall be removable from office, if, upon impeachment, he shall be found guilty of any official misdemeanor.

SEC. 4. In case of vacancy by the death, resignation, refusal, or inability to serve, or absence from the State, of a judge of this court, his place may be filled by the grand committee, until the next annual election; when the judge elected shall hold his office as before provided.

SEC. 5. The judges of the supreme judicial court shall receive a suitable compensation for their services, which shall not be diminished during their continuance in office.

SEC. 6. The judges of the supreme judicial court shall, in all trials, instruct the jury in the law.

SEC. 7. There shall be annually elected by each town, and by the several wards in the city of Providence, a sufficient number of justices of the peace, or wardens, resident therein, with such jurisdiction as the General Assembly may prescribe. And said justices, or wardens (except in the towns of New Shoreham and Jamestown), shall be commissioned by the Governor.

SEC. 8. The courts of probate in this State, excepting the supreme judicial court, shall remain as at present established by law, until the General Assembly shall otherwise prescribe.

ARTICLE XII.

Of Education.

SECTION 1. The diffusion of knowledge as well as of virtue among the people being essential for the preservation of their rights and liberties, it shall be the duty of the General Assembly to promote public schools, and to adopt all other means to secure to the people the advantages and opportunities of education, which they may deem necessary and proper.

SEC. 2. The money which now is, or which may hereafter be, appropriated by law for the formation of a permanent fund for the support of public schools, shall be securely invested, and remain a perpetual fund for that purpose.

SEC. 3. All donations for the support of public schools, or for other purposes of education, which shall be received by the General Assembly, shall be applied according to the terms prescribed by the donors.

SEC. 4. The General Assembly shall make all necessary provisions by law for carrying this article into effect. They are prohibited from diverting said moneys or fund from the aforesaid uses; and from borrowing, appropriating, or using the same, or any part thereof, for any other purpose, under any pretence whatsoever.

ARTICLE XIII.

Of Amendments.

The General Assembly may propose amendments to this constitution by the votes of a majority of all the members elected to each House. Such propositions shall be published in the newspapers, and printed copies of such propositions shall be sent by the Secretary of State, with the names of all the members who shall have voted thereon, with the yeas and nays, to all the town and city clerks in the State; and the said propositions shall be by said clerks inserted in the warrants or notices by them issued for warning the next annual ward and town meetings in April; and the clerks shall read such propositions to the electors when thus assembled, with the names of all the Representatives and Senators who shall have voted thereon, with the yeas and nays, before the election of Representatives and Senators shall be had. If a majority of all the members elected to each House, at said annual meeting, shall approve any proposition thus made, the same shall be published and sent to the electors in the mode provided in the act of approval; and, if then approved by three-fifths of the electors of the State present, and voting thereon in town and ward meetings, it shall become a part of the constitution of the State.

ARTICLE XIV.

Of the Adoption of this Constitution.

SECTION 1. This constitution, if adopted, shall go into operation on the first Tuesday of May, in the year one thousand eight hundred and forty-two. The first election of Governor, Lieutenant-Governor, Secretary of State, Attorney-General, and General Treasurer, and of Representatives and Senators, under said constitution, shall be had on the third Wednesday of April preceding. And the town and ward meetings therefor shall be warned and conducted as is now provided by law. All civil, judicial, and military officers now elected, or who shall hereafter be elected, by the General Assembly or other competent authority, before the said first Tuesday of May, shall hold their offices, and may exercise their powers, until that time, or until their successors are qualified to act. All statutes, public and private, not repugnant to this constitution, shall continue in force until they expire by their own limitation, or are repealed by the General Assembly. All charters, contracts, judgments, actions, and rights of action, shall be as valid as if this constitution had not been made. The present government shall exercise all the powers with which it is now clothed until the said first Tuesday of May, one thousand eight hundred and forty-two, and until their successors, under this constitution, are duly elected and qualified.

SEC. 2. All debts contracted, and engagements entered into, before the adoption of this constitution, shall be as valid against the State as if this constitution had not been formed.

SEC. 3. The supreme judicial court, established by this constitution, shall have the same jurisdiction as the supreme judicial court at present established; and shall have jurisdiction of all causes which may be appealed to, or pending in, the same; and shall be held at the same time and places, and in each county, as the present supreme judicial court, until otherwise prescribed by the General Assembly.

SEC. 4. The towns of Jamestown and New Shoreham shall continue to enjoy the exemption from military duty which they now enjoy, until otherwise prescribed by law.

Done in convention, February 19, 1842.

HENRY Y. CRANSTON,

President of the Convention.

THOMAS A. JENCKES, *Secretary.*

WALTER W. UPDIKE, *Assistant Secretary.*

STATE OF RHODE ISLAND AND PROVIDENCE PLANTATIONS,

In Convention, February 19, A. D. 1842.

Resolved, That the constitution framed by this convention be certified by the president and secretaries, and, with the journal and papers of the convention, shall be deposited in the office of the Secretary of State; that the

Secretary of State cause said constitution, together with this resolution, and all the acts and resolutions of the General Assembly relating to this convention, to be printed and distributed according to law; and that said constitution be submitted to all the people authorized to vote for general officers under the same, for their ratification or rejection, at town and ward meetings, to be holden in the several towns and in the city of Providence, on Monday, Tuesday, and Wednesday, the twenty-first, twenty-second, and twenty-third days of March, A. D. 1842. The several town and city clerks shall issue the necessary warrants for said meetings. Said meetings shall be kept open for the reception of votes from the hour of nine o'clock in the forenoon, until seven o'clock in the afternoon; and in the city of Providence and town of Newport, until nine o'clock in the evening, on the days appointed. At said town and ward meetings every person voting shall have his name written on the back of his ballot; and said ballots shall be sealed up in open town or ward meetings, and, with lists of the names of the voters, shall be returned to the General Assembly at their session to be holden on the fourth Monday of March next.

Read and adopted, February 19, 1842.

THOMAS A. JENCKES, *Secretary.*

APPENDIX D.

CONSTITUTION

OF THE

STATE OF RHODE ISLAND

AND

PROVIDENCE PLANTATIONS.

We, the people of the State of Rhode Island and Providence Plantations, grateful to Almighty God for the civil and religious liberty which He hath so long permitted us to enjoy, and looking to Him for a blessing upon our endeavors to secure and to transmit the same unimpaired to succeeding generations, do ordain and establish this constitution of government.

ARTICLE I.

Declaration of Certain Constitutional Rights and Principles.

In order effectually to secure the religious and political freedom established by our venerated ancestors, and to preserve the same for our posterity, we do declare that the essential and unquestionable rights and principles hereinafter mentioned shall be established, maintained and preserved, and shall be of paramount obligation in all legislative, judicial, and executive proceedings.

SECTION 1. In the words of the Father of his Country, we declare that "the basis of our political systems is the right of the people to make and alter their constitutions of government; but that the constitution which at any time exists, till changed by an explicit and authentic act of the whole people, is sacredly obligatory upon all."

SEC. 2. All free governments are instituted for the protection, safety and happiness of the people. All laws, therefore, should be made for the good of the whole; and the burdens of the state ought to be fairly distributed among its citizens.

SEC. 3. Whereas Almighty God hath created the mind free; and all attempts to influence it, by temporal punishments or burdens, or by civil incapacitations, tend to beget habits of hypocrisy and meanness; and whereas a principal object of our venerable ancestors, in their migrations to this country, and their settlement of this state, was, as they expressed it, to hold forth a lively experiment, that a flourishing civil state may stand, and be best maintained, with full liberty in religious concernments: we, therefore, declare that no man shall be compelled to frequent or to support any religious worship, place, or ministry whatever, except in fulfillment of his own voluntary contract; nor enforced, restrained, molested, or burdened in his body or goods; nor disqualified from holding any office; nor otherwise suffer, on account of his religious belief; and that every man shall be free to worship God according to the dictates of his own conscience, and to profess and by argument to maintain his opinion in matters of religion; and that the same shall in nowise diminish, enlarge, or affect his civil capacity.

SEC. 4. Slavery shall not be permitted in this state.

SEC. 5. Every person within this state ought to find a certain remedy, by having recourse to the laws, for all injuries or wrongs which he may receive in his person, property, or character. He ought to obtain right and justice freely and without purchase, completely and without denial; promptly and without delay; conformably to the laws.

SEC. 6. The right of the people to be secure in their persons, papers and possessions, against unreasonable searches and seizures, shall not be violated; and no warrant shall issue, but on complaint in writing, upon probable cause, supported by oath or affirmation, and describing as nearly as may be, the place to be searched, and the persons or things to be seized.

SEC. 7. No person shall be held to answer for a capital or other infamous crime, unless on presentment or indictment by a grand jury, except in cases of impeachment, or of such offences as are cognizable by a justice of the peace; or in cases arising in the land or naval forces, or in the militia when in actual service in time of war or public danger. No person shall, after an acquittal, be tried for the same offence.

SEC. 8. Excessive bail shall not be required, nor excessive fines imposed, nor cruel punishments inflicted; and all punishments ought to be proportioned to the offence.

SEC. 9. All persons imprisoned ought to be bailed by sufficient surety, unless for offences punishable by death or by imprisonment for life, when the proof of guilt is evident, or the presumption great. The privilege of the writ of *habeas corpus* shall not be suspended, unless when in cases of rebellion or invasion the public safety shall require it; nor ever without the authority of the General Assembly.

SEC. 10. In all criminal prosecutions, the accused shall enjoy the right to a speedy and public trial, by an impartial jury; to be informed of the nature and cause of the accusation, to be confronted with the witnesses against him, to have compulsory process for obtaining them in his favor, to have the assistance of counsel in his defence, and shall be at liberty to speak for himself; nor shall he be deprived of life, liberty, or property, unless by the judgment of his peers, or the law of the land.

SEC. 11. The person of a debtor, where there is not strong presumption of fraud, ought not to be continued in prison after he shall have delivered up his property for the benefit of his creditors, in such manner as shall be prescribed by law.

SEC. 12. No *ex post facto* law, or law impairing the obligation of contracts, shall be passed.

SEC. 13. No man in a court of common law shall be compelled to give evidence criminating himself.

SEC. 14. Every man being presumed innocent, until he is pronounced guilty by the law, no act of severity which is not necessary to secure an accused person shall be permitted.

SEC. 15. The right of trial by jury shall remain inviolate.

SEC. 16. Private property shall not be taken for public uses, without just compensation.

SEC. 17. The people shall continue to enjoy and freely exercise all the rights of fishery, and the privileges of the shore, to which they have been heretofore entitled under the charter and usages of this State. But no new right is intended to be granted, nor any existing right impaired by this declaration.

SEC. 18. The military shall be held in strict subordination to the civil authority. And the law martial shall be used and exercised in such cases only as occasion shall necessarily require.

SEC. 19. No soldier shall be quartered in any house, in time of peace, without the consent of the owner; nor, in time of war, but in a manner to be prescribed by law.

SEC. 20. The liberty of the press being essential to the security of freedom in a state, any person may publish his sentiments on any subject, being responsible for the abuse of that liberty; and in all trials for libel, both civil and criminal, the truth, unless published from malicious motives, shall be sufficient defence to the person charged.

SEC. 21. The citizens have a right in a peaceable manner to assemble for their common good, and to apply to those invested with the powers of government for redress of grievances, or for other purposes, by petition, address, or remonstrance.

SEC. 22. The right of the people to keep and bear arms shall not be infringed.

SEC. 23. The enumeration of the foregoing rights shall not be construed to impair or deny others retained by the people.

ARTICLE II.

Of the Qualifications of Electors.

SECTION 1. Every male citizen of the United States, of the age of twenty-one years, who has had his residence and home in this state for one year, and in the town or city in which he may claim a right to vote, six months next preceding the time of voting, and who is really and truly possessed in his own right of real estate in such town or city of the value of one hundred and thirty-four dollars over and above all incumbrances, or which shall rent for seven dollars per annum over and above any rent reserved or the interest of any incumbrances thereon, being an estate in fee-simple, fee-tail, for the life of any person, or an estate in reversion or remainder, which qualifies no other person to vote, the conveyance of which estate, if by deed, shall have been recorded at least ninety days, shall thereafter have a right to vote in the election of all civil officers and on all questions in all legal town or ward meetings so long as he continues so qualified. And if any person hereinbefore described shall own any such estate within this state out of the town or city in which he resides, he shall have a right to vote in the election of all general officers and members of the general assembly in the town or city in which he shall have had his residence and home for the term of six months next preceding the election, upon producing a certificate from the clerk of the town or city in which his estate lies, bearing date within ten days of the time of his voting, setting forth that such person has a sufficient estate therein to qualify him as a voter; and that the deed, if any, has been recorded ninety days.

SEC. 2. Every male native citizen of the United States, of the age of twenty-one years, who has had his residence and home in this state two years, and in the town or city in which he may offer to vote, six months next preceding the time of voting, whose name is registered pursuant to the act calling the convention to frame this constitution, or shall be registered in the office of the clerk of such town or city at least seven days before the time he shall offer to vote, and before the last day of December in the present year; and who has paid or shall pay a tax or taxes assessed upon his estate within this state, and within a year of the time of voting, to the amount of one dollar, or who shall voluntarily pay, at least seven days before the time he shall offer to vote, and before said last day of December, to the clerk or treasurer of the town or city where he resides, the sum of one dollar, or such sum as with his other taxes shall amount to one dollar, for the support of public schools therein, and shall make proof of the same, by the certificate of the clerk, treasurer, or collector of any town or city where such payment is made: or who, being so registered, has been enrolled in any military company in this state, and done military service or duty therein, within the present year, pursuant to law, and shall (until other proof is required by law) prove by the certificate of the officer legally commanding the regiment, or chartered, or legally authorized volunteer company in which he may have served or done duty, that he has been equipped and done duty according to law, or by the certificate of the commissioners upon military claims, that he has performed military service, shall have a right to vote in the election of all civil officers, and on all questions in all legally organized town or ward meetings, until the end of the first year after the adoption of this constitution, or until the end of the year eighteen hundred and forty-three.

From and after that time, every such citizen who has had the residence herein required, and whose name shall be registered in the town where he resides, on or before the last day of December, in the year next preceding the time of his voting, and who shall show by legal proof, that he has for and within the year next preceding the time he shall offer to vote, paid a tax or taxes assessed against him in any town or city in this state, to the amount of one dollar, or that he has been enrolled in a military company in this state, been equipped and done duty therein according to law, and at least for one day during such year, shall have a right to vote in the election of all civil officers, and on all questions, in all legally organized town or ward meetings: *Provided*, that no person shall at any time be allowed to vote in the election of the city council of the city of Providence, or upon any proposition to impose a tax, or for the expenditure of money in any town or city, unless he shall within the year next preceding have paid a tax assessed upon his property therein, valued at least at one hundred and thirty-four dollars.

SEC. 3. The assessors of each town or city shall annually assess upon every person whose name shall be registered a tax of one dollar, or such sum as with his other taxes shall amount to one dollar, which registry tax shall be paid into the treasury of such town or city, and be applied to the support of public schools therein; but no compulsory process shall issue for the collection of any registry tax: *Provided*, that the registry tax of every person who has performed military duty according to the provisions of the preceding section shall be remitted for the year he shall perform such duty; and the registry tax assessed upon any mariner, for any year while he is at sea, shall, upon his application, be remitted; and no person shall be allowed to vote whose registry tax for either of the two years next preceding the time of voting is not paid or remitted as herein provided.

SEC. 4. No person in the military, naval, marine, or any other service of the United States shall be considered as having the required residence by reason of being employed in any garrison, barrack, or military or naval station in this state: and no pauper, lunatic, person *non compos mentis*, person under guardianship, or member of the Narragansett tribe of Indians, shall be permitted to be registered or to vote. Nor shall any person convicted of bribery, or of any crime deemed infamous at common law, be permitted to exercise that privilege, until he be expressly restored thereto by act of the general assembly.

SEC. 5. Persons residing on lands ceded by this state to the United States shall not be entitled to exercise the privilege of electors.

SEC. 6. The general assembly shall have full power to provide for a registry of voters, to prescribe the manner of conducting the elections, the form of certificates, the nature of the evidence to be required in case of a dispute as to the right of any person to vote, and generally to enact all laws necessary to carry this article into effect, and to prevent abuse, corruption and fraud in voting.

ARTICLE III.

Of the Distribution of Powers.

The powers of the government shall be distributed into three departments: the legislative, executive and judicial.

ARTICLE IV.

Of the Legislative Power.

SECTION 1. This constitution shall be the supreme law of the state, and any law inconsistent therewith shall be void. The general assembly shall pass all laws necessary to carry this constitution into effect.

SEC. 2. The legislative power, under this constitution, shall be vested in two houses, the one to be called the senate, the other the house of representatives; and both together, the general assembly. The concurrence of the two houses shall be necessary to the enactment of laws. The style of their laws shall be, *It is enacted by the general assembly as follows:*

SEC. 3. There shall be two sessions of the general assembly holden annually: one at Newport, on the first Tuesday of May, for the purposes of election and other business; the other on the last Monday of October, which last session shall be holden at South Kingstown once in two years, and the intermediate years alternately at Bristol and East Greenwich; and an adjournment from the October session shall be holden annually at Providence.

SEC. 4. No member of the general assembly shall take any fee, or be of counsel, in any case pending before either house of the general assembly, under penalty of forfeiting his seat, upon proof thereof to the satisfaction of the house of which he is a member.

SEC. 5. The person of every member of the general assembly shall be exempt from arrest, and his estate from attachment in any civil action, during the session of the general assembly, and two days before the commencement and two days after the termination thereof, and all process served contrary hereto shall be void. For any speech in debate in either house, no member shall be questioned in any other place.

SEC. 6. Each house shall be the judge of the elections and qualifications of its members; and a majority shall constitute a quorum to do business; but a smaller number may adjourn from day to day, and may compel the attendance of absent members in such manner, and under such penalties, as may be prescribed by such house or by law. The organization of the two houses may be regulated by law, subject to the limitations contained in this constitution.

SEC. 7. Each house may determine its rules of proceeding, punish contempts, punish its members for disorderly behavior, and, with the concurrence of two thirds, expel a member; but not a second time for the same cause.

SEC. 8. Each house shall keep a journal of its proceedings. The yeas and nays of the members of either house shall, at the desire of one fifth of those present, be entered on the journal.

SEC. 9. Neither house shall, during a session, without the consent of the other, adjourn for more than two days, nor to any other place than that in which they may be sitting.

SEC. 10. The general assembly shall continue to exercise the powers they have heretofore exercised, unless prohibited in this constitution.

SEC. 11. The senators and representatives shall receive the sum of one dollar for every day of attendance, and eight cents per mile for traveling expenses in going to and returning from the general assembly. The general assembly shall regulate the compensation of the governor, and all other officers, subject to the limitations contained in this constitution.

SEC. 12. All lotteries shall hereafter be prohibited in this state, except those already authorized by the general assembly.

SEC. 13. The general assembly shall have no power, hereafter, without the express consent of the people, to incur state debts to an amount exceeding fifty thousand dollars, except in time of war, or in case of insurrection or invasion; nor shall they in any case, without such consent, pledge the faith of the state for the payment of the obligations of others. This section shall not be construed to refer to any money that may be deposited with this state by the government of the United States.

SEC. 14. The assent of two thirds of the members elected to each house of the general assembly shall be required to every bill appropriating the public money or property for local or private purposes.

SEC. 15. The general assembly shall, from time to time, provide for making new valuations of property, for the assessment of taxes, in such manner as they may deem best. A new estimate of such property shall be taken before the first direct state tax, after the adoption of this constitution, shall be assessed.

SEC. 16. The general assembly may provide by law for the continuance in office of any officers of annual election or appointment, until other persons are qualified to take their places.

SEC. 17. Hereafter, when any bill shall be presented to either house of the general assembly, to create a corporation for any other than for religious, literary, or charitable purposes, or for a military or fire company, it shall be continued until another election of members of the general assembly shall have taken place, and such public notice of the pendency thereof shall be given as may be required by law.

SEC. 18. It shall be the duty of the two houses, upon the request of either, to join in grand committee for the purpose of electing senators in congress, at such times and in such manner as may be prescribed by law for said elections.

ARTICLE V.

Of the House of Representatives.

SECTION 1. The house of representatives shall never exceed seventy-two members, and shall be constituted on the basis of population, always allowing one representative for a fraction exceeding half the ratio; but each town or city shall always be entitled to at least one member; and no town or city shall have more than one sixth of the whole number of members to which the house is hereby limited. The present ratio shall be one representative to every fifteen hundred and thirty inhabitants, and the general assembly may, after any new census taken by the authority of the United States or of this state, re-apportion the representation by altering the ratio; but no town or city shall be divided into districts for the choice of representatives.

SEC. 2. The house of representatives shall have authority to elect its speaker, clerks and other officers. The senior member from the town of Newport, if any be present, shall preside in the organization of the house.

ARTICLE VI.

Of the Senate.

SECTION 1. The senate shall consist of the lieutenant-governor and of one senator from each town or city in the state.

SEC. 2. The governor, and in his absence the lieutenant-governor, shall preside in the senate and in grand committee. The presiding officer of the senate and grand committee shall have a right to vote in case of equal division, but not otherwise.

SEC. 3. If, by reason of death, resignation, absence, or other cause, there be no governor or lieutenant-governor present, to preside in the senate, the senate shall elect one of their own members to preside during such absence or vacancy; and until such election is made by the senate, the secretary of state shall preside.

SEC. 4. The secretary of state shall, by virtue of his office, be secretary of the senate, unless otherwise provided by law, and the senate may elect such other officers as they may deem necessary.

ARTICLE VII.

Of the Executive Power.

SECTION 1. The chief executive power of this state shall be vested in a governor, who, together with a lieutenant-governor, shall be annually elected by the people.

SEC. 2. The governor shall take care that the laws be faithfully executed.

SEC. 3. He shall be captain-general and commander-in-chief of the military and naval forces of this state, except when they shall be called into the service of the United States.

SEC. 4. He shall have power to grant reprieves after conviction, in all cases except those of impeachment, until the end of the next session of the general assembly.

SEC. 5. He may fill vacancies in office not otherwise provided for by this constitution, or by law, until the same shall be filled by the general assembly, or by the people.

SEC. 6. In case of disagreement between the two houses of the general assembly, respecting the time or place of adjournment, certified to him by either, he may adjourn them to such time and place as he shall think proper: provided that the time of adjournment shall not be extended beyond the day of the next stated session.

SEC. 7. He may, on extraordinary occasions, convene the general assembly at any town or city in this state, at any time not provided for by law; and in case of danger from the prevalence of epidemic or contagious disease, in the place in which the general assembly are by law to meet, or to which they may have been adjourned, or for other urgent reasons, he may, by proclamation, convene said assembly at any other place within this state.

SEC. 8. All commissions shall be in the name and by the authority of the state of Rhode Island and Providence Plantations; shall be sealed with the state seal, signed by the governor, and attested by the secretary.

SEC. 9. In case of vacancy in the office of governor, or his inability to serve, impeachment, or absence from the state, the lieutenant-governor shall fill the office of governor, and exercise the powers and authority appertaining thereto, until a governor is qualified to act or until the office is filled at the next annual election.

SEC. 10. If the offices of governor and lieutenant-governor be both vacant, by reason of death, resignation, impeachment, absence, or otherwise, the person entitled to preside over the senate for the time being shall in like manner fill the office of governor during such absence or vacancy.

SEC. 11. The compensation of the governor and lieutenant-governor shall be established by law, and shall not be diminished during the term for which they are elected.

SEC. 12. The duties and powers of the secretary, attorney-general, and general treasurer shall be the same under this constitution as are now established, or as from time to time may be prescribed by law.

ARTICLE VIII.

Of Elections.

SECTION 1. The governor, lieutenant-governor, senators, representatives, secretary of state, attorney-general, and general treasurer shall be elected at the town, city, or ward meetings, to be holden on the first Wednesday of April, annually; and shall severally hold their offices for one year, from the first Tuesday of May next succeeding, and until others are legally chosen, and duly qualified to fill their places. If elected or qualified after the said first Tuesday of May, they shall hold their offices for the remainder of the political year, and until their successors are qualified to act.

SEC. 2. The voting for governor, lieutenant-governor, secretary of state, attorney-general, general treasurer and representative to congress, shall be by ballot; senators and representatives to the general assembly, and town or city officers, shall be chosen by ballot, on demand of any seven persons entitled to vote for the same; and in all cases where an election is made by ballot or paper vote, the manner of balloting shall be the same as is now required in voting for general officers, until otherwise prescribed by law.

SEC. 3. The names of the persons voted for as governor, lieutenant-governor, secretary of state, attorney-general, and general treasurer shall be placed upon one ticket; and all votes for these officers shall, in open town or ward meetings, be sealed up by the moderators and town clerks and by the wardens and ward clerks, who shall certify the same and deliver or send them to the secretary of state; whose duty it shall be securely to keep and deliver the same to the grand committee, after the organization of the two houses at the annual May session; and it shall be the duty of the two houses at said session, after their organization, upon the request of either house, to join in grand committee, for the purpose of counting and declaring said votes, and of electing other officers.

SEC. 4. The town and ward clerks shall also keep a correct list or register of all persons voting for general officers, and shall transmit a copy thereof to the general assembly, on or before the first day of said May session.

SEC. 5. The ballots for senators and representatives in the several towns shall, in each case, after the polls are declared to be closed, be counted by the moderator, who shall announce the result, and the clerk shall give certificates to the persons elected. If, in any case, there be no election, the polls may be reopened, and the like proceedings shall be had until an election shall take place: Provided, however, that an adjournment or adjournments of the election may be made to a time not exceeding seven days from the first meeting.

SEC. 6. In the city of Providence, the polls for senator and representative shall be kept open during the whole time of voting for the day, and the votes in the several wards shall be sealed up at the close of the meeting by the wardens and ward clerks in open ward meeting, and afterwards delivered to the city clerk. The mayor and aldermen shall proceed to count said votes within two days from the day of election; and if no election of senator and representatives or if an election of only a portion of the representatives shall have taken place, the mayor and aldermen shall order a new election, to be held not more than ten days from the day of the first election, and so on until the election shall be completed. Certificates of election shall be furnished by the city clerk to the persons chosen.

SEC. 7. If no person shall have a majority of votes for governor, it shall be the duty of the grand committee to elect one by ballot from the two persons having the highest number of votes for the office, except when such a result is produced by rejecting the entire vote of any town, city or ward, for informality or illegality, in which case a new election by the electors throughout the state shall be ordered; and in case no person shall have a majority of votes for lieutenant-governor, it shall be the duty of the grand committee to elect one by ballot from the two persons having the highest number of votes for the office.

SEC. 8. In case an election of the secretary of state, attorney-general, or general treasurer should fail to be made by the electors at the annual election, the vacancy or vacancies shall be filled by the general assembly in grand committee, from the two candidates for such office having the greatest number of the votes of the electors. Or, in case of a vacancy in either of said offices from other causes, between the sessions of the general assembly, the governor shall appoint some person to fill the same until a successor elected by the general assembly is qualified to act; and in such case, and also in all other cases of vacancies not otherwise provided for, the general assembly may fill the same in any manner they may deem proper.

SEC. 9. Vacancies from any cause in the senate or house of representatives may be filled by a new election.

SEC. 10. In all elections held by the people under this constitution, a majority of all the electors voting shall be necessary to the election of the persons voted for.

ARTICLE IX.

Of Qualifications for Office.

SECTION 1. No person shall be eligible to any civil office, (except the office of school committee,) unless he be a qualified elector for such office.

SEC. 2. Every person shall be disqualified from holding any office to which he may have been elected, if he be convicted of having offered, or procured any other person to offer, any bribe to secure his election, or the election of any other person.

SEC. 3. All general officers shall take the following engagement before they act in their respective offices, to wit: You being by the free vote of the electors of this State of Rhode Island and Providence Plantation, elected unto the place of do solemnly swear (or affirm) to be true and faithful unto this State, and to support the constitution of this state and of the United States; that you will faithfully and impartially discharge all the duties of your aforesaid office, to the best of your abilities, according to law: So help you God. Or, this affirmation you make and give upon the peril of the penalty of perjury.

SEC. 4. The members of the general assembly, the judges of all the courts, and all other officers, both civil and military, shall be bound by oath or affirmation to support this constitution, and the constitution of the United States.

SEC. 5. The oath or affirmation shall be administered to the governor, lieutenant-governor, senators, and representatives, by the secretary of state, or in his absence, by the attorney-general. The secretary of state, attorney-general, and general treasurer shall be engaged by the governor, or by a justice of the supreme court.

SEC. 6. No person holding any office under the government of the United States, or of any other state or country, shall act as a general officer, or as a member of the general assembly, unless at the time of taking his engagement he shall have resigned his office under such government; and if any general officer, senator, representative, or judge shall, after his election and engagement, accept any appointment under any other government, his office under this shall be immediately vacated; but this restriction shall not apply to any person appointed to take depositions or acknowledgment of deeds, or other legal instruments, by the authority of any other state or country.

ARTICLE X.

Of the Judicial Power.

SECTION 1. The judicial power of this state shall be vested in one supreme court, and in such inferior courts as the general assembly may, from time to time, ordain and establish.

SEC. 2. The several courts shall have such jurisdiction as may, from time to time, be prescribed by law. Chancery powers may be conferred on the supreme court, but on no other court to any greater extent than is now provided by law.

SEC. 3. The judges of the supreme court shall, in all trials, instruct the jury in the law. They shall also give their written opinion upon any question of law whenever requested by the governor, or by either house of the general assembly.

SEC. 4. The judges of the supreme court shall be elected by the two houses in grand committee. Each judge shall hold his offices until his place be declared vacant by a resolution of the general assembly to that effect; which resolution shall be voted for by a majority of all the members elected to the house in which it may originate, and be concurred in by the same majority of the other house. Such resolution shall not be entertained at any other than the annual session for the election of public officers; and in default of the passage thereof at said session, the judge shall hold his place as is herein provided. But a judge of any court shall be removed from office if, upon impeachment, he shall be found guilty of any official misdemeanor.

SEC. 5. In case of vacancy by death, resignation, removal from the state or from office, refusal or inability to serve, of any judge of the supreme court, the office may be filled by the grand committee, until the next annual election, and the judge then elected shall hold his office as before provided. In cases of impeachment or temporary absence, or inability, the governor may appoint a person to discharge the duties of the office during the vacancy caused thereby.

SEC. 6. The judges of the supreme court shall receive a compensation for their services, which shall not be diminished during their continuance in office.

SEC. 7. The towns of New Shoreham and Jamestown may continue to elect their wardens as heretofore. The other towns and the city of Providence may elect such number of justices of the peace, resident therein, as they may deem proper. The jurisdiction of said justices and wardens shall be regulated by law. The justices shall be commissioned by the governor.

ARTICLE XI.

Of Impeachments.

SECTION 1. The house of representatives shall have the sole power of impeachment. A vote of two thirds of all the members elected shall be required for an impeachment of the governor. Any officer impeached shall thereby be suspended from office until judgment in the case shall have been pronounced.

SEC. 2. All impeachments shall be tried by the senate; and when sitting for that purpose, they shall be under oath or affirmation. No person shall be convicted, except by vote of two thirds of the members elected. When the governor is impeached, the chief or presiding justice of the supreme court, for the time being, shall preside, with a casting vote in all preliminary questions.

SEC. 3. The governor, and all other executive and judicial officers, shall be liable to impeachment; but judgment in such cases shall not extend further than to removal from office. The person convicted shall, nevertheless, be liable to indictment, trial, and punishment, according to law.

ARTICLE XII.

Of Education.

SECTION 1. The diffusion of knowledge, as well as of virtue among the people, being essential to the preservation of their rights and liberties, it shall be the duty of the general assembly to promote public schools, and to adopt all means which they may deem necessary and proper to secure to the people the advantages and opportunities of education.

SEC. 2. The money which now is, or which may hereafter be appropriated by law for the establishment of a permanent fund for the support of public schools shall be securely invested, and remain a perpetual fund for that purpose.

Sec. 3. All donations for the support of public schools, or for other purposes of education, which may be received by the general assembly, shall be applied according to the terms prescribed by the donors.

Sec. 4. The general assembly shall make all necessary provisions by law for carrying this article into effect. They shall not divert said money or fund from the aforesaid uses, nor borrow, appropriate, or use the same, or any part thereof, for any other purpose, under any pretence whatsoever.

ARTICLE XIII.

Of Amendments.

The general assembly may propose amendments to this constitution by the votes of a majority of all the members elected to each house. Such propositions for amendment shall be published in the newspapers, and printed copies of them shall be sent by the secretary of state, with the names of all the members who shall have voted thereon, with the yeas and nays, to all the town and city clerks in the State. The said propositions shall be, by said clerks, inserted in the warrants or notices by them issued, for warning the next annual town and ward meetings in April; and the clerks shall read said propositions to the electors when thus assembled, with the names of all the representatives and senators who shall have voted thereon, with the yeas and nays, before the election of senators and representatives shall be had. If a majority of all the members elected to each house, at said annual meeting, shall approve any proposition thus made, the same shall be published and submitted to the electors in the mode provided in the act of approval; and if then approved by three fifths of the electors of the state present, and voting thereon in town and ward meetings, it shall become a part of the constitution of the state.

ARTICLE XIV.

Of the Adoption of this Constitution.

Section 1. This constitution, if adopted, shall go into operation on the first Tuesday of May, in the year one thousand eight hundred and forty-three. The first election of governor, lieutenant-governor, secretary of state, attorney-general, and general treasurer, and of senators and representatives under said constitution, shall be had on the first Wednesday of April next preceding, by the electors qualified under said constitution. And the town and ward meetings therefor shall be warned and conducted as is now provided by law. All civil and military officers now elected, or who shall hereafter be elected, by the general assembly, or other competent authority, before the said first Wednesday of April, shall hold their offices and may exercise their powers until the said first Tuesday of May, or until their successors shall be qualified to act. All statutes, public and private, not repugnant to this constitution, shall continue in force until they expire by their own limitation, or are repealed by the general assembly. All charters, contracts, judgments, actions and rights of action shall be as valid as if this constitution had not been made. The present government shall exercise all the powers with which it is now clothed, until the said first Tuesday of May, one thousand eight hundred and forty-three, and until the government under this constitution is duly organized.

SEC. 2. All debts contracted and engagements entered into, before the adoption of this constitution, shall be as valid against the state as if this constitution had not been adopted.

SEC. 3. The supreme court, established by this constitution, shall have the same jurisdiction as the supreme judicial court at present established, and shall have jurisdiction of all causes which may be appealed to, or pending in the same; and shall be held at the same times and places, and in each county, as the present supreme judicial court, until otherwise prescribed by the general assembly.

SEC. 4. The towns of New Shoreham and Jamestown shall continue to enjoy the exemptions from military duty which they now enjoy, until otherwise prescribed by law.

Done in convention, at East Greenwich, this fifth day of November, A. D., one thousand eight hundred and forty-two.

JAMES FENNER, *President.*
HENRY Y. CRANSTON, *Vice-Pres't.*

THOMAS A. JENCKES,
WALTER W. UPDIKE, } *Secretaries.*

ARTICLES OF AMENDMENT.

ADOPTED NOVEMBER, 1854.

ARTICLE I.

It shall not be necessary for the town or ward clerks to keep and transmit to the general assembly a list or register of all persons voting for general officers; but the general assembly shall have power to pass such laws on the subject as they may deem expedient.

ARTICLE II.

The governor, by and with the advice and consent of the senate, shall hereafter exclusively exercise the pardoning power, except in cases of impeachment, to the same extent as such power is now exercised by the general assembly.

ARTICLE III.

There shall be one session of the general assembly, holden annually, commencing on the last Tuesday in May, at Newport, and an adjournment from the same shall be holden annually at Providence.

ADOPTED AUGUST, 1864.

ARTICLE IV.

Electors of this state who in time of war, are absent from the state, in the actual military service of the United States, being otherwise qualified, shall have a right to vote in all elections in the state for electors of president and vice-president of the United States, representatives in congress, and general officers of the state. The general assembly shall have full power to provide by law for carrying this article into effect; and until such provision shall be made by law, every such absent elector on the day of such elections, may deliver a written or printed ballot, with the names of the persons voted for thereon, and his christian and surname, and his voting residence in the state, written at length on the back thereof, to the officer commanding the regiment or company to which he belongs; and all such ballots, certified by such commanding officer to have been given by the elector whose name is written thereon, and returned by such commanding officer to the secretary of state within the time prescribed by law for counting the votes in such elections, shall be received and counted with the same effect as if given by such elector in open town, ward, or district meeting: and the clerk of each town or city, until otherwise provided by law, shall, within five days after any such election, transmit to the secretary of state a certified list of the names of all such electors on their respective voting lists.

ADOPTED APRIL 7, 1886.

ARTICLE V.

The manufacture and sale of intoxicating liquors to be used as a beverage shall be prohibited. The general assembly shall provide by law for carrying this article into effect.

ARTICLE VI.

All soldiers and sailors of foreign birth, citizens of the United States, who served in the army or navy of the United States from this state in the late civil war, and who were honorably discharged from such service, shall have the right to vote on all questions in all legally organized town, district or ward meetings, upon the same conditions and under and subject to the same restrictions as native born citizens.

ADOPTED APRIL 4, 1888.

ARTICLE VII.

SECTION 1. Every male citizen of the United States of the age of twenty-one years who has had his residence and home in this state for two years, and in the town or city in which he may offer to vote six months next preceding the time of his voting, and whose name shall be registered in the town or city where he resides on or before the last day of December, in the year next preceding the time of his voting, shall have a right to vote in the election of all civil officers and on all questions in all legally organized town or ward meetings: *Provided*, that no person shall at any time be allowed to vote in the election of the city council of any city, or upon any proposition to impose a tax, or for the expenditure of money in any town or city, unless he shall within the year next preceding have paid a tax assessed upon his property therein, valued at least at one hundred and thirty-four dollars.

SEC. 2. The assessors of each town and city shall annually assess upon every person, who, if registered, would be qualified to vote, a tax of $1, or such sum as with his other taxes shall amount to $1, which tax shall be paid into the treasury of such town or city and be applied to the support of public schools therein: *Provided*, that such tax assessed upon any person who has performed military duty, shall be remitted for the year he shall perform such duty; and said tax assessed upon any mariner for any year while he is at sea, or upon any person who by reason of extreme poverty is unable to pay said tax, shall upon application of such mariner or person be remitted. The general assembly shall have power to provide by law for the collection and remission of said tax.

SEC. 3. This amendment shall take in the constitution of the state, the place of sections 2 and 3 of article II, "Of the qualification of electors," which said sections are hereby annulled.

ADOPTED JUNE 20, 1889.

ARTICLE VIII.

Article V. of the amendments to the constitution of this state is hereby annulled.

ADOPTED NOVEMBER 8, 1892.

ARTICLE IX.

SECTION 1. Hereafter the general assembly may provide by general law for the creation and control of corporations: *Provided, however*, that no corporation shall be created with the power to exercise the right of eminent domain, or to acquire franchises in the streets and highways of towns and cities, except by special act of the general assembly upon a petition for the same, the pendency whereof shall be notified as may be required by law.

SEC. 2. This amendment shall take in the constitution of the state the place of section 17 of article IV., "Of the legislative power," and shall be deemed to be in amendment of said section and article.

ADOPTED NOVEMBER 28, 1893.

ARTICLE X.

SECTION 1. In all elections held by the people for state, city, town, ward or district officers, the person or candidate receiving the largest number of votes cast shall be declared elected.

SEC. 2. This amendment shall take in the constitution of the state the place of section 10 of article VIII, "Of elections," which said section is hereby annulled.

APPENDIX E.

---

*THE DORRIAD.

THE ATTACK ON THE ARSENAL.

THH' impatient chief looked on with ire,
Blanched was his cheek, but tenfold fire
Was flashing in his eye.
He threw his martial cloak aside,
And, *waddling* up — he meant to *stride* —
"Give me the torch," with fury cried,
"And, d—— it, let me try!"
He seized the match with eager hand,
While backward his brave soldiers stand;
Three times he waved it in the air,
The cursed Algerines to scare,
And bid them all for death prepare;
Then down the glowing match-rope thrust,
As though he'd have the cannon burst.
Had they not *put the ball in first*,
It very likely would.

But, hark! what sounds astound the ear?
Why turns each hero pale with fear?
What blanches every lip with fright?
What makes each "General" look so white?
And e'en the Governor looks not quite
As easy as a Governor might.

The mingled toll of twenty bells,
The solemn note of warning tells;
And through the ranks the word has past,

---

* By Henry B. Anthony. *Providence Journal*, Jan. 7 and 13, 1843; May 22, 1892. S. S. Rider & Brother, 1870.

"The ALGERINES have come at last!
They're turning out in every street,
Their tyrant swords we soon shall meet.
Already in the torches' glare,
Their bayonets gleam in MARKET SQUARE.
WEYBOSSET trembles 'neath their tread,
Thro' WESTMINSTER their ranks are spread;
And all SOUTH MAIN and BENEFIT,
With spears and flashing swords are lit.
The INFANTRY are on the route,
The NATIONAL CADETS are out,
And those all-fired MARINES, about
Two hundred men, all tall and stout.
Nor PROVIDENCE alone is stirred—
Far down the BAY the news is heard.
GREENWICH hath sounded the alarms;
NEWPORT and BRISTOL are in arms.
The KENTISH GUARDS, that know not fear,
And half of WARREN's half way here.
From PAPOOSE-SQUAW the platoons pour,
From NOOSENECK HILL, from SAUKET'S SHORE,
    From MONTHAUP's grassy side.
And if we linger here till light,
From ALUM POND to KINGSTON HEIGHT,
    Will pour one living tide.
Down LOUISQUISETT's stony steeps,
Where dark MOSHASSUCK slowly creeps,
    The note of warning peals;
From swift PAWTUXET's farthest floods,
And next we'll know, all HELBURN WOODS
Will be upon our heels."

Enough was said, enough was heard,
They needed not another word.
Away, like frightened sheep, they ran,
And save himself, they cried, who can.
Foremost to start, swiftest to run,
Was the brave band of BUFFINGTON.
Their gallant leader was not there;
Saltpetre he could never bear.

While all was safe, there was not one
More fiercely brave than BUFFINGTON.
No other Captain talked so loud,
No other Captain stepped so proud;
And had you seen him at the head
Of his bold volunteers, you'd said
That if the *State* withstood his arms,
    At least the *hen-roosts* stood no chance;
What could the yeomen from their farms,
    When such a knight took up his lance?
But when he heard the firelock click,
He suddenly was taken sick;
And when he found with grape they'd loaded,
His valor all at once exploded.

As pauses in the upper air
    The carrier pigeon, just let fly,
And circling for a moment there,
    Starts home with never-erring eye,
So DISPEAU paused; but not in doubt
    If he should run or he should stay;
But only paused till he found out
    The quickest and the shortest way.
Then, straight as ever pigeon darted,
He turned, and for his home he started,
Down the steep hill rolled like a bucket,
Nor stopped until he reached Pawtucket.
His men had sworn not to desert
    Their gallant leader, come what might,
And when they saw how he "cut dirt,"
    True to their oath, they joined the flight.
    Like hunted deer they flew
O'er Christian Hill, down BROADWAY'S height
    And ATWELL'S AVENUE.
If some few chanced to lag behind,
The fault was in their legs and wind.

When the "INVINCIBLES" turned tail,
The other corps began to quail,
    And looked which way to fly.

The "HARMONIOUS REPTILES" turned about,
The "PASCOAG RIPGUTS" joined the rout,
With Glocester's chosen chivalry.
Up looked the "JOHNSTON SAVAGES,"
(For they had thrown upon the ground
Their carcasses at the first sound
Of "fire," and shut up both their eyes.)
Some on all fours and some upright,
They joined in the disastrous flight.

Of all the leaders who went forth
To court the dangers of that night,
CARTER alone and HORACE PEARCE
Remained until the morning light.
But where, you'll ask, was PARMENTER?
And where was BURRINGTON?
From honor's post did BAILEY stir?
Did JOHN S. HARRIS run?
Where was the eloquent JOHN A.?
Where was the mighty DUTEE J.?
And say, did LEVI run away?

Vain questions! seek not, Algerine,
The motives of such men to scan.
Know that great patriots seldom mean
To share the dangers that they plan.
Enough for them to point the way
And leave the rest to meaner clay.
These men, in the beginning, saw
They were for *council*, not for *war*.
They kept within their proper sphere,
And never went to danger near
Enough to run away.
Too well they loved the *people* dear,
Not to regard their *servants'* fate.
They saved themselves to save the State,
And kept out of the fray.
Yet doubt not that they were as bold,
As those whose warlike deeds I've told,
And had they been as frightened, would
Have run as fast as they.

Far from this scene of fearful strife,
The DOCTOR passed his quiet life.
For though the Algerines he spurned,
For though with patriot fire he burned,
    And in the battle, to be won,
He longed to take the foremost part,
Yet ill, he knew, the healing art
    Could spare her favorite son.
Around his brow the laurel green
    Was tainted by no battle breath,
He never harmed an Algerine,
    Unless he physicked him to death.
Peaceful the triumphs of his name,
And beer and hot drops all his fame!

Anxious the DOCTOR spent that night,
    And anxious spent the day,
For well he knew the hour of fight
    Had come and passed away.
But if the "people" in their might,
    Had risen from the fray,
Or scattered, in inglorious flight,
    They crushed and broken lay,
He knew not, and his manly heart
Longed in their fate to bear a part,
    Whatever it might be,
Whether their triumph he should sing,
    Or their defeat bewail.
While thus he stood, a man rushed in,
Fresh from the battle's dust and din,
"News from the 'people's' cause I bring,
    This paper tells the tale."
A light on JOHN A.'s visage sped;
He snatched the paper, but he read
    Defeat instead of victory.
Trembling with fear, despair and rage,
He shook aloft the damp NEW AGE,
    And shouted Sover*inn*uity.
Run, DISPEAU, run; down, GOVERNOR, down,
Were the last words of DOCTOR BROWN.

THE CHEPACHET CAMPAIGN.

THERE'S gathering on Rhode Island's shore;
There's mustering on each hill;
From every plain her yeomen pour;
Spears every valley fill.
The people, rousing in their might,
Are armed for vengeance and for fight;
And woe unto the Algerine,
Whose luckless neck may stand between
The people and their right.

On Diamond Hill the beacon-light
Is blazing fierce and high;
The answering flame on Acote's height
Is flashing to the sky.
O'er Chepi-Chuck the banners flout
And rings the warning cry;
And hark! the signal-gun speaks out
From Holmes's Brewery.

From Chipinoxet Point they throng,
From Quidnick Pond they pour along,
From Petaquamscut's stream;
From fair Woonasquatucket's banks;
From Devil's Foot, the patriot ranks
With swords and bayonets gleam.

In Baker's Hollow, see, they meet,—
They're thronging fast in Federal street,
And Shingle Bridge and Scrabbletown,
Beneath their weight are breaking down.

From Yawgoo Pond, from Rice's Mill,
From Mishnick Swamp, from Shannock Hill,
From Nipmuck's quarried height,
From broad Quidneset's plain they start,
All swift of limb, and true of heart,
All eager for the fight.

And from those regions dark and hilly,
In Glocester and "Burrillvilly,"
Where old romance her charms hath thrown,
And wonder claims the land her own;
Where savage tribes are said to roam,
And savage beasts still keep their home;
Where, startling up from rock and glen,
    Fierce cannibals their faces show,
And "Anthropphagi, and men
    Whose heads beneath their shoulders grow."

For now the martial Governor Dorr
Hath buckled on *that sword* for war,
And swears he is determined for
    The Algerines to rout.
With him D'Wolf and Potter stand,
And Charley Newell draws his band,
    And General Sprague so stout.

Brave Elder Bullet takes the field,
And many a heart untaught to yield,
    Beats eager for the fray;—
His war-steed Sheldon mounts upon,
The "tricksy Ariel" urges on,
    And Slocum points the way.

Foremost in courage and in skill,
With laurels won on Federal Hill,
The Woonsocket Light Infantry
Press on for Dorr and victory.
Each soldier true, to fear a stranger,
Or "fearing nothing except danger."

But not alone on native ranks
    Did freedom's sacred cause recline;
The cry of "Beauty and the Banks,"
    Aroused the patriots o'er the line;
Connecticut her heroes sent;
New York her fiercest warriors lent;
With eloquence the Five Points rung;

The Pewter Mug delighted hung
On Slamm's appeals, on Hopkins' tongue.

Mike Walsh, with twenty Spartans true,
To Governor Dorr's assistance flew,
And patriotic gifts were made,
The cause of freedom's hope to aid.
What Allen gave, beyond my reach is;
But Vanderpool gave — several speeches!
Two virtues, in old Sparta's code,
With most conspicuous lustre glowed,
Courage in war, thieving in peace,
Such were the glories of old Greece.
If Michael's Spartans did not quite
Their Grecian namesakes match in fight,
In courage, and in lofty feeling,
They more than made it up in stealing.
And well thy barn-yards, Foster, and
    Full well thy hen-roosts, Glos'ter, know
The prowess of the Spartan Band,
    The weight, the force of Michael's blow.

Cleveland, Connecticut's great chief,
Promised assistance and relief;
    And Morton pledged his name,
Should Heaven and clams give him the power,
The suffrage folks might, in that hour,
    Old Massachusetts claim.

And Hubbard, mightiest of the host,
New Hampshire's Solon and her boast,
By his great ancestress had sworn —
        (That Old Mother Hubbard,
        Who went to the cupboard
        To get her poor dog a bone,)
The suffrage banner should be borne,
His granite hills upon.

Ne'er men so true in cause so good,
As those on Acote's height, that stood
    Burning with patriot rage.

Ill would it suit my humble verse,
Their many virtues to rehearse.
Rather to Charlestown's records go,
Rather let Moyamensing show,
And Auburn's glowing page,
Rather let Blackwell's Island tell
The story that it knows full well,
How budded 'neath its tender care,
The flowers that cast their fruitage there.

The Governor saw with conscious pride,
The men who gathered at his side;
That bloody sword aloft he drew,
And "list my trusty men," he cried—
"Here do I swear to stand by you,
As long as flows life's crimson tide;—
Nor will I ever yield, until
I leave my bones upon this hill."

His men received the gallant boast
With shouts that shook the rocks around.
But hark, a voice! old Acote's ghost
Calls out, in anger, from the ground,
"If here your bones you mean to lay,
Then d——n it, I'll take mine away."

Not mine to sing that dreadful night,
When, scattered in disastrous flight,
The patriot forces left the height;
Not mine to sing that dreadful day,
When all the "people" ran away,
And left the Algerines full sway,
To plunder as they might;
Nor mine, to sing in mournful tunes,
That "cooking stove," "them silver spoons,"
Sad trophies of the fight.

Some future poet yet shall stand,
And high the vengeful strain shall lift;
Shall sing the horrors of that band,

Which, seized with sacrilegious hand,
"Them lasting garters," Rispy Tift.
Tremble, ye Algerines: the hour
Is hastening, when, with sovereign power,
The people shall their rights demand,
And rise in vengeance through the land.
Morton, with twice ten thousand men
For Governor Dorr, shall cross the line;
Dispeau's broad banner shall again
O'er serried ranks of thousands shine;
The exiles shall their footsteps turn
Where freedom's hopes forever burn.
On Acote's height, o'er Dexter's Plain,
Freedom's wild shout shall burst again,
And franchised freemen join the cry,
For beauty, banks and liberty.
Brown, shall his snow-white charger mount,
Spencer, "undaunted," thousands count;
And if Wales finds that *Paixhan Gun*,
The cause is safe, the State is won!

APPENDIX F.

BIBLIOGRAPHY.

THE following list of books, pamphlets, magazines, and newspapers contains nearly all the material bearing upon the subject of this monograph. Burke's Report and the current newspapers furnished the great mass of facts for the story. The proceedings of Congress and of the Rhode Island General Assembly have been of value, as well as a few of the pamphlets. It should be remembered, however, that partisanship lay at the bottom of every publication, and that no statement made in any of the books or periodicals can be accepted without due precaution. The contest was remarkably bitter, and there were absolutely no unprejudiced observers. The secondary material furnished by magazine and general histories is in general not based on a careful examination of sources.

SECONDARY MATERIAL.

Arnold, Samuel G.—*History of the State of Rhode Island and Providence Plantations.* 2 Vols., New York, 1858–60.

Bancroft, George.—*History of the United States.* 10th Ed., Vol. II, Boston, 1888.

Congdon, Charles T.—*Reminiscences of a Journalist.* Boston, 1880.

Cooley, Thomas M.—*Constitutional Limitations upon the Legislative Powers of the States.* Boston, 1868.

Durfee, Thomas.—*Gleanings from the Judicial History of Rhode Island* (Rhode Island Historical Tracts). Providence, 1883.

Elliot, Jonathan.—*Debates.* Philadelphia. 5 Vols.

Frieze, Jacob.—*A Concise History of the Efforts to Obtain an Extension of Suffrage, 1811–42.* Providence, 1882.

Goodell, William.—*The Rights and Wrongs of Rhode Island.* Oneida Institute.

Greene, G. W.—*A Short History of Rhode Island.* Providence, 1877.

Greene, W. A. and others.—*The Providence Plantations for 250 Years.* Providence, 1886.

Jameson, John A.—*The Constitutional Convention; its History, Powers, and Modes of Proceeding.* New York, 1867.

Kettell, Samuel.—*Daw's Doings*, or *The History of the Late War in the Plantations. By Sampson Short-and-Fat.* Boston, 1842.

King, Daniel.—*Life of T. W. Dorr.* Boston, 1859.

Perry, Eliz. A.—*History of the Town of Glocester.* Providence, 1886.

Poore, B. P.—*Charters and Constitutions.* 2 Vols., Washington.

Rawle, William.—*A View of the Constitution of the United States.* 1825.

Rhode Island.—*Colonial Records.* 10 Vols., Providence, 1856–1865.

Rhode Island.—*Manual*, 1896–97. Providence, 1897.

Richardson, Erastus.—*History of Woonsocket.* Woonsocket, 1876.

Sergeant, Thomas.—*Constitutional Law.* 1822.

Staples, W. R.—*Rhode Island in the Continental Congress.* Providence, 1870.

Story, Joseph.—*Commentaries on the Constitution of the United States.* Boston.

Tyler, Lyon G.—*Letters and Times of the Tylers.* 3 Vols., 1897.

Wharton, Francis.—*A Treatise on Criminal Law.* 3 Vols., Philadelphia, 1871.

Wilson, Bird.—*Works of James Wilson.* Philadelphia, 1803–4. 3 Vols.

GENERAL MATERIAL.

Adams, John Quincy.—*The Social Compact.* (Pam.) Providence, 1842.

Address of the Democratic Members of the Legislature of Massachusetts to their Constituents and the People of the Commonwealth, with a History of the Proceedings of the Late Session, 1843. (Pam.) Boston, 1843.

Address to the Freemen of Rhode Island. By "A Republican Farmer." (Pam.)

Address to the People of Rhode Island. From the Convention, March 12, 1834. (Pam.) Providence, 1834.

Anthony, H. B.—*Defense of Rhode Island, her Institutions, and her Right to her Representatives in Congress.* (Pam.) Washington, 1881.

Anthony, H. B. (Ed.)—*The Dorriad.* (Poem.) Providence, 1870.

Anthony, H. B. (Ed.)—*The Great Slocum Dinner.* (Poem.) Providence, 1870.

Aristides (Pseud.)—*Political Frauds Exposed, 1836–38.* (Pam.)

Arnold, Lemuel H.—*Reply to John Whipple.* (Pam.) Providence, 1845.

[Bolles, John A.]—"*The Affairs of Rhode Island.*" *A Review of Pres. Wayland's Address.* (Pam.) Providence, 1842.

Bowen, Francis.—*The Recent Contest in Rhode Island.* (Pam.) Boston, 1844.

Bradley, Charles S.—*Method of Changing Constitutions.* (Pam.) Boston, 1885.

Burges, Tristam.—*Address of a Farmer.* (Pam.)

Circular to the People.—Issued March, 1842. (Broadside.)

Cleaveland, C. F. and others.—*Letters to Governor King.* (Pam.) Fall River, 1842.

Conspiracy to Defeat the Liberation of Governor Dorr—or the Hunkers and Algerines Identified and their Policy Unveiled. (Pam.) New York, 1845.

Cowell, Benjamin.—*Letter to Samuel W. King, May, 1842.* (Pam.) Providence, 1842.

Curtis, George Ticknor.—*Merits of T. W. Dorr and George Bancroft as They are Politically Connected.* (Pam.) Boston, 1844.

Davis, Thomas.—*Rhode Island Politics and Journalism.* (Pam.) Providence, 1866.

Dorr, T. W.—*The Right of the People of Rhode Island to Form a Constitution. "The Nine Lawyers' Opinion."* (Appended to Rider, S. S.—*Bibliographical Memoirs of three Rhode Island Authors.* Providence, 1880.)

Durfee, Thomas.—*Some Thoughts on the Constitution of Rhode Island.* (Pam.) Providence, 1884.

Eventful Day in the Rhode Island Rebellion. By "A Looker On." (Poem.) Providence, 1842.

Facts for the People. (Pam.) Providence, 1842.

Four Traitors, The. (Broadside.) 1845.

Goddard, William G.—*Address to the People of Rhode Island, May 3, 1843.* (Pam.) Providence, 1843.

Goddard, William G.—*Letter to James F. Simmons, April 1, 1845.* (Pam.)

Hallett, Benjamin F.—*Argument before the Supreme Court, January, 1848. Right of the People to Establish Forms of Government.* (Pam.) Boston, 1848.

Hazard, Benjamin.—*Report on the Extension of Suffrage.* 1829. (Pam.)

How the People's Constitution was made for Rhode Island without the Aid of the Law or the Legislature. 1841. (Pam.)

Important Resolutions Suppressed. March 29, 1845. (Broadside.)

Jewett, C. C.—*The Close of the Late Rebellion.* (Pam.) Providence, 1842.

Knight, N. R. and others.—*Address to the People of the United States.* 1844. (Pam.)

Pett, Edward W.—*Sermon Preached July 21, 1842.* (Pam.) Providence, 1842.

Pitman, John.—*Reply to Marcus Morton.* (Pam.) Boston, 1842.

Pitman, Joseph H.—*Report of the Trial of T. W. Dorr for Treason.* (Pam.) Boston, 1844.

Potter, E. R.—*Considerations on the Rhode Island Questions.* (Pam.) Boston, 1842.

Potter, E. R.—*Speech on the Memorial of the Democratic Members of the Rhode Island General Assembly.* (Pam.) Washington, 1844.

Randall, Dexter.—*Democracy Vindicated and Dorrism Unveiled.* (Pam.) Providence, 1846.

Review of the Proceedings in the Massachusetts Legislature, for 1843, with an Appeal to the People Against the Violent Course of the Majority, by the Whig Minority. (Pam.) Boston, 1843.

Rhode Island.—*Acts and Resolves.* 1841–1854.

Rhode Island.—*Acts and Resolves.*—Digest of 1730.

Rhode Island.—*Acts and Resolves.*—Digest of 1752.

Rhode Island.—*Acts and Resolves.*—Digest of 1798.

Rhode Island.—*Constitutional Convention, 1842, Journal of.* Providence, 1859.

Rhode Island.—*House Journals*, 1841–1843. (Mss.)

Sawyer, F.—*Facts Involved in the Rhode Island Controversy.* (Pam.) Providence, 1842.

Sheffield, W. P.—*Mode of Altering the Constitution. Reply to C. S. Bradl*
and Abraham Payne. (Pam.) Newport, 1887.

Social Reform Society.—*Address to the Citizens of Rhode Island, Who are Denied the Right of Suffrage.* (Pam.) 1840.

Suffrage Association, Rhode Island.—*Constitution of.* (Pam.) Providence, 1840.

Tucker, Mark.—*Discourse Preached on Thanksgiving Day.* (Pam.) Providence, 1842.

Turner, George.—*Case of T. W. Dorr Explained.* (Pam.) 1845.

Turner, George.—*Report of the Trial of T. W. Dorr for Treason.* (Pam.) Providence, 1844.

United States.—*Congressional Globe*, II Session, 27th Cong., Vol. IX.
Congressional Globe, I Session, 28th Cong., Vol. XIII.
Congressional Globe, II Session, 28th Cong., Vol. XIV.
House Documents, I Session, 28th Cong., Vol. V.
House Journal, I Session, 28th Cong.
House Journal, II Session, 28th Cong.
House Reports, I Session, 28th Cong., No. 581, called *Causin's Report.*
House Reports, I Session, 28th Cong., No. 546, called *Burke's Report.*
Senate Documents, II Session, 27th Cong., Vol. IV.
Senate Documents, II Session, 28th Cong., Vol. II.
Senate Journal, I Session, 23d Cong.
Senate Journal, II Session, 27th Cong.
Senate Journal, I Session, 28th Cong.
Senate Journal, II Session, 28th Cong.

Vinton, Francis.—"*Loyalty and Piety,*" *a Discourse preached July 21st, 1842.* (Pam.) Providence, 1842.

Wayland, Francis.—*The Affairs of Rhode Island.* (Pam.) Providence, 1842.

Wayland, Francis.—*Discourse Delivered on July 21st, 1842.* (Pam.) Providence, 1842.

Whipple, John and Webster, Daniel.—*Arguments before the Supreme Court, January, 1848.* (Pam) Providence, 1848.

Whipple, John.—*Address on the Approaching Election, March 22d, 1843.* (Pam.) Providence, 1843.

[Whipple, Frances H.]—*Might and Right, By a Rhode Islander.* Providence, 1844.

Young, Durham.—*Scourge No. 1. Address to the Whigs of Rhode Island, with Political Portraits.* (Pam.) 1842.

PERIODICALS AND NEWSPAPERS.

The American, V, 391. H. W. Jenkins—The Rhode Island Suffrage.

Brownson's Quarterly Review, I, 532—Review of "Might and Right."

Democratic Magazine, XXII, 193.—The Rhode Island Question—Sovereignty of the People.

Democratic Review, X, 602.—The Rhode Island Affair.

Democratic Review, XI, 70.—The Rhode Island Question.

Democratic Review, XI, 201.—T. W. Dorr.

Democratic Review, XV, 122.—Rhode Island—Its Rightful Governor and Unrighteous Government.

Historical Magazine, II, 290.—The Rhode Island Question.

Narragansett Historical Register, VI, 145. Elisha Dyer—Reminiscences of Rhode Island in 1842, as connected with the Dorr Rebellion.

Narragansett Historical Register, VII, 25. Swan, J. C.—Newport Artillery in 1842.

Narragansett Historical Register, VII, 201.—Newport in 1842—Editorials from Newport Newspapers.

Narragansett Historical Register, VII, 208.—History Makers—An Answer to General Dyer's Article.

Narragansett Historical Register, VIII, 305. Noah J. Arnold—History of Suffrage in Rhode Island.

New Englander, I, 85.—The War in Rhode Island.

New England Magazine, II, 389. C. H. Payne—The Great Dorr War.

Newport Historical Magazine, I-IV.—Notes.

New Princeton Review, IV, 213. W. L. Gifford—Dorr Rebellion.

North American Review, LVIII, 371. Francis Bowen—Dorr Rebellion.

North American Review, CXLII, 332. Abraham Payne and W. F. Sheffield—Constitutional Reform in Rhode Island.

Providence Evening Chronicle, 1842.

Providence Manufacturers and Farmers Journal, 1820–30.

Providence New Age, 1840–42.

Providence Express, 1842.

Providence Gazette, 1821–24.

Providence Journal, 1840–54.

Rhode Island Historical Magazine, V-VII.—Notes.

Book Notes.—Notes.

INDEX.

www.ingramcontent.com/pod-product-compliance
Lightning Source LLC
LaVergne TN
LVHW090545110826
845146LV00001B/28

* 9 7 8 1 4 2 5 5 7 3 4 9 2 *